The Methuen Drama Book of
Trans Plays

The Methuen Drama Book of Trans Plays

Sagittarius Ponderosa
The Betterment Society
how to clean your room
She He Me
The Devils Between Us
Doctor Voynich and Her Children
Firebird Tattoo
Crooked Parts

Edited and with an introduction by
LEANNA KEYES, LINDSEY MANTOAN,
and ANGELA FARR SCHILLER

methuen | drama

LONDON · NEW YORK · OXFORD · NEW DELHI · SYDNEY

METHUEN DRAMA
Bloomsbury Publishing Plc
50 Bedford Square, London, WC1B 3DP, UK
1385 Broadway, New York, NY 10018, USA
29 Earlsfort Terrace, Dublin 2, Ireland

BLOOMSBURY, METHUEN DRAMA and the Methuen Drama logo are trademarks of Bloomsbury Publishing Plc

First published in Great Britain 2021
Reprinted 2021 twice, 2022

A catalogue record for this book is available from the British Library.

ISBN: HB: 978-1-3501-7920-2
       PB: 978-1-3501-7921-9
       ePDF: 978-1-3501-7922-6
       eBook: 978-1-3501-7923-3

Typeset by RefineCatch Limited, Bungay, Suffolk
Printed and bound in Great Britain

To find out more about our authors and books visit www.bloomsbury.com and sign up for our newsletters.

Contents

Acknowledgments

Creating a book is always a community undertaking and this one certainly benefited from expertise, labor, and collaboration from multiple corners. We'd like to thank Dom O'Hanlon and Peter Warren at Bloomsbury for their guidance and support. We had some truly exciting conversations with Lauren Whitehead and appreciate her engagement with this book. Sara Brady has been an invaluable resource and sounding board. Finally, we thank all of the artists and scholars whose work is included herein for their creativity and for sharing a bit of themselves with the world.

Biographies

Marquis Bey (they/or any pronoun) is an Assistant Professor of African American Studies and English at Northwestern University. Bey's work concerns black feminist theorizing, transgender studies, critical theory, and contemporary African American literature. Bey is the author of the forthcoming *Black Trans Feminism* (Duke University Press) and *The Problem of the Negro as a Problem for Gender* (University of Minnesota Press).

j. chavez (they/them) is a recent graduate from Western Washington University with a BA in Theatre. They are an award-winning playwright from the Pacific Northwest. They are the Founder and Artistic Director of Haus of Hazard Theatre Productions in Bellingham, Washington. When they aren't making theatre, j. chavez can be found drinking coffee, hanging out with friends, and performing as drag queen Sue Nami-Meadows. Check them out at: jchaveztheatre.weebly.com.

Mashuq Mushtaq Deen (he/they) is a resident playwright at New Dramatists, a Playwrights Center CORE Writer, and a 2019 Lambda Literary Award Winner. His full-length plays include *Flood* (upcoming: Kansas City Rep, 2021), *The Empty Place* (NYU/New Dramatists joint commission), *The Betterment Society*, *The Shaking Earth* (postponed production, National Queer Theater, 2021), and *Draw the Circle* (productions: PlayMakers Rep Theatre, Mosaic Theatre, Rattlestick Playwrights Theater; published: Dramatists Play Service; winner of the Lammy). Deen's work has been presented/developed/supported by a number of institutions including Sundance Institute/Ucross, Blue Mountain Center, The Public Theater, NYTW, MacDowell Colony, Bogliasco Foundation, Helene Wurlitzer Foundation, Target Margin Theatre, among others. He is represented by the Gurman Agency.

Ty Defoe (*Giizhig*) (he/him/they/we) is from the Oneida and Ojibwe Nations of Wisconsin and resides in New York City. They are a writer, lyricist, scorpio, two-spirit IndigiQueer interdisciplinary shape-shifting artist. They have been published by Routledge, *Pitkin Review*, *Thorny Locust Magazine*, and HowlRound, and they are a TransLab Fellow. Tydefoe.com or AllMyRelations.Earth.

Angela Farr Schiller (she/her) is the Director of Arts Education at the three-time Southeastern Emmy® Award-winning ArtsBridge Foundation for the Cobb Energy Performing Arts Centre, in Atlanta, GA. She researches the intersections between race and performance. She formerly served as an Assistant Professor, the Resident Dramaturg, and the Coordinator of Undergraduate Research for the Department of Theatre & Performance Studies at Kennesaw State University. She also works as a Dramaturg-in-Residence with Atlanta-based Working Title Playwrights (WTP), the leading new play development organization in the Southeast, with a focus on new play development. https://www.angelaschiller.com.

Stephanie Hsu (she/her) is Associate Professor of English and American Studies at Pace University, and a founding member of Q-WAVE, a grassroots organization for queer women and trans/gender-nonconforming folks of Asian/South Asian/Pacific Islander descent in New York City.

MJ Kaufman (he/they) is a writer from Oregon currently living in Brooklyn. A few years ago they founded Trans Lab, a fellowship for TGNC Theater Artists with Kit Yan. Their plays have been seen at the Public Theater, WP Theater, InterAct, Colt Coeur, National Asian American Theater Company, and in Russia and Australia among others. They have received residencies from the MacDowell Colony, The New Museum, and SPACE on Ryder Farm. They are a graduate of Yale School of Drama and they have also written for Netflix. They like to bike, cook, and play with their dog Milkshake.

Leanna Keyes (she/her) is a multi-hyphenate theater artist with a primary focus on queer and trans people, aiming to authentically portray the full complexities of queer life (past, present, and future). She was a playwright in residence at Crosstown Arts in Memphis and has been commissioned by Valiant Theatre in Chicago. Her plays have been performed and studied at universities around the United States, including at Carnegie Mellon in the curriculum of "American Women Playwrights of the 20th and 21st Centuries." Get in touch and view productions: leannakeyes.com.

Raphaël Amahl Khouri (he/they) is a queer transgender Jordanian documentary playwright and theatremaker living in Berlin. They are the author of several plays, including *She He Me* (Kosmos Theatre, Vienna, 2019), *Ich Brauche Meine Ruhe* (Politik im Freien Theater Festival, Munich, 2018), and *No Matter Where I Go* (Beirut, 2014). Khouri is also a part of the Climate Change Theatre Action and their play *Oh, How We Loved Our Tuna!* was read internationally as part of the initiative. Khouri's work has been published in several US journals, as well as *Global Queer Plays* (Oberon Books, 2018), *Skrivena Ljubav* (Samizdat, 2018), and *Queer Dramaturgies: International Perspectives on Where Performance Leads Queer* (Palgrave, 2016). Khouri's work also appears in the anthology International Queer Drama published by Neofelis Verlag.

Finn Lefevre (they/them) is a dramaturg and facilitator whose work focuses on trans and queer communities. They currently serve as a lecturer at the University of Massachusetts Department of Theater and have previously taught in the Theater Department at Keene State College and the Department of Ethnic and Gender Studies at Westfield State University. They earned their MFA in Dramaturgy and a Graduate Certificate in Advanced Feminist Studies from the University of Massachusetts, and BS in Theatre Studies from the University of Evansville. They facilitate applied theatre workshops on trans naming, microaggressions, and community healing. www.finnlefevre.com

Lindsey Mantoan (she/her) is Assistant Professor of Theatre and Resident Dramaturg at Linfield University. She researches contemporary US character, both on the national and individual level. She is the author of *War as Performance: Conflict in Iraq and Political Theatricality* (Palgrave, 2018) and co-editor with Sara Brady of *Vying for the Iron Throne: Essays on Power, Gender, Death, and Performance in HBO's* Game of

Thrones (McFarland, 2018) and *Performance in a Militarized Culture* (Routledge, 2017). In 2019 she won Linfield's Allen and Pat Kelley Faculty Scholar Award and in 2020 she won the Mid-America Theatre Conference's Robert A. Shanke Award for Theatre Research. She is an occasional contributor to CNN.com.

Yasmin Zacaria Mikhaiel (she/they) is a dramaturg, journalist, and oral hxstorian who grew up in/around Chicago. Their multi-disciplinary work as a queer, fat, brown femme endeavors to amplify and archive stories that go lost/stolen/forgotten. Select bylines include arts criticism and essays with *American Theatre* magazine, *Chicago Reader*, *Rescripted*, *Austin Chronicle*, and *Sightlines*. They received a BFA in Dramaturgy & Dramatic Criticism from DePaul University (2017) and are currently pursuing an MA in Performance as Public Practice at the University of Texas at Austin. Mikhaiel is the recipient of the 2020 Texas Educational Theatre Association Founders Scholarship. Learn more at www.yasminzacaria.com and follow them on Twitter @ yasminzacaria.

Melory Mirashrafi (she/they) is a dramaturg, actor, and director from Hillsboro, Oregon. Since graduating from Linfield University in 2019, they have interned with the American Conservatory Theater in San Francisco, and were the 2019–2020 Literary Apprentice for the Huntington Theatre Company in Boston. Their work focuses on Iranian and Muslim diaspora theatre, and their writing has appeared in Oregon ArtsWatch, Public Books, and at the ATHE 2019 National Conference in the Women/LGBT+ Early Scholars Panel.

Ali-Reza Mirsajadi (he/they) is a scholar, artist, and activist working at the intersections of critical race studies, gender and sexuality, and the Middle East. Their first two book projects are on the work of post-revolutionary Iranian playwrights and directors, and they are the founder and chair for ATHE's Middle Eastern Theatre focus group. They are an Assistant Professor of Theatre Studies at The Theatre School at DePaul University, and they hold a PhD in Theatre and Performance Studies from Tufts University.

Courtney Elkin Mohler (she/her) is Assistant Professor of Theatre and serves as the Director of the Social Justice, Diversity and Vocation Fellowship at Butler University. Her research, teaching, and professional work as a director and dramaturge focus on Native American drama and theatre for social justice. She has published articles in *Theatre Topics, Ecumenica, Modern Drama,* and *Text and Presentation*, and co-authored *Critical Companion to Native American and First Nations Theater and Performance: Indigenous Spaces* (Bloomsbury, 2020) with Jaye T. Darby and Christy Stanlake.

Azure D. Osborne-Lee (he/they) is an award-winning black queer theatre maker from south of the Mason–Dixon Line. He holds an MA in Advanced Theatre Practice (2011) from Royal Central School of Speech and Drama as well as an MA in Women's and Gender Studies (2008) and a BA in English and Spanish from the University of Texas at Austin (2005). They are the recipient/winner of Parity Productions' 2018

Annual Commission, Downtown Urban Arts Festival's 2018 Best Play Award, and the 2015 Mario Fratti-Fred Newman Political Play Contest. Find out more at: azureosbornelee.com.

Jesse Daniel O'Rear (he/him) is a scholar and artist of performance that centers the lived experiences of trans people in the United States. He received his PhD in Theatre from the University of Texas at Austin where he wrote his dissertation on live performance of autobiographical material by trans artists. He currently holds a position as Visiting Assistant Professor of Performance Studies at Texas A&M University.

Jaclyn Pryor (they/them) is a physical theatre artist and performance studies scholar specializing in devising and queer/transgender cultural production. Their first book, *Time Slips: Queer Temporalities, Contemporary Performance, and the Hole of History* (2017), examines the capacity of performance to rewrite histories of racial and sexual violence, as well as to reveal queer futures not determined by past harm. They received their PhD in Theatre from the University of Texas at Austin with an emphasis on performance as public practice. They currently teach in the Department of Integrative Arts at Penn State, Abington. More at jaclynisaacpryor.com.

Sharifa Yasmin (she/her) is a trans Egyptian-American director and playwright from South Carolina. She has completed fellowships with The Drama League, Actors Theatre of Louisville, Manhattan Theatre Club, Geva Theatre, and Hypokrit Theatre, and is a 2020 Eugene O'Neill national directing fellow. Yasmin graduated cum laude from Winthrop University with a BA in Theatre Performance and a minor in Sociology. She uses these areas of study to produce pieces of theatre that are not only powerful, but focus on socio-economic issues and marginalized communities. Her work reflects the intersection of queerness and Arab-American identity. www.sharifayasmin.com.

Play Synopses

Sagittarius Ponderosa by **MJ Kaufman**

Archer's not out to his family, but when his father falls ill he has to move back to his childhood home in central Oregon. At night under the oldest Ponderosa pine, he meets a stranger who knows the history of the forests and the sadness of losing endangered things. As Archer accepts big changes in his family, he discovers the power of names and the histories they make and mask. *Sagittarius Ponderosa* is a play about changing names, love potions, and tilling up the soil to make room for new growth.

The Betterment Society by **Mashuq Mushtaq Deen**

Three women on a godforsaken mountain wrestle with the elements, with each other, and with a world that does not value their way of life. As their resources dwindle, Gertie, Lynette, and Doreen try to redefine what it means to be civilized—a mission that forces them to confront what they value and what they're willing to sacrifice.

how to clean your room (and remember all your trauma) by **j. chavez**

Spencer begins to clean their room and reflect on their relationships with the people around them. Who can and can't we control in our lives, does caring mean anything beyond words, and does infatuation go both ways? A play in two cycles with anxiety, depression, and puppets.

She He Me by **Raphaël Amahl Khouri**

She He Me follows the lives of three Arab characters who challenge gender. Randa is an Algerian trans woman who is expelled under the threat of death from her homeland because of her LGBT activism there. Omar is a Jordanian gay man who, rather than body dysphoria, suffers social dysphoria when it comes to the strict codes of masculinity imposed and expected of him by both the heterosexual and gay people around him. Rok is Lebanese and a trans man. Through humor and horror, the three characters come up against the state, society, family, but also themselves.

The Devils Between Us by Sharifa Yasmin

In a small town in the boonies of South Carolina, a closeted young man named George is trying to figure out how to keep his late father's business running, only to be faced with a ghost from his youth. A young Muslim, whom he knew as his boyhood lover Latif, has returned as Latifa to take care of her estranged father's funeral. Forced to confront devils both have been avoiding, they find that their only way out of the past is through each other.

Doctor Voynich and Her Children by Leanna Keyes

This "prediction" is set in America years after reproductive health care has been made illegal. Doctor Voynich and her apprentice Fade travel the countryside in a converted ambulance dispensing harmless herbs by day and providing family planning services by night. Fade tries to help local youth Hannah complete her abortion, using forbidden knowledge from an ancient manuscript, before her mother and the sheriff can nail them for the "attempted murder of an unborn person." This play about mothers and daughters is poetic, sexy, vulgar, queer, and a little too real.

Firebird Tattoo by Ty Defoe

Sky Red Rope goes on a quest to find her father, ultimately finding out she is queer by getting a tattoo. This play features themes of queer two-spirit identity on the Indigenous reservation in Anishinaabe territory.

Crooked Parts by Azure Osborne-Lee

Crooked Parts is a family dramedy set in yesterday and today. Freddy, a black queer trans man, returns to his family home in the South after his fiancé breaks up with him. Once there, Freddy must navigate the tension created by his transition and his brother's serial incarceration. Meanwhile, in his past, thirteen-year-old Winifred struggles to balance her relationship with her mother with her desire to better fit in with her peers. *Crooked Parts* is poignant, queer, funny, and definitely, definitely black.

Introduction: In a Trans Time and Space

Leanna Keyes, Lindsey Mantoan, and Angela Farr Schiller

A cisgender man dons a Santa costume and prances on tables singing about killing a dog for money. The character presents as a woman for the duration of the musical; most of the cast refers to her with male pronouns. The character, of course, has AIDS, and, of course, dies tragically, which teaches the rest of the cast an important lesson about following your dreams. The man wins a Tony. The cis male writer wins two Tonys, three Drama Desk Awards, and the Pulitzer.

A cisgender man plays a character who undergoes a botched gender confirmation surgery to be with the man that she loves. The man leaves her after only a year. Later, another man whom she has fallen in love with abandons her after discovering she isn't a cis woman. She breaks down onstage and removes her wig, makeup, and dress, as if her gender is only a theatrical costume. The man who originates the role wins an Obie; the man who stars in the Broadway production wins a Tony.

This is a pattern that recurs year after year, at theaters of all sizes, and also on screen (where such egregious representation is more widely disseminated). Cis actors performing tragic trans characters written by cis people isn't meaningful trans representation; trans art by trans people, by contrast, avoids inflicting trauma on trans characters to teach cis people important life lessons or make a point. In the shadow of the problematic history of trans representation, one of the questions we received most often when creating this book was, "How are you defining a 'trans play'?" When writing about something as vast and personal as gender, and particularly transness, it becomes difficult to define strict borders around what "is" and "isn't" a trans play. Asking whether Wilson Jermaine Heredia or John Cameron Mitchell or Neil Patrick Harris gave authentic trans performances is the wrong question. The right question is: do trans people recognize themselves in the art? In the cases of *Rent* (which premiered on Broadway in 1996) or *Hedwig and the Angry Inch* (which premiered off-Broadway in 1998 and premiered on Broadway in 2014), we can recognize that actual trans people and cis-written characters like Angel and Hedwig exist in different circles on the same blurry Venn diagram. Trans art by trans people and art with trans characters by cis people can both explore the way people experience gender—but the positionality matters.

Defining or putting strict borders around "trans theater" is beyond the scope of a single anthology, and might not even be a useful project to undertake. For the purposes of this book, we employed three metrics when curating plays: 1) that the play be authored by a trans playwright, 2) that the play feature at least one prominent trans character, and 3) that the play offer experiences of trans humanity that move beyond a central focus on surgeries and death. Marquis Bey argues in this book that "trans *lives* in all their nuance and complexity, all their vicissitudes, are still often eclipsed by popular mythologies of extravagant balls and surgeries, skewed life chances, and death" (p. 387). While we wholeheartedly acknowledge that there are important plays by playwrights with a range of gender identities that do pivot around these themes, this anthology endeavors to expand the field and spectrum of contemporary theater by offering stories about trans characters for whom their transition or death is not the central dramatic arc.

The eight plays in this anthology span themes ranging from gender identity and expression to racial and religious attitudes toward love and sex. These texts represent a variety of performance modes and genres and they call for innovative theatrical approaches to telling trans stories. Some firmly reside in the realm of American realism, many playfully weave together elements of magical realism, and others stand as post-apocalyptic considerations of current and even past traumas and delineations of identity. Geographically, it is important to point out that most of the playwrights included in the anthology are U.S.-based, in an acknowledgment that context matters. Trans performance, history, legality, identities, and expression differ widely between communities within the U.S. and around the world.

Although it is perhaps more standard for an anthology of plays to contain only one introduction, written by the editors, we opted to include introductions to every play in this book. We felt strongly that the art deserved scholarly attention from many voices. There are precious few critical engagements with trans dramatic art and these introductions contribute to a growing body of scholarly criticism. The intro writers situate the plays within a broader theatrical landscape, analyze the plays' themes, and provide important theoretical and historical context. They also build bridges between theory and practice that we hope will prove enlightening for artists, theorists, scholars, and audiences. Almost all of our intro writers are trans, which was important to us given that two of the three editors of the anthology are cis. We hope that publishers amplify more trans voices going forward.

Language in Time and Space

As the introductions to the specific plays in this volume indicate, these pieces maintain a preoccupation with temporality as a complex experience through which trans lives might be investigated and embodied. Queer and trans temporalities eschew linearity in favor of backward folds woven together with leaps of futurity. In their monograph *Time Slips*, Jaclyn Pryor explains, "Queer and transgender subjectivities remind us that it is possible to live, at least in part, outside of or in opposition to the time of capital, and to challenge timelines that presume the inevitability of linear gender and sexual development" (2017: 5). Indeed, the notion of transition seems inextricably linked to an engagement with time. In an explication of the many meanings and interpretations of transition, Julian Carter writes: "This is the promise of transition, as the term continues to expand from its psychiatric and surgical usage: that we can live in the time of our own becoming and that possible change is not restricted to the narrow sphere of our conscious intention" (2014: 236–237). The myriad approaches to transition and time displayed in this book challenge not only theatrical genealogies of damaging trans representation but also linguistic limitations associated with identity.

Our title for this introduction builds on Jack Halberstam's *In a Queer Time and Space*, and his articulation that "queer uses of time and space develop, at least in part, in opposition to the institutions of family, heterosexuality, and reproduction. They also develop according to other logics of location, movement, and identification. If we try to think about queerness as an outcome of strange temporalities, imaginative life schedules, and eccentric economic practices, we detach queerness from sexual identity" (2005: 1). Trans uses of time and space develop along similar yet distinct patterns, with tensions and joy in the interstices of family, geography, identity, and community. The scripts in this book reveal the playfulness of language and nonlinear time and space.

We take an expansive view of the word "trans," recognizing that this is an imperfect word to group together experiences of many people across many cultures across many eras—past, present, future, and the particular trans experience that invites those temporalities to coexist in a single body. And yet even the word "trans" holds contradictions and complexity for a community that doesn't always agree on whether it encompasses nonbinary gender (we understand it to do so), and how it converses with prior language and identity conceptions (see Deen and Hsu's introduction in this volume). In their introduction to the edited volume *Nonbinary: Memoirs of Gender and Identity*, Micah Rajunov and Scott Duane explain the nuances of language: "Within gender diverse communities, there is overlap and disagreement as to what the words we use actually mean, and who can share a given identity. For instance, do nonbinary people belong in the transgender community? Some people say yes, some no. We walk a tightrope between acknowledging these lines and finding utility within them, while claiming that such boundaries are artificial" (2019: xxii). Language slips, much like Pryor's articulation of the way time slips, "already haunted by improperly buried ghosts as well as liberatory futures not yet performed" (2017: 4).

In a brilliant debate published in 2019 in *Transgender Studies Quarterly*, Andrea Long Chu and Emmett Harsin Drager stake positions on the topic of what trans theory might be and do, with Chu declaring, "Let's face it: Trans studies is over. If it isn't, it should be. Thus far, trans studies has largely failed to establish a robust, compelling set of theories, methods, and concepts that would distinguish itself from gender studies or queer studies" (2019: 103). In their reply, Drager focuses on narrative form: "In trans studies, it seems to me that we are telling a story of our victimhood (tragedy) or a story of our resistance (romance)" and they suggest that other types of narratives might be a mode through which original theories might emerge (104–105).

Indeed, when curating these plays, we were aware that, in much the same way that narratives featuring gay characters have had a long and painful history of killing off gay characters (think, for example, of Lilian Hellman's play *The Children's Hour*), narratives with trans characters frequently kill them off, often because the stories are based on the lives of real people who are already deceased. Jesse O'Rear persuasively demonstrates the way this phenomenon serves to reaffirm the gender binary, analyzing the play *I Am My Own Wife* (Wright 2003); the films *Boys Don't Cry* (Peirce 1999), *The Danish Girl* (Hooper 2015), *Dallas Buyers Club* (Vallée 2013), *The Crying Game* (Jordan 1992); and the musical *Rent* (Larson 1996). O'Rear argues:

> Each of these performances take audiences on the narrative journey of the transgender person's life which, inevitably, ends with their death. There are two other qualities that all of these performances have in common as well: All of these performances feature a transgender character portrayed by a cisgender actor and all of the actors in the transgender roles were given at least one award nomination for their performance. The audience, therefore, is presented with the body of a cisgender actor who performs the symbolic death of their character, at

which point they can return to their own identity (gendered and otherwise) in order to receive an award for their performance. The transgender body, however, effectively remains disposed of through the death of the character.

(O'Rear 2016: 12–13)

While the plays herein represent some dark and challenging moments, they resist the reductive and violent representation of trans stories historically perpetuated by cisgender artists. The characters here are not "the brave victim stuck in the wrong body," as so often happens when cis artists write trans characters (Scharf 2018).

Instead, the plays collected here offer a range of forms and aesthetics, and they resist not only gender binaries but also the binary formal choice between trans tragedy and trans romance. In this way, these plays are already in conversation with the growing body of trans theater, including works by Olivia Dufault (*Year of the Rooster* (2013)), Taylor Mac (*Hir* (2016)), Shakina Nayfack (*Manifest Pussy*, first performed in 2016), Travis Alabanza (*Burgerz* (2018)), Basil Kreimendahl (*Orange Julius* (2018)), Kit Yan (*Interstate*, first performed in 2018), Aziza Barnes (*BLKS* (2020)), and others, and previous works by playwrights in this book, such as Mashuq Mushtaq Deen's *Draw the Circle* (2018).

Arguably the most famous trans theater artist is Taylor Mac, a 2017 finalist for the Pulitzer Prize for Drama and a recipient of a MacArthur "Genius Grant." Mac, whose pronouns are judy, created the durational performance *A 24-Decade History of Popular Music* (2016) and the Broadway play *Gary: A Sequel to Titus Andronicus* (2019). Judy's play *Hir* (2016) follows a veteran's journey home from war to discover that his mother is tormenting the family's formerly abusive patriarch, now incapacitated by a stroke, and his sibling has transitioned and now has hir/ze pronouns. Set in the theatrical style of "absurd realism," the piece displaces overseas military conflict onto the suburban domestic gender front, resulting in a hilarious and incisive investigation of oppression and liberation.

Holding hands with the legacy of trans theater artists who have been paving the way for decades, this anthology is not the first or only one to publish trans plays. Oberon Books's *Global Queer Plays* (2018) includes seven plays from across the world, labeled by their country of origin (India, Kosovo, Jordan, France, Taiwan, Egypt, and Argentina). The collection responds to the *Daily Telegraph* article "The Five Gay Plays that Changed the World" (Williams 2017), all of which were U.S. or U.K.-based. The book includes *No Matter Where I Go*, a play by Raphaël Amahl Khouri (whose *She He Me* can be found in Part Two of this book) that represents real queer women delivering papers at a conference at the American University of Beiruit and sharing their experiences of having to defend their identities to "a well-meaning but often ignorant Western audience" (Oberon 2018: 8). The book also includes Mariam Bazeed's personal memoir *Peace Camp Org*, about a young Mariam journeying from their oppressive home "to the increasingly absurd setting of a peace-themed summer camp in Maine" (Oberon 2018: 7). *Global Queer Plays* span themes related to gay marriage and queer family issues to trans identity—although collectively the plays focus more on queerness in a broad sense than specifically on transness. Similarly, Mark Gatiss's carefully curated *Queers: Eight Monologues* puts forward short texts investigating gay life and Fintan Walsh's *Queer Notions: New Plays and Performances from Ireland* includes plays, experimental performance documentation, and a visual essay.

This book, *The Methuen Drama Book of Trans Plays*, is the first collection of exclusively trans plays. We have organized the plays in this book into three sections: Disembodied Articulations, Fraught Spaces, and Familiar/Familial. Certainly numerous other themes connect these pieces, and we could have organized them differently. We considered a more chronological grouping, such as: Trans Then, Trans Now (*Crooked Parts, Sagittarius Ponderosa,* and *The Devils Between Us*); Trans Today (*She He Me, how to clean your room,* and *Firebird Tattoo*); and The Future is Trans (*Doctor Voynich and Her Children* and *The Betterment Society*). While these themes may seem more in line with "a trans time and space," there's a Western patriarchal linearity to such an organizational structure. Recurring motifs, jumps across temporalities and geographies, and simultaneous resonances connect these plays. We also eschewed sorting the plays by gender or pronouns of the playwright. Dropping plays by gender-expansive playwrights into neatly delineated gendered silos would be reductive. Gender and pronouns are real; barriers between them are constructs. The sections we've divided the book into focus on thematic connections across plays and offer starting points for theoretical analysis.

Disembodied Articulations

The works of MJ Kaufman, Mashuq Mushtaq Deen, and j. chavez form the first grouping in this anthology: "Disembodied Articulations." All three of these plays use puppetry as a way to explore emotions, relationships, and histories in a powerfully physicalized display. The book opens with MJ Kaufman's *Sagittarius Ponderosa*, which could be categorized as a homecoming play, or a puppet play, or a surreal piece in which scenes in different locations run simultaneously. Archer returns to his childhood home when his father falls ill, and the family negotiates personal and collective journeys in the shade of a massive ponderosa pine. The piece weaves ancient wisdom into the essential fabric of the family's growth and transition. *The Betterment Society* by Mashuq Mushtaq Deen, an allegory made manifest, engages with the fraught tension that arises between the forces of masculinity and femininity and the pathway forward that transcends them both. Rounding out this grouping is *how to clean your room (and remember all your trauma)* by j. chavez. Sliding between the present and past, chavez's memory play challenges the normative understanding of time and our overdetermined reliance on linearity. Constructed as a play in two cycles, Spencer begins to clean their room and reflect on their relationships with the people around them. These plays investigate what lives in the body and what might be best encountered through disembodied figures, displacing trauma, fear, and hope onto puppets and other nonhuman objects.

Fraught Spaces

The second section of the book, Fraught Spaces, combines plays with radically different approaches to space and place. Raphaël Amahl Khouri's *She He Me* has virtually no stage directions or indicated setting, and Sharifa Yasmin's *The Devils Between Us* is set in an auto mechanic's shop in the U.S. South. Both of these plays feature characters who are drawn to dangerous places, driven to confront villains close to home even, or perhaps especially, when it's hazardous. Khouri's play, based on interviews, follows three Arab characters, Rok, Randa, and Omar, who have migrated, either by choice or force, from the country of their origin. As they relate stories from their past, including confrontations with family, law enforcement, and religious leaders, these characters challenge gender and also geopolitical dynamics and assumptions. Yasmin's play investigates what happens when Latifa returns home to South Carolina to bury her father, but unexpectedly reunites with her childhood lover, George. Having transitioned, she has to navigate both new and old violence, as well as her own relationship to forgiveness. These two plays ask: what happens when trans bodies cross a border they're not meant to cross?

Familiar/Familial

Leanna Keyes's *Doctor Voynich and Her Children*, Ty Defoe's *Firebird Tattoo*, and Azure D. Osborne-Lee's *Crooked Parts* share compelling thematic DNA, fundamentally asking us to consider how much of family lives in the blood and how much lives in the ineffable resonances between souls. Keyes's prediction play takes place in a near-future America after reproductive healthcare has been made illegal. The titular Doctor Voynich travels with a young apprentice named Fade, whom she adamantly disavows as anything more than a student, believing that keeping their clandestine work safe takes priority over emotional ties. *Firebird Tattoo* tells the story of Sky: young, Ojibwe, two-spirit, queer, and desperately trying to figure out where she fits in (geographically and socially). When she meets a queer stranger off-rez and begins to recognize parts of herself in this young woman, she also gains new insight into the lives of her family members. *Crooked Parts* deals with coming home again and learning the ways in which the familiar can become alien, and rediscovering the familiar in what seems so changed. Late-twenties black writer Freddy Clark returns to his family home and reconnects with his parents and brother, relearning how to be in a relationship with relatives who haven't seen him since he transitioned. Collectively, these plays rebuild traditional ideas of family into new queer-informed structures without discarding the deep and meaningful connection that home can provide.

The Growing Trans Ecosystem

We put this anthology into the world hoping that it does more than inspire regional theaters to tokenize trans plays, perhaps subbing one into the season's April "gay" slot. AJ Schwartz argued in HowlRound, "Beyond just scoring a theatre company some diversity points, we can expand the scope of the art being made." Schwartz calls on theaters to engage with trans theater beyond simply putting more trans people on payroll, arguing, "We need to be given the creative freedom to explore gender in the text, staging, and design just as much as in the audition" (2020). By incorporating trans plays that range from unproduced to workshopped to single production to reviewed in the *New York Times*, we offer a vision of trans artistry that looks beyond what the overwhelmingly cis, predominantly white gatekeepers of the U.S. theater scene have already deemed "producible." Almost none of the decision-makers at professional or even community theaters are trans, and so for the most part only certain trans narratives have been produced on traditional stages. We look to a future of theater in which trans people have the power to tell their own stories for their own communities, rather than relying on cis artistic directors catering to cis sensibilities.

Publishing these playwrights is important to us in itself, and we're excited about the ripple effect that these plays will create. The plays in this book open possibilities for a wide range of artistic choices and provide opportunities for trans directors and designers to explore what might be meant by trans aesthetics. Creating an accessible body of work helps expand the talent base and provide material support in contracts and personal artistic development to trans artists of all stripes. These eight new plays provide opportunities for trans actors to play trans roles, and for trans directors to take the reins on work directly about their community. Trans art will only get better as more of it is created, published, and produced, and as more artists develop the field.

References

Alabanza, Travis. 2018. *Burgerz*. London: Oberon Books.

Barnes, Aziza. 2020. *BLKS*. New York: Dramatists Play Service.

Deen, Mashuq Mushtaq. 2018. *Draw the Circle*. New York: Dramatists Play Service.

Dufault, Olivia. 2013. *Year of the Rooster 2013*. New York: Dramatists Play Service.

Gatiss, Mark. 2017. *Queers: Eight Monologues*. London: Nick Hern Books.

Halberstam, Jack. 2005. *In a Queer Time and Place*. New York: NYU Press.

Hooper, Tom, director. 2015. *The Danish Girl*. Focus Features.

Jordan, Neil, director. 1992. *The Crying Game*. Miramax Films.

Kreimendahl, Basil. 2018. *Orange Julius*. New York: Dramatists Play Service.

Mac, Taylor. 2016. *Hir*. New York: Dramatists Play Service.

O'Rear, Jesse. 2016. "The Spectacle of Transformation: (Re)Presenting Transgender Experience Through Performance," MA Thesis, University of Texas at Austin.

Oberon Books, Inc. 2018. *Global Queer Plays*. London.

Peirce, Kimberly, director. 1999. *Boys Don't Cry*. Fox Searchlight Pictures.

Pryor, Jaclyn. 2017. *Time Slips: Queer Temporalities, Contemporary Performance, and the Hole of History*. Evanston, IL: Northwestern University Press.

Rajunov, Micah and Scott Duane. 2019. *Nonbinary: Memoirs of Gender and Identity*. New York: Columbia University Press.

Scharf, Nitsan. 2018. "A Call for Exciting Trans Theater." Howlround.com, December 18. https://howlround.com/call-exciting-trans-theatre.

Schwartz, AJ. 2020. "Trans Theater is More Than a Cast List." Howlround.com, March 24. https://howlround.com/trans-theatre-more-cast-list.

Vallée, Jean-Marc, director. *Dallas Buyers Club*. 2013. Focus Features.

Walsh, Fintan, ed. 2010. *Queer Notions New Plays and Performances from Ireland*. Cork: Cork University Press.

Williams, Holly. 2017. "The Five Gay Plays that Changed the World." *The Telegraph*, July 9. https://www.telegraph.co.uk/theatre/what-to-see/five-gay-plays-changed-world/

Wright, Doug. 2004. *I Am My Own Wife*. New York: Dramatists Play Service.

Part One
Disembodied Articulations

Waiting, Watching, and Witnessing as Queer Praxis in *Sagittarius Ponderosa*

Jesse D. O'Rear

Sagittarius Ponderosa is a play about transition.

In the inaugural issue of *Transgender Studies Quarterly*, Julian Carter writes the following in their contributed essay on the word "Transition":

> 'Transition' differs from 'sex change' in its inherent reference to duration rather than event, from 'assuming a dress' in its attention to the embodied self who dresses, and from 'coming out' in its disengagement from politically radical and street subcultures; yet conceptual residue from these earlier vocabularies adheres to the term as the activities it encompasses expand. [. . .] Transitions are brave work. Like birth, like writing, gender transition is when hopes take material form and in doing so take on a life of their own.
>
> (Carter 2014: 235–236)

Essentially, what Carter identifies in this passage is that "transition" as a term in application to trans subjects rejects a linear chronological progression. To "transition" is not to move from one point to the next, nor to make a singular change to one's wardrobe or expression, nor to make an announcement that changes one's identity or the way one is perceived in public. Subsequently, Carter acknowledges that "transition" does not encompass a singular set of actions. By pluralizing the term in their essay, Carter highlights that there is no singular definition of what it means to "transition."

At the crux of *Sagittarius Ponderosa* is this: "Transitions are brave work."

Sagittarius Ponderosa focuses on a family in the midst of a collective transition, within which each member experiences their own individual transition(s) over the course of the script. To center the play around transitions requires that we remember that transitions are moments of movement, not fixed points in time. Where this play finds its tension and its growth are in the characters' resistance to, and eventual embrace of, "duration rather than event."

Sagittarius Ponderosa asks—and requires—us to consider the stillness of transition. As José Esteban Muñoz states in his 2009 book *Cruising Utopia*, "waiting" is an action to the marginalized: "Those who wait are those of us who are out of time in at least two ways. We have been cast out of straight time's rhythm, and we have made worlds in our temporal and spatial configurations" (p. 182). "Time" for queer subjects is something that we know we are not guaranteed, constantly in a state of either fighting to acquire or keep our legal rights and our dignities in an actively queerphobic/racist/classist/colonial/imperialist society. Additionally, and relatedly, due to the very legal and social discriminations and economic hurdles faced by queer and trans people in the U.S., we also face a shortage of time in our lifespans. Lack of adequate healthcare, as well as our community's relationship to the onset of and continuing HIV epidemic, leaves few of us with the ability to view "time" as something of which we have an abundance.

Contrary to "straight time's rhythm," "queer time" exists in opposition to the measurement and passage of time which Elizabeth Freeman (2010) deems "chrononormativity" in its service to capitalist colonial and patriarchal hegemony. Similarly, Jack Halberstam's *In a Queer Time and Place* (2005) theorizes "queer time" in relation to risk and failure as queer modes of living in the face of the productive body endorsed by capitalism.

Chrononormativity expects the *movement* of transition but toward a purpose that reinforces and supplements capitalism—and, consequently, racist patriarchal heteronormativity, all of which are inextricably tied to it. Bound up in and reiterated by notions of "the American dream," chrononormativity seeks to create seekers and generators of capital, as opposed to interdependent community members, out of its participants. This expectation seeps into every crevice of our indoctrination into capitalism, even into our understandings of health and wellness. As Halberstam explains, "in Western cultures, we chart the emergence of the adult from the dangerous and unruly period of adolescence as a desired process of maturation; and we create longevity as the most desirable future, applaud the pursuit of long life (under any circumstances), and pathologize modes of living that show little or no concern for longevity" (2005: 4). As such, physical and mental maturity is linked to a reduction in behavior considered to involve risk—whether that be physical, social, or economic risk. More so than a concern over health and well-being, chrononormative longevity aims to ensure an enduring and docile population of laborers and consumers.

The transitions in *Sagittarius Ponderosa* guarantee no such thing. The story follows a genderqueer main character, Archer/Angela, who returns to live with his parents at age twenty-nine after a span of time spent living elsewhere. Archer's Mom is a housewife with dreams of being a gardener, though much of her time is spent tending to Archer's father (Pops) as he battles an unnamed health condition related to his love of processed sugar. Grandma, Pops's mother and a widow, lives in her own house nearby, hard of hearing and desperately dreaming that Archer, who she still perceives as her granddaughter, will soon get married. Every character is fueled by a relationship to the passage of time: resistance to, longing for, rejection of, fear toward what may be ahead, behind, or right in front of them.

Each of the interior spaces—Mom, Pops, and Archer's house and Grandma's next door—exist as part of the Ponderosa Forest. One eponymous Ponderosa, under which Archer and his love interest Owen spend their time together, is also present on stage. According to the script, regarding the Ponderosa: "She never goes away" (p. 18).

In fact, as Owen points out, the Ponderosa lives and ages in spite of the capitalist death drive while also in danger because of it. Owen, Archer's paramour and a Ph.D. student, is learning about and trying to reinstate prescribed burning, a process of forest fire prevention practiced by the Northern Paiute on whose land the forest—and the play itself—is set. Owen himself claims some Native ancestry, and laments not being more connected with that part of his heritage. Without that practice, coupled with the devastating effects of global environmental destruction, the Ponderosas cannot continue to thrive—or, eventually, even survive.

Prescribed burning, as Owen describes, helped to "keep the trees healthy and the forest sparse" so that naturally occurring wildfires, inevitable in the summer heat, would not destroy the entire forest (p. 40). It was a process of preparing for what was inevitable in nature; a moment of transition through loss to prevent a transition to extinction.

But Owen reminds us: "[Now] we don't do that and that's why there're so many less of the trees" (p. 40). Colonizers, in their theft of the land, prohibited the vital tending of the land by its human communities. The advancement of industrialism and capitalism-fueled globalization destroys the land and increases the temperature of the earth, the phenomenon known passively as "climate change." As a result, the forest dwindles. A 400-year-old tree faces extinction because of the egomaniacal greed of murderous settlers who arrived 200 human years into this Ponderosa's life.

Owen also points out to Archer that the Ponderosa experiences time differently than humans: "A year for us is like an hour for them, you know?" (p. 21). And for the characters in *Sagittarius Ponderosa*, time seems as if it is passing so quickly. In the span of the single play, the characters experience a year of loss, grief, love, and joy. The audience is, in many ways, like the Ponderosa. We experience in one hour of our own time an entire year's worth of life on stage.

The Ponderosa stands on stage as a reminder of the subjective passage of time. What occurs under her boughs are but a blink of an eye to the tree. For Archer and Owen, it feels that way, too, but for different reasons: Owen will leave soon, returning to school, and Archer has just arrived, to be in the forest indefinitely as this part of his life demands.

The Ponderosa never leaves. She remains on stage for the entirety of the production. She has been in that forest for at least, according to Owen's best guess, 400 years. She will (hopefully) continue to be in that forest long after Pops, Grandma, Mom, and even Archer's lifespan ceases. She waits, and has waited, and will wait. She watches, has watched, and will watch. She witnesses, has witnessed, and will witness. The Ponderosa is the queerest character in the play.

What is transition to a being like the Ponderosa pine? How does the Ponderosa ask us to reconsider our own relationships to time, to the cycles of life, to our expectations of ourselves and of each other? Grandma expects that Archer will soon be married, because that is what she expects of women at Archer's age. Yet she, herself, is left husbandless at her age due to the life cycle of death. Her own son makes the transition from life to death before she does, disrupting the expected cycle that a child will bury his mother, not the other way around.

What is the human cycle of life and death to the Ponderosa pine? What is the capitalist timeline of life, the slow march toward death during which we are expected to hit markers of productivity and success as defined by our accumulation of capital, to the Ponderosa pine? What is chrononormativity to the Ponderosa, other than a weapon used in the continual destruction of herself, her family, and her home?

Likewise, what are these concepts to trans people? What is the transition from adolescence to adulthood when some of us will experience the effects of puberty twice: once against our will when we are young and a second time with our consent when we are older? And whether or not we choose to pursue transition by medical means, how are we served by a narrative of maturity equivalent to a reduction in risk when simply being trans in a transphobic culture is risky behavior?

Every one of us, of all genders and sexes, transitions through multiple phases and stages of our lives. Our identities and expressions of our selves shift constantly, even sometimes within a day, depending on the context in which we find ourselves in every moment. Gender-related transitions have garnered attention for the grand physical changes that often accompany or characterize these particular shifts in identity and expression. Yet trans people are not the only people who make changes—to our names, our bodies, or our expressions of our selves. And we are not the only ones who scoff in the face of chrononormativity.

The same can be said of each member of Archer's family. They are all waiting in and for transition. Waiting for death, waiting for (re)birth, waiting for love, waiting for salvation, waiting to find something: the self, the past, the future, each other. And these moments of waiting are moments of transition—in the sense that moments of transition are also always moments of waiting.

The structure of the nuclear family attempting to stagger their way through a series of tumultuous transitions hearkens to another "trans play:" Taylor Mac's 2014 script *Hir*. Much like *Sagittarius Ponderosa*, *Hir* focuses on a main character who returns to his family's home to find it the site of numerous transitions. However, *Hir* places as its central character a member of the hegemonic class: white, cisgender, heterosexual, military veteran Isaac. When he arrives, the house is disorganized and dirty. His father, formerly emotionally and physically abusive to all members of his family, is dressed in clownish drag and is kept silent and perpetually confused by the effects of a stroke and a cocktail of drugs which Isaac's mother feeds him every day.

The play's trans-identified character is Isaac's brother, Max, who he previously thought to be his sister. Max uses gender neutral pronouns (ze/hir) and takes testosterone. It seems as though Max's gender transition and subsequent political radicalization is the catalyst for hir mother's transition from passive wife and victim of domestic abuse to how we see her in the play: the home's powerful matriarch, depicted as delusionally delighting in acts of physical, emotional, and social retribution against her abuser.

While *Hir* uses gender transition as the gateway to explore a world that is confusing and unsettling to a member of the hegemonic class (Isaac: white, cisgender, heterosexual, participant in U.S. imperialism), in many ways, *Sagittarius Ponderosa* decenters Archer's transness. Archer transitions in other ways—back to his parents' home, into being a fatherless adult, between employment opportunities—but he begins and ends the play in the same position with regard to his gender. There are no conversations about Archer's gender identity or status with regard to transition.

Pops begins the play in a moment of transition, moving from a diet heavy in processed sugar to something less sweet. Very quickly into the play, he transitions from Robert to Robert Jason, at his doctor's behest, to help grapple with the chronic illness in his body. His wife attempts to keep him on a strict schedule, also at his doctor's behest, with a dictated sleep schedule, which Robert Jason frequently rejects. Then, he embarks on the transition from life through death. In transitioning through death, he takes on new life as Peterson, his mother's late-in-life companion.

Archer resists the transitions of the culture in which he has been raised. By identifying himself through astrology, he rejects the Gregorian calendar: "I'm also grateful for my name. And for it being the month I was born in. [. . .] I mean the astrological month. Sagittarius time" (pp. 19–20).

Sagittarius is the most mature of the fire signs. He is the Archer, the Hunter, the Explorer. Sagittarius energy brings with it the urge to travel, the yearning to seek and find things outside of one's comfort zone. Sagittarians do not fare well when asked to stay put.

But rather than an arrow, the symbol of the constellation, Archer is more like a boomerang: he leaves home, then returns. The American cycle of adulthood expects that with maturity comes leaving the family home. Returning to the nest has become a critique slung at the millennial generation, an implication that we are unfit for the trials and tribulations of being a "grown-up" in "the real world." Archer also defies what could be considered a normative narrative of queerness: the young queer adult who leaves their hometown to find community in a chosen family of other queers in a new but exciting atmosphere.

Archer does not explain why he has returned home. He references "family stuff" to Owen, and we can infer that this has to do with his father being unwell. But there is tension within the house around such things: in their final conversation, Pops accuses Archer of being part of the "police state" for refusing to drive to the store for some candy in the middle of the night; and after Pops' death, during one of their arguments Archer accuses Mom of wishing that he would move out. And Archer's attitude at the beginning of play does not inspire much confidence that moving home was a choice made of his own free will.

Grandma yearns for Archer to fulfill chrononormative ideals. Grandma's concerns come from a place of love—she wants Archer to be married because she does not want him to be alone. But she is unable—or unwilling—to envision him as queer, trans, and happily partnered. Her worldview only encompasses what she understands as the markers of security in a colonial capitalist context: cisgender heterosexual monogamous marriage. When she attempts to give Archer a love potion in his tea, comprised of "something old" with "ancient wisdom," he swaps his cup with hers, leaving her to drink the potion before he meets with Owen under the Ponderosa again. Archer dodges his grandmother's attempts at a spiritual intervention, instead arriving at his own romantic conglomeration of ancient wisdom, bringing an old book on the history of the land's trees to his true paramour, the student attempting to recover a practice from his own temporarily lost lineage in order to save the ancient wisdom held by the forest.

Carter reminds us: "Transitions are brave work."

After Pops dies, Archer and his mother go through his things, deciding what to keep and what to sell. This process, in its own way, is a form of prescribed burning. To prune away the kindling so that the forest can continue to grow; to safely light the sagebrush to prevent future fires from burning without end; for the family to mourn what is lost, so that they can preserve what is left. When Archer goes through the box of his grandfather's things, discovered in Grandma's home, it reminds us of the grieving process she has gone through, offstage and presumably before the start of the play. This is a transition that she has braved, and even still, the process is not over. Transitions, remember, do not take us from one point to another—simply through.

We witness the grief that Archer and his Mom endure. The loss, inevitably, brings them closer together, once they are both able to grieve in their own way, at their own pace. Attempting to force each other's grief, to fit the image or timeline of the other's, leads only to a heightened sense of tension between the two. Once again: we each transition on our own time, in our own ways. There is no "normal" within states of transition. Nor is there, truly, a normal outside of transition—if there even is a space outside of transition at all.

Both Archer and his mother relive the final conversations that they had with Pops before his death. In these moments, memory becomes tangible; they speak their words out loud. In Mom's mourning, she speaks the words she said to him. In Archer's case, he relives Pops' side of the conversation, but offers fresh responses. He tells Pops his name: Archer. He calls Pops by his name: Robert Jason. Pops finally acknowledges Archer's name, wishes him a happy birthday, and then we transition—in the theatrical sense of the word—to the last scene, set at the Thanksgiving dinner table, one year later.

The play ends back at the Thanksgiving table for Archer and his family. The seasons change, though we do not witness them doing so. However, Mom makes reference to the bountiful harvest that her garden has experienced, with Archer's help and Owen's helpful advice in his fleeting meeting with her during his failed goodbye to Archer the previous winter. Interesting that the play begins and ends at the dinner table, the gathering space for the nuclear family, however un-nuclear it may find itself now. (Interesting also that the play, which makes explicit reference to the destructive nature of colonialism, still depicts its main characters celebrating colonial violence.)

Grandma and Peterson have found love together, as he joins her at the family table. The plants in Mom's garden have grown, with Archer's help. Archer has also acquired a job in town, for which he gives thanks, suggesting that, at least for now, this Sagittarius has planted some roots in this forest. What lies ahead for each of them is unknown, but for now, there is growth to be had in the wait.

References

Carter, Julian. 2014. "Transition." *TSQ: Transgender Studies Quarterly 1*, 1–2:235–237.

Freeman, Elizabeth. 2010. *Time Binds: Queer Temporalities, Queer Histories.* Durham, NC: Duke University Press.

Halberstam, J. Jack. 2005. *In a Queer Time and Place: Transgender Bodies, Subcultural Lives.* New York: NYU Press.

Mac, Taylor. 2014. *Hir.* Hanover, NH: Smith & Kraus.

Muñoz, José Esteban. 2009. *Cruising Utopia: The Then and There of Queer Futurity.* New York: NYU Press.

Sagittarius Ponderosa

MJ Kaufman

Characters

Actors
Archer Genderqueer. Archer to himself, Angela to his family. Twenty-nine.
Pops Archer's dad. Sixties.
Grandma She doesn't hear very well. Eighties
Owen Semester intern at the nature conservancy. Twenty-nine.
Mom Archer's mom. Sixties.

Puppets
Peterson Cute pot-bellied puppet, manipulated by Pops.

Casting Policy

Archer should be played by a transmasculine spectrum actor.

Where

Central Oregon desert on the edge of a Ponderosa Pine forest. The forest is also Archer's family house and Grandma's room at the old folks home. There are always multiple settings going on at once. It's important that the rhythms, the kinetic energy across different spaces be coordinated.

There's a gigantic majestic Ponderosa Pine. She never goes away.

Scene One

*The family (***Mom***, ***Pops***, ***Archer***, ***Grandma***) sits around the table. It's best if their table is set against a dark winter sky with snow falling. There's a turkey.*

Mom   Angela?

Archer   Snow.

Biker Mice from Mars.

3 Musketeers Bars.

That's it.

Pops   That's it?

Archer   I mean yeah, I guess so. There's probably more. Come back to me.

Pops   Laur?

Mom   My family.

My health.

My beautiful garden and all the food it gave us this fall. In particular the chives and the green tomatoes I brought in just this afternoon.

Archer   Like one tomato, singular.

Mom   Well one tomato is better than none!

And it was my first time with tomatoes, now I know they need more sun.

So, where was I? The garden.

Which was fun to make—no matter how much anything grew.

My husband getting better.

My lovely if occasionally obnoxious daughter.

Bob?

Pops   Oh, well, turkey, of course. Cranberry sauce, sweet potatoes, and still having a job even if I can't do it most days. Pumpkin pie, chocolate mousse—

Archer   Mom didn't make chocolate mousse.

Pops   I mean, in the world, in general. And my soft armchair with a wide enough seat for my whole big belly. Twenty-four-hour ESPN news that you can watch in the middle of the night.

Any last things, Angie?

Archer   Yes. I'm also grateful for my name. And for it being the month I was born in.

Mom   It's November. You were born in December. I would know.

Archer   I mean the astrological month. Sagittarius time. (*He nods at* **Grandma**.) I'm grateful for winter and graphic novels and IHOP burgers. Grateful for big beach towels and Dad being with us and, uh, coming home.

Grandma?

Grandma?

Grandma   Yes?

Pops   MOM, SAY SOMETHING YOU'RE GRATEFUL FOR.

Grandma   Grateful?

Pops   GRATEFUL. SOMETHING YOU'RE GRATEFUL FOR.

Grandma   Well. I am most grateful for one thing:

My granddaughter's going to be married!

Everyone looks at **Grandma** *with confused looks.*

Scene Two

Archer *stands next to the Ponderosa pine. He sits. He's feeling sleepy. He smells the tree's bark. Maybe the moment he smells it the whole theater does. That unmistakable butterscotch Ponderosa scent.*

Lights up on **Mom** *and* **Pops**' *bed.* **Pops** *turns on his bedside lamp and hobbles out of bed. He checks on* **Mom** *to make sure she's out as cold as possible. She doesn't respond to his poking. She rolls over and starts snoring.*

Pops *hobbles over to the big easy chair where he sits down and turns on the twenty-four-hour ESPN. The glow illuminates his eyes.*

In the old folks home **Grandma** *turns on the same station at the same time and we see her illuminated by the glow somewhere else onstage.*

They both listen to the twenty-four-hour ESPN while **Archer** *sleeps under the tree.*

There is a knock on **Grandma**'s *door.*

She gets up. A newspaper falls from above. In her mind it was just slid under her door. She picks it up. There is a note on it. She reads it.

Owen *enters the forest. He notices* **Archer** *sleeping under the Ponderosa.*

Owen *stands there for a minute while* **Archer** *sleeps.*

Archer *jerks awake.*

Owen   Sorry.

Archer   Sorry.

Owen   Nice smell, huh?

Archer   Huh?

Owen   The tree.

Archer   Oh. Yeah.

Owen   You shouldn't sleep out in the snow. It's dangerous. Hypothermia, you know.

Archer   Yeah. You're right. I'm just so, uh, sleepy. I can't ever sleep in my bed.

Owen   Big. Huh.

Archer   What?

Owen   The tree. It's the biggest in this forest.

Archer   Oh, is it?

Owen   I mean yeah. According to the nature conservancy. And we should know.

Archer   Oh.

Owen   I mean, we scout and measure. And this is definitely the biggest one. Biggest Ponderosa pine around. Oldest one. Might be like 400.

Archer   You think it's gotten bigger in the last few years?

Owen   Um . . .

Archer   I mean, like since I was in high school. How much bigger do you think the tree's gotten.

Owen   I'm just a semester intern. I wouldn't know.

Archer   Oh.

Owen   But I doubt that a tree like this could grow that much in such a short time. It's a short time for a tree, it's a longer time for humans. A year for us is like an hour for them, you know?

Archer   Wow.

Owen   You're from here?

Archer   Yeah.

Owen   Like, you were born here?

Archer   Not under this tree but . . . yeah.

Owen   You still live here?

Archer   I just came home.

Owen   For Thanksgiving?

Archer   No. For good. Or for a while anyway.

Owen   Oh. Like home home, or like got your own apartment in your hometown?

Archer   Home home.

Owen   Wow. Gotta say. I kinda admire that.

Archer   Don't. I don't really have a choice this time. Family stuff.

Owen   Okay, sure.

Archer   I mean, where I was living before . . . it was time to leave anyway.

Owen   Uh huh.

Archer   Just, didn't really expect to come back here next.

Archer *has a purple flannel handkerchief hanging out of his back pocket.*

Owen *notices it.*

Archer *notices* **Owen** *noticing it.*

Owen   What's your name?

Archer   Archer. Or Angie, whatever you want.

Owen   I like Archer. Where's it from?

Archer   It's like a thing, it has to do with Sagittarius and stuff. Because Sagittarius is like a hunter, a seeker, you know? And I really identify with that. So I took the name.

Owen   You a Sag?

Archer   Yeah.

Owen   I'm a Leo. Another fire sign.

Which means we're uh . . .

Archer   Compatible?

Owen   Yeah.

Wanna fuck?

Grandma *turns up the radio and settles in to listen excitedly.*

Herbalist (*voiceover*)   Welcome to Herbalist Earnestine's Late Night Potion hour! Herbal cures and magic solutions for every need and care! Tonight we'll be continuing our series on love potions. Getting ready to make a mix for that special someone.

Owen   Sorry. Was that too forward?

Archer   No. No, it wasn't.

Owen   I have condoms.

Sorry. I'm being too forward.

Just, uh, you're cute.

And it's a holiday and I'm far from home.

Even though I'm Twenty-nine. I still miss home on a holiday.

Fucking makes it better.

Archer   I had three years of missing home on holidays.

They turn towards each other.

Herbalist (*voiceover*)   Remember—you can make a love potion out of everything! Look for plants and foods with a sexy feel. A romantic vibe.

To get you inspired, let's review the top five aphrodisiacs of all time:

Grandma *gets eager to make a note of this.*

Herbalist (*voiceover*)   Asparagus, artichoke, banana . . . I can't remember the others. Oh boy. We'll come back to that.

As we know, for a love potion you need:

Something old

Something new

Something borrowed

Something . . .

No. That's for a wedding.

But you do need something old. I'd recommend gingko! Gingko is a plant that's older than humans. A plant that lived among the dinosaurs. You can order it from your local herbiary or natural food store.

Grandma *looks around confused.*

Herbalist (*voiceover*)   In any case, it is important that your potion contain something old.

So, keep your eyes open! Be creative with your old ingredient. Is there something in your midst with a dose of ancient wisdom?

Grandma*'s eyes wander out the window and settle on the Ponderosa pine.*

Archer *and* **Owen** *wake up from sleeping in the snow under the tree.*

Owen   You were asleep.

Archer   Was I?

Owen   We both were. We slept in the snow. Which is what I told you not to do.

Archer   I wasn't cold.

Owen   Two fire signs. Of course we're not cold.

The sun's rising now so I gotta go to work.

Archer   Work.

Owen   I work on holidays. S'why I can't go home.

Archer   Oh. Early work.

Owen   Nature conservancy. Gotta take a core sample from like ten different trees and then get back to the desk to answer questions.

Archer   Right now?

Owen   Every morning.

Archer   How come?

Owen   It's my dissertation. Gotta see if this tree's gonna make it.

Archer   This tree?

Owen   This tree. This forest.

Archer   What do you mean "gonna make it"?

Owen   Well it used to be able to survive wild fires. Used to have a bark like armor. But now the forest eco-system's changed. There's too many trees too close together, too much overgrown brush acting as kindling to the forest fire. More than there should be. Fires are intense now. We're not sure the tree would survive anymore.

Owen *kisses* **Archer**.

Owen   It was nice to meet you.

He disappears.

Archer *brushes himself off.*

He stands up to walk home.

Scene Three

At home **Mom** *is up making breakfast.* **Pops** *sits in the living room. It seems like no one in the house ever sleeps.*

Pops   That insurance commercial with the fake-tan lady ran ten times in the last hour.

Mom   Shredded wheat or steel-cut oats?

Pops   We outta Lucky Charms?

Mom   Bob. Sugar.

Pops   Steel-cut oats takes an hour and shredded wheat gets stuck in your throat.

Mom   Well, you can wash it down with one of those probiotic smoothies you love so much.

Pops   It's important to disobey your doctor sometimes.

Mom   Only if you're actually obeying him most of the time.

Pops   How about a half-and-half bowl of sugar cereal and shredded wheat?

Mom   Disgusting. Whatever you want.

Archer *enters.*

Mom   Angie, is that you?

Archer   Hi.

Mom   Did you just come in from outside?

Archer   I went for a walk.

Mom   Alone? Honey, that's not safe. It's not safe to go for a walk alone so early in the morning.

Archer   Who says?

Mom   I say.

Archer   I'm twenty-nine.

Mom   Also you forgot to empty the recycling.

Archer   What's Pops doing?

Mom   That's your chore now. You've got to do the recycling every week. We all have to help out around here. Also I'm going to need your help tearing up the garden and turning over the beds.

Barb said the restaurant's looking for someone to do a little marketing work, and I thought of you with all your fancy art skills. Want me to talk to her about you?

Archer *stares at* **Pops**.

Mom *looks up and notices.*

Mom   Bob.

Archer   Dad?

Pops   Huh?

Archer   He was just asleep.

Pops   Did you say something?

Mom   Go back to sleep. He needs his sleep. Doctor stresses that every time we see him.

Pops   What's going on?

Archer   Mom thinks I shouldn't be going out for walks at night but I'm twenty-nine. What do you think?

Pops   Leave him alone.

Mom   Who?

Pops   Leave him alone. I mean her. Leave Angie alone.

Mom   I just don't want you to get eaten by a coyote, that's all. Can I make you some cereal?

Archer   No thanks.

Mom   Yogurt?

Archer   I hate yogurt.

Mom   Eggs, anything? You need your protein.

Pops   I have an announcement to make.

Mom   Are you on one of those hunter-gatherer diets?

Pops   Would everyone please listen to me right now?

Mom *and* **Archer** *slowly turn their heads to* **Pops**.

Pops   I just had a dream. And as a result I am going to change my name. As soon as possible.

And I would like the whole family present. I'm going to do it this afternoon. So let's all get together then.

Mom   Bob?

Pops   This is something my doctor suggested. And I had completely forgotten. Until just now when I remembered in my dream.

Archer   Your doctor?

Pops   My doctor. Suggested I take a new name. Because he's Jewish. And it's something that Jews do when they are very sick. Because supposedly if you take a new name the angel of death won't be able to find you. And anyway he said it might be meaningful for me. And I think it would be. And I just had a dream. So I'm going to do it.

Archer   What's your new name going to be?

Pops   Jason.

Mom   Jason?

Pops   Robert Jason. You keep your old name. You just add on a new one. Is how he explained it. The doctor.

Mom   Will I still be allowed to call you Bob?

Pops   Bob Jason.

Mom   Bob Jason?

Archer   Why Jason?

Pops   I like Jason.

Archer   Such a best friend in second grade name.

Mom   Are you naming yourself after someone?

Pops   No.

Mom   You just chose it because you like it?

Pops   No I chose it because of its meaning.

It means healing.

Scene Four

*That afternoon. The family (**Mom**, **Pops**, **Archer**, and **Grandma**) sits around the dining-room table. They are a little dressed up. **Pops** is wearing his Halloween shirt with lots of funny striped colors.*

Archer   Do you want to call your doctor first?

Mom   Your father wants to do it now.

Archer   I know but don't you want to check how the doctor would do it in case there's something—

Pops   I want to do it my way. It's for me.

On this day November 28, I will be taking a new name.

I will no longer be just Robert. Which is a name that has served me well. And has given me many other names. Including Rob, Robby, and Robo-cop. And means, "bright glory." And is the name of many an important leader, scientist, artist, and otherwise important figure throughout history. And gave me my primary moniker since the age of ten which has been Bob. A one-syllable name, which I always liked. Because you can say it quickly. And it always made me think of bobbing for apples. Bending with a distinct goal and popping back up again. After getting splashed with water.

Basically, it's all served me very well.

My new name will be Robert Jason. Jason means health, healer, healing. Jason is the one who sought the golden fleece. Jason is two syllables and slides around in your mouth in a kind of satisfying way.

At least I think so. You're the ones that will be saying it a lot.

So. Let's practice. Let's all go around and practice calling me by my new name.

Mom   Hello. Robert Jason.

Archer   Hey, Bob Jason.

Pops   MOM, CALL ME—

Grandma   Hello. Jason.

Pops   Thank you.

Scene Five

The same night. **Archer** *is getting his coat and getting ready to leave. He checks his phone and his wallet. His keys aren't in his pocket. He looks for them.*

From the dark he hears:

Pops   Where're you going?

He's startled.

He looks around.

He still doesn't see **Pops**.

Pops *switches on a lamp.*

Archer   Going to take Grandma home.

Pops   And then?

Archer   Plans with friends.

Pops   You should bring her some leftovers.

Archer   She took home lots yesterday.

Pops   Just don't want 'em to go to waste.

Angela. Do you, uh, still want to be called that?

Archer   Huh?

Pops   Never mind.

Archer   No, what?

Pops   Just seems, I don't know, did you want a different nickname or something?

Archer   Where'd you get that idea?

Pops   Nowhere.

I mean.

I just changed my name so why not you!

Never mind. You remember the recycling?

Okay, Alix Weaver. She asked me because she saw something on Facebook.

Archer   Wow. Didn't know she was even home. Where'd you see her?

Pops   The grocery store.

Archer   Since when do you go to the grocery store?

Pops   Since I sometimes want a pack of Reeses peanut butter cups and a ginger ale.

Archer   Pops, you gotta cut back on the sugar

Pops   You're as bad as your mom, lay off.

Archer   Your doctor said.

Pops   Haven't had any sugar for two weeks, okay? Didn't know this was a police state all of a sudden.

Archer   Whatever.

Pops   Go take Grandma home.

Archer   I'm sorry.

Pops   Just go take Grandma home.

Archer *watches* **Pops** *exit.*

Grandma *sets up her room.*

Archer *moves to* **Grandma***'s room.*

Grandma   Stay and have a cup of tea with me.

Archer   I'D LOVE TO BUT I HAVE PLANS WITH FRIENDS.

Grandma   Just a little cup of tea? Look!

She points to the TV.

Archer   What?

Grandma   That baseball player. Isn't he attractive?

Archer *looks.* **Grandma***, as quickly as she can, pulls out a vial and empties it into* **Archer***'s cup of tea.*

Grandma   Don't you think? Don't you think he's attractive?

Archer   Not my type I guess.

Grandma   Want some tea?

Archer   Not really.

Grandma   Peterson has a single grandson.

Archer   Who's Peterson?

Grandma   What?

Archer   WHO'S PETERSON?

Grandma   Oh, the gentleman across the hall. We both get the *New York Times* but they made a mistake and started sending only one paper for this floor even though there's two of us. Now we share. Anyway. His grandson is very strong looking, very attractive. I hear he's in construction. Isn't that interesting?

Archer   WHAT ARE ALL THOSE BOXES?

Grandma   Hmm?

Archer   THOSE BOXES. IN THE CORNER. I HAVEN'T SEEN THEM BEFORE.

Grandma   Louie's stuff. Grandpa's stuff.

Archer   FROM WHERE?

Grandma   Storage unit. I wanted some of his stuff.

Archer   LIKE WHAT?

Grandma   His books . . . some things for you.

Archer *gets up and starts looking through the boxes.*

He comes to a book he wants to keep.

Archer   CAN I TAKE THIS ONE?

Grandma   Sure.

Come sit down. Don't you want your tea?

Archer *shakes his head.*

Suddenly he stands up and points.

Archer   Look! Behind you!

Grandma   What?

She turns around. **Archer** *quickly switches their teacups.*

Grandma   I don't see anything.

Archer   THERE'S SOMEONE THERE. SOMEONE PASSED BY YOUR DOOR, I SAW IN THE WINDOW.

Grandma   Who?

Archer   I DON'T KNOW.

Grandma   But there's no one there.

Archer   GONE NOW.

Grandma   Hmm.

She turns around and takes a drink from the tea that used to be **Archer***'s.*

Grandma   Probably Peterson.

Lights up on the Ponderosa pine. **Owen** *enters and sits down under the tree. He looks around and waits.*

Grandma   Want a snack? I have so many leftovers.

Archer   I DON'T REALLY LIKE THAT KIND OF FOOD.

Grandma   Meat? You don't like meat again?

Lights up on **Mom** *and* **Pops***' bed. They're in their pajamas crawling in.*

Mom   Okay. We can write down 8 p.m. in your journal, which is going to be great. Doc's gonna be thrilled. And I know you can't sleep past 8 a.m. but this way you'll have slept for twelve hours. If you sleep through the night.

Pops   Yup.

Mom   'Night, Robert Jason. I love you.

Pops   Love you.

They kiss. **Mom** *rolls over and konks out immediately. She snores loudly.*

Pops *stares at the ceiling.*

Lights out on them.

Grandma   Well. If you ever want to meet Peterson's grandson just let me know.

Archer   SURE.

Grandma   I could arrange for him to come tomorrow night if you wanted to come back for dinner?

Archer   I HAVE PLANS TOMORROW NIGHT.

Grandma   Oh, plans with who?

Archer   FRIENDS.

Grandma   Which friends?

Archer   I'M LATE. I HAVE TO GO.

Grandma   Well, just think about it.

So nice of you to take me home.

Archer   NICE SEEING YOU, GRANDMA.

Grandma   Come see me again.

They hug.

Archer *exits.*

Grandma *sits down on the couch with the love potion tea that she doesn't know has a love potion in it.*

Lights up on **Pops** *getting out of bed.*

Archer *enters the forest at the same time.*

Pops *hobbles over to his armchair. He hobbles at the same rate that* **Archer** *walks to the Ponderosa pine. Father and son move in unison.*

Pops *arrives at his armchair.* **Archer** *arrives at the Ponderosa pine.* **Owen** *is there.*

Owen   Hey.

Archer   Oh. Hey.

Owen   I was hoping you'd come again.

Archer   I hoped you would come again too. I brought this.

He takes out the book.

Owen   A history of Oregon forests.

Archer   From an old box of my Grandpa's books. I thought it might be interesting for you. Cuz it's old. And, like, your dissertation.

Owen   Sure! When's it published—oh wow '65. Yeah I wonder how they were thinking about wildfire at that time. That was before most of our research on prescribed fire. You know, like controlled burns. This is cool. I can really nerd out about this stuff.

Archer   Glad you like it.

Archer   By the way, what's your name?

Owen   I didn't tell you? Owen.

Archer   What does that mean?

Owen   I think it means, um, young warrior. Or something like that.

Archer   You don't connect to it that much?

Owen   Not really.

Archer   Why don't you go by something else? Or change it or something?

Owen   Well. I don't know. I like the way it sounds. And it sounds like me. Because I've been called it my whole life, you know. So it sounds like my name.

Archer   Mmm hmm.

Owen   Hey, I, uh, don't mean to be, like coming on strong by being here and stuff and, like, we don't have to fuck again or anything, I just thought it would be cool to see you again.

I mean we could do anything we want to do.

Archer   What if we just sit under the tree and see what happens?

Owen   Oh. Yeah.

Archer *leans into the tree.*

Pops *leans into the chair.*

Mom *relaxes in bed.*

Grandma *leans into her couch.*

Three generations fall asleep.

They are all having the same dream.

Then suddenly there is a knock on the door.

Grandma, **Mom**, *and* **Archer** *wake up.*

Owen   What? Is everything okay?

Archer   I just heard something.

Owen   What?

Archer   I don't know.

I think I was asleep.

Owen   You were.

Everything's okay.

There is another knock on the door.

Grandma, **Mom**, *and* **Archer** *sit up.* **Pops** *does not.*

Owen   What do you keep hearing?

Archer   I don't know.

Owen   Did you have a bad dream?

Archer   I guess. I can't remember it.

I can't go back to sleep now.

My heart's beating too fast.

There is another knock on the door.

Grandma *slowly moves to her door.*

Cautiously she answers it.

There's no one there.

She turns around to shut it when suddenly **Peterson** *puppet falls from above.*

He lies still on the floor. As he falls **Pops** *stands, stiffly, not like himself but like a marionette. He moves in slow motion to the* **Peterson** *puppet.*

Grandma *turns and stares at the* **Peterson** *puppet.*

Grandma   Peterson? Is that you? I was sleeping. I'm sorry I didn't hear you knocking.

Are you okay?

Did you fall?

Get up. Peterson?

Oh. Oh no, I'll call someone. I'll call the nurse on duty.

She turns to go back into her apartment and get the phone.

Pops *arrives at* **Grandma**'*s door.*

She doesn't see him.

He picks up the **Peterson** *puppet.*

Peterson   Anna?

Grandma   Peterson?

Peterson   Sorry, I can't hear very well.

Grandma   Are you okay? Did you fall?

Peterson   I came to bring you the newspaper.

Grandma   I can still call someone if you want.

Peterson   I'm fine, don't worry about me.

Grandma   It would be good to check in with someone. After a fall like that. You never know what could have happened.

Peterson   Would you like to read the newspaper together?

Grandma   You should at least visit the nurse tomorrow.

Peterson   I thought we could read together.

Sit next to each other and read.

Sometimes it's nice to read in company.

He sits down on the couch and sets the paper on his lap.

He pats the space next to him.

Grandma *sits down next to him.*

He opens the paper.

He begins to read.

Grandma *stares at* **Peterson**.

Peterson *notices* **Grandma** *staring at him.*

He stops turning pages and stares at her.

Peterson   Glad we can share.

So silly, a newspaper.

Only useful for one day.

After you've read it, what will you do with it?

Pops *puts the puppet down and looks at* **Grandma**.

She doesn't see him.

Archer   I need to go home.

Owen   Okay.

Archer   Thanks for letting me sleep on you.

Owen   No problem.

Archer   Come back tomorrow.

Owen   Of course.

Pops *throws* **Peterson** *offstage and starts walking home.*

Archer *walks home.*

They walk at the same rhythm.

Pops *walks slower and slower.*

He does a very slow dance of approaching the armchair, a Butoh dance.

He takes a deep breath.

And collapses into it.

Archer *approaches his father in the armchair.*

He studies him.

He comes closer.

Archer   Dad.

DAD.

Scene Six

Mom, **Archer**, *and* **Grandma** *dressed in black.* **Archer** *holds the mic.*

Archer   Hello?

Hi, everyone.

Hi. Okay. Hi. Here we um. So we want to thank all of you for being—and I mean especially the neighbors and the church and stuff because without you I mean, well anyway thanks. And I wrote down some things to say.

So um.

He reaches into his pocket and pulls out a crumpled piece of paper. He un-crumples it slowly and stares at it.

Archer No dad on the block could throw a tougher curveball!

No dad in the city could whistle louder at a little league game.

No dad in the country could make better chocolate chip pancakes.

No dad in the world could do a better Kermit impression.

That's all I got.

Mom It means so much to see all of you here. I know this is sooner than we all thought. I don't have anything prepared. I didn't think I would have to . . . so quickly. And I'm not good at these kind of public speaking things. Angela will . . .

She can't go on.

She pulls away.

Archer *steps forward.*

Archer Pops would have been psyched to see you all here. I mean, uh, Robert Jason would have. He would have, uh, wanted us to serve breakfast because he always felt it was superior meal with the best cuisine offerings, namely bacon. So, uh, there'll be a buffet in the next room. And he would have wanted us to play Michael Jackson. For obvious reasons.

Before we proceed, GRANDMA. DO YOU HAVE ANYTHING TO ADD?

Grandma I would like to add. Well.

I would like to add.

That I am so excited for the wedding.

Scene Seven

Mom's *room.* **Mom** *and* **Archer** *go through* **Pops**' *clothes.* **Pops** *watches them.*

Mom I don't want to do it but I'd rather do it than not do it.

Archer Is there anything that you know right off the bat you want to keep?

Mom Nothing. Get rid of it all.

Archer What if I want something?

Mom What? Want one of your dad's old work shirts?

Archer Yeah.

Mom   Why would you ever want something like that?

Archer   I don't know.

Mom   You don't want them. They're grody.

Archer   They came out of the washing machine an hour ago.

Mom   They're way too big for you.

Archer   That's the point.

Mom   And where would you wear them anyway?

Archer   I don't know. Anywhere. The bar.

Mom   This shirt?

Archer   What's so funny about that?

Mom   Nothing.

Archer   Fine. I'm donating them.

Mom   I don't even want to watch.

Archer   This his stuff too? (*He points to a pile of clothes on the floor.*)

I mean, clearly it is, the clothes he was wearing . . .

I guess I'll go through it.

Okay.

You want his, uh, watch?

Mom   No.

Archer   Really?

Mom   We should probably keep it. It's a nice watch.

Archer   I mean yeah, I think it's got like real gold.

Pops *laughs.*

It makes **Mom** *and* **Archer** *laugh.*

Mom   No. That is not real gold.

They giggle for a moment.

Archer   Whatever. I want it.

Mom   Check the pocket of the jeans.

In the pocket is a wrapper for a Reese's Peanut Butter Cup.

Mom   Of course.

Archer   He snuck out to get it.

Mom   No kidding he snuck out. He snuck out every night for sugar.

Archer   Mom?

Mom   What else is under there?

Archer   Are you okay?

Mom   Let's just finish this.

Archer *gets to the Halloween shirt that* **Pops** *was wearing at his re-naming ceremony. He holds it up.*

They both giggle.

So does **Pops***.*

Mom   I can't even remember who gave him that shirt.

Archer   It was Grandma, I thought.

Mom   That's right. It was his Halloween shirt.

Archer   And this. From the funeral home.

Mom   His wedding ring.

Archer   Grandma really thinks I'm getting married, huh?

Mom   Maybe tomorrow you could take her the hearing aid and have a talk.

You should probably set her straight about everything.

Archer   What do you mean everything?

Mom   She just shouldn't get her hopes up.

Archer   About what?

Mom   About . . . you know.

Archer   What's that supposed to mean?

Mom   Do you think you could take Grandma her hearing aid tomorrow?

Archer   Guess so.

Mom   Are we done here?

Archer   I am.

Scene Eight

Mom *stands next to her bed and stares.*
She starts to climb into her side.
It's not right.

She rolls over to **Pops***' side.*

It's also not right.

She walks slowly to **Pops***' armchair.*

She stares at it.

She sits down in it.

She turns on the TV. It is twenty-four-hour ESPN.

In her room **Grandma** *makes yesterday's newspaper into a tablecloth.*

There is a knock at **Grandma***'s door.* **Grandma** *stands up.* **Peterson** *is there, manipulated by* **Pops.**

He holds the New York Times.

Grandma   Oh. Is it, uh? The newspaper again?

Peterson   Nice to see you again.

Grandma   How was your day?

Peterson   Lovely weather.

Grandma   I re-used the newspaper.

Peterson   I see you re-used the newspaper.

Would you like to go with me on the Goodwill bus tomorrow?

Grandma   I'd like to introduce my granddaughter to your grandson.

Peterson   I need a new suit. I was going to look for one there. (*He sits down on the couch.*) I'd enjoy going somewhere with you.

He begins turning the pages in the paper.

Grandma *sits down next to him.*

They read together.

Archer *enters and approaches the Ponderosa. He sees* **Owen.**

Archer   Want some of my 3 Musketeers bar?

Owen   Um. No thanks.

Archer   I don't usually like processed sugar things like this but 3 Musketeers is special.

Owen   Oh yeah?

Archer   Best chocolate bar.

Because of the gray mushy stuff on the inside.

Sorry about the other night.

Owen   Everything okay?

Archer   No. Nothing's okay.

Peterson   Lots of economic problems in the EU, huh?

Grandma   I always like to read about those tycoons getting embarrassed.

Peterson *turns some pages.* **Grandma** *catches something.*

Grandma   Stop, the nuptials. Let's look at these.

Archer   Don't be quiet tonight.

Owen   Okay.

Archer   Talk to me. Talk a lot.

Owen   Sure.

Archer   Tell me about this tree.

Owen   Oh. What do you want to know?

Archer   Anything at all. Just talk about it.

Owen   Oh. Well, uh. It's called Ponderosa. It was named by some Scottish colonizer guy. But, I mean, it precedes all that. It's native. He named it Ponderosa, which means heavy, because its bark is so heavy. When I hear the name I think of the word "ponder," like "to think." So I really think of it as a thinking tree.

And uh, for hundreds of years there were healthy forests of Ponderosas because the Native Americans did this thing called prescribed burning, where they would set the forest on fire in a controlled way. And it would burn away the sagebrush and keep the trees healthy and the forest sparse enough that when it got really hot and there were real fires the forests could survive.

And, well, now we don't do that and that's why there're so many less of the trees. That and climate change—it's warmer now so there're more fires. So I'm like researching that practice and trying to restore it. And my great-great-grandparents might have done it. Because some of my ancestors are from right around here we think—Paiute nation. I mean, that's what the colonizers called them, northern Paiute, I don't know what they called themselves, what band they were part of or anything. It's really hard to figure out. And prolly not the same as the Native folks I've met through my research. It's been great to connect to them. But it makes me wish I got to know my own family better. Everyone from that side's dead and I never talked to them anyways and yeah now instead I'm paying a lot of money to the U and asking other people's grandparents to teach me what they could have taught me if I thought to ask them when I was younger.

But there's lots of stuff the U can't teach me. What they called themselves. What dialect they spoke. What they would have called this tree.

Grandma   Look at all those young people getting married.

All those families getting bigger.

Someone gets another father, another mother . . .

another child.

So much to celebrate.

My family just gets smaller.

Peterson   Diana told me your son died.

Grandma   Yes, my granddaughter's single.

Peterson   I'm so sorry to hear that.

Grandma   Yes, if you bring your grandson, we could introduce them.

Peterson   Let me know if you need anything.

Grandma   HOW ABOUT TOMORROW NIGHT?

Peterson   TOMORROW? YES I'LL COME BACK TOMORROW NIGHT!

Grandma   WITH THE GRANDSON?

Peterson   What?

Scene Nine

Grandma *and* **Mom** *in the old folks home. The next afternoon.* **Pops** *watches them.*

Mom   Here. Your hearing aid.

Grandma   What?

Mom   Here.

Grandma   What's this?

Mom   DID ANGIE COME OVER?

Grandma   Not today.

Mom   She said she was going to bring you the hearing aid. But she clearly didn't.

Grandma   It doesn't work.

Mom   Of course it works, just adjust it.

Grandma   It's broken.

Mom   It's brand new!

Grandma   No more, thanks.

Mom   Are all those boxes more of Louie's stuff?

Grandma   What?

Mom   LOUIE'S?

Grandma   Yes. And my stuff too.

Mom   We should get rid of it.

Grandma   I'll give it to Angela. She'll want my nice clothes.

Mom   SHE WON'T WANT THEM.

Grandma   She'll need a dress when she gets married.

Mom   SHE'S NOT INTO THAT.

Grandma   What?

Mom   SHE DOESN'T WEAR DRESSES.

Grandma   She's going to fall in love soon, you'll see.

Mom   I WISH YOU'D TURN ON THE HEARING AID.

Grandma   I put it in. It's broken.

Mom   Have you tried that button?

Grandma   When you're my age you'll understand none of these things actually work.

Mom   This one, this button—

Grandma   Don't touch me.

Mom   The one right behind your—

Grandma   Ow!

Mom   SORRY.

Grandma   DON'T SHOUT AT ME!

Mom (*whisper*)   Sorry.

I think it's on.

Grandma   When it's on there's a buzzing. That's what the world sounds like with a hearing aid. Buzz buzz buzz.

Mom (*whisper*)   I'll go now.

Grandma   I don't want her to be alone.

When she's old.

Mom   No, of course not.

Grandma   You think she wants to be alone? When she's old?

Mom   No, no of course not.

Grandma   She doesn't know what it will be like. If she doesn't get married.

Mom   But you and I were both married.

Grandma   Yes?

Mom   And now we're both alone. (*Beat.*)

So. When do you want to move those boxes?

Tomorrow? Next weekend? (*She picks up a newspaper.*)

Who's Peterson?

I think you're getting someone else's newspaper.

Scene Ten

Mom *and* **Pops'** *bed.* **Archer** *stands outside the door.*

Archer   Barb wants to come over.

Mom   I'm not home.

Archer   You didn't want to see anyone yesterday.

Mom   I already saw Grandma today. By the way you forgot to take her the hearing aid. If you say you're going to do something please do it. Like the recycling.

Archer   Okay.

Mom   And can you please turn your video games down? Sounds like an amusement park out there.

Archer   Sorry.

Did you tear up your garden?

I think I'm gonna go grocery shopping.

Mom   Make sure you get yogurt.

Archer   I hate yogurt.

Mom   Well, it's for me, not you.

She starts replaying her last conversation with **Pops**.

Mom   Okay. We can write down 8 p.m. in your journal, which is going to be great. Doc's gonna be thrilled. And I know you can't sleep past 8 a.m. but this way you'll have slept for twelve hours. If you sleep through the night.

'Night. . . I love you.

Pops   Love you.

Archer   Do you want any, like fruit or anything?

Mom   Angela, please.

Archer   What? I just wanted to know if you wanted any fruit!

Mom   Give me a break.

Archer   Geez fine.

But he stays outside the door.

Mom   'Night . . . I love you.

Pops   Love you.

In her room **Grandma** *watches ESPN.*

There is a knock on her door.

Peterson *is there.*

Peterson   Hello.

Grandma   Thank you for coming back.

Peterson   It's a lovely night.

Grandma   I'm happy to see you.

Peterson   Do you need help moving those boxes somewhere?

Grandma   Yes. I would love your help with that. Soon. Maybe tomorrow.

Archer *arrives at the tree.* **Owen** *'s there.*

Archer   Hey.

Owen   Hey. Cool sweatshirt.

Archer   Huh?

Owen   Is it weird that I'm here again?

Archer   You always ask if that was too weird or too much.

Owen   Sorry. I mean I shouldn't apologize.

Archer   That's usually a girl thing.

Peterson   What section do you want to read tonight?

Grandma   Anything you want.

Peterson   I'd be happy to read anything.

Health columns. Science section.

Grandma   I'd love to look at the nuptials again.

Archer   I have to tell you something.

Owen   Me too.

Archer   Oh.

Owen   You go first.

Archer   It's my birthday tomorrow.

Owen   Oh. Wow.

Archer   What were you going to say?

Owen   Um. That I'm leaving tomorrow.

Archer   Oh. Leaving for where?

Owen   Home. Semester's over.

Archer   I was gonna ask if you would come with me to have dinner with my grandma. For my birthday.

Grandma   I like the wrinkles on your hands.

Peterson   Your face is different to me tonight.

Grandma   I like the long line on your palm.

Peterson   You can't hear me and I can't really hear you.

I'd like to tell you all kinds of things.

Grandma   I see that line every time you turn a page.

Peterson   For instance, that your nose is very beautiful. I like the crooked part.

Grandma   This afternoon I worried you wouldn't come tonight.

Peterson   I have so many questions about your life. If we could hear each other I'd ask.

Grandma *touches her hearing aid.*

Peterson   What's that?

Owen   I was gonna ask if I could see you earlier because I'm leaving at 7.

Archer   Wow. Well, um, I can see you earlier. But you can't come to dinner with my Grandma.

Owen   Yeah.

Archer   Which is, uh, too bad. Cuz she's always bugging me about boyfriends and stuff.

Owen   I'd make a good grandma boyfriend.

Archer   Like, seriously.

Wow. You're leaving already.

Owen   Yeah.

Archer   That was quick.

Owen   I know.

Archer   Damn.

That sucks.

If you're not here I don't want to be here.

Owen   Don't say that.

Archer   This place is terrible.

Owen   This place has awesome trees.

Archer   There's nothing left here.

Owen   Didn't you have some family something that made you come—

Archer   It's over. The family thing's over.

Owen   You gonna go back to, uh, where was it?

Archer   Nothing to go back to there.

Owen   Where do you want to go?

Archer   I don't know.

Owen   You know, uh, what they say you're supposed to do when you're lost in the woods? Start a fire. And stay put. Kinda counter-intuitive. But that's what they say about people who survive. They stayed put long enough to get found.

Scene Eleven

Morning. **Archer** *and* **Mom** *sit at the table.*

Pops *sits at the head of the table.*

They don't see him.

Mom   If you want you can eat in bed.

Archer   I can't.

Mom   But you're not even eating now.

Archer   I forgot I hate eggs.

Mom   Did you go out last night?

Archer   For a walk.

Mom   Were you out with friends all night?

Archer   I wasn't out all night.

Mom   I heard you come in at 4 a.m. I always hear you come in because you crash into my lamp.

Archer   Well, it's, like, right in front of the door.

Mom   Who are you out there with?

Archer   Neither of us is going to take a single bite of egg, huh?

Mom   Let me get some salsa to put on it.

Archer   We don't have any salsa.

Mom   Didn't you go to the grocery store?

Archer   Yeah but I didn't get . . . you didn't tell me to get anything.

Mom   Yogurt.

Archer   Well I got yogurt.

Mom   How long are you going to be here for?

Archer   What's that about?

Mom   If it's longer than a month I suggest you find an avenue for gainful employment.

Archer   Who's done all the shopping this last week?

Mom   Look. If you say you're going to bring Grandma her hearing aid bring Grandma her hearing aid. If you say you're going to take out the recycling take out the—

Archer   Maybe we could practice saying something nice to each other or—

Mom   Or just eat in silence.

Archer   Maybe we should stay in separate rooms.

Mom   What?

Archer   So we don't fight all the time.

Mom   We don't fight all the time.

Archer   I'll just stay in the kitchen.

Mom   Does that leave me the living room?

Archer   Leaves you like the whole house.

Mom   What about when you have to go to the bathroom? Are you going to walk through my living room to get there?

Archer   Unless you find me a chamber pot.

Mom   Not at the dinner table.

Archer   We're eating breakfast.

I mean we're actually not.

Mom   Why don't I clear the table?

Archer   You're not even going to try it?

Mom   It was a sweet thought, okay.

Archer   Dad would have at least tried it.

Mom   He could eat anything.

Archer   Fine, I'll move out.

Mom   That's not what I—

Archer   You've been saying that this whole time.

Archer *exits.*

Mom *starts to clear the table.*

There's a knock at the door.

Archer (*offstage*)   And I'm not getting that.

Mom *waits.*

There is another knock.

Archer (*offstage*)   Seriously.

Mom *goes to the door.*

Pops *follows her.*

Owen *is there.*

Mom   Can I help you?

Owen   I'm looking for Archer.
Is he here?

Mom   Who?

Owen   Archer.

Mom   Archer?

Owen   Yeah.

Mom   You got the wrong house.

Owen   Oh, really?

Mom   Yup.

Owen   Oh darn. I really thought he said it was here. I wanted to surprise him.

Mom   Nope. Not here.

She turns around to leave.

Pops *stands in her way.*

Owen   Can I ask, just outta curiosity—did you take a lawn mower to your garden?

I, uh, saw a lawn mower out there in the garden and it looks a bit ripped apart. So I was just wondering if—you did that?

Mom   Yes. I did that.

Owen   Oh cool. Is that like a technique for something? I mean, for like gardening, is that supposed to help with something?

Mom   Sure.

Owen   Oh. What does it do?

Mom   Tears out all the dead stuff so you can start all over.

Owen   Oh, I see, like after the frost comes, you mean? You didn't want to try to let anything survive?

Mom   It's all dead. I checked. And I'd rather get rid of it.

Owen   What were you growing?

Mom   Uh, tomatoes. Chives. Cucumbers. Broccoli. Brussels sprouts.

Owen   Oh, that's great. Did you, um, get anything? Like, um, anything worth harvesting?

Mom   Well, I got a tomato and a few cucumbers and a teeny tiny broccoli.

Owen   Well, that's great!

Mom *clearly does not think that was great.*

Owen   You could, uh, try growing chard. That grows really well around here, it's pretty hardy, can usually survive a fair amount of frost. And, you know, next spring you could start the broccoli and the Brussels sprouts inside. Did you do that this time? Cuz that's really important actually.

Mom   What is?

Owen   Letting the seedlings get a good start. Inside. Where it's warm. I'd start them in like March. And then put them in the ground in May. Depending on how warm it is. I'd say wait til it's pretty warm to plant them outside.

Well, uh, I was gonna surprise Archer with these flowers. But I don't know where he is. So, um, maybe you'd like them?

He holds out some odd-looking flowers that were clearly not bought from a florist.

Mom *stares at them.*

Owen   Want 'em?

Mom   Um.

Yes. Actually.

Owen *hands them to her.*

Mom   Thanks.

Owen   You have a good day.

He leaves. **Mom** *takes the flowers. She puts them on the table. She arranges them for a moment.*

Archer *enters.*

Mom   These were for someone named Archer.

Scene Twelve

Lights up on **Grandma** *in her apartment preparing for company.*

Peterson *knocks on the door of* **Grandma**'*s apartment.*

Grandma   Hello! So glad you could make it. My granddaughter will be here any minute.

Peterson   My grandson will join us later.

Grandma   We'll be having lasagna tonight. I made it myself. My granddaughter doesn't like food out of a box. And it is her birthday after all. And I wanted to show you my famous lasagna recipe. It has a secret ingredient. Does your grandson like food out of a box?

Peterson   His name is Michael.

Grandma   I knew he would be just like my granddaughter. I just knew it.

Ask her about comic books. She likes those.

Archer *knocks on the door.*

Grandma *answers.*

Archer   Hi, Grandma.

Grandma   You look skinnier.

This is Peterson. We're having non-box food. Lasagna. With the secret ingredient. Peterson, do you like sun-dried tomatoes?

Peterson   I don't know if I've ever had them.

Grandma   But you've been alive so many years! How could you have missed sun-dried tomatoes?

Archer   Where'd all those boxes go? All those boxes of Grandpa's—

Peterson   Is your granddaughter coming too? Or just your grandson?

Grandma   WHAT?

Peterson   WHERE'S ANGELA? YOUR GRANDDAUGHTER?

Grandma   Oh! THIS is Angela. THIS is my granddaughter.

Archer   Hi. Nice to meet you.

Grandma   I'll go check on that lasagna. I'll be right back.

Peterson   What grade are you in, Angela?

Archer   I graduated.

Peterson   What?

Archer   I GRADUATED.

Peterson   Oh, oh. I see. From college too?

Archer   YES.

Peterson   My grandson Michael graduated from college too. He'll be arriving soon. Your grandmother said you like comic books.

Archer   Graphic novels.

Aren't you warm? Can I take your coat?

Peterson   I'm fine thank you.

He unzips his coat.

Underneath he's wearing **Pops***' Halloween shirt.*

Archer   Whoa. Where'd you get that shirt?

Peterson   Michael will be so pleased to meet you.

Grandma *comes back.*

Grandma   Only another twenty in the oven. How about some crackers?

Peterson   Smells delicious.

Archer   Grandma, I think I actually have to go.

Grandma   I know how you like olives, Angela.

Archer   I forgot I made plans with friends.

Grandma   Michael will be arriving soon.

Archer   I'd be glad to meet him another time.

GOODBYE, GRANDMA.

NICE TO MEET YOU, PETERSON.

He exits.

Peterson   Your granddaughter had to leave?

Grandma *notices his shirt.*

Grandma   Peterson.

Where did you get that shirt?

You smell like someone else today.

Who's that behind you?

She glimpses **Pops** *behind* **Peterson.**

Peterson *looks behind himself. He doesn't see anything.*

Grandma   I need to know who you smell like.

She sinks her nose into his shirt.

Pops *puts the puppet down.*

He hugs his mother.

Archer *arrives home.*

He hangs up his coat.

From the dark he hears:

Pops   Where're you going?

He looks around.

He still doesn't see **Pops.**

Pops *moves from* **Grandma***'s room to the house.*

He switches on a lamp.

Pops   Where are you going?

Where are you going?

Archer   I'm not going anywhere.

Pops   Where are you going?

Archer   I'm staying here.

Pops   And then?

Archer   I don't know.

Pops   You should bring her some leftovers.

Archer   No one eats in this house.

Pops   Just don't want 'em to go to waste.

Angela. Do you, uh, still want to be called that?

Archer   No.

Pops   Do you, uh, still want to be called that?

Archer   I don't want to be called that. I don't.

Pops   Never mind.

Just seems, I don't know, did you want a different nickname or something?

Archer   Yes.

Pops   Nowhere.

I mean.

I just changed my name so why not you!

Never mind. You remember the recycling?

Archer   Pops. I do have a new name. Like you.

Pops   Hey. Can you do me a favor?

Can you give me a ride to the grocery store?

Archer   It's Archer now. Archer's my new name.

Pops   Since I sometimes want a pack of Reeses' Peanut Butter Cups and a ginger ale.

Archer   Call me Archer, please.

Pops   You're as bad as your mom, lay off.

Haven't had any sugar for two weeks, okay? Didn't know this was a police state all of a sudden.

Archer   Pops.

Pops   Go take Grandma home.

Archer   POPS.

Pops   Just go take Grandma home.

Archer   ROBERT JASON.

Pops *freezes.*

Pops   Good night, Archer. Happy birthday.

He exits. **Archer** *stares after him.*

Scene Thirteen

Archer, **Mom**, **Grandma**, *and* **Peterson** *sit around a table with a turkey on it. Behind them is the big Ponderosa and snow falling.*

Mom   Archer?

Archer   Well, okay.

Don't even know where to start. So much.

Let's see. This delicious dinner. Especially the pumpkin pie. And the turkey.

My job. Which, by the way, thanks, Mom. Graphic novels. Sagittarius time. All the fun we got to have in the garden this summer. Ponderosa pines.

Mom   Okay. Well, um. Of course, my health, my family.

Food from the garden. A lot more this year than last. First of all the chard. Which is still growing despite the frost. And can be made into so many delicious dishes—I didn't even think I liked chard! Two little broccolis as opposed to just one last summer. Still figuring out that broccoli plant.

And *multiple* green tomatoes. Good thing I got them a little more sun.

Grateful for Archer helping me with the garden this summer.

And for us all being able to be together. Tonight.

Grandma   I'm grateful for Peterson.

Peterson   I'm grateful for Anna.

Grandma   And for the *New York Times*.

Peterson   Hear! Hear!

Mom   Anything else?

Peterson *looks behind himself. He sees* **Pops**.

The whole family sees him.

Pops   The recycling.

The way a forest recycles.

And how we were recycled.

Pops *exits.*

End of play.

Generations of Language:
Mashuq Mushtaq Deen in Conversation
with Stephanie Hsu

Mashuq Mushtaq Deen and Stephanie Hsu

Deen   I have strong feelings about language. I am stubborn about it, threatened by it, see its limitations and also its beauty. I fight with my friends about few things but I will draw my line in the sand when it comes to language. As a transgender man, I came out in a different era and with different language. There were very few words with which we had to imagine a future, but the words we had were lifesavers. Now there are many more words, but the words are policed. Words like *stone butch* (a term I first encountered in Leslie Feinberg's *Stone Butch Blues* in the early nineties, it refers to a masculine woman who doesn't like to be touched in certain ways) and *transsexual*, which once created space for my possibility, are now out of vogue.

And though I've known you for more than fifteen years, the fact that we're about to have this conversation in an *academic* context makes me wary. It's important to me that my work is accessible to a broad audience on an emotional level. The *-ese* with which academics speak to each other is very specialized, and . . . very heady, and though the head can be useful, I prefer to rely on the heart.

And then finally, as an artisan of words—a play*wright*—I know intimately that words are, in the end, deeply flawed and inadequate (and therein lies their beauty, kind of like humans). So I come into this conversation with you tentatively. That said, we've known each other a very long time—as individuals, organizers, and professionals—and you already know most of my secrets.

Steph   When we met in the early 2000s, I was in grad school and the field of queer and trans studies was merely a decade old. Genderqueer is a term that I identified with back then, but now I like saying that I'm a queer woman who is androgynous (another word that resonates curiously across different eras, especially in relation to Asian bodies such as mine). While you became a playwright, I became a writer of literary criticism and a teacher. My work is usually done later and behind your back, like a secretive thing, which I believe is a reason for the tension I've often witnessed between artists and academics who make them objects of study. I wonder, however, if you're not right about a necessary opposition between what we're calling the heart and head in the development of queer and trans culture. Maybe academics risk forgetting that language has limits when we choose esoteric words or create new ones out of perceived urgency or need. We could stand to remember that the sharp, analytical language we use to carve space in the world for ourselves and our communities can still cut both ways.

The dynamic of conflict or in-fighting with those who are closest to us is central to your play that we're introducing, *The Betterment Society*, which you note is "an allegory that steps out of itself and meets us in the flesh" (p. 65). I'm interested in taking these allegorical steps with you, starting by exploring the main oppositions or primal conflicts in Gertie, Lynette, and Doreen's world.

Deen When I set out to write *The Betterment Society*, I had in mind to interrogate the urban/rural divide. I had been thinking about how we often judge the other by the values that make sense in our own milieu. So this division between rural and urban America is where I thought the primal conflict was going to be. But after I wrote it, I realized I had written about a titanic war between the forces of masculinity (in Gertie) and femininity (in Lynette), and a precarious future caught between the two (in Doreen).

This Nietzsche quote often comes to mind: "Whoever fights monsters should see to it that in the process he does not become a monster. And when you look long into an abyss, the abyss also looks into you" ([1966] 1989: 89). Lynette is in danger of turning into all the things she despises about Gertie, and similarly, so are we. We want to topple the system of toxic masculinity, but there is a lazy rhetoric these days—and again, this is where I take language very seriously—that levels its weapons at broad swaths of people with blanket statements about how all men are chauvinistic, predators, etc. To me, this is lazy, and it misses the point that we all participate in propping up the system of toxic masculinity, women included. I think with this play, I must have wanted to take away that too easy divide between men and women and look instead at the way the forces are playing out within us. Personally, I feel that war within myself in painful ways.

Steph I'm also wary of the monolithic approach to gender that we find in certain critiques of masculinity or "the" heteropatriarchy, because the power you're talking about isn't an essential characteristic of one type of body. That's why it's so evocative that this gender war takes place between women. There is also a Town where the mountain-dwelling poor go to sell off parts of their bodies, and aside from this, "there's a very good possibility that there is nothing—*literally* nothingness," you state in the notes to the play (p. 64). Gertie's masculinity is forged in this rural dystopia where all is focused on survival, any desire for change is stifled, and every encounter with the doctors in Town leaves them with a little less of themselves. I'd like to touch on those forms of embodiment that are defamiliarized here. I have to ask, is this a world without the possibility of gender transition?

Deen I would say . . . on this mountain, there is no imagination yet that has created the possibility of a gender transition. And, perhaps, much of what makes gender transitions possible and needed in our world doesn't exist here.

Gertie is a stone butch (a term of old); she has already transgressed (our) gender boundaries, and in this world there's no conflict around that. This is a place without men. These women are not defined in opposition to men, but only in relation to each other. Being female here doesn't mean anything other than what they do—hunt, fish, shoot things, build things, sometimes sleep with each other, etc.

Before I transitioned, I had to first imagine the possibility existing. It was a complicated reckoning with myself and with the world that I live in. I used to ask myself, if I lived on a desert island, would I need to physically transition? And that answer, too, was complicated . . . But this necessity of imagination—I don't think this is limited to gender transition, I think this is true for all kinds of dreamings which someday lead to becomings. In any world, one has to imagine something into being.

Steph The racial imaginary of this world is especially open to possibility. Why is it important to you that no more than two of the three women should be played by actors who are visibly of the same race or ethnicity?

Deen The simple answer is that I'm a playwright pushing against the institutional bias towards white actors, and the assumption that non-white actors have to be in service of telling a story about ethnic difference or identity.

The more organic reason is that the play lives in metaphor. If all the actors are from the same ethnicity, the play begins to feel located in a known geography, and audiences begin to think we're in Appalachia or in some other mountain community. By having, ideally, three different ethnicities in the roles, the play is able to transcend geography. Age adds to this: Gertie is as old as the mountain and Lynette's not far behind. This is not a war between a specific Gertie and a specific Lynette; this is a war between larger forces in the world.

When audiences spend too much time locating the play in a "real" or known world, they miss the metaphor. I'd rather they look at our world and this world and notice that the massive differences point to the glaring similarities—for instance, the way these forces of masculinity and femininity are at war.

The masculine and feminine are energies are out of balance in our world. The mapping of those forces onto male and female bodies exacerbates that imbalance. If I've learned anything as a transgender man, it's the importance of balance. There are those who say men and women are the same. I would not be the first person to argue that *equality* does not equal *sameness*. I hope we can cultivate a balance of these very different energies within ourselves, and also in the world. Each has something to teach us, and out of balance, they can both be destructive.

Steph The theory and practice of gender equality is how I'd describe the work of feminism, and I can't help but see in these three characters the three generations or waves of the U.S. feminist movement. For instance, their volatile relationships bring to mind some of the conflicts that defined second-wave feminism, including debates over separatist communities and access to womyn's land, questions of childbirth and reproductive rights, and pressures to assimilate to one (white, straight, cis) model of "liberated" womanhood. The "Betterment Society" initiated by Lynette tries to practice domestic or feminine arts (quilting, singing, etiquette lessons, but also gossiping) for the stated purpose of self-improvement, but Gertie always manages to reveal the limits of this mode of sociality or gendered bonding. Convened during breaks in their labor at a subsistence living, these women's group meetings seem to mock the idleness of conventional femininity and pull-yourself-up-by-the-bootstraps meritocracy—and they usually devolve into screaming matches and threats of gun violence, which I want to take as funny, absurdist commentary on the art of feminist "processing."

Deen I don't think I'm making fun of feminist processing, but you may be right that I'm poking gently at a certain expectation by those women's magazines of old, and so a certain pressure that was placed on poor women, to cultivate themselves through (sometimes) arbitrary activities that were unrelated to the very real and very demanding work of the home, as if what they were doing wasn't already enough. I think Gertie is wise to this, actually. And yet, on the other hand, there is a way that if Doreen and Lynette were quilting, it would work fine, and if Doreen and Gertie were hunting together, that would also work fine, but something about all three of them around the same activity exacerbates the fault lines that already exist in their relationships. And because these are the only three people on the mountain, they are forced to reckon with each other, and in that way, this could be seen as an absurdist commentary on the relegation of these activities to certain bodies.

This reminds me of my school days and gym class: There were people who *hated* gym and, much like Gertie, took every opportunity to declare how stupid it was. But I think, in reality, gym was hard for them, and rather than be "bad" at it, they were contemptuous of it. I can't help but wonder if that's why Gertie torpedoes every attempt at Lynette's "Betterment Society" meetings: If she only has one hand, how can she possibly sew?

Steph The way you describe Gertie's predicament is all the more fascinating to me because I know you didn't intend it, but there's a resonance between this imagined bodily cutting and the practice of elective amputation by a subculture of people who identify as transabled—which I mention only because controversial comparisons have been drawn between transability and the medicalization of trans identity. Writers and activists such as Jasbir Puar and Eli Clare have carefully argued that disability, transness, and this subculture are different mirrors of the extreme degree to which capitalist exploitation and alienation extracts value from the body in fragments and parts. Puar uses the term "trans piecing" to emphasize how the medical-industrial complex has determined which surgeries are curative in restoring the body to wholeness, and which body modifications are pathological because they reduce the body's apparent productivity (2017: 45). As a trans man with cerebral palsy, Clare compares his experience of gender dysphoria to transabled people's accounts and concludes, "I have to say that I don't fully grasp their desire, but I do know that it is real and unrelenting. I could be one of those people who ask endless questions . . . Or I could quiet myself and sit with what I don't understand" (2017: 175). There's something about Town's unfathomable market demand for body parts supplied by the mountain poor, and Gertie more than anyone else, that contains and allows us to sit with these critical insights.

Deen I think audiences can definitely read a critique of capitalism embedded in the play. But for me, the selling of body parts in this play has illuminated the way traditionally masculine men in our world have often sacrificed parts of themselves—emotional facility, for example—in exchange for power or domination. And I don't think it's always a conscious choice. And so it's striking to me that we can actually see parts of Gertie that are missing, in a way that we often don't see (but which still exist) in our day-to-day life.

Steph There's another character in the play, Lil'ope, who can only be seen by Doreen, the youngest of the old women. Composed of multiple dancers' or movers' bodies, called into being by Doreen's willful imagination, and existing in a liminal space between the world of the play and our own, Lil'ope seems to embody the gender fluidity that's characteristic of third-wave feminism—and this figure is inspired by the unicorn, if we take the hint from the epigraph you selected, Rilke's so-called unicorn sonnet from *Sonnets to Orpheus*. In the casting notes, you specify Lil'ope's gender pronoun: "Himher is not the same thing as the current term 'genderqueer,' though it's possible that there is overlap" (p. 64). To create Lil'ope is to construct a newly gendered being by playing with sameness and difference across multiple bodies, and you challenge us to think about what kinds of gender presentations we could create with three (or more) bodies. What do you see when you imagine himher?

Deen (laughs) As a playwright, what I imagine in my head and what I see on stage are sometimes two very different things. But I can hope. I see a moving thing, something that can't quite be pinned down, something that defies language and definitions. Lil'ope is multiplicitous—is truly fluid, in the sense of movement. Heshe is possibility without limitation, constantly in motion. I see three or seven or seventeen bodies in space, all wearing the same simple costume, all presenting the same neutral mask—available for the audience's projections. And so Lil'ope is as multiplicitous as all the bodies in motion playing Lil'ope, *but is also* as multiplicitous as the audience. And yet is one being.

You bring up the term genderqueer. It makes me wonder if there aren't many ways to find balance. Genderqueer is one way. Perhaps I'm another. I am historically, biologically, and emotionally *both genders,* though I don't present or identify as genderqueer.

Steph I've learned from you the importance of recognizing that when I identified as genderqueer and in identifying as a woman now, I've never experienced gender dysphoria. Still, I think we agree that the notion of having a choice in our gender or sexuality can be misleading, because our desire for self-definition is constant—it's language that changes. It's been almost two decades since the publication of the groundbreaking anthology *GenderQueer: Voices Beyond the Sexual Binary*, edited by trans activists Riki Wilchins and Clare Howell along with Joan Nestle, a founder of the Lesbian Herstory Archives and an expert on butch/femme culture. Another inaugural collection, *Nonbinary: Memoirs of Gender and Identity*, was produced just a couple of years ago by Micah Rajunov and Scott Duane, and this book features the voices of nearly three dozen writers, including parents of nonbinary-identified youth. When we try to imagine genderqueerness and emerging forms of identity and expression—agender, androgyny, nonbinary gender, and so on—as opposed to old school terms, I wonder whose bodies don't fit which descriptions, and how we get better at imagining these possibilities.

Deen I often feel like the words that make sense to me are now forbidden by a new generation of word-makers. Words like *stone butch* or *transsexual* are words that are a part of my journey, my history. And I do feel like a man, even if that seems too binary for others. The policing of language around our identities has become militant. And on one hand, I get it: It's so hard to assert yourself in an unfriendly, unwelcoming world. But on the other hand, I agree with Carmen Aguirre's essay "This is Not a Rhetorical Question: Neoliberal Identity Politics in Current Casting Practices" (2020), that the idea that one can possess or claim ownership of an identity makes it a commodity, and reinforces the capitalist structure we live within. In the essay, she's sourcing the original theory of identity politics which came out of the second-wave women of color group, the Combahee River Collective, and was a much more nuanced interrogation of the role of identity politics in our collective liberation than current rhetoric often is. Now what I often experience is the white-washing I mentioned above (with regards to casting), or tokenization, or the wielding of identities as weapons in this current "cancel culture" we live in. (And by "cancel culture," which is a relatively new term for me, I mean a culture of fear around language and identity that leaves little room for intention and shared humanity.)

Steph You're right to mention that women of color feminism and its theory of intersectionality grew in direct opposition to second-wave feminists who were white, straight, and cis, and whose transphobic ideology persists today in the attitudes of trans-exclusionary radical feminists or TERFs, which is another new word. It can feel as if queer folks of our generation are caught in between these waves of gender politics and in the undertow of so much cancelation. To me, your work in theater and your queer activism have always appealed to a collective optimism and even a sense of spirituality. Your autobiographical play *Draw the Circle* features a Muslim prayer, and *The Betterment Society* invokes the metaphor of church. Like Rilke's unicorn, whose horn comes into existence because the people who love it always leave a space for it to emerge, the metaphor or imaginary figment can be very real in how it exerts a cultural force.

Deen I think Lil'ope and queer people, we're both like unicorns. At one time, we needed some space to be made so that we could find our way into the world, we needed to be fed with the possibility of being, maybe it was a person, or a word, or tawdry talkshow, or a website for trans people (there weren't very many websites when I was coming out). And for those who came first, long before I did, maybe they created possibility out of sheer nothingness. But now, here we are, and because we're now the magical unicorns, we're able to create space for others: We create the possibility of more freedom for all people. When I talked to mostly straight audiences, for instance, after performances of *Draw the Circle*, the conversation was not that "I am so different from them and they need to understand me"; it's rather that "we are so very much the same." I, a person who defied language, was able to find my way into the world. They can, too. They now have more freedom to imagine the kinds of men and women and *people* that they inherently are, and those boxes that they were put into as children, they can let those boxes go. Obviously this is easier said than done, but what I mean is that we—queer people, trans people, unicorns—by our very being, create the possibility. And that is magic. Lil'ope opens up a space that allows the possibility of dreams and songs and poetry and feelings . . . the possibility of finding each other in the dark.

Steph That brings us back to the possibility of nothingness which frames this world, or the possibility of *not* finding ourselves in each other. *The Betterment Society* has two possible endings—one of which is a gunshot—and the audience unknowingly makes the choice. What is at risk for the audience that does not sing along, and what is being offered to the audience that does?

Deen The risk for the audience that declines to sing is that the world will remain the same. This place is brutal, and it will continue to be so in knowable ways. The cycle of devastation will continue. And we, too, will be the same: The walls of the theater remain standing, but the heart is not filled with song. For the audience that *does* sing, they have taken a shared risk together, to sing out loud, to be heard by their neighbor, to experience that moment where the audience is aware of itself in an act of generosity—that experience is one they can take with them; they have risen beyond, through, above the mere walls of the theater. They have created a kind of church, maybe a better church than ever there was.

And this is a digression, but I want to come back to language for a moment here: Because language is a flawed tool, the idea that we can get it right or say it perfectly is a flawed supposition. What theater teaches me is that life is messy—people are flawed and language is inadequate—but we can still wade through the mess together and find a way forward. In that way, life requires a kind of humility. Maybe that's the church I envision, one of shared humility, and it probably won't be shiny, but it can still be durable, beautiful even.

And then, from that place, when we raise our voices in song or applause, in tears or laughter, we are in a room with other people experiencing our shared humanity. That knowing of the One amongst the Many, and the Many joined together as the One, that is the sacredness of theater.

References

Aguirre, Carmen. 2020. "This is Not a Rhetorical Question: Neoliberal Identity Politics in Current Casting Practices." Howlround.com, May 21. https://howlround.com/not-rhetorical-question.

Clare, Eli. 2017. *Brilliant Imperfection: Grappling with Cure*. Durham, NC: Duke University Press.

Nestle, Joan, Clare Howell, and Riki Wilchins. 2002. *Genderqueer: Voices Beyond the Sexual Binary*. Boston: Alyson Books.

Nietzsche, Friedrich. [1966] 1989. *Beyond Good and Evil*. New York: Vintage Books.

Puar, Jasbir K. 2017. *The Right to Maim: Debility, Capacity, Disability*. Durham, NC: Duke University Press.

Rajunov, Micah and Scott Duane, eds. 2019. *Nonbinary: Memoirs of Gender and Identity*. New York: Columbia University Press.

The Betterment Society

Mashuq Mushtaq Deen

Music by Nell Shaw Cohen

Lyrics by Mashuq Mushtaq Deen

Characters

Gertie Ornery. Abrasive. Leathery. She's as old as the mountain.

Lynette (lye-NET) She's got some maternal qualities, but that doesn't mean she's warm and fuzzy. She's almost as old as Gertie and she's pregnant and there's nothing particularly surprising about those two things being true at the same time.

Doreen Earnest. Pragmatic. A hard worker. Secretly, she has a great sense of wonder and curiosity about the world that she keeps to herself. She's a mixture of a little bit schooled and a little bit wise. She's not *quite* as old in age as the others, but she's an old soul.

The other character is Lil'ope (lil-LOPE), played by three or more movers/dancers; they are all dressed the same, wearing neutral masks, moving in synchronicity. They never speak. Together, they are Lil'ope, a magical creature of *possibility*. They present as himhers (which in the world of the play means something like, "the potentiality without the definition"). Himher is not the same thing as the current term "genderqueer," though it's possible that there is overlap.

Casting Policy

All three main characters are played by older women (trans or cis), with no more than two of any one ethnicity. The actor playing Gertie should be as old-school butch as you can get. These are tough, rural women. Any one of them could and would: shovel shit, toss a goat over their shoulder, shoot a shotgun. They are *not* smooth, shiny, sophisticated, or urban. The dancers/movers playing Lil'ope can be any gender and any age.

Where

1. What some would call a godforsaken mountain. Down from the mountain is Town. There are a very few mountains around this Town, and outside of that, there's a very good possibility that there is nothing—*literally* nothingness, like the map peters out and becomes graph paper, that kind of nothingness.
2. The theater we are in.

When

Not specified.

Playwright Notes

To the Players The pace is lively; it clips along most of the time. A lot happens in the silences. If there is a music to the play, and there is, then the stage directions are how the music is scored. Also, this is a place of survival, and as such there's no time sit idle and jaw. These characters are always productive, always mending, fixing, repairing, working.

To the Audience This play is an allegory that steps out of itself and meets us in the flesh. I want to destroy a church—what we think of as "church"—and build a new one, which is our heritage as theater makers: We are a kind of church. But is it a building that we go to, or is it community that we make, together? And I don't think it's enough to show up and sit in a seat; I think it has to do with participation, with stepping outside what's comfortable, what's expected. We are always in danger of becoming the very monsters we are fighting. What would it mean to find another way? What would it cost? And why don't we ever talk about God?

Acknowledgments

Many thanks to the generosity of Jessi Hill, Nell Shaw Cohen, Lori Wolter Hudson, Jeannette Yew, and to the many collaborators who gave their time and talents to the development process.

I do think that women could make politics irrelevant. By as a kind of spontaneous cooperative action, the like of which we have never seen. Which is so far from people's ideas of state structure and vital social structure that it seems to them like total anarchy. And what it really is is very subtle forms of interrelation which do not follow a sort of hierarchical pattern which is fundamentally patriarchal. The opposite of patriarchy is not matriarchy, but fraternity. And I think it's women who are going to have to break this spiral of power and find the trick of cooperation.

—Germaine Greer, recorded speech, Sinéad O'Connor's
Universal Mother album

This is the creature there has never been.
They never knew it, and yet, none the less,
they loved the way it moved, its suppleness, its neck,
its very gaze, mild and serene.

Not there, because they loved it, it behaved as though it were.
They always left some space.
And in that clear unpeopled space they saved
it lightly reared its head, with scarce a trace

of not being there. They fed it, not with corn, but only
with the possibility of being.
And that was able to confer such strength,

its brow put forth a horn. One horn.
Whitely it stole up to a maid – to be
within the silver mirror and in her.

—Rainer Maria Rilke, *Sonnets to Orpheus, Part Two*

Chapter 1: Quilting

A theater. An old one. Maybe it was once a church, but now it's a theater. There is a stage. The stage is set like so:

A godforsaken mountain. A place of vulgarity and simplicity and survival.

Down from the mountain there is Town. Outside of that, there is a very good possibility that there is nothingness.

A one-room house. Nothing is new in this house.

There are a lot of guns: revolvers, shotguns, rifles. There's an umbrella stand by the door filled with guns instead of umbrellas; one of the woodpiles is a pile of guns instead of wood.

A circle of three chairs.

Gertie *and* **Doreen**.

Gertie *is old and tough and mean. She has an eye patch and is missing a hand. She also uses a cane, but more to hit things with than because you notice her limp, and she always has at least one gun on her.*

Doreen *is not so mean. She seems to have all her parts.*

Gertie   She's ruining my mountain!

Doreen   We're trying something new.

Gertie   Fuck new!

Doreen   We're supposed to think positive thoughts, that's what she said.

Gertie   I'm trying. They're giving me a headache.

Doreen   Maybe don't try hard—try different? Like sometimes when the door is shut and you push and push and push but it won't open. It'll hurt your shoulder to keep pushing, so you gotta walk round back or climb in a window or sometimes just sit down on the step until someone comes along with a key or a crowbar.

Gertie   Why can't you just carry a crowbar with you? I always have a crowbar. I don't sit on no steps waiting for other people.

Doreen   It was just an example.

Gertie   You know, I think certain brains are made for positive thinking, like yours—it's soft—and certain brains are made for hard thinking, for doing—

Doreen   —for crowbars.

Gertie   Did you ever see me wait for someone to open a door for me!

Doreen   No.

Gertie   No! And you never will! And let that be a lesson to you!

Doreen   I feel like you're mad at me.

Gertie   I ain't mad at you!

Doreen   You sound mad.

Gertie   A raised voice is not mad, it's clarity, it's emphasis!

Doreen *has heard this refrain before.*

Gertie   Everything is not about you, Doreen, stop being so goddamned sensitive all the time.

Doreen   I'm trying, Gertie.

Gertie   Well, try harder!

Doreen   I will.

Enter **Lynette** *carrying stuff. She is not quite as old as* **Gertie**, *but older than* **Doreen**.

Gertie   For fuck's sake—!

Lynette   Watch your language, Gertie.

Gertie   Where in the devil's hell you been?

Lynette   I ain't been to hell, Gertie, and I told you to watch your mouth.

Gertie   We been growing old waiting on you.

Lynette   Bettering ourselves takes patience.

Gertie   I got better things to do than watch my nails grow.

Doreen   Lynette, you alright? You look a little peakéd.

Lynette   You know, Doreen, I've always admired your vocabulary—"peakéd," what a lovely word. That's just the sort of thing I'm talking about—*education.* (*She puts the box down.*) That's a good way to start. And so, with no further ado, welcome, ladies, to the first meeting of the Betterment Society of, well, of here. (*Unfolds a piece of paper.*)

Gertie   What's that?!

Lynette   I wrote a little speech.

Gertie   What for?!

Lynette   I wanna start things right. On the right foot. And since not everyone is as *eloquent as you,* Gertie, I wrote it down so I would say it right. Is that alright with you?

Gertie   It's just the two of us, what do you need—

Lynette   Is that *alright with you,* Gertie?

Doreen   It's alright with me, Lynette. Makes it seem real official.

Lynette   Thank you, Doreen.

Clearing her throat and reading.

"For too long, we women—we *ladies*—have been focused on survival. Instead of just surviving, it's high time we thought about *thriving*. I am starting this here first ever Betterment Society so that we will have a place for us to improve ourselves. We will learn about the *finer things* and in due course, we will become *finer people*. Let it be recorded that the very first members were Miss Doreen and Miss Gertie, and that the society was founded by Miss Lynette."

Doreen *claps.*

Gertie   That's a lot of words. A lot of words that said nothing. You beginning to sound like one of them po-li-ti-cians.

Doreen   I think it was nice, made it feel special, like the first day of school.

Lynette   And it is like the first day of school. We are here studying to be better people. Today is lesson one. We're gonna have us a quilting circle.

Gertie   Quilting?!

Lynette   Quilting is something that ladies do together. We take a lot of nothing, like scraps from old clothes, and we turn it into something—a quilt. As we quilt, we talk about comings and goings, we learn from each other and our experiences, and we, we *bond*.

Gertie   You ain't said nothing about "quilting" when you asked me to come to this meeting!

Lynette   It's all different things, and today is quilting!

Gertie   I don't know how to quilt!

Lynette   We're here to learn—

Gertie   I don't wanna know how to quilt!

Lynette   Now, Gertie, you promised, you promised you'd be nice!

Gertie   I am being nice! This is me being nice!

Lynette   You promised you would participate!

Gertie   You didn't say nothing about no quilting, no "ladies' society"!

Lynette   I said we were gonna improve ourselves.

Gertie   You said you needed my help.

Lynette   And I do. Ain't no one else here to help me except you two—

Gertie   "AIN'T NO ONE ELSE"? So you did that whole song and dance cause I was the only choice you had?!—

Lynette   I—

Gertie   —You hiked up your skirt for me, but you would've done it for anyone, is that it? Is that it, Lynette?

Gertie *puts her hand on her gun.*

Doreen   Now, Gertie, take it easy—

Gertie   I feel used, Lynette. I feel like you took me for a ride.

Lynette   Who took who for a goddammed *ride*, Gertie? I did something for you and you promised to do something for me. Now you keep your goddammed word, Gertie, or else!

Gertie   Or else what?!

Lynette   OR ELSE!

The standoff is tense. **Gertie**'s *hand is still on her gun.* **Doreen** *steps between them.*

Doreen   Should I pass these around? . . . How many do you think? (*She places squares of fabric on the chairs.*) One, one, one . . . two, two, two . . . three, three, three—how about three to start?

Lynette   I think it's four.

Doreen   Four, four, four.

Lynette   . . . Thank you, Doreen.

Doreen   You're welcome, Lynette.

Gertie   So what do we do with this stuff?

Lynette   We sew the pieces together into squares. And then we sew those squares together to make a quilt. And the squares should have designs. And sometimes the designs tell a story and sometimes they're just pretty.

Doreen *threads her needle.* **Lynette** *does the same.* **Gertie** *tries.*

Lynette *and* **Doreen** *sew.*

Gertie *still can't thread the needle. She's getting frustrated.*

Doreen *takes the needle from* **Gertie**, *threads it, gives it back.*

Gertie   Now what?!

Doreen   You sew them together. Right, Lynette?

Lynette   Right. I think so. Yes.

Gertie   You don't know?!

Lynette   I'm learning same as everyone else.

Doreen   I remember this—this was Gertie's shirt the year my momma passed. That was a long time ago. Remember, Gertie, you used to let me wear it.

Gertie   It was the only way I could pry you off my leg. We used to have to wash you and it together, you never would let it go.

Doreen   Where'd you find it?

Lynette   Gertie never throws nothing away.

Gertie   It's wasteful to throw good things away.

Lynette   At some point things stop being *good* and they start being *trash*.

Silence and sewing.

So much silence.

More silence.

Doreen   This is nice.

Gertie   What's nice?

Doreen   Talking. Us talking.

Gertie   I don't hold no store in talking.

Doreen   I like it. What else are we supposed to do, Lynette?

Lynette   I think we're supposed to tell each other things, like things we're struggling with, and get advice.

Doreen   Like secrets?

Lynette   No, not secrets. "All ladies should have secrets." (*Whispering.*) (That's what diaries are for.)

Doreen (*whispering back*)   (Diaries!)

Gertie   I can hear you.

Lynette   (Diaries take a lot of reading and writing though.)

Doreen   (Oh. Right.)

Gertie   I can still hear you.

Lynette   (Maybe that can be something for down the line.)

Gertie   I ain't gonna learn how to READ and I ain't gonna learn how to WRITE more than what's necessary.

Lynette   And how much reading is that?

Gertie   I can get me the right bullets for the right gun. I can buy something and I can sell something. That's all I need.

Lynette   Don't you ever want to better yourself, Gertie? Learn something more? Be something better?

Gertie   Why'd I want to be better than I am? What's wrong with what I am?

Lynette   Ain't nothing wrong with you, but don't you dream of the future? Of a better life? Of leaving some kind of legacy behind?

Gertie   Legacy? For what?

Lynette   For "whom."

Gertie   Whom what?

Doreen   Like if we had children, Gertie, we could leave them better off than how we grew up. More learning, schooling, so maybe they could have a better life.

Gertie   A better life? That's the biggest load of hog shit I ever heard. There ain't nothing worse than an uppity child who thinks she's better than her momma. And she ain't better. A good momma works *hard*, on the *land*, has a simple *mind* and a strong *back*—like your momma, Doreen, she was a good woman.

Lynette   But she worked hard so that Doreen wouldn't have to, not in the same way. She sent Doreen to school even though she ain't had no schooling of her own.

Gertie   And what that schooling got you, Doreen? You got a better life cause of it?

Lynette   Maybe if her momma ain't 'a been working so hard, she would've had time to be loving to Doreen! To tell her she loved her—

Gertie   *Loved* her? Ain't no one can tell you that. If you don't know it then nothing nobody says can change that. If Doreen don't know love, that's on her. And when you know, then you know and can't no one take it away from you. Is that what all this *betterment* is about? Not feeling *loved*?!

Lynette   We may not feel loved, but at least our children could.

Gertie   We ain't got no children, ain't never had no children, ain't got no use for no children. I'd just as soon shoot one as look at them as kick them down the mountain. They are useless, hungry, whiny creatures that come from the devil.

Lynette   Doreen was a child when she came here!

Gertie   It weren't her fault her momma died on her!

She puts her hand on her gun.

Something's happening here and I don't understand it and I don't like it.

Doreen (*she's figured it out and knows* **Gertie** *will take it hard*)   Um, I think what Lynette's trying to say is that she's with child.

Gertie *draws her gun. She doesn't know if she should point it at* **Doreen** *for telling her, or* **Lynette** *for it being true.*

She settles on **Lynette**.

Gertie   It better be mine. Is it mine?! I ain't never got 'a woman knocked up before, but I done some stuff with you that I ain't done with other women . . . Am I gonna be a daddy?

Lynette   No, Gertie, you're not the daddy.

Gertie   There ain't no one else on this godforsaken mountain! How'd you get knocked up?! . . . You ain't givin me a lot of reasons not to shoot you. (*She thinks for a moment.*)

Lynette *gets weak.* **Doreen** *helps her.*

Gertie What's wrong with her?! What's wrong with you, Lynette?!

Doreen She's with child, Gertie. It makes her sick in the stomach.

Gertie *puts her gun down.*

Gertie Yeah, makes me kind of sick in the stomach, too.

She sits. **Lynette** *sits.* **Doreen** *remains standing.*

A beat, and then:

A large, old, abandoned bell rings. Only **Doreen** *hears it.*

The work of life continues in the dim background as **Doreen** *steps out—*

AN INTERLUDE

—and into a liminal space.

She looks at **Gertie** *and* **Lynette**,

at the set,

and then at the edge of the set.

She reaches out to touch the fourth wall . . .

Lights lag, but shift to follow her.

Doreen (*to* **Gertie** *and* **Lynette**) You can't hear it.

I hear it.

A distant strain of music is heard.

I can hear it.

Oh . . .

Blackout.

Chapter 2: Manners

The outside of a ramshackle cabin, sitting—literally—atop a godforsaken mountain. A ramshackle outhouse nearby.

Doreen I'm glad we're going to have another meeting. I like the idea of bettering ourselves.

Gertie Don't get no lofty ideas.

Doreen I won't get no lofty ideas. I like it though. All of us spending time together.

Gertie You're hopeless, Doreen.

Doreen I don't know, I think maybe I'm hopeful.

Gertie   You can't eat hope, or nail it up into a house, or put it on to keep out the cold.

Doreen   I know. I just like the idea that things are possible.

Gertie   You're old enough to know better than that.

Doreen   I guess. How come you came back for the second meeting?

Gertie   Well, it wasn't to better nothing—I'm as better as I'm gonna get. I'm like a piece of jerky, I'm just gonna get tougher and chewier and at some point you'll have to spit me out and bury me. I came back cause Lynette's been avoiding me and me and her need to have some words.

Doreen   You aren't really gonna shoot her, are ya?

Gertie   Depends. I like to think Lynette can be reasonable, but if not, I'm leaving my options open.

Doreen   You'd miss her.

Gertie   There's lots of places to shoot a person, you don't got to kill 'em.

Doreen   What do you think we're doing this time?

Gertie   Fighting probably.

Doreen   To better ourselves. What kind of thing are we doing to become better people.

Gertie   Fighting probably. I sure as shit ain't quilting.

Doreen   I thought maybe we could sing.

Gertie   I *hate* singing.

Doreen   I didn't know that.

Gertie   Hate it! Over my dead body will I raise my voice in song.

Doreen   All kinds?

Gertie   All kinds of what?!

Doreen   All kinds of music? Do you hate all kinds?

Gertie   I don't know, I ain't heard all the kinds yet, but all I heard so far.

Doreen   How come you hate it so bad?

Gertie   You're asking a lot of questions.

Doreen   I got me a curiosity inside.

Gertie   How long you had *that* affliction?

Doreen   I don't know. I always had it in me I think, I just keep it to myself.

Gertie   Hmph. (*To outhouse.*) LYNETTE, WHAT IN GODDAMNED HELL IS KEEPING YOU?

Lynette *yells from the outhouse.*

Lynette   GET OFF MY GODDAMNED BACK, GERTIE!

Gertie   I'M AT YOUR DAMNED MEETING, AIN'T I? DOREEN AND I ARE THE FOUNDATION OF YOUR STUPID SOCIETY AND WHERE THE HELL ARE YOU? WE'RE GETTING BETTER WITHOUT YOU. I'M SO MUCH BETTER ALREADY I CAN'T HARDLY STAND IT.

Lynette (*from outhouse*)   YOU ARE MEAN, GERTIE, MEAN AND EVIL, AND I HATE YOU WITH EVERY FIBER OF MY BEING, I HOPE YOU DIE DIE DIE! AAARGHHHH!

Gertie   She'll be out soon.

Doreen   Gertie?

Gertie   What?

Doreen   How come you hate singing?

Gertie   How come you care so much why I hate singing?

Doreen   I don't know. I guess I can't imagine why anyone'd hate it.

Gertie *looks at her for a long, hard moment. Is answering her questions worse? Or is listening to more of her questions worse? It's hard to tell.*

Gertie   Church.

Doreen   What church?

Gertie   When I was little my momma took me to church—we had a church back then, oh feels like a century ago. Probably was a century ago. Sometimes we had as many as six or seven people in those pews. There was a lot of talking at that church, and a lot of guilting—and then some singing—and the singing made people feel something, something soft—and then they passed the plate and took our money, money we didn't even have it to give, they took it. It was cause of the singing, I know it.

Doreen   But what if it wasn't church singing, what if it was just regular singing?

Gertie   Ain't no such thing—when people raise their voices together, it's all the same.

Doreen   I bet singing together is a powerful thing. But maybe you could use it for good, instead of to steal from people.

Gertie   Famous last words. Don't mess with it, that's my advice. People start singing and the next thing you know, LYNETTE'S KNOCKED UP, I WOULDN'T BE SURPRISED IF THAT'S HOW IT HAPPENED.

Lynette (*from outhouse*)   THAT AIN'T HOW IT HAPPENED!

Gertie   Churches and whorehouses, I don't trust 'em. People are looking for salvation—looking to rise up out of themselves. It's bad news. And there's always someone twinkling their fingers on the piano. You hear people singing together, you turn around and walk away.

They wait, surrounded by the sounds of the mountain.

Doreen   So what do you think we're gonna do at the meeting to better ourselves?

Gertie   YOU EVER COMING OUT OF THERE, LYNETTE?

The outhouse does not respond.

Gertie   *I don't know*, Doreen, why don't you ask her.

Doreen   LYNETTE, IF YOU'RE NOT FEELING WELL, I HAVE ANOTHER IDEA FOR WHAT WE COULD DO FOR THE MEETING. Not singing, Gertie, something else.

Gertie   What something else?! Why you got so many ideas today, Doreen?! You always been so quiet, and now all of a sudden you have "ideas" and "curiosities"—what's wrong with you?!

Doreen   Nothing's wrong with me I don't think. I don't know what's gotten into me, maybe the idea of Lynette having a child has made me wonder about the world, has made me feel wonder about all kinds of things. Wonder about you, Gertie, and if you were ever young like me. Wonder about Lynette and her baby and what it's like to make a new person. Wonder about people all over and if they're basically the same or basically different.

Gertie   You know, if I shot you in the foot, you wouldn't wonder about nothing except the pain in your foot.

Doreen   Oh I don't mind the wondering, it don't hurt none. I can put it away when I have chores to do, but it makes the world feel kind of big and also kind of small all at the same time. I kind of like it and it kind of hurts, but not in a bad way.

Gertie   You've just said more words than I have ever heard you say at one time in your entire life.

Doreen   I don't think I like saying them as much as I like holding them inside me. The words change somehow when you say 'em out loud.

Lynette *enters from the outhouse dabbing the corner of her mouth. She has composed herself.*

Lynette   The second meeting of the Betterment Society can now come to order, Miss Lynette presiding. In attendance are Miss Doreen and, well—(*She gives* **Gertie** *the evil eye then ignores her.*)—I thank you for your patience, Doreen, I was feeling unwell momentarily, but it has thankfully passed.

Doreen   Wow, Miss Lynette, you sound real nice, like a real lady.

Lynette   You too, can be a lady, my dear Doreen, with just a little bit of effort.

Gertie   What about me? You gonna make a lady out of me, too?

Lynette   What was that sound? It sounded like an ugly old bullfrog. Doreen, would you please tell that ugly old bullfrog that no matter how many times it gets kissed by a princess, it will always be *ugly* and *old* and a *bullfrog*.

Gertie   You gonna make me mad, Lynette, with all your games. I don't have time for games.

Doreen   I think Gertie wants to be a part of the meeting, too.

Lynette   If she wants to, then she may. Far be it from me to keep her from high society.

Gertie   You ain't no high society lady, you're just the same old mountain girl you'll always be: smart enough to know better, but too stupid to keep her britches on.

Lynette   Gertie, you can be at my meeting if you want to be, but you mind that mouth of yours.

Gertie   I don't give a damn about your stupid meeting, I want to know and you're gonna tell me!

Lynette   It ain't none of your business, Gertie.

Doreen   Lynette, what kind of things are we learning today?

Lynette   We are learning about manners, Doreen, something that is sorely lacking around here.

Gertie   Bringing another mouth to feed into my house is damn well my business.

Lynette   I thought it was *our* house?

Gertie   It's *our* house cause I say it's *our* house, which means it's goddamned *my* house first!

Lynette   Maybe I should leave then. You wouldn't last five minutes without me.

Gertie   You wouldn't last five minutes off this mountain.

Lynette   I could move to Town.

Gertie   Ha! The only thing you'd be good for is the whorehouse, but who knows, maybe you'd be good at it. Or, maybe you'd end up a stump, no hands, no feet, sleeping with the dogs for a stale piece of bread.

Lynette   Fuck you, Gertie.

Gertie   You done already fucked someone. I ain't playing at seconds.

Lynette   Gertie, I am with child and I am gonna give birth to this child and that is that. If you don't like it, you can go ahead and shoot me, but otherwise, I have an important meeting to attend to.

Gertie   I only asked whose the child was.

Lynette   I don't know, Gertie. Just some fella.

Gertie   Did he step onto my mountain, or did you step off it?

Lynette   I wouldn't leave the mountain.

Gertie   Well, who was he?!

Lynette   I don't know!

Gertie   Well, if I don't know who it was, how will I find him and kill him?

Lynette   You can't.

Gertie   What if he comes looking for you?

Lynette   He won't.

Gertie   How do you know?

Lynette   He won't, I just know.

Doreen   . . . So we're gonna learn about manners today?

Lynette   Yes. We are. Manners are what separate the civilized from—(*Looks at Gertie.*)—the uncivilized.

Doreen   Manners like saying please and thank you?

Lynette   Yes, like that. Manners like washing your hands before a meal, saying "please pass the salt," using the right fork, these are things that civilized people— well-bred people—do.

Gertie   How many forks you need to eat a meal?!

Doreen   I got a question about civilization.

Lynette   What about it?

Doreen   Well, civilization is supposed to be better, right? I mean what Lynette said, that's what people think, that we are uncivilized people and people down the mountain, people in town, are civilized, are better than us, better off than us.

Gertie   I don't think that.

Doreen   And down the mountain is where you go when you need to buy things or sell things.

Gertie   What're you getting at?

Doreen   Well, I was just wondering, those people in Town, they need you to bring them food cause they can't grow any of their own, right?

Gertie   So?

Doreen   And so it seems like the things that grow, grow out here on the mountain with us. And down there, they can make bullets and guns and stuff, but they can't make food.

Gertie   You sure do tell a slow story, Doreen.

Doreen   Well, it just seems to me that their lands down there in civilization ain't very fertile—and I know you don't like no church talk, Gertie, and this ain't church talk, this is just a little bit of God talk—but ain't God, ain't he—

Gertie   God's too mean to be a man.

Doreen   —Ain't she, ain't God, supposed to have punished the wicked people with land that done dried up and couldn't grow nothing? And weren't God supposed to love the good people and give them fertility, so that their herds would not diminish?

Gertie   Yeah, that's pretty basic—if you got a good life, then you must of done something good, and if you got a shit life then you must of done fucked up somewhere.

Doreen   Well, my question is, well, on the one hand, in Town, they got lots of people and their herds don't seem to be diminishing, but on the other hand, they don't have no fertility, they can't even get knocked up like Lynette, right? That's what you said.

Gertie   Right.

Doreen   So do we live on a godforsaken mountain, or do we live in paradise?

Lynette   This ain't no paradise, Doreen, no one would ever mistake this rotten spot for paradise.

Doreen   But you're with child, ain't that a blessing, a little bit of green popping up through fallow earth? So I can't quite make out if civilization is a good thing or a bad thing, in the grand scheme of things.

Gertie   Some times a child is a blessing, like you were to your momma. And sometimes a child is a curse, like the way I was to my folks. And that is wholly different from whether it's better to live up here on the mountain or in Town. (*To* **Lynette**.) Is it a blessing on you, Lynette?

Lynette   I ain't known a blessing in my whole life.

Gertie   It's gonna be a curse on us, and it ain't gonna be its own fault, but it's gonna be that way just the same. Who's gonna care for it and feed it and clothe it? That child is gonna grow up knowing that it's the reason there ain't enough to eat, why their momma is ragged and tired to the bone.

Lynette   I could do it all. I could take care of this child and still do my chores. And it's only for a few years and then the child'd be able to do its own chores, it'd be another pair of hands working alongside.

Gertie   Maybe. . . . But in the meantime, how you gonna keep up with your chores?

Lynette   I'll figure it out.

Doreen   I'll help!

Gertie   You gonna have the baby here?

Lynette   We could do it. . . . I think we could do it.

Gertie   Maybe. . . . I been around a long time. You've been around almost as long as me, almost as long as people have been on this land. And in that time, I've set bones, made poultices for a fever, but I ain't no doctor, I ain't delivered no babies . . . Now animals, they don't need no help, not really, but I know how to stick my good hand in and give a calf a yank to get her out, but people babies?

Lynette   You could do it.

Gertie   People babies are a helpless mess. Sometimes they don't wanna come out at all.

Lynette   Then I'll go to Town.

Gertie   You never been to Town. You sure you want to start?

Lynette   I want this baby.

Gertie   Now, going to Town, that takes money. This ain't a godforsaken mountain for nothing—we ain't had much rain this year, it's a miracle anything comes up at all. We don't have much to sell, not even for the essentials.

Lynette   I know that.

Gertie   You willing to sell something to get that money?

Lynette   Sell myself, you mean?

Gertie   I sold my hand. I sold my eye. I need what I got left to shoot. 'Sides, I ain't the daddy. The fella who got you knocked up, he got any money?

Lynette   No, no, he ain't had any money. I had to kill him, Gertie. I felt like you, I felt like the devil.

Doreen   Why'd you have to kill him, Lynette?

Gertie   Cause he would have followed her home and been another mouth to feed. Am I right?

Lynette   Oh you are always right, Gertie, and you know it. It's the most *endearing* quality about you.

Gertie   So?

Lynette   I don't know, I need a minute to figure it out.

Gertie   You're a healthy girl.

Lynette   I ain't been a girl in a long time.

Gertie   Fine, a healthy woman then. You got assets. (*She raps her eye patch with her knuckles.*) I did it. Reckon I did it for us though, not for no selfishness like this, but you're a grown woman, like you said, it's probably about your turn by now . . . Of course, there is one thing you could sell and stay whole—

Lynette   I ain't selling the baby! Get that out of your head!

Gertie   People sell their babies. You wouldn't be the first.

Lynette   This baby is mine! You the meanest thing on this mountain—

Gertie   I keep you alive—!

Lynette   —and maybe you keep us alive, but this baby, she's gonna be my hope, she's gonna be my light.

Gertie   Says you.

Lynette   Says me.

A beat.

An old, abandoned bell rings—only **Doreen** *hears it.*

The work of life continues in the dim background as **Doreen** *steps out—*

AN INTERLUDE

She comes to the edge of the playing space.

She hesitates—

then steps beyond it

and, well, that's far enough for right now.

The same strain of music can be heard again—not much, just a taste.

There are rustlings in the dark of the theater.

She sits on the edge of the stage, between the set and the audience

—a middle space.

Doreen (*ss* **Gertie**)   Are you steppin off my mountain?!

(*As herself:*) No, Gertie, I'm just steppin off my mind, I think. Or maybe my heart. I can't quite tell the difference.

(*As* **Gertie***:*) It's a dark place off the mountain! You step off once, and before you know it you're lost!

(*As herself:*) I won't get lost. I'm stayin close by. Just want look at it, you know, the edge, see what the other side feels like.

(*As* **Lynette***:*) What does it feel like then?

(*As herself:*) Like darkness. And fear. And like it could swallow me up. And also like . . . God, like music. Am I crazy?

(*As* **Gertie***:*) There's no room for crazy on this mountain. (*Mimes shooting a revolver from each hand.*) Pchoo-pchoo!

Blackout.

Chapter 3: Helping Out

Outside the ramshackle house.

Doreen *is sewing—she's almost finished sewing together a cloth doll out of scraps from the quilting scene, and maybe some burlap of canvas sacks. You couldn't say for certain if the doll was a girl doll or a boy doll; the most you could say was that it was, well, scrappy.*

The mountain is colder; autumn is beginning to make way for winter.

Lynette *enters from inside the house. She's weary under the weight of a very large belly.*

Doreen   You sure are pregnant, Lynette.

Lynette   Ain't truer words ever been said.

Doreen   He's gonna be a big baby.

Lynette   She's gonna be a big baby.

Doreen   Gertie says it's a boy for sure.

Lynette   Gertie's wrong.

Doreen   What if it's two babies? Or three babies? All at once? Triplets or quintuplets?

Lynette   Then they're gonna kill me trying to get out. And Gertie will kill me if they don't.

Doreen   You look tuckered out.

Lynette   I am. Sooner I meet this child the better.

Doreen   Look what I made, Lynette! It's a doll. I made it for the baby. Whether it's a girl or a boy or a little of both, it's gonna need a friend up here on the mountain, someone to keep it company.

Lynette   You're sweet, Doreen. Too sweet for your own good.

Doreen   Do you think I should name it, or wait and let Baby name it?

Lynette   That might take some years, babies don't talk at first.

Doreen   Oh, yeah, I forgot that, I was just so excited for it to get here. I hope it grows fast. It'd be nice to have someone else to talk to. I won't be the youngest anymore.

Lynette   Don't bully her too much, Doreen, I'd like her to stay sweet. If that's possible on this mountain.

Doreen   I won't. I'll teach her things. And I'll only be mean when I'm really cross, you know, to toughen her up, but not too much.

Lynette *gets a contraction.*

Doreen   You alright, Lynette?

Lynette   I reckon we're getting close to time.

Doreen   Can I do anything?

Lynette   Can you have this baby for me? Then I reckon not.

They sit in silence.

Doreen (*holding up the doll*)   I think I'll name her Hope.

Enter **Gertie** *from the woods.*

Gertie   I reckon that's about right. It'll get torn apart, peed on, puked on, sucked on and spit out, and that's about right for what happens to hope around here.

Lynette   Don't listen to her, Doreen.

Doreen   I did think Lilith could be a backup name. Do you like that one better, Gertie?

Lynette   It's almost time.

Gertie   Keep your britches on. I have a few more things to do before we leave.

Lynette   It's not up to me, Gertie, this baby's coming when it wants to—

Gertie   Well, you best teach it that that ain't how it works up here on the mountain.

Lynette   What's got your panties in a twist?

Gertie *aims her gun at* **Lynette**.

Gertie   Don't even. I don't care if you are pregnant, or even if you were the last living human being on this world other than myself, I'll still shoot you.

Lynette   I'm pregnant Gertie, I'm about to give birth to another human being, I'm a little on edge myself, okay? I hurt, I ache, I can't really breathe, I have to pee every five minutes, life is not a bowl of roses.

Gertie *lowers the gun.*

Gertie   Who's fault is that?

Lynette   Mine. It's all mine.

Doreen   What's the matter, Gertie?

Gertie   What's the matter?! We ain't got enough to sell, that's what's the matter! We're low on propane. Something's wrong with Alberta, and she ain't had no milk in two days. And the cold's coming in, I can feel it . . . And Lynette would like me to drop everything to take her into Town so she can bring another mouth to feed into the world.

Doreen   It might be a boy. You said you wouldn't mind having a boy around here.

Lynette *is about to protest, but* **Doreen** *shushes her.*

Gertie   Well. now, I suppose a little boy wouldn't be all bad. Course I'd have to beat him a lot when he's young. But he'd grow up strong. And he wouldn't go getting himself *pregnant*. And boys are easy to control. They think with their peckers. They love their peckers. Makes 'em dumb. But simple-dumb, not stupid-dumb. And when he gets to about thirteen, I'll grab him by the pecker, give it a half twist, and say, "You step out of line, I'll twist your pecker clean off, cook it up and feed it to you for dinner, you got that, boy?" . . . Girls are harder. Too smart. Too moody. Too independent.

Doreen   I knew a boy in school, when I was little, he was as smart as me.

Gertie   And where is he now?

Doreen   I don't know. They all left. Another mountain maybe?

Gertie   Gone to Town, more like. Mistake, you ask me. A waste.

Doreen   I liked him. We used to call him Mud. He was smart.

Gertie   A boy like that, well, he's a girl—maybe in a boy's body, but a girl nonetheless. The girl part makes him smart. And dangerous.

Lynette   We're all girls, Gertie.

Gertie   And three's the limit.

Lynette   What about the baby?

Gertie   That baby's a boy. Besides, you're not really anything til you're about eight or nine. You're just a runt.

Lynette   I think you want this baby, Gertie. I think you've gotten soft on it.

Gertie   Don't you call me soft.

Lynette   It's a compliment, Gertie.

Gertie   Well, I ain't asked for it. I'm practical is all.

They're silent for a minute, listening to the mountain.

Doreen   I miss our Betterment Society meetings. You reckon we can start those again when you come back?

Lynette   I'd like that, Doreen.

Gertie   We ain't got time for no foolishness—you think chores and a baby is gonna be easy? You think there's a mamaw's or papaw's where you can drop him off at? And don't go looking at Doreen, I need Doreen working.

Lynette   My baby's a girl.

Gertie   IT'S A PAIN IN MY ASS IS WHAT IT IS!

Doreen   I'll help out.

Gertie   You can help out now—clean these guns for me.

She throws **Doreen** *the shotgun and a small pistol.*

Doreen *starts cleaning the guns.*

Gertie Maybe Lil'ope there'll help you.

Doreen She's too young yet for guns, right Lil'ope?

Gertie You're never too young to protect yourself. You got five fingers and a good eye, you can shoot a gun.

Lynette You gotta be able to lift it up first.

Gertie Where there's a will, there's a way.

Lynette *has another contraction.*

Lynette Mmsdfghrptmmph. You done listening to yourself talk yet?!

Gertie I guess. You made up your mind?

Lynette . . . You got an extra eye patch for me?

Gertie *is quiet.*

Gertie I never wanted to see this day come.

Lynette We all gotta grow up someday.

Gertie I've always thought your eyes were real pretty. Even when they're hard, they're still pretty.

Compliments are mighty rare and mighty uncomfortable, and tend to derail a good fight.

Lynette Well.

Gertie Well . . . Best get a move on. It's a half day down the mountain and I ain't delivering no baby.

Lynette You will if you have to.

Gertie I'll let you die first.

Lynette I'd scream so loud you'd do it just to shut me up.

Gertie (*she smiles*) You would, just to spite me.

Lynette I would.

Gertie Doreen.

Doreen *gives* **Gertie** *the guns.*

Gertie You hold down the mountain.

Doreen I will.

Gertie And clean those other guns.

Doreen I will.

Gertie And shoot anything we can eat, and anything that talks—you hear me?

Doreen   Yeah.

Gertie   I mean it. I don't care if it's your long lost girlboy friend from when you were in school, you shoot him, you hear?

Doreen   Okay.

Gertie   Doreen's getting to be a good shot, you know.

Doreen   I'll teach Lil-ope to shoot. Then there'll be two of us.

Lynette   Gertie—(**Lynette** *looks at her hands, wiggles her fingers.*)—I reckon I don't need all these fingers. Let's get some extra propane while we're there.

Gertie *looks at her with a glisten in her eyes.*

Lynette   It's gonna be a hard winter, let's at least be warm.

Gertie   We're gonna be twins.

Lynette   That's a horrid thought. And Gertie—you make sure they take care of my baby, I mean it, whatever it takes.

Gertie   Let's hope it don't come to that.

Lynette   You point that gun at them and make them do their jobs.

She points her gun at **Gertie**.

Lynette   Promise me. I want this baby, Gertie. I want this baby so bad I can taste it.

Gertie   You shoot if you need to, but if you're coming, then let's go.

She exits.

Lynette *lowers her gun and exits after* **Gertie**.

Doreen *is left on stage with Lil'ope.*

She goes inside, comes out after a moment carrying an armful of guns, stacks them on the porch like firewood.

She puts one in Lil'ope's lap—just a small one.

Doreen   Well, Lil'ope, looks like it's just you and me then.

Gertie trusts us so we gotta do a good job. I'm good with guns so it's easy for me. Gertie trusts me with her guns. But you—you're new at it. You're gonna make some mistakes at first, but don't get down, don't pout, don't complain, don't cry, just do it better next time.

You stick with me. I'll show you the ropes. And when Baby is here, well you'll have a friend, someone to boss around and also to look after—cause you're the older one—you'll have to show Baby around. Don't be too hard on himher cause it's hard learning new stuff, but don't be easy neither, because its a hard world and you want 'em to be tough enough to survive it. Like me, for instance, my skin is kind of thick, but also kind of thin, and so sometimes I'm too sensitive. Gertie hollers at me then, when I'm too sensitive because she knows she won't be around forever and she wants me to be tough like her, so I'll survive.

It's a tough life, Lil'ope.

But at least up here on the mountain, it's beautiful, too. Hard beautiful. Nature is a stern parent.

"What about in Town?" you ask? Well, I guess they're crazy down there. There's tons of people. Hundreds of them. And they don't look at each other none, and they don't got no trees or flowers to look at neither, but all the same, sometimes they have an extra eye, maybe one to watch all their money, cause they're all rich, all of them. I don't know what else you'd do with an extra eye. And everybody's super fancy cause of all their money— except those that live in the brothel, but you should kill yourself before you do that. And they have funny faces, like makeup and stuff but tattooed to their faces forever, and big boobs and big peckers and fourteen fingers each so they can push more buttons and do more things and they never stop, never ever stop to smell the rain or a flower, but then they ain't got no flowers neither. They're sort of half human and half plastic now. That's what Gertie says. I've never been there myself. But you know, I wonder what it's like to visit somewhere like that, I wouldn't want to live there mind you, but just to see it.

Or other mountains, you know? . . . Are there other mountains? . . . Maybe places where they sing—not bad-singing like at church—but good-singing, like for the joy of it.

I wonder what joy feels like.

Lil'ope, you ain't cleaning hard enough. Put your elbows into it!

I didn't give you no elbows, did I? Well, no use complaining, best make due with what you got.

I suppose this was what Lynette was talking about, us talking about our trials and tribulations, and bonding.

Well, sure, Lil'ope, I don't see why not. We can have us a meeting of the Betterment Society, just the two of us. In the absence of Miss Lynette, our founder, and Miss Gertie, Miss Doreen is presiding, and Miss Lil'ope is in attendance. A new member!

Welcome, Miss Lil'ope.

Today we're gonna be learning about Helping Out. With Baby coming, you're gonna need to know how to help out. Helping Out means doing your chores, but also doing other people's chores because they're too busy, or maybe they're sick, like Lynette's been. Helping Out means not complaining. And it especially means not talking too much! You put your head down and do what needs to be done. Got it?

Let's practice.

They do.

Some moments go by in this way.

The clang of a faraway bell.

Doreen *looks up.*

She steps out—

AN INTERLUDE

—and to the edge, as if she sees something in the distance. A short strain of music, similar to before.

She sees something approaching from the darkness of the theater.

Slowly,

slowly,

in a tentative but graceful way, it approaches.

It's Lil'ope—multiple bodies moving in unison, wearing masks, but one energy, one magical creature.

Lil'ope—each mask—has the same button eyes that the doll has.

Lil'ope comes to stand in front of **Doreen**. *Lil'ope is tentative,* **Doreen** *has never seen anything like this creature before.*

Blackout.

Chapter 4: It's Hard to Better Yourself Because It's Cold

Inside the ramshackle house.

Lynette *sits in a chair in the corner, staring out the window. She is whole, and not pregnant.*

A new blanket covers her. In fact, there are a few new things, small things, like the blanket, around the house.

Gertie*'s smoking a pipe.*

Doreen *stands in the doorway, looking out.*

Gertie   Are you coming or going?

Doreen   It's turning wild out there.

Gertie   Well, if you wanna turn wild with it, out with ya. But otherwise, close the door.

She does.

Doreen   I hate winter. Nothing grows. Everything's cooped up like we are.

Gertie   That's what makes spring sweet. You gotta encounter some things you hate so you can know what you love.

Doreen   Is Lynette gonna talk to us today, you reckon?

Gertie   Lynette? Lynette! LYNETTE! . . . No, I don't reckon she is.

Doreen   She ain't talked for so long I've about forgotten what her voice sounds like.

Gertie   Hear that, Lynette? You're traumatizing the child.

Lynette *doesn't answer.*

Gertie   Well, it's better than when she was crying and carrying on. I didn't think that would ever end. Keening, that was, 'bout split my head in two.

Doreen   She was sad, Gertie. Sadder than I've ever seen a person be. I think her heart was broken, like the kind of broken that never heals. I was scared watching her.

Gertie   Lynette's tough, whether she knows it or not. Like me. Though she'd hate me saying that. Because she hates me, I know it. But I did what had to be done! I always do what has to be done. You can hate me for it, but you're also alive cause of it. I didn't have no choice, Lynette.

Lynette *doesn't answer.*

Gertie   Fine. You wanna wallow and feel sorry for yourself, you go right ahead. You got all winter to sit here. Doreen and I will cover your chores because that's what we do: What needs to be done. What the land demands. What life demands. Shit goddamn it.

She stomps around. Goes outside. Comes back in. Sits again.

You warm, ain't you? You got heat? A new blanket? Food enough for the winter? And you got all yourself still, ain't you? Life is about sacrifice. I've had to do it time and again, when you all been sick and needed something. I got one eye and I'm short a hand, but you don't see me carrying on, do you? Do you?!

She jams her pipe in her mouth.

Lynette *hasn't moved.*

Doreen   I sure was looking forward to having a baby around.

Gertie   Don't you start!

Doreen   I was gonna teach himher to read. And fish. And farm. And hunt. I was gonna be a big sister. And maybe someday I would've gone traveling, oh, I don't know where to, but somewhere, just so I could have come back and told himher about it.

The other two don't notice as **Lynette** *wipes her eye.*

Gertie   At least you got Lil'ope here.

Doreen   Yeah. She's nice. She does everything I tell her. Sometimes I'm mean to her just to see if she'll sass me back, but she never does. Kind of takes the fun out of being a bully.

Gertie *gets an idea:*

Gertie   Have you made Lil'ope a member of the society yet?

Doreen   The society? (*Catching on.*) Oh! Well, I told her all about it. How Miss Lynette started it, and how we're gonna better ourselves. And how every meeting is something new to learn. And I invited her to one meeting, but it doesn't feel official unless Miss Lynette invites her in, cause she's the founder.

Lynette *says nothing.*

Gertie   . . . Well, maybe we could have ourselves a meeting and Lynette will feel like joining us.

Doreen   You think?

Gertie   I'd rather her be yelling at me, or cussing, or even her stupid meeting than this. I can't stand this.

Doreen   Well, you know, I've always wanted to sing—

Gertie *groans.*

Doreen   I think there's something powerful in singing, and it seems like it might lift us up, and maybe it would lift the dark cloud that's on Lynette. Right, Lil'ope? You like singing, right? We've been singing a little when it's just the two of us.

Gertie   I hate singing, Doreen, you know I do.

Doreen   I know, but I thought about that—you could just hum or tap your foot or something. And then, maybe the song will bring you joy, and then if you feel like it, you might join in.

Lynette   I *hate* joy. I *hate* singing. I *hate* this room. I *hate* this mountain. I *HATE* Gertie. And if you start singing, I'll hate you too, Doreen.

They look at **Lynette** *for a moment, speechless.*

Doreen   Lynette, you're back!

Lynette   I ain't back. I'm a changed woman. That old Lynette's gone. Gertie killed her.

Gertie   I could've lied to you and told you the baby died in birth. I didn't do that.

Lynette   Cause I'd have known you were lying.

Gertie   Cause I don't lie. I ain't never lied to you, even when you'd of wanted me to.

Lynette   No, you sell babies! You murdered everything good in me. Now I'm like you, bitter and hateful. You think this mountain is big enough for two hateful, bitter people?

Gertie   You're a whole person, ain't you?

Lynette   *WHOLE*?!

Gertie   You know what I mean!

Lynette   You took the one thing that was *mine*, the *one* thing . . . and you took it away from me.

Gertie *storms out.*

Doreen   Lynette, I'm sorry. I know you really wanted that baby.

Lynette *doesn't respond.*

Doreen   I know it's not the same, but you can have Lil'ope, if you want. She doesn't talk a lot, but she doesn't cry neither. And she listens real good when you talk to her, and she's real nice, like a real friend.

Lynette   . . . My breasts hurt. They turned rancid, the milk inside them, it turned to poison. I wish Gertie would suck on my breasts one more time cause then she would die.

She stares out the window again.

Doreen *takes Lil'ope into her arms and rocks her and coos to her quietly.*

Gertie *enters in a huff.*

Gertie   You know, if you really loved that baby—loved it for itself and not for what it was gonna be for you, you'd be glad! That child is gonna have all the food it can eat! Clothes that are new! A warm house! Its own bedroom! Everything she wants, she'll get!

Lynette   She was a girl?

Gertie   . . . Yeah, she was a girl.

Lynette   I had a girl . . .

Gertie   I didn't have a choice.

Lynette   You had a gun, didn't you?

Gertie   Part of knowing how to shoot a gun is knowing when to put it down and walk away.

Lynette   Would they have killed you? I wish they had.

Gertie   Part of knowing how to shoot a gun is never walking into a situation where you're outgunned in the first place! Who asked you to get pregnant?! Three's the limit! We don't have room for four women on this mountain!!

Doreen   Lil'ope is a girl.

Gertie   Shut up, Doreen! Lil'ope is a goddamned doll.

She takes the doll from her and rips its eye off, then throws the doll to the floor.

Gertie   See, a doll! Get it together!

Doreen (*quietly*)   (I know. I know she's a doll. We're all kind of dolls, ain't we.)

Gertie *gets a gun, throws it to* **Lynette**.

Gertie   Lynette, if you want to shoot me, then shoot me! Otherwise, get over it. I know it's hard, but it is what it is. Life goes on.

Lynette   I'm not gonna shoot you.

Gertie   Ain't we better off? In the grand scheme of things, ain't we?

She faces **Lynette**. **Lynette** *faces out.* **Doreen** *cradles Lil'ope as she sits on the floor.*

The clang of an old, abandoned bell.

As the work of life continues in the dim background, **Doreen** *hears the bell and steps out—*

AN INTERLUDE

*—***Doreen** *steps into the middle space.*

There also is Lil'ope, all of them,

with their hands over the same eye on their masks.

Doreen   Your eye, tsk.

. . . Sometimes I hate this mountain. I mean I love this mountain, but I hate, I hate the feeling that God's out there, whatever God is, and I can't get off this mountain to find her . . . I wish I could show them, you know. This. You. This place in my heart that feels so big, and I look out, and I think, maybe it's not empty in here, maybe there's other people here, maybe that's what all of that is—(*She looks at the audience.*)

—and this place is where we all are, each of us alone, but also together, like music. Maybe this is what God is. Or when God made churches, maybe this is what she meant, for us to make music. Together . . . But then sometimes the song gets so faint I can't hardly hear it anymore, it all just goes quiet, and I get so scared that the door has closed and it was all just make-believe.

Lil'ope responds, all the actors synchronized together, with movement and synchronized sound.

Doreen   Maybe.

Blackout.

Chapter 5: Travel and Leisure

It's early spring. The outside of this ramshackle house. The ramshackle outhouse is nearby.

Gertie *is on the porch, in a chair, covered with a blanket. She's sick. She has a gun in her lap.*

Occasionally, she hears something and takes aim, but then puts the gun down again.

Doreen *enters from the woods. She has Lil'ope strapped to her back in a sling.*

Doreen   How do you feel, Gertie?

Gertie   Hmphrph.

Doreen   I heard you fire, but I didn't see nothing. It must of got away.

Gertie   I hit it.

Doreen   I think you're so sick it's throwing off your aim.

Gertie   If I shot it, I hit it.

Doreen   I know, Gertie. You're the best shot in three mountains. But I looked and I couldn't see nothing. Was it a squirrel?

Gertie   Skunk.

Doreen   I didn't smell nothing neither.

Gertie   Hmrhmph.

Doreen (*to make* **Gertie** *feel better*)   Maybe a bobcat got there before I did and is having lunch right now.

Doreen *takes Lil'ope out of her sling and puts her down in a little chair.*

Lil'ope has an eye-patch.

Doreen   You stay put, ya hear? You hungry? No? Okay then. I'll be right back.

She goes to the outhouse.

Gertie *and Lil'ope just sit there, like a matching set in matching chairs, one big and one little.*

Lynette *enters.*

Lynette   You ain't pulling your weight, Gertie.

Gertie   I shot something.

Lynette   You missed.

Gertie   I didn't miss.

Lynette   You missed.

Enter **Doreen** *from the outhouse.*

Doreen   You all done in the barn, Lynette?

Lynette   For today.

Doreen   Lynette's fixing the barn roof. She did a good job, you'd a been proud of her.

Lynette   It's not finished yet.

Doreen   Alberta is gonna be so happy.

Lynette   She better show it with some milk.

Doreen   I know it ain't spring yet, and the ground's still hard, but it feels good to be outside.

Lynette   You weren't made for cooped up living, Doreen.

Doreen   I reckon not. I gotta see the big sky to really breathe.

Gertie *takes aim—shoots—click—she's out of ammo. She's frustrated.* **Doreen** *gets some and puts it near her.* **Gertie** *reloads and takes aim—too late, the target is gone.*

Lynette   You better hit something soon, Gertie.

Doreen   She will. Gertie's the best shot in three mountains.

Lynette   She *was* the best shot. I think she's losing her touch.

Doreen   She's just sick, Lynette. She needs to rest a while.

Gertie   I ain't sick.

Doreen   You are too sick, Gertie. You need anything? Another blanket?

Gertie *coughs and shakes her head.*

Lynette   Did you get your chores done, Doreen?

Doreen   I did. We both did—Lil'ope helped.

Lynette   Well?

Doreen   The seedlings are started, another couple of weeks we can put 'em in the ground. Wood pile is still pretty high. Animals fed. No milk from Alberta yet, but soon I think.

Lynette   We're gonna need meat soon.

Gertie   I'll get the meat.

Lynette   Gertie couldn't hit water if she fell out of a boat.

Gertie   I could hit you.

Lynette   Really? Let's see.

Gertie *turns away.*

Doreen   Lynette, I was wondering, do you think we could better ourselves today?

Lynette   There is no betterment, Doreen. That was a stupid fantasy I had. I'm rid of my fantasies. Gertie was right. There ain't no place on this mountain for fancies like that.

Doreen   Do you ever wish you didn't live on this mountain?

Lynette   What do you mean?

Doreen   I don't know. You been to Town . . . you ever want to live there?

Lynette *thinks about it.*

Lynette   No. Gertie's right. The only thing for us in Town would be the whorehouse. We don't look right, we don't sound right, we ain't educated enough. And anyway, you need a lot of money down there. You can't grow your food. There's laws against even trying, probably cause it'd all come up poisoned.

Doreen   Laws against growing food?

Lynette   There's laws against everything there. Can't carry more than one gun at a time. Can't leave your kid on the porch alone for five minutes. I reckon Gertie's right, they're half plastic down there.

Doreen   Lynette, you ever think about Baby Girl and what she's doing?

Lynette (*after a pause*)   No. She's ain't mine no more. She probably has a name. She's probably half plastic by now, too.

Doreen   Well, what about on another mountain? You ever think about seeing what's there?

Lynette   Why? It's the same thing. Another Gertie, different hair, different size, but same ornery, same spit. There's another Lynette too, not as pretty, but same otherwise.

Doreen   Is there a Doreen?

Lynette   Likely. Another Doreen.

Doreen   And Lil'ope?

Lynette   No, probably not a Lil'ope.

Doreen   I think about other places sometimes. I wonder if they see the same sky, the same stars, the same little weeds. I just wonder.

Lynette   Gertie's right, you're too soft, Doreen.

Doreen   I'm not.

Lynette   It's gonna hurt when life smacks you in the face.

Doreen   I'm tough, I can get smacked a few times, I don't mind.

Lynette   Suit yourself.

Doreen   Lynette, you mind if I have a meeting with Lil'ope?

Lynette   You should be out hunting for meat.

Doreen   There's still time. It'll be better hunting at dusk anyways.

Lynette   You're a mess, Doreen. You know Lil'ope's a doll, right? She's not real, you know that.

Doreen   I know.

Lynette   If you've lost your mind, I'll shoot you myself.

She exits.

Doreen *stares out at the land.*

Doreen   Alright, Lil'ope, time for the meeting of the Betterment Society. Miss Doreen presiding. Gertie, you want to attend the meeting?

Gertie *coughs badly, then puts her head back.*

Doreen   Miss Gertie will be attending but not participating as such at today's meeting. Our topic for today's meeting is Travel and Leisure. Miss Doreen and Miss Lil'ope in attendance.

"What is Travel and Leisure?" That's a good question, Lil'ope. Travel and Leisure are things people do when they're rich or when they're young. Most people aspire to be rich.

Gertie   Not me.

Doreen   Except Gertie. You set off on your own—it's important to be on your own—and in the really, really old days, you might have stowed away on a ship, and then become a sailor, sailing the high seas, traveling from port to port. You might even have liked it so much you became a pirate. If you were super-rich, you'd go to a place called "Europe" and do something called "Summer in Europe."

'Course nowadays, travel is different. You might go from the mountain down into Town, but many of those people are never heard from again. Maybe they ended up at the brothel. Or maybe they were sold for parts. I don't think I'd like the brothel, except for the music—I'd like the music.

Gertie, have you ever been anywhere?

Gertie *coughs.*

Doreen   Gertie doesn't hold much store in travel or leisure, but she's been to Town lots, and she likes it better up here.

Lil'ope—where would you go if you could? . . . You want to travel to mountain ranges, and maybe find another sorry stuffed doll like yourself? . . . Yeah, I can understand that. It's a tough life out there, though. Especially all by yourself.

But maybe they have schools on those other mountains. Maybe they have churches—not bad ones, but good ones—maybe they pass the plate and everyone takes something, like a dollar, or a good wish or something.

But you can't just think of yourself, Lil'ope, that's selfish. We live in a community and we depend on each other.

And ain't no one gonna care about you when you leave this godforsaken mountain—right Gertie? . . . Gertie?

She checks **Gertie**—*she's got a bad fever.*

Doreen   LYNETTE . . . You look after Gertie, Lil'ope.

She exits looking for **Lynette**.

Gertie *rouses herself, stumbles from her chair, goes to the outhouse, makes it about halfway inside and passes out.*

Enter **Lynette** *and* **Doreen**.

They see **Gertie** *and get her out.*

Doreen   She looks like she's gonna die.

Lynette   Maybe we should let her.

Doreen   She's tried all the poultices already, nothing works. She never been this sick before.

Lynette   Nope, I don't think she has.

Doreen   Maybe she needs a doctor?

Lynette   She hates doctors.

Doreen   I know she does.

Lynette   She'd rather die on the mountain than see a doctor in Town.

Doreen   I know it, but I don't want her to die. I wish I was a doctor.

Lynette *thinks on it.*

Lynette   Put her in the wagon.

Doreen   You gonna take her to Town? You sure you wanna go down there? . . . Can I come?

They get **Gertie** *in the wagon.*

Lynette   No. Someone's gotta take care of the things here. You wouldn't like it, Doreen. Doctors, well the ones we see, they ain't noble or nothing. They're a business. They'll try and talk the legs right off ya. You're young and vulnerable. I don't want them getting their hands on you.

Doreen   I just wanna see it.

Lynette   Someday. Hopefully, not anytime soon. Find us some meat. We'll need it.

Doreen   I will.

Lynette   Get on then.

She exits with **Gertie** *in the wagon.* **Doreen** *watches them go. Lil'ope in the chair.*

The clang of an, old abandoned bell.

Doreen *hears it, and steps out—*

AN INTERLUDE

—and into the middle space.

Lil'ope is there, more mischievous, more curious.

All of Lil'ope is wearing an eye-patch on the same side of their masks.

They examine both the stage space, the doll-size Lil'ope, all kinds of things. This is a moment when though they move in a similar fashion, they are free to split up to explore the space separately.

They respond sometimes to what **Doreen** *says, and wherever they are, they do this with synchronized movement or sound.*

Doreen   Am I crazy, Lil'ope? I feel like I might be. I feel like I'm on a ledge on the far side of the mountain, and I feel . . . I feel the breeze and maybe it could carry me away, but I also feel like if I'm not as sure-footed as a goat, I'm gonna fall right off this ledge and die.

Lil'ope responds.

Doreen *looks at the audience, makes eye-contact.*

Doreen   I look out, at all of them, and I wonder—are they real? Or real enough? Can they see each other, or are they like me, on their own mountains somewhere, or just, somewhere else alone.

Lil'ope responds.

Doreen   Lil'ope, if I'm crazy, you'd be doing me a mercy to put me out of my misery.

Lil'ope responds.

Doreen   Yeah, I think so, too.

Do you think they can hear it, Lil'ope? Maybe that's why I can see them? Maybe they know where God lives, what her song sounds like?

Lil'ope responds.

Doreen   Do you think there is a God?

A moment, maybe the strain of music again.

Blackout.

Chapter 6: One Big Happy Family

Outside. A beautiful spring day. A ramshackle house on a godforsaken mountain. A front porch.

Lynette *sits in a chair, a shotgun across her lap.*

Gertie is propped up on the porch steps. She has no legs. She has two fingers. She is trying to figure out how to shoot a gun with the fingers she has left. She is clumsy, immobile, and frustrated.

Lil'ope is in her little chair.

Lynette   Want your pipe?

Gertie *doesn't answer.*

Lynette   Well, do you or don't you? . . . You still have your tongue, don't ya? They asked for it, but I said the mountain wouldn't be the same without your carrying on . . . Suit yourself.

She lights the pipe, smokes it.

This is disgusting.

She keeps smoking it.

Enter **Doreen** *from the woods. She's carrying dead critters.*

She tosses the animals down, puts her gun up, takes a moment to take in the mountain.

Lynette   It's a hard mountain, but sure is a pretty view.

Doreen   Yup.

Gertie *drops the gun she's been fiddling with.*

Doreen *picks it up and gives it back to her.*

Doreen   It was a good day to hunt, you would've liked it, Gertie.

Gertie   Hmphrh.

Doreen   If we didn't have so much to do around here, I would have gone around yonder to the lake and tried for some fowl. Next time.

Lynette   Don't take it personal, she ain't talking to nobody today.

Doreen   I don't take it personal.

Lynette   Did you get all your chores done?

Doreen   I did. And Alberta gave milk again, I think she's feeling better now that it's spring.

Lynette   Garden's planted. Animals are happy. We have meat. It's a good life we have here, ain't it, Gertie?

Gertie *continues to fiddle with the gun.*

Lynette   You ain't pulling your weight, but you'll probably need some time to get used to your new situation. All things considered, Doreen and I are holding down the mountain just fine on our own. It's like you ain't even necessary. But we like you, so don't you worry, we're gonna keep you around. I think in time, you might get good at some of the household chores, cooking, cleaning. I think you'll like it.

Doreen   It's a lot of work, though, just the two of us. I wish we had that baby now. I sure could use another pair of hands in the garden.

Lynette   Lil'ope not pulling her weight neither?

Doreen   Lil'ope don't weigh nothing at all. Besides, she ain't real. I mean you're real, Lil'ope, real enough to provide comfort to me. And she's trying to give Gertie some comfort, too. But she ain't real enough to pull weeds with me.

Lynette   I bet Gertie wishes we had the baby now too, don't you, Gertie? Another young-something running round the mountain, cutting up and causing trouble . . . be nice.

Gertie   You the meanest most spiteful person I ever met, Lynette. I should of let you die on that birthing table. I should've killed you when you were a wee thing. But you'll get yours. One day, you'll get yours.

Lynette   Oh now, Gertie, you know I ain't had no choice. You was sick. They said you would've died if I hadn't brought you in.

Gertie   You should've let me die.

Lynette   Now, Gertie, I couldn't do that . . . And you know, we did have some money, but that was *my* money, I reckon, since it was from the sale of *my* baby. And I just didn't think it'd be right to let you profit from the sale of *my* baby. So when it came time to pay, we looked at what we had. Well, what *you* had . . . left. Not much. And old and gnarly, all of it. But in the end, we made it work. And now, well we got ourselves a nice little nest egg even, putting our little fortunes together. Not much to spit at, but enough to heat us in the winter, buy us some new tools, keep ammo in the guns. We'll be alright I think.

Gertie   When I figure out how to fire this gun, I'm gonna kill you.

Lynette   I was a naive little girl for a lot of my life, but you made me grow up, Gertie. I wanted to better myself, but you know, I think I'm better enough. I thank you for that lesson, Gertie.

Doreen   Gertie, I think I might be able to rig up the wagon if you want to come hunting with me next time.

Gertie   There's only one thing I want to shoot.

Lynette   Gertie, if you're gonna shoot me, then shoot me already, but if not, get over it. Life's rough and you learn to move on. Isn't that what you said?

Doreen   I think she'd get over it quicker if she could move around more. I know she always said she loved this mountain, but I think she loved coming *back* to this mountain. She liked to wander and hunt and forage and then she liked to come back and see this place here, and turn around and look out at it all.

Lynette   Well, I ain't stopping her. I even got her these.

She pulls out two small tree trunks, cut a few feet long, and throws them over the porch railing to the ground below.

She can carve herself some new legs even. I'm not heartless. And frankly, she's a pain in the ass. The sooner she can take care of herself the better. We all got chores to do, we all gotta pull our weight. Right, Gertie? You taught me that. No matter what. No matter what life throws at you. Pull yourself up and get on with it. What do you think, Lil'ope? You agree?

Gertie *fiddling with her gun.* **Lynette** *sitting in the chair on the porch. Lil'ope in the little chair.*

The clang of a bell.

As the work of life continues in the dim background, **Doreen** *steps out—*

THE LAST INTERLUDE

—and into the middle space.

Lil'ope is there.

Doreen *puts on a brave face but you can feel she's vulnerable.*

Doreen   I'm kinda scared. That this is all there is, you know? That I'm imagining this, this, all of us sitting together in a room, on the tallest mountain, in a church maybe.

I'm not sure I know what God is, or what a real church is supposed to look like. But—I look out at you, and you look so different from me, and also not different at all. And here we are maybe. Together. And in my heart, this is what church could feel like—a good church, not a stealing church. And we'd sing, all together like, we'd sing that song that's so deep in our hearts we can't quite make out the words but we would try.

She takes the guitar.

Because that's all you can do, is try. All we can do is ask for help . . . from God, from each other. Maybe it's all the same thing in the end. So I'm asking you. Straight out. All of you, and I guess I'm asking God, too—if she can hear me—to help me to believe.

Because otherwise I really am crazy.

Lil'ope spreads throughout the audience. Offering plates appear. Air violins. And yet Lil'ope still feels very much like they are one entity, the language of their movements is the same.

The offering plate—good wishes, a dollar or something—are offered to the audience, and they are encouraged to take.

Doreen
    COME TO THE EDGE
    IT'LL BE ALRIGHT

COME TO THE EDGE
IF IT'S DAY OR NIGHT

COME TO THE EDGE
IF YOU'RE SCARED AT ALL
COME TO THE EDGE
IF YOU WANT TO FALL

COME TO THE EDGE
AND I'LL PUSH YOU OFF
TRUST IN YOUR HEART
THOUGH YOUR HEAD ASKS WHY
IF YOU FEAR THE FALL
WE WILL, NEVER FLY

Lil'ope (all of them) spreads throughout the audience, stops as one and sings, quietly there, lifting up the song.

Doreen and Lil'ope:
COME TO THE EDGE

Doreen
YOU'VE DREAMT ALONE FOR SO LONG NOW
ARE YOU TIRED YET?

Doreen and Lil'ope
COME TO THE EDGE

Doreen
I'LL PUSH YOU OFF

Doreen and Lil'ope
TRUST IN YOUR HEART
THOUGH YOUR HEAD ASKS WHY
IF YOU FEAR THE FALL
WE WILL, NEVER FLY

TRUST IN YOUR HEART
THOUGH YOUR HEAD ASKS WHY
IF YOU FEAR THE FALL
WE WILL, NEVER FLY

TRUST IN YOUR HEART
THOUGH YOUR HEAD ASKS WHY
IF YOU FEAR THE FALL
WE WILL, NEVER FLY

LA LA LA LA (*etc.*)

Ending One:

If the audience joins her—either by coming to the edge and/or by singing along at the end, then she will have courage . . .

Doreen   I knew I wasn't crazy . . .

*She walks back into the scene with **Gertie** and **Lynette**.*

Doreen *goes into the house to get her jacket. She comes out.*

Lynette's *cleaning a shotgun. She cocks it and sights along the top, checking it, as she says:*

Lynette   Where you going, Doreen?

Doreen   I don't know. I don't rightly know.

She exits.

The theater lights up like a cathedral.

Fade to black except the cathedral.

End of play.

[OR]

Ending Two:

If the audience leaves her completely on her own, then she won't have courage, and she peters out before the end of the song.

Doreen   . . . I guess I really am crazy.

*She walks back into the scene with **Gertie** and **Lynette**.*

Doreen *goes into the house to get her jacket. She comes out.*

Lynette's *cleaning a shotgun. She cocks it and sights along the top, checking it, as she says:*

Lynette   Where you going, Doreen?

Doreen   No where.

She sits down on the steps.

They look out.

She pulls out her gun and points it at Lil'ope, who are gathered together again, one unarmed creature.

Blackout.

Gunshot.

End of play.

Come to the Edge

From THE BETTERMENT SOCIETY

Lyrics by Mashuq Mushtaq Deen

Music by Nell Shaw Cohen

($.= 60)

Come to the edge__ It'll be_ al - right Come to the edge__ If it's day or night__ Come to the edge__ If you're scared at all Come to the edge If you want to fall Come to the edge__ And I'll push you off Trust in your heart__ Though your head asks why__ If you fear the fall__ We will nev - er fly

(Instrumental)

Come to the edge_____ You've dreamt a - lone__ for so long now_ Are you tired yet?

Come to the edge___ I'll push you off

Trust in your. heart Though your head asks why___ If you fear___ the

fall___ We will, nev - er fly fly_____

La la la la_____ la la la la___ la

La la la la_____ la la la la___ la

how to tell time (when you are trans and processing trauma)

Finn Lefevre

j. chavez begins their play *how to clean your room (and remember all your trauma)* with this epigraph from *Lemonade*, Beyoncé's visual album: "The past and the future merge to meet us here. What luck. What a fucking curse" (2016). The epigraph reads like a warning for what is ahead—both the luck and the curse—while simultaneously asking us to let go of our normative understandings of time.

Within this play exists the future, the past, and maybe even the present. chavez does not welcome us into this temporality, does not offer us a roadmap or timeline to follow, does not provide us with markers to track our steps. Instead, they ask us to reorient ourselves to the stars—to mark time in cycles instead of days, to locate memories in objects instead of calendars, to swirl around in the muck of time and see what sticks.

This structure is not that unusual for a memory play—many memory plays offer glimpses of time and jump around in a central character's narrative. Similarly, in this play we don't encounter traumas as Spencer faced them; rather we join them as they piece together fragmented memories from different times.

What is more unique about this particular memory play is that we are asked to see these memories through Spencer's eyes, and (given Spencer's own admitted memory faults) not as the immutable "truth" of these events as some sort of archive, but accept them as Spencer's own reconstructions. That Spencer openly admits to their unreliability as a narrator allows us to forgive them their fudged histories, instead focusing on how their brain has chosen to present them to us, in what order, with which details emphasized and which removed.

This structure speaks to a current edge in trans theory, trans temporality. Queer temporalities have been analyzed and theorized extensively: in *In a Queer Time and Place*, Jack Halberstam offers us space outside of normative or "family time," and reminds us that queer lives exist in asynchrony to expected uses of time within a capitalist model (2005: 10). In *Feeling Backward*, Heather Love gives language to the queer yearning for the past, making space for us to feel and articulate the shame of this reaching, to reject the concept of a "progressive" linearity to time (2007: 30). Trans theorists have taken up these and other non-normative temporalities to explore the way time functions differently in trans lives. Trans theorists have examined the cyclical nature of hormonal transition, the asynchrony of adult puberties, the rep&rev (as borrowed from Suzan-Lori Parks 1995: 8–11) of coming out, the coexistence of past and present, the contra-punctuality of queer time, the arrested time of knowing but not living as your gender, and more.

This play toys and tangles with many of these temporalities.

Spencer's intimate relationship to the objects they uncover in their room call back to Love's connections between "feeling backward" and the queer camp aesthetic. Love defines these connections as "defiant refusals to grow up, in explorations of haunting and memory, and in stubborn attachments to lost objects" (2007: 7). It's not that Love is suggesting we don't grow, but that the idea of growing *up* implies expecting ourselves to progress in a linear, incremental fashion. It suggests we let go of pieces of ourselves, move past our past. But growth is messy, complicated, and doesn't move in only one direction. Growth doesn't mean letting go of our whole past, and in the case of Spencer it actually means a much closer connection to an understanding of their past. This tension appears in moments like Spencer's simultaneous embarrassment towards and desire to reclaim and refashion their old poetry book, or in Spencer's "stubborn attachment" to memories that are already faded and distorted.

Much of this "stubborn attachment" comes out in trauma work. Trauma work, or any processes by which someone faces, works through, and reconciles with their own trauma, is central to this play. Trauma can also deeply affect the memory, leaving blank spots, revised sections, or suddenly reemerging. Memories are often "triggered" (used here to mean brought to the forefront of consciousness in a painful, abrupt, or disruptive way) by tokens that connect to that moment: the smell of smoke on an old flannel shirt transports Spencer to a memory of a house party, for example. For trauma, this triggering can turn objects into portals, smells into flashbacks, senses into memories, and over time Spencer's room becomes a graveyard.

Their attempts to not solely destroy or remove all of the offending objects show desire to reconcile past with present, to not just salvage but savor. They reassert these attachments, not only keeping their old poetry book but allowing a piece of it to weave into a new poem they write.

Piecing these parts of the self together feels like "re-membering." Black feminist scholars Laura Trantham Smith and Hortense Spillers (among others) have taken up this idea of "re-membering," of embodied experience creating flesh memories, of people collecting and collaging assemblages of self (Smith 2010: 103–106). Trans people, whether or not we partake in medical, surgical, or other physical forms of transition, are in a constant process of negotiating our bodies in a cis-centric world. As a person of color, Spencer's body is also subjected to the dis-ordering process of white supremacy. Re-membering the way Spencer does, then, could be read as a trauma response.

Healing from trauma, like transitioning, may not follow a linear path. The winding, circling tango of healing is echoed by chavez's choice of dramatic structure, chavez introduces us to traumas from a side view, never straight on, the way trauma seeps into surrounding pockets of memory—mundane moments become the locus of loss. Spencer doesn't flashback to the exact moment of loss; they remember instead a night looking at the stars, a stilted conversation, a last hug. They don't show us the immeasurable traumas of living as a nonbinary person of color, instead recalling discrete moments of misgendering, of medical gatekeeping, of every day microaggressions, of the ways trauma altered their mood, their conversations, their memories.

Spencer's constant refrain that they might soon be dead (or should be dead or wish to be dead) is also rooted in their experience of trans temporality. Taking up Jasbir K. Puar's analysis of "prognosis time" or the expected shortened lifespan of people with non-normative bodies, trans people can also exist in this state (an argument I've taken up in previous publications) (Puar 2009: 166). Many trans people grow up believing our lives might be short, even occasionally internalizing unsubstantiated rumors about lifespans of trans people being only twenty-four years (a statistic I've heard more times than I can count and have as of yet been unable to find any data to support). Every year a trans person lives past the age they expect to die is bonus time—time that is unexpected and often unplanned.

Imagine living your entire life expecting to only live to be twenty-four. Did you plan for twenty-five? For middle age? For retirement? Probably not. Puar argues that our own understanding and internalization of state and circumstance-determined lifespans directly impacts our ability to hope (2009: 163–5). We are surrounded by images of violence against trans people, of trans suicidality. For trans people operating on prognosis time, the few years before hitting twenty-four carry many parallels to the last years for others whose lives are expected to end soon (long-term terminal illness patients, for example). Trans people during this time can be frantic and panicked, unprepared for the future, unable to conceptualize the future, apathetic, or stalled.

Combine this internalized fear of early mortality with an edge of suicidality and it's not surprising that Spencer believed they were not long for this world. That belief propels them through many of the memories they show us—it's a constant joke, a recurring justification, a way to dissociate. No reason to plan ahead if there is no ahead. Must savor this hug because there won't be another. Mark this moment, it's certain to be the last.

how to be a human (even if everyone else is puppets)

Beyond its connections to contemporary trans temporality theories, this play also speaks to current trends in puppetry.

Trans and queer performance theorists have named and unpacked a number of ways performers can extend their bodies. Lip sync, for example, is theorized as a bodily extension (DeLanda 2016) that can offer the performer a broader vocal range, more status (depending on what is synced), and the capability to haunt the present space with the specter of the original voice (Popat et al. 2017: 101–103). Prostheses have been described as bodily extensions that also take up embodied meaning, part of a complex assemblage of material and immaterial objects that make up a trans body (Clarkson 2019; Preciado et al. 2018).

Like prosthetics and lip syncing, puppets also expand the capabilities of the human body. Puppets can take shapes no actor could, exist in bodies impossible to inhabit. Since the late 2000s/early 2010s, puppets have been popping up in more and more trans performances. Puppets have been used to create a liminal stand-in for a lost baby and all the possibility she represented (à la Mashuq Mushtaq Deen's *The Betterment Society*), to offer a bit of magic to bring spirits to life (MJ Kaufman's *Sagittarius Ponderosa*), to explore the monstrous and impossible (M Sloth Levine's *The Interrobangers*), to perform beyond the capabilities of the human body (Taylor Mac's *The Lily's Revenge*), to centralize and celebrate normally marginalized figures (Spiral Q Theater's *Peoplehood Parade*), to meld fairytale fantasy with real life tragedy (Sam Max's *Pidor and the Wolf*), and more. The first two of these texts, *The Betterment Society* and *Sagittarius Ponderosa*, are available in this anthology, on pages 63 and 17 respectively.

In *how to clean your room*, chavez's use of puppets goes hand in hand with their exploration of mental health. Spencer's bouts of dissociation, depression, and anxiety have altered their memories, in which people are now replaced by puppets. As you read the play, if you track the appearance of the puppets, you will start to notice patterns in their use. The puppets appear most in those memories where Spencer was dissociating, unable to connect, unable to see the other person for their full, complex, imperfect humanity. The puppets become the fragmented, simplified bits Spencer remembers of the real people.

Visibly, the puppets' features are limited by a "cartoonish" palette "closest to Muppets" (p. 115), and physically their gestures may not replicate that of the human body, but their words should not be limited by the fact that they are puppets. And yet, Spencer recounts to their therapist that their memories are full of holes—words they didn't listen to, whole ideas they wished the friend would say instead of what they did. The puppets become a visual symbol of the mental and emotional distance Spencer felt from the humans they represent.

Every character in the play takes a turn or several as a puppet. Everyone except Spencer. And this is important—though there are other trans and queer characters in the play, it's important that there is one trans figure who is not *ever* de-anthropomorphized.

So often trans characters are made to be the least nuanced role, often reduced to oversimplified narratives where transness is their sole attribute. Trans characters whose identities expand beyond their gender feel rare. Nonbinary characters are rarer still. chavez has written a nonbinary character whose experience of the world is impacted by their transness, but whose identity is complex and intersectional and not solely rooted in their anatomy. Spencer is solid and human in a play full of puppets, but they are never made to be *just* a body. chavez doesn't even describe Spencer's body in the casting notes, only that they are a person of color and in need of meds. This absence of the usual descriptors (AMAB/AFAB/transmasculine/transfeminine/on hormones/pre-op/visible stubble/a few curves/etc., etc., etc.) opens up so much space to explore, so much room for an actor to bring their own experience of body to the role, but it also forecloses essentialist desires to interpret behaviors in terms of gender assigned at birth. If you read closely, the text does hint at Spencer's assigned gender at birth, but the fact that it isn't centralized indicates a devaluation of that kind of casting focus or performance mode.

how to track the stars (and other patterns to look for)

This play is full of other patterns as well. The play begins with a note about the stars. chavez tells us the sky is visible and reminds us throughout the play that the stars are going through their cycles. Since each scene jumps forward and backward and around in time, the stars' cycles are similarly disjointed, and yet patterns start to emerge. Stars are brighter when Spencer is not alone—especially when they are with a close friend. Stars are dim when they feel anxious and depressed, and gone entirely when they are most alone. The stars seem to serve a similar function to Spencer's emotion tracking system. They appear and disappear not with the cycle of some chrono-linear sense of time, but with the cycles of mental health Spencer goes through.

That we are given stars to chart Spencer's emotional journey is also familiar—tracking stars, the moon, and astrology are all frequently taken up as queer acts, as deeply rooted in a queer sense of the world. There's something very trans about stars; stars shine for centuries beyond their death, their transformations both explosive and nearly invisible unless you look closely, their relative positions to other stars building complex systems of interconnection. Through their stubborn attachment to what I can only assume is not an actual archival record of the night sky, Spencer reveals the stars as another part of their queer assemblage of self.

There's also something very lonely about the stars, about Spencer checking in with the stars and noting their absences, about remembering the stars but not your friends' faces, about the queer longing for something so impossibly distant and yet ever-present. In one of the most affecting moments of the play, Spencer's embrace with puppet-Greg, chavez's stage directions describe the stars as being "just bright enough," and yet for what, chavez does not tell us (p. 157). We are left only to wonder what might have happened if they hadn't been bright enough.

Notes like these pepper the script, chavez's voice a central figure in its own right. They speak to us in sparse poetry, symbols left untranslated, using a delicately light hand for a play that often feels so heavy. Their light hand is especially noticeable in the punctuation; some lines end in a comma, asking us to imagine what more there was to be said, what exists beyond the spoken. The way the lines are broken up on the page, the punctuation, the blank spaces all indicate a rhythm, though irregular. This irregular rhythm echoes back to the stage direction of "irregular breathing" that begins the first cycle (p. 116), and carries through the indicated breaths throughout the piece. Follow these breaths and you will start to see patterns, scenes where the words seem to tumble out without any air, scenes where breaths are shared, scenes where only the character played by a puppet is given a moment to breathe. Who is being defended and who is wielding breath like a weapon?

Puppet breathwork can have a profound impact on an audience. Never has a puppet felt more alive to me than when I watched Joey of Handspring Puppet Company's *War Horse* take his first breath on stage. Just as lip syncing relocates the origin of the recorded sound within a performer in the eyes of the audience, text spoken by a puppeteer becomes voice for a puppet. Breathwork like this, then, in contrast with their "cartoonish" aesthetic, amplifies the "inhumanly human" quality of these puppets. They are at once sharing breath with Spencer and simultaneously creating physical distance between Spencer and any human they share the stage with.

how to clean your room (and remember all your trauma)

If this play was reconstructed as an instruction manual, as the title suggests, it might look something like this:

1. Realize you have a problem. Is it the room? Is it you?

    a. Both. Definitely both.

2. Pick up an object in your room.

    a. It's garbage.
    b. Blame yourself for your life being garbage.

    c. Throw away garbage. Try not to throw away self.

    d. Maybe you overreacted.

3. Check the stars.

4. Pick up an object in your room.

    a. The object belongs to someone else. Remember that person.

    b. Vaguely. Maybe simplified. You know what, actually, just make them a puppet. You can't really remember what they looked like anyway. You were too sucked up in your own shit at the time.

    c. Beat yourself up for not remembering them properly.

    d. Beat yourself up for not being a great friend to them.

    e. Let yourself remember that they loved you anyway.

5. Check the stars again. Don't be surprised if they have disappeared.

6. Repeat steps 2–5 in any order until satisfied.

    a. Maybe this is enough for now.

7. Finished.

    a. The whole room isn't clean, but that's ok.

    b. Check the stars again. They might have changed. They're always doing that.

    c. Do you feel better?

how to read this play (and hopefully produce it)

Step 1. Let it take up space.

This play exists in space. Both outer and specifically Spencer's room. The space is queered, rearranged and revalued, dis- and re-articulated. Though not described as site-specific, this play takes up so many of the techniques of site-specific work, locating lived experience in space, examining the ways we interact with and are influenced by our environment.

Step 2. Don't unpack it.

Unpack, verb, an overused word in queer theory meaning taking something apart and analyzing it closer.

    I don't mean don't analyze the play. But this play lives in its complexity, in its reflexivity. Don't try to take the scenes apart and put them in chrono-linear order and think that will reveal something. I mean, it might, but not as much as is revealed by our desire to do so.

Step 3. Let it breathe.

Let the puppets breathe. Let them feel just as alive as the people and notice when they don't.

Let the words find the rhythm and poetic quality of chavez's writing. Let them ebb and flow and breathe.

Let yourself breathe too.

Step 4. (Re)member.

This play serves as an exercise for Spencer in re-asserting agency over their own memory, body, and futurity. Integrating lost, distanced, fragmented memories-histories-ancestries is a process of re-membering, of pulling your limbs back together.

Every body in the room contains a piece of this story, and each embodied knowledge must be utilized to make the play.

The body re-members.

The body heals.

References

Beyoncé, Jack White, Weeknd, James Blake, Kendrick Lamar, Warsan Shire, MeLo-X (Musician), Kahlil Joseph, and Onye Anyanwu. 2016. *Lemonade*. [Explicit version]. Parkwood Entertainment.

Clarkson, Nicholas L. 2019. "Incoherent Assemblages: Transgender Conflicts in US Security." *Surveillance & Society* 17 (5): 618.

De Landa, Manuel. 2016. *Assemblage Theory: Speculative Realism*. Edinburgh: Edinburgh University Press.

Halberstam, Judith. 2005. *In a Queer Time and Place: Transgender Bodies, Subcultural Lives*. New York: New York University Press.

Lefevre, Theo F., Priscilla Page, Harley Erdman, and Chris Baker. 2017. *Transgressive Acts: Adapting Applied Theatre Techniques for a Transgender Community*. University of Massachusetts Libraries.

Love, Heather. 2007. *Feeling Backward: Loss and the Politics of Queer History*. Cambridge, MA: Harvard University Press.

Parks, Suzan-Lori. 1995. *The America Play, and Other Works*. First edition. New York: Theatre Communications Group.

Popat, Sita, Sarah Whatley, Rory O'Connor, Abbe Brown, and Shawn Harmon. 2017. Bodily Extensions and Performance. *International Journal of Performance Arts and Digital Media* 13 (2): 101–104.

Preciado, Paul B., Kevin Gerry Dunn, and Judith Halberstam. 2018. *Countersexual Manifesto: Critical Life Studies*. New York: Columbia University Press.

Puar, Jasbir K. 2009. "Prognosis Time: Towards a Geopolitics of Affect, Debility and Capacity." *Women & Performance* 19 (2): 161–172. doi:10.1080/07407700903034147.

Smith, Laura Trantham. 2010. "From Rupture to Remembering: Flesh Memory and the Embodied Experimentalism of Akilah Oliver." *MELUS* 35 (2): 103–120.

Spillers, Hortense J. 1987. "Mama's Baby, Papa's Maybe: An American Grammar Book." *Diacritics* 17 (2): 65. doi:10.2307/464747.

how to clean your room
(and remember all your trauma)

j. chavez

Characters

Spencer
Greg
Al
Derek
Casey
Brian
Quinn
Mother
Therapist
Doctor

Casting Policy

Spencer is best played by a nonbinary person of color.

Greg, Al, Derek, and Casey are best played by a white man. They can be the same actor.

Brian and Quinn are best played by any gender and any race. They can be the same actor.

Mother, Therapist, and Doctor are best played by an older woman of color. They can be played by the same actor.

Setting

The bedroom is always relevant, but should be transformed into various locations with the items inside. A desk chair is now an office chair, a dirty dish has become a clean dish at a diner; think creatively.

A night sky can be seen above the playing space.

Time

Right now.

Playwright Notes

The puppets are humanly inhuman. They are cartoonish in nature and are closest to Muppets.

Some sounds like lo-fi music, a bell, anything simple to signify the change of scenes.

All other actors beyond Spencer are chorus. When they speak as a chorus, they can be puppets, or not. They are puppets in scenes. Chorus lines can be divided up how you feel.

Punctuation and capitalization are important, in dialogue and stage directions.

A period at the end means nothing more to be said.

A comma means there's more to be said.

Railroad track // indicates that a character starts speaking over another.

Asterisks indicate the actor is not using a puppet.

> *The past and the future merge to meet us here. What luck. What a fucking curse.*
>
> —Beyoncé's Lemonade, *The Visual Album*

Cycle One

Scene

A messy room that hasn't been cleaned in a while. Unpacked boxes from months ago, blankets, dirty and/or clean clothes cover the room, books, worksheets from classes, pages of poetry, journals, dishes. The bed is unmade. The walls, if there are any, are covered in posters and art. It's a mess.

1.

the stars are dim,
what begins is a cacophony of irregular breathing.
around the room.
panic, at the fullest extent.
sensory overload.
it does not calm down,

2.

the stars go through their cycles,

Spencer* *enters*

Chorus   Spencer enters
they are in need of meds
and a hug

Spencer* *throws backpack on the ground*

wades through all the dirty clothes

sits at their desk, or on their bed, or the floor

pulls out a journal

Spencer*   Four? . . .
No, no today's like a six,
Six.

Haven't written any poetry in weeks, which isn't bad, but it could be better. I think I only write when I'm sad and I'm not that sad right now. Talked with Al on the phone earlier today. Always good to get back in touch with him. Thought I saw Greg today in the store, but it was just someone who looked like him. It was a polarizing moment, ya know, seeing someone but it not being them. But I didn't feel numb afterwards, so that's a step in the right direction. I think? I don't know. What do I know? I don't know the different soil types that I need to know for my exam next week, god. I cannot fail this class, Dr. Albertson will kill me. Doing better than before, but not by much.

puts journal away

begins to stream some show on their laptop

no wifi

Spencer*   Goddamnit!
Hey! Is the wifi working?
. . .
Brian!

Brian* (*offstage*)   WHAT?!

Chorus   Brian walks into the room
Brian is Spencer's roommate.
very well-kept
and very tired

Brian* *enters*

Spencer*   What's wrong with the wifi?

Brian*   Nothing it's,
Oh, my god dude
It's a goddamn mess in here

Spencer*   No it's not.

Brian*   Is that my good salad bowl?

Spencer*   Oh that's the good salad bowl?
I was wondering what you meant
by good salad bowl

Brian*   Spence, you need to clean this up
There are ants

Spencer*   There aren't any ants

Brian*   This is a nightmare in here

Spencer*   Hey, don't call my room a nightmare dude

Brian*   But it is dude, you need to clean it sometime
It's like something died in here

Spencer*   it's me

Brian*   Rank.
You need to clean this,
Landlord is doing an inspection tomorrow
and if she sees this fucking mess, she'll probably evict you
and maybe me too

Spencer*   I'll clean it,
I promise

Brian*   Good.

Spencer*   but, is something wrong with the wifi?

Brian*   Not that I know of
mine has been working fine

Spencer*   Can you go check it out

Brian*   You're the one with the problem,
you go check it out

Spencer*   I don't know how that shit works.

Brian*   You don't know how to do anything.

Spencer*   Oh fuck off

Brian*   I don't have time
I'm gonna go see Derek

Spencer*   ...

Brian*   Spencer,

Spencer*   I know, we worked it out,
I've moved on,
I was in a dark place
Blah blah blah

Brian*   Thank you

Spencer*   I hardly see him anymore really

Brian*   Well maybe one day you two can go back to being best friends

Spencer*   I don't know
Maybe one day.
Why not fix the wifi on your way out,
it won't take that long

Brian*   Do it yourself

Spencer*   Haha, no

Brian*   Jesus dude, you gotta get this cleaned

Spencer*   It's fine

Brian*   I can't see your floor

Spencer*   It's an organized mess.
I can locate anything

Brian*   Then where are my drumsticks I lent you last month

Spencer* Those are under
. . .
that pile of clothes

Spencer *begins to rifle through some clothes*

throwing them onto the bed and rearranging everything

finds dishes, random scraps of paper, and other odds and ends, but not the drumsticks.

Brian* I'll just get them back another time

Spencer* No no, they're here
I'll find them

Brian* I'm gonna go
See you later dude

Brian* *begins to exit,*

Brian* Before I forget,
rent is due
and you need to pay it on time.
Okay

Spencer* Thank you for the reminder

Chorus Brian leaves,
to go hang out with Derek . . .

Spencer *is left attempting to find the drumsticks*

They turn on some soft indie music to clean,

they find an old flannel that smells like smoke

3.

Chorus Two.
"Saw Derek at the party last night . . ."

The music becomes bad and loud college house show music, muffled by the walls

the stars aren't bright,

Chorus Derek appears.
he is "alternative,"
he smokes cigarettes
edgy
Spencer's old best friend
they are outside of a house show

Derek *lights a cigarette*

Spencer   ...

Derek   ...

Spencer   ...

Derek   ...

Spencer   ...

Derek   ...

Spencer   The stars look nice ...

Derek   Yeah ...

Chorus   Quinn, who is
a lot
appears. Spencer's dumbest friend

Quinn *joins* **Spencer** *outside*

Quinn   Spencer!
There you are
Come back inside

Spencer   I'm fine out here

Quinn   What if it was shots?

Spencer   Not right now,
I'm not feeling shots

Quinn   Are you okay?

Spencer   Yeah, I'm uh, I'm just
having a moment

Quinn   Okay, what's up
You're only ever like this,
When, when a
You know

Spencer   It's not that,
It's
....
No it's nothing I'm fine

Quinn   Do you want to be left alone

Spencer   No, can you just stand here
and look at the stars,

Derek *leaves into the house after finishing his cigarette*

Quinn   He's gone now

Spencer   It's not him,
It's me

Quinn   Fuck him, and his shitty attitude

Spencer   I'm not mad at him

Quinn   You should be,
Smoking cigarettes, abandoning you
What a fucking ass

Spencer   Quinn,
Just chill out

Quinn   You right,
I just don't want you to get hurt
Again,

Spencer   He's not like the others,
I hurt him and he just
Did what he had to do

Quinn   Men ain't shit

Spencer   I just, I
I don't know
. . .
Can you go grab me a drink?

Quinn   Of course.

Quinn *goes back into the house*

Chorus   Quinn is gone

The stars aren't shining,

4.

Chorus   Five.
"Night time is always great with Al . . ."
enter Al.
Spencer's longest best friend
they are in a field looking at a starry night.

the stars are bright,

Al   I value loyalty

Spencer   Really?

Al   Yeah, loyalty.
I want a friend who I know

will remain by my side through it all.
You don't agree?

Spencer   I mean, yeah, I agree,
but I would say I value humor more than loyalty
I want someone to laugh with

Al   Huh?

Spencer   No no no, hear me out. I want someone to be loyal in a friendship,
but humor brings people together. It like,
makes me feel good

Al   That makes sense.

Spencer   And how can a friend be un-loyal anyway?

Al   Talking about them behind their back.
I don't think that's loyal at all.
You could easily go behind my back
and be a complete jerk and ruin my reputation

Spencer   you need a reputation before it gets ruined

Al   Oh oh, I see, sorry I can't be popular like you

Spencer   Barely popular

Al   Everyone likes you

Spencer   That's so not true, everyone however, likes you

Al   Not everyone likes me

Spencer   Name one

Al   . . .
Becca //

Spencer   // Becca doesn't count

Al   She most certainly does

Spencer   She still ignoring you?

Al   Yep, it would be fine if she wasn't my partner in English

Spencer   Ouch
it could be worse

Al   I really don't see how it can be

Spencer   She could murder you

Al   She's not gonna murder me
I mean, I don't think she is

Spencer   Only I'm allowed to murder you

Al   A bit morbid don't you think

Spencer   All I am is morbid

Al   Don't die yet, you're too young

Spencer   Oh but I'm an old soul
I'll die any day now.
A whole bonfire, glitter, a live band.
A spectacle for the ages

Al   The only way you know how to go,

Spencer   I'm thinking for my funeral there's an open casket
and on my face, is googly eyes

Al   Googly eyes?

Spencer   Googly eyes.

Al   I make no promises

Spencer   Uh, if I put it in my will,
you have to

Al   That's not how that works

Spencer   It so is,
it's my dying wish

Al   you can only give people things, not make them do things

Spencer   I'm dead, so they have to

Al   You're wrong though

Spencer   I'm never wrong!
How dare you, accuse me
of that buffoonery

Al   Look it up

Spencer   No

Al   Oh, you scared that I'll be right

Spencer   Uh, no
My phone is dying,
And I don't wanna just sit on my phone
I want to, you know, live
in the moment

Al   Oh so now you want to be alive?

Spencer   Fuck, caught in the act of living

take me to jail cop,

Al   You wouldn't last a day in jail

Spencer   Says you, I'll run that place in three days

Al   Okay, yeah, I'll give you that

Spencer   . . . .

Al   . . . .

Spencer   I'm gonna miss everyone
I'm gonna miss you.

Al   Huh

Spencer   I'm thinkin about leaving,
I'm like, scared

Al   You'll be fine.
I'll miss you too
I'm just a plane ride away
It's just across the country, no big deal

Spencer   I'll keep in contact

Al   You better, don't abandon me

Spencer   How could I ever

Al   What's the next question,
we got a little side tracked

Spencer   one second, gotta look back at my phone
uh, uh,
uh
ah yes, what is one thing you love about yourself?

Chorus   Al is gone

Spencer* *cleans up a bit*

5.

Chorus   Seven.
"I need to go see a doctor . . . ."
Doctor appears.
they are in her office
she is very helpful.

Spencer   My heart races and I get,
like sensory overload

Doctor   What's that like?

Spencer   I can feel everything.
it's like,

Spencer *then attempts to describe*

the feeling with sound effects and hand motions.

Spencer   I know that doesn't make sense
but that's what's happening.
It's like, the color light blue, and a breath, like,
one that doesn't make it all the way to the spine
at the same time

They keep repeating this until the **Doctor** *gets it, maybe they do, maybe they don't*

Spencer   That doesn't make sense, I'm sorry,
I'm trying, I'm sorry
This is just how I am

Doctor   It's okay. You're fine
Is there anything in particular that has been causing you stress?
Even little things can stack up over time

Spencer   I mean, I've had a pretty shitty month
I've been so busy with,
with just about everything

Doctor   like what

Spencer   Oh so much. Classes in general
are slowly killing me
I feel like I'm going insane with all the world
And I'm behind on everything

Doctor   Have you gone in for help?
Teachers are willing to help you with anything

Spencer   It's not that I need help,
I just need more time in the day

Doctor   Do you find time in your day to do homework

Spencer   Not really . . .
Okay, I know I should be doing my homework
But I got a job
And I spent the last month doing interview after interview
It was so much

Doctor   I think you need to take more time for yourself

Spencer   Once this quarter is over, I can

Doctor   It seems like the last month took a toll on you

Spencer   Just an absolute shit ton of things
Wait, can I swear in here?

Doctor   Yes you can

Spencer   Cool sool. I don't mean to swear
It just kind of
comes out naturally. One time,
this like family asked me for directions
and like, a child was there and I said
like shit or something and I didn't even realize
. . .
Um yeah
. . .
But um. . . .
Wait, where was I?

Doctor   You were talking about being busy

Spencer   Ah yes, booked and busy. I,
I just have had a lot this quarter,
this month really. Interviews, presentations,
I might fail physics and get kicked out of school
Which, I like, really, really don't wanna do

Doctor   Have you tried medication?
Because the symptoms you described
sound like you could benefit from some

Spencer   No.
I don't need medication.
I've gone this far in my life without them and I just feel like it'll
change me, or ya know,

Doctor   Not every medication is like that,
but if you do ever want some let me know.

Spencer   Awesome . . . cool
cool, uh
I do, uh, I have one request though

Doctor   Yes?

Spencer   Could you help me drop my physics class?
I need to, if I
Ya know, want to stay here,

Doctor   okay.

Spencer   but,
I know I am going to fail this physics class
And I just, I don't want to, I'm scared

Doctor   Why are you going to fail?

Spencer   I just don't get it. It's really difficult and it's not like other classes. It causes me so much stress just thinking about it.

Doctor   I can email the office if you need me to

Spencer   That would be nice.
If I can like drop this class
it would make my life so much easier.
just thinking about it, makes me
it makes me so anxious

Doctor   Try some guided meditation, and make sure you drink water.

Spencer   . . . .

Doctor   . . . .

Spencer   . . . .

Doctor   You are drinking enough water each day, aren't you?

Spencer   Yes! Sort of,
I drink water with every meal
and I cut back on soda,

Doctor   Are you drinking alcohol?

Spencer   I'm not gonna get in trouble if I am?

Doctor   No. This is confidential

Spencer   Cause I don't wanna like,
go to jail

Doctor   You won't

Spencer   uh, yeah, I have.
I told myself I was going to cut back. because
I feel as though I've been drinking a lot this month

Doctor   Why's that?

Spencer   Mainly stress,
But it's like how I bond and make connections, you know

Doctor   Okay, have you actively tried
not drinking?

Spencer   Well no, but I don't think it's a true problem
But I also don't want to make it one.
And I'm not even twenty-one yet, so
like, I can't buy alcohol so my intake is kinda limited

Doctor   Well, it sounds like you just need a break from things,

I'll email the student life office about dropping a class

Spencer   Thank you so much
It means a lot

Doctor   Here is my card. Call me, email me, or text me if you need anything.
If you have any questions about meds, feel free to let me know.

Chorus   Doctor is gone

Spencer* *exits to put the laundry in the washer*

eventually returns to keep cleaning

6.

Chorus   Seven.
"What even is Speed Friend Dating . . ."
Greg appears

Greg *and* **Spencer** *sit across from each other*

Spencer   I would prefer to stay home,
I mean, I want to travel,
I think it would be so cool to like
see the world, but I don't have the money

Greg   Travelling is so fun dude,
and fuck money, you don't need a shit ton
I get it though, but get some friends together and just drive somewhere
Not everything needs to be international

Spencer   I've also never left the country so

Greg   Really?

Spencer   No,
I never got a passport, and I just kinda
didn't get around to getting one

Greg   When you can, there are
beautiful places all over

Spencer   Where have you been?

Greg   All over, I love climbing
and I'm constantly in search of the best climbing spots

Spencer   Where are the good ones?
I honestly don't know anything about climbing

Greg   There's Santa Barbara, California.
Oh and Baraga, Michigan.

Krabi, Thailand.
Greece. Spain. Mexico has great places.

Spencer   And you've been to these places?
Who takes you there?

Greg   Most of those places I actually go alone
I look em up online, ask around from friends
And just go

Spencer   Isn't that dangerous?
Like, doing any of that alone
don't get hurt

Greg   I'm a hundred percent safe.
I actually work for our outdoor center leading people on climbing excursions

Spencer   That's so dope, like
legit cool

Greg   It's nothing
I mean, I love my job and I love doing it regardless
but the pay does help

Spencer   I still need a job
my mother doesn't think I need one right away,
So I can, like adjust to life
but I want my own income
It's like, "God Mom, can't I just jump out of the nest?
If I die, I die"

Greg   Oh I get that,
It's like, let me make my mistakes,
The worst that can happen is death.

Spencer   That doesn't sound too bad haha

They laugh

Spencer   You're like, really cool
We should hang out sometime

Greg   I agree,
Put your number in my phone

They exchange numbers

Spencer   Beep beep beep
Done and done

Greg   I'm heading to the pass later this week
with some of the other girls on the floor.
Do you want to join?
Get some climbing in

Spencer   I'm so afraid of heights,
I don't think I could do it

Greg   Oh come on,
I'll make sure you're safe

Spencer   I believe you,
I just, I know my limits

Greg   What's the highest you've climbed?

Spencer   One time at my old work I had to climb a ladder
and I think I made it, like
half way up?

Greg   How tall though?

Spencer   Maybe a six-footer

Greg   Oh my god,
I know you can get over that fear,
I can help you

Spencer   People have been trying for years,
There's no way to help me

Greg   Is it like,
A fear of failure
cause we can start you out on a climbing wall
Something short and simple

Spencer   Well, I mean yeah, and fear of hurting myself.
I don't want to like, get really injured

Greg   You won't be injured unless you're unsafe,
and I won't let you be unsafe.

Spencer   Are you sure?

Greg   Yes.

Chorus   Greg is gone

Spencer* *goes back to cleaning, this time focusing on trash*

7.

Chorus   Seven.
"Got drinks with Quinn . . ."
Quinn appears. A bar, drunk

Spencer   Do we take another shot!

Quinn   Um, I think the fuck we do

Where's the bartender

Spencer   Bartender!

Quinn   tar
bender

Spencer   Did you just fucking say tarbender

Quinn   Yeah, what of it

Spencer   idiot.
but
He's uh, down there I think
we can just wait

Quinn   What're we getting shots of

Spencer   Fireball

Quinn   Fireball!

Spencer/Quinn   Fireball!

Spencer   I have a secret

Quinn   Dish it

Spencer   No i can't

Quinn   Do it

Spencer   Okay, ya got me
If I, like, just got hit by a bus,
I wouldn't be mad

Quinn   Oh my god same,
Like, just let it, just plow over me

Spencer   I don't need to be dead, I just
need a break

Quinn   Something to take the edge off
just, be fucking like comatose

Spencer   What a way to live,
by not being alive
. . .
God I wish I was fucking dead

Quinn   I am right there with you,
if a clawfoot tub could
just fall from the sky and
kill me on sight
I wouldn't be mad

Spencer   Why the fuck would a clawfoot tub fall from the sky

Quinn   You know, like in old movies
or cartoons, where they lift it into the sky
and then it falls on a pedestrian
I want to be that pedestrian

Spencer   I would want to die quickly and easily, no pain
maybe in my sleep

Quinn   well we gonna die tonight,
We going to get dumb fucked up

Spencer   We need shots right the fuck now

Quinn   Where is that bartender!

Spencer   Tar bender! Tar bender!

Spencer/Quinn   Tarbender!
Tarbender!
Tarbender!

Spencer   We need to fucking die,

Quinn   To dying!

Spencer   To fucking killing myself ehehe

Quinn   Throw it back for dead bitches

they laugh

Quinn *is gone*

Spencer* *is alone in their room*

they find an old poetry book

8.

Spencer*   the sky was lilac
when I wanted to kill myself
the sun, draped golden over the hills
when I wanted to end it all
the clouds huddled together
when I was in pain
a crowded bus
a busy evening
a night with people i loved
and i felt alone
the only thing
keeping me alive

is a promise i made
to my friends
the world felt my pain
and turned it into beauty
as a way to distract me
from myself

Spencer* *cleans*

9.

Chorus   Four.
"My mother is a little worried . . ."
Mother appears.
she and Spencer are exactly alike
she's a bitch.
she's motherly.
home.

Mother   Grampy and Grandmum say hi
they got your poetry book in the mail

Spencer   Oh did they like it

Mother   They said it was a little dark
they're a little worried

Spencer   Did you let them know that I was fine

Mother   Yes,
I'm also a little worried about you

Spencer   There's no need to be worried,
yes I was in a dark place when I started those
they helped me get out of it

Mother   Okay, it just seems like you still aren't over
some deaths in your life

Spencer   Of course I'm not over them but I came to terms with them
that's what the book is all about
rebounding and dealing with my problems

Mother   Okay, okay
I just want you to know we love you

Spencer   I love you too

Mother *does some dishes*

Mother   You know, your father would be proud of you

Spencer   Would he?

Mother   Yes, you're an accomplished poet,
And all he wanted was to see you and the others succeed

Spencer   It never felt like he wanted me to succeed

Mother   Oh you don't know that. He wanted his son to be happy

Spencer   Mom, you know I'm not your son

Mother   You're always going to be my son.

Spencer   But I'm not. I'm not your son, I'm your kid

Mother   But //

Spencer   No buts. I am nonbinary mom.

Mother   Wel how am I supposed to tell my coworkers about the things my son does

Spencer   You say my child, Spencer, did this really cool thing

Mother   Can you just put yourself in my shoes?

Spencer   What shoes? The one where I disregard your identity.
I can call you Joanne.

Mother   I am your mom, call me mom, not Joanne

Spencer   But put yourself in my shoes. Your name is Joanne,
So I'm calling you Joanne.

Mother   Don't do that,

Spencer   Disrespect you?

Mother   Yes.

Spencer   Well now you know how it fucking feels

Mother   Watch your language mister

Spencer   Goddamnit Joanne, I am not a man. I am not your son.
What do I need to do to make you understand

Mother   . . . .

Spencer   . . .

Mother   . . .

the stars are dim

Spencer   I need to uh,
get going,
I don't want to miss my flight

Mother   You sound a little sick,

I give Rick a shot of apple cider vinegar and lemon juice every morning
He insists that he hates them but I put them in his smoothie
clears his sinuses. It's just a cap of the apple cider vinegar and then a cap of lemon
then drink it with water
super simple

Spencer . . . .

Mother   I'll give you some money and you can pick some up
take it in the morning and at night, it will help

Spencer   Okay, I'll pick it up when I fly back

Chorus   Mother is gone.

Spencer* *sits in their room for a bit*

They find some old photos

10.

Chorus   Seven.
"I'm glad to have Casey in my life . . ."
Casey appears.
the drunkest friend,
he's charming
he's everything Spencer loves and wants to be
it is 1 a.m. his house

Casey *is tipsy/drunk*

Casey   Finish that beer!

Spencer   I don't know if I can
I'm bad at drinking beer

Casey   Impossible
no friend of mine will be bad at drinking
In this house we chug all our beers

Spencer   I don't even like the taste of beer

Casey   take a deep breath and throw the can back

Spencer   Uh, okay, I'll try

Spencer *sloppily chugs the whole can of shitty beer*

Casey   Atta kid

Spencer   Oh that was,
Ugh,
oh rank

I'm gonna vomit

Casey   No vomiting allowed
Not until after we shotgun a beer

Spencer   After we what?!
I have no idea what that means

Casey   Oh I have so much to teach you

Spencer   let's do this!

Casey   I am the best
no one else at this school knows how to party
but you have the potential

Spencer   You think so?

Casey   I know so,
you have the right kind of energy
and persistence
I love that about you

Spencer   Dude,
I look up to you so much
Like, you just, you're so cool
Like, I know that's cheesy // but

Casey   Shotgun the beer!
Go!

Casey *successfully shotguns the beer, and* **Spencer** *shotguns it like someone who has never shotgunned a beer before*

Spencer   Oh I am definitely going to vomit now
Oh fuck here it comes

Spencer *runs out of the room to vomit.*

Eventually returns

Spencer   Thank you dude,
Thank you so much
I'm happy when I'm with you.
You're my best friend

Casey   You're mine too bro,
After I graduate and leave,
You'll be right in my place
teaching someone how to drink.
Just like I did years before.

The stars are bright,

Spencer   Thanks.

Casey   I love you

Spencer   I uh, oh my god,
I love you so much
That, that means the world
Like the world to me

Casey   I'm always here for you

Spencer *starts tearing up*

Casey   Hey, hey is everything okay?

Spencer   Dude, I was in such a dark place
last quarter
And you really helped me

Casey   You're gonna get through it
I know you are
Do you know why,
You're strong.
And it's going to be okay, and I'm proud of you

Spencer   You're too good to me. When I thought I was going to flunk out you
helped me. I forgot to tell you that, but you really did. I didn't know how to go on.
God, All those people I was tutoring, they loved me and fucking Gabriella from HR
wanted to fire me. I, ugh, she was waiting for me to slip up. I was a good tutor. I liked
my job and my students liked me. I'm just mad at myself for messing up. But I did
what I had to do. I left, and I'm in a better place, with you. And, we could do this, like
quarterly, like, ya know, get together and decompress, just the two of us, it would be
like a bonding thing, and I would just love that

Casey   Yeah, that sounds awesome
I'll be right back,
I need to shit

Casey *leaves*

the stars aren't as bright

Chorus   Spencer sits alone
. . .
for awhile
. . .
waiting
Casey is gone.

Spencer* *continues to clean and vibe to music*

11.

Chorus Five.
"Learned a lot at poetry club today . . ."
A classroom

Quinn *appears, the poems can be seen by all*

She is teaching the audience

Quinn Welcome to poetry club, I'm your president Quinn
Yes yes, snaps snaps, poetry lingo, haha we have fun here
Today we're gonna try a new form,
It's called the golden shovel.
In his poetry book *Lighthead*, Terrance Hayes, a brilliant poet,
took the iconic poem "We Real Cool" by Gwendolyn Brooks
and gave it new life, new breath, new meaning
he gave her credit for her words and reinvented them
It's a very very easy process, and that's what we're going to do today.
You take a simple ten- to fifteen-word phrase
that, inspires you, or speaks to you
then take each word and make that the last word of each line
in your new poem.
It's a way to pay homage to a phrase or piece you like
An example, my phrase is
"I can't remember the last time I felt undying, unconditional love, from someone"
So if I take the first word, "I"
my first line would be

"Is this all that I"
Then the next line would start with whatever I want,
but that line would need to end with "can't"
It'll be something like this.
"is this all that i
am? i just can't
shake it. to remember
that the
time we spent was our last.
i wanted more time.
is it because i
am selfish? i felt
lost after you. your undying
love for books. your unconditional
love for people. your love
came directly from
your heart. i wanna be that someone"

I chose that first line from one of my favorite plays

And I recreated it to honor not only the playwright
but a friend I had lost.
Poetry can be so much for so many people
and I want you all to fall in love with it
there's so many forms and ways to express emotions
I could go on, but I'll let you write

Chorus   Quinn is gone

Spencer *writes poetry*

Spencer   "The sky was lilac when I wanted to kill myself." Hmmm. what can I do,
what can I do. Hmm. . . .
. . .
. . .
. . .
Nothing
. . .
"it was the
blue of the sky
that is and was
and will always be lilac"
. .
What the fuck does that mean
God

They continue writing. Then **Spencer*** *cleans up some notes*

12.

Chorus   Six
"I'll see you all in therapy . . ."
Therapist appears,
She's gentle, and kind
Her office

Spencer   So imagine it, me
dying
having a panic attack
in an urgent care

Therapist   Ok

Spencer   And like, I have no idea what's happening
bitch, I.
can I swear?

Therapist   Yes

Spencer   So, I'm like, uh dying and it was really fucking with me

I couldn't breathe
my back hurt
my heart was beating so fast everyday
I had no idea why,
dude in urgent care could like
see my back muscles tensing.

Therapist   Has anything happened recently?

Spencer   Just stress, when I was at the doctor they told me to like fucking relax
So he gave me muscle relaxers and I popped those pills
I just took them when I got home from class
cause I couldn't take them before
they made me drowsy and I was like uh fucking kill me

Therapist   . . .

Spencer   Oh my god, I didn't mean it like that,
I don't actually want to kill myself

Therapist   Okay, just making sure

Spencer   I know you have to like,
report that if you hear it,
trust me, I won't kill myself
I do not have the time

Therapist   . . .
What brought you in?

Spencer   My mother told me I should seek some help.
Stuff has been pretty "hard" recently

Therapist   What do you mean by "hard"?

Spencer   Things are just hard. I don't know.
Everything is so confusing
. . .
I just, don't feel anyone wants to talk to me,
or that any of my friends like me. I'm stressing them out, and I can see it. I don't want
to do that though. I want be a support for them, but I think I'm just hindering them,
and it honestly feels like shit. I feel like people only pity me and don't actually want
to be my friend

Therapist   Why would they pity you?

Spencer   Cause I'm that sad friend who like, you feel bad for. The stupid guy who
like, is a loner and doesn't know how to hang out with people. I don't know how
people do it, they like just make plans, but my mom always said to never invite
yourself over, so I'm like scared to do that

Therapist   Why be scared?

Spencer   It seems needy, and clingy, and I don't want to be that. I want to be something else, you know. I don't want to be known as that friend you regret bringing along. It hurts, I feel like people are talking about me behind my back

Therapist   Why do you feel that way?

Spencer   I don't know why I feel the way that I do, I just do

Therapist   You say "I feel" a lot, but sometimes those feelings aren't really there. You "feel" like people don't like you, you "feel" alone, but are you really?

Spencer   I don't think I am but //

Therapist   // no buts, try saying and,
Yes and

Spencer   I hate improv

Therapist   Humor me

Spencer   I don't think I am alone, and
I think no one wants to be around me

Therapist   . . .

Spencer   . . . .

Therapist   What I'm getting is that you don't want to be your true self. Already I could tell that you don't want to show the real you. There's honesty hiding in you, you may have said some truthful things but you made a joke out of it. You had a smile, you pretended to be hurt, you pretended to show what you consider to be truth. But // that

Spencer   // And

Therapist   And, that's not what's going on.
I believe that you put fierce first because the world can't stop you if you don't show weakness

Spencer   . . .

Therapist   . . .

Spencer   Okay,
I'm afraid that when I'm open, people leave me. And it's happened before already. I don't want it to happen again. I feel like, if I'm confident, then no one can hurt me. I want people to think I'm honest, but it's never true honesty. Does that make sense. Like false honesty, to like, make them feel like they know me, but it's not the real real me.
. . .
. . .
I don't even think I know the real real me because I've lied to myself.

Therapist   That was much more honest,

Chorus   Therapist is gone

Spencer* *picks up trash*

13.

Chorus   Three
"Read my poetry at open mic tonight . . ."

Spencer *is on a stage, with a mic*

Spencer   Hi uh,
I've never done this before
I'm gonna read a couple of poems, they're
uh, not good
I'm sorry in advance
this first one is called silence

"I learned to live in silence
when I want one thing
but need another
this is the price I paid
for the iPhone 7"

I uh, wrote that after I
upgraded phones
you don't care though

um, this next one is called
my actions

"I am so tired
I am so exhausted
I am so lost

my actions
and decisions
have consequences
I made my bed
so I slept in it

that nap was a mistake"

uh, this one is a bit longer
Sorry
uh content warning to
subtle abuse

"It was a repeat
I'd seen it before
Though I was younger

I knew

Same poison,
different person
Slowly pulling the life out of you
Slowly pulling the life out of me
Linked together through a bond unbroken
I would fall with you

I would fall harder
Chained to you at the heart
Pull me down,
pull me down,
pull me down
Your arms wrapped around me ensuring safety

Your hand reached for another drink
And another
And another
And another

Smoke fills the air
Masking my eyes
Blinding my perception of you
Night has consumed daylight
Stillness

I sit there
Watching over you
The resemblance to my father is uncanny

Your eyes closing slowly
As the moon makes her way across the sky
The only light in this darkness
Reflected from a better time

The chain tightens around my heart
I fall to my knees asking for forgiveness
Hands clasped together around a new bottle
But I come back to you again
Attaching the chain around my neck
I fall after you slowly
With heavy love in my heart

One day you'll truly crash
And I'll be right by your side
Like I always was
And always will be

And I'll stare down at you
The same I did when I was younger

A point of view I know all too well

With your hands across your chest
A bottle in one
A cigarette in the other
The two most important things in your life
Right by your heart

It was all over again
It was all the same
It was all a repeat"

Thank you,
I'll uh, go

The mic is gone

Spencer* *is still going through trash,*

finds a bunch of crushed beer cans

14.

Chorus   Eight
"Casey and I hung out last night . . ."
his house,
it's a power hour

Casey *appears*

he and **Spencer** *are both drunk*

many beer cans surround them

there is a visible timer going

they take a shot of beer every minute.

Casey/Spencer   Woooooooo!

Casey   I just, see so much in you

Spencer   Thank you

Casey   I,
am very glad to have you

Spencer   Same,
oh
. . .
Oh my god
I might vomit

Casey   Don't, we don't have paper towels or toilet paper

Spencer   How do you not have either of those?
Do you have rags?

Casey   No,
. . .
But we have these streamers

Spencer   Streamers,

Casey   yeah

Spencer   Are you fucking kidding me

Casey   Sorry

Spencer   Uh okay,
okay
vomit averted

Casey   You know what I'll say it
I only have like, three good friends and you,
you're one of them.
I feel like the other idiots around here
just don't get it
but you do. You understand me

Spencer   I feel like I've grown so much
with people like you

Casey   You haven't grown
you've changed

Spencer   But for the better. Having you in my life
It makes me happy.
You make me happy. I feel so,
so connected.

Casey   Same, I do, I really do.
You have so much power
You're a strong individual

Spencer *begins drunkenly tearing up*

Casey   Woah woah, are you okay?

Spencer   I'm just, so emotional
I'm like happy
and sad
at the same time
Like that Kacey Musgraves song

Spencer *drunkenly hums "Happy and Sad" by Kacey Musgraves*

Spencer   but you literally are my best friend dude.

I really don't know if I would be alive if it weren't for you
And your, just, kind heart,
I fucking am so happy to have you in my life
I don't mean to be emotional, but
I am, it's too late, I'm emotional

Casey   It's okay to be emotional,
sometimes

Spencer   I'm always emotional,
I don't know why

Casey   Have you tried talking to someone?

Spencer   Well I'm talking to you

Casey   Not just me, like therapy

Spencer   I don't need therapy, I have my friends

Casey   Dude,

Spencer   But it won't help me

Casey   You don't know if you don't try

Spencer   I don't need it

Casey   I see you get stressed so much and
it seems like you need to control your anxiety

Spencer   but it isn't stopping me from doing anything
I can still function

Casey   Can you though?
I've seen you

Spencer   I'm fine!
I have my friends, they keep me in check
things like this,
these calm me down
being around you, makes me happy
. . .
I like being happy

Casey   I like when you're happy
come here you fool

Chorus   They embrace,
it is, it was
and will be
great

the stars are bright,

Spencer   Hey,
Uh
I have a crazy idea

Casey   Hit me with it

Spencer   I remember like, awhile ago, you mentioned
needing a new roommate
and my current housing situation
is shitty, and it's very difficult to find a place with the other gang
and
you're my best friend
. . . do you
want to live together
next year

Casey   yes, dude, of course
yes.
I propose a toast
to us,
we will take on the world
one shot at a time

they take a shot, this time of hard liquor

Chorus   Casey is gone

Spencer* *cleans beer cans and streamers*

15.

Chorus   Eight
"I just wish he'd listen to me . . ."
Derek appears.
a coffee shop

Spencer   You said you would stop

Derek   When this pack is done

Spencer   oh my god, Derek,
You're being so fucking stupid
and an asshole.
you're acting just like my old abuser
who I told you smoked cigarettes

Derek   I'm not like him,
God, you are being so fucking selfish.

Spencer   How am I being selfish,

I'm just trying to watch out for you

Derek   Of course you are, you're always trying to watch out for me
I'm an adult Spencer, I can make my own decisions

Spencer   I know, I know
you can, I just want
I want you to be careful

Derek   you are so controlling,
you know that right

Spencer   What?!

Derek   I can't even have a piece of mind with you
and your clinginess
consuming my life

Spencer   I'm clingy?! Wow, this is new
Let's talk about how you are a fucking
douchebag. You don't know how to love anyone
because you can't even love yourself

Derek   Look who the fuck is talking.
I know more about love and what it means to,
to actually care about someone not for my own
personal gain

Spencer   well,
you only fuck women to feel some sort of goddamn pleasure in your sad excuse of a
life
you piece of shit. All I wanted was to be your friend and all you did was fucking push
me aside
like I was nothing. All the times I helped you, all the times you passed out on the floor
and I got you water and a bowl to vomit in

Derek   I didn't fucking ask
for any of that. Okay! None of it
you took it upon yourself to make it seem like
like we were more.
we weren't

Spencer   wait,

Derek   And you dump all your baggage on me like it's nothing,
sometimes I'm not even in a good head space

Spencer   Why didn't you tell me?
You knew I was anxious about that kind shit

Derek   Exactly, if I told you to back down,
You probably would have went and hurt yourself,
Do you understand the pressure that puts on me,

Constant fear that if I say one wrong thing,
Miss one text, do something wrong
That you'll fucking go and kill yourself

Spencer   dude, I didn't
I didn't mean it // like that
you know, I care

Derek   Exactly, you didn't mean it
You didn't truly think about how I felt
The stress I'm under

Spencer   I'm sorry, okay
I just care, so much

Derek   That's your problem
you care so much, but only about yourself

Spencer   Dude, i'm //
sorry

Derek   You only cared about me to make yourself feel better
You used me
You used me to make yourself feel better
that if you "cared" for me
That I would have to be there for you, but if I knew
If I knew that you would bring all your baggage and dump it on my front door
I would not have been your friend.
You said you never wanted to treat me
like you were treated
Well,
I hope one day I never treat anyone like the way you treated me.
I never asked to be on a pedestal, I didn't want that
Because you never asked. You're selfish
Spencer,
You're an absolutely selfish person,
And I wish you the best
Because i really wish we could have been best friends
and I will miss you
but I can't be around you until you learn to be by yourself

Spencer   . . . .

Derek   . . . .

Spencer   . . .

Derek   . . . .

the stars are dim

Spencer   I uh, I love you dude,

Derek   Bye.

Chorus   Derek is gone

16.

Spencer* *continues cleaning up trash*

Chorus   it's quiet
the night sky is back
Al is back

the stars are bright,

Chorus   Eight
"I know something is up with Al . . ."

Al *appears*

Al   It's been really good,
I haven't made many new friends
but, it's going along

Spencer   How haven't you made any new friends
don't you talk in classes and shit

Al   Not really
there's not a lot of
interaction between psych majors

Spencer   Make a study group

Al   I study better alone

Spencer   Don't become some sad loser
who doesn't have friends.
I mean other than me

Al   And I am fine with that
you're still my best friend

Spencer   And you are mine.
I just think college is that time
where you meet new people
learn new things
Ya know

Al   I just want to get my degree
and get out

Spencer   It's your first year, you shouldn't be thinking that

Al   but I am

I'm not at college for other people
I'm here for me

Spencer   And having other friends is important
It's vital
keeps your mind sharp and happy

Al   I am happy
and my mind is fine

Spencer   That is good to hear, but I'm not here

Al   I know you aren't

Spencer   I'm across the country
I can't always be here
it's a miracle I'm even back home for break
I never like being here,

Al   yeah,
I know

Spencer   I'm sorry dude.
You know I love you

Al   I miss seeing you

Spencer   I miss you too
we need to Facetime more
so we can like,
actually see each other

Al   I would like that.
you're just . . . busy

Spencer   I'll always make time for you
you know this

Al   I know I know

Spencer   . . .

Al   . . .

Spencer   . . .

Al   . . .
I've been meaning to tell you
but Becca and I got back together

Spencer   Oh really?
That's, uh
fun

Al   Yeah, we talked it all out, and we

kind of settled some stuff

Spencer   Well that's really cool
are you happy?

Al   I am,
Um, yeah, yeah
I am

Spencer   But you don't really seem so happy
Are you okay

Al   I'm fine. But, uh
okay,
I don't know how else to phrase this
but
um
Did you tell Becca I was cheating on her?
to get her to break up with me?

Spencer   No dude! Why would I do that?

Al   Are you sure?

Spencer   Yes I'm sure
I couldn't do something like that to you

Al   Don't lie.
Don't lie to me
Becca told me

Spencer   . . .

Al   When we had our talk she told me why she broke up with me
I had to explain that I didn't cheat and she said that you told her I was

Spencer   Okay listen,
Please

Al   I don't want to listen
Honestly. It's fucked up what you did

Spencer   I did it for you,
for us, for
I don't know

Al   I really love Becca, and now it's harder for her to trust me!
I don't know if I can ever get that trust fully back

Spencer   Dude, just wait a second. I have to explain.
I, uh, I didn't really mean to.
I was hanging out with her and Sarah, and
We got drunk
and I kind of just said something I shouldn't have said

Al   Now that's something I can believe.
You being drunk and making stupid decisions. It all makes sense now

Spencer   It all makes sense?

Al   You're always drunk. Always!
You're just a functioning alcoholic

Spencer   I am not an alcoholic!

Al   Actually //

Spencer   // I can guarantee that I am not an alcoholic

Al   You say that now,
But you're in denial // about some stuff

Spencer   Denial? What would I be in denial about

Al   You're in denial about becoming your father,
so you drink to cope

Spencer   You leave my father out of this

Al   I'm just watching out for you dude
you know I care about you

Spencer   Yeah, I know,
but sometimes you don't show it

Al   Oh I do,
but I'm not blackout drunk when I do

Spencer   Again with the drinking,
Maybe we should talk about the fact
that you literally never reach out to me

Al   I do reach out

Spencer   Ha ha, no you don't
I'm always the initiator
It's always me who asks if you're free

Al   I'm busy

Spencer   Off fucking Becca I guess!

Al   No.
Avoiding you!

a loud buzz of the washer drowns everything out

Al *is gone*

Spencer *is alone*

they exit their room to go change the laundry

the stars brighten,

Intermission

Cycle Two

17.

a home, the stars are dim,

Mother *appears*

Chorus   Two
"My mother gave me a call on my birthday, but I didn't answer . . ."

Mother   Hi sweetie, happy birthday. The big twenty-one. I can't believe it's been twenty-one years. Time sure does fly. I still feel like you're in the first grade, when you didn't have any friends in the neighborhood yet. But, thank goodness I met the Davises, it was also nice they could watch you during the summer while I was at work. You were such a nervous little boy, not wanting to make friends. But I knew you were outgoing. You just needed a push in the right direction. Your father would be proud. He's watching from up above, making sure that you're okay, cause Lord knows I can't keep track of all you kids. He's able to watch you all, now that you're all, uh, off in the world. It still scares me that you're across the country for school, but I know it'll all be fine. I'm just proud of you. I am. Have fun tonight, please don't go all out though. You're young, enjoy life, but be safe.

Hangs up phone

Mother*   That's all I want from you kids, to be safe. I know I can't protect you all the time, and I know you're all going to be okay. I want you to be okay. I love you. Have a good day. There's always so much I want for my son, I mean, kid. But there's a lot I can't tell them to make sure they stay safe. Lying to them has been, the hardest thing I've ever done. Little white lies, we all do it. But it's the big ones. There's one, one in particular I haven't told them, and I don't know how. But their father, before he passed, their father and uncle would pretend to be gay, and they would go on dates, with other men, and lure them into alleys and beat them up. To near death. I don't think my kid would be alive if, if their father was still alive. After Steve died, I was heartbroken. But only one of them can be alive at once, and I'm glad it's Spencer. But every day, I'm afraid that I won't have Spencer for much longer. It's scary being their mother. Every message could be a final goodbye from them. Every word could be their last breath. I'm scared

Mother* *exits*

Spencer* *comes back to their room*

begins cleaning out the closet

taking out all the clothes, shoes, and other odds and ends

eventually finds an old photo of **Greg**

18.

Chorus   Seven.
"Reunited and it feels amazing . . ."
Greg appears
A coffee shop just up the hill

Greg   It's really good,
like I love it

Spencer   Oh that is so
so refreshing to hear
Like, you have no idea

Greg   I'm proud of you
You're really good at poetry

Spencer   Oh, no, no
No I'm not

Greg   You shut up and stop being humble

Spencer   I just think, that
it's something, that isn't awful

Greg   Are you gonna like publish it, or something

Spencer   God no, I
have no idea how to do that
and like, no one wants to read this
It's just sad

Greg   People love sad shit
And this is also absolutely hilarious too

Spencer   Well no one knows how to make sad shit funny like me

Greg   Truth.
But I really believe that people will read this

Spencer   Again, thank you,
but I want to let it sit more.
Before I let the world see it

Greg   Either you get that published,
Or you come climbing with me

Spencer   Woah, no no
Both are terrifying

Greg   Come on dude,
Take a risk, take a risk, take a risk

Spencer   I ain't trying to die on a cliff
in the middle of bumfuck nowhere

Greg   Again with the dying
You won't die

Spencer   You read that book,
I'm suicidal
I might jump for any reason

Greg   That's your brain being a dumb idiot.
I want to take you climbing
to see the world

Spencer   Okay, okay
I'll go // maybe
But with a few conditions

Greg   Yeah you will! It's going to be a blast
You're going to love it
We can go next weekend
Fuck yeah dude!

Spencer   On the conditions // that

Greg   Yeah, totally

Spencer   The conditions that it's a small and easy expedition
Nothing too high, or treacherous

Greg   I know the perfect place
If we go later in the day,
you will see one of the most beautiful sunsets
in your entire life

Spencer   I love a good sunset

Greg   I know

Spencer   And you promise I'll be safe

Greg   I will keep you safe,
I promise
We won't even need climbing gear,
It's gonna be simple with some mild bouldering

Spencer   Okay,
okay

Greg   I'm so excited for you
to try something different.
That's all I want from you
To do something new
and exciting
for me.

Spencer   I will,
for you

Chorus   they embrace,
it is, it was
it will be

the stars are just bright enough

Chorus   Greg is gone
Greg is gone
Greg is gone.

Spencer* *is alone in their room, with nothing*

19.

Spencer*   my heart fell five hundred feet
never to climb back up again.
scared, that if I love
like that again
I won't recover

from here,
where I stand
the world looks too big to climb
but I wanna climb it,
For you

the mountains you left untouched,
the trails you never discovered,
the world that kept existing
without you

if I fall,
maybe I'll see you

again
april showers
brought me
funeral flowers

Spencer* *goes back to cleaning, still organizing the closet*

20.

Chorus   Nine.
"I just want him to respond . . ."
Al appears
he and Spencer can't see one another
there's distance

Spencer   Just pick up, pick up, pick up pick up

Al *sees his phone ringing, but doesn't pick up*

Spencer   Fucking christ
dude, what did I do to you, what the fuck
goddamnit
dude
I'm just trying to talk to you

Al *still does nothing*

Spencer *calls again*

Al *looks at it, still doesn't pick up*

Spencer   Oh god, he's mad
He's mad at me, I know he's mad
I'm mad
I'm pissed
at myself
Jesus, of course he doesn't want to fucking talk to me
I wouldn't even want to, fuck
I can't believe I lied to him
I ruined his whole relationship. I'm sorry dude
But I also didn't call him often,
Goddamnit. I still love you dude, I still love you, you can be mad,
but I just want to talk to you
If anything, I mean I definitely did.
God why me, why fucking me, I mean, yeah, me of all people, it makes sense.
AAGGGHHHHH

Spencer *calls again, leaves a voicemail*

Spencer   Hey Al.
I fucked up. I can never take back what I did and I don't need you to forgive me. I just want to hear from you again. I want to hear your voice. Even if it's you yelling at me. You're the most genuine friend I had. You're the only person to make me feel like I wasn't crazy, like I, like I'm at my most calm with you. I'm sorry about everything. Telling Becca to break up with you wasn't even the worst thing I did to you. I was a shitty friend. I'm sorry, from the bottom of my heart. I guess this is goodbye.

Spencer *hangs up the phone and is overcome with emotion*

Spencer   I'm gonna call him again,
no Spencer that is a bad idea, no, yes, no, yes, no yes
Fuck me
I'm gonna do it

Spencer *calls him one more time*

Al *picks up*

Spencer   Oh my god,
Al

Al   Hey,
I got your voicemail

Spencer   . . .

Al   . . .

Spencer   I'm uh
I'm
. . .
Just glad to hear your voice

Al   . . .

Spencer   . . .

Al   . . .

Spencer   . . .
. . .
Say something,
please.

Al   . . .
How is,
life

Spencer   good, really good
I'm still breathing,
. . .
you?

Al   good,
I uh, I made some friends at school

Spencer   that's so fucking cool dude

Al   Yeah yeah, they're really nice

Spencer   How did you meet them

Al   One of them asked to study
and then a little group of us got together

Spencer   Proud of you

Al   Thanks,
I took your advice

Spencer   I'm glad
. . .
Man, I'm sorry

Al   I can't say it's okay.

Spencer   I get that. I fucked up

Al   What you did really fucked me and Becca up

Spencer   I know. You don't have to forgive me

Al   I'm not going to

Spencer   . . .

Al   I think back sometimes
to the nights on the field looking at the stars
talking about life,

Spencer   and death.
God it's been so long

Al   Only like five years

Spencer   Only five?! That's so much longer than I thought

Al   Time flies

Spencer   I miss you
A lot

Al   I miss you too

Spencer   . . .

Al   . . .

Spencer   . . .

the stars dim

Al   I love you dude

Spencer   I love you too

Chorus   Al is gone

Spencer* *goes back to organizing,*

21.

Chorus Ten
"I broke . . ."

Derek *is here.*

They are both at a party, behind the house

both a little tipsy, but not drunk

Spencer *is hyperventilating, and repeating motions, and twitching at the neck, and*
mutters the last word until their next line

the stars are brighter than ever,

Chorus The night sky is out
Derek is here.

Spencer   I know know know she isn't okay! okayokay

Derek She's fine
She got into an Uber and got home safe

Spencer   No, no, no no no no

Derek What makes you say she isn't home
safe?

Spencer   She called me, and uh, she called me, and uh, she called me,
crying, crying, crying, crying,
says she fell and she fell and she fell
hurt herself, self self

Derek Do you want to call her back

Spencer   selfselfselfselfself self

Derek Just breathe okay, it will be okay
It will be okay
repeat after me
it will be okay

Spencer   It will be okay
Okayokayokay okay
It will will willwill be okay

Derek Take some deep breaths with me

Spencer   . . .

Derek   . . .

Spencer   . . .

Derek   . . .

Spencer   . . .

Derek   How are you feeling?

Spencer   I don't know know know knowknowknowknow
One,twothreefourfivesixseven
Seven knows seven knows knows knows

Derek   Do you want a hug,

Spencer   That would be nice nice nice

Derek   Okay

Chorus   They embrace,
it is, it was,
and will be
okay

Spencer   Thank you, thank you thank you
I'm sorry, sorry, sorry, sorry, sorry

Derek   You don't need to apologize

Spencer   but I do, i do, i doidodo

Derek   deep breaths

Spencer   Oh godgodgodgodgod I can't cantcan'tcan't dude I can'tcan't

Derek   Look at me, you are amazing
you have helped me so much
you're extremely caring
you care so much, it astounds me how much you care
I am so glad you're here, with me
God, you're so great. I am so glad we became friends
It's okay to not be okay

Spencer   But it isn't! Isn't isn'tisn'tisn't

Derek   Shhhh
Thank you for being my friend, for being my best friend,
being with you makes me happy
spending time with you makes me happy
I want you to be happy
it's all I want for you
I want you to feel like I feel
safe, cared for
you are that for me, and I want to be that for you
okay?

Spencer   Okayokay okayokayokay

Derek   Never forget that,

wherever you are, know that I still care.
God, I'm still thinking about how amazing
and caring, and absolutely phenomenal you are

Spencer   Dude, thank you thank you thank you thank you thank you you you
youyouyou

Derek   What can I do for you right now

Spencer   Can you just, just just
stand with me me me me mememe stand with me

Derek   Yeah, I can do that

Spencer   . . .

Derek   . . .

Spencer   . . .

Derek   . . .

They look at the sky together

Spencer   I like, looking at the stars
It, makes me feel good good good good

Derek   . . .

Spencer   . . .
Can you get me some water

Derek   Yeah, hydrate,
please

Spencer   Yeah yeah yeah

Derek *exits to get water,*

Spencer *continues looking at the stars,*

Spencer   . . .
Fuck, me.
fuck fuck, how could I fucking do that to him goddamn
Goddamnit
breathe
breathe
. . .

a long, long moment of looking at the stars and controlling breath

Derek *returns*

Derek   Here you go,
sorry that took me awhile,
Kevin, uh, didn't know where the cups were

it's his house,
so you would think

Spencer   It's fine. Thank you
for everything.
wait with me for a bit?

Derek   yeah,
I can do that

Chorus   they enjoy each other's company
and look at the stars,
Derek is gone.

the stars aren't so bright,

Chorus   Then Spencer is alone

finds their old poetry book

flips through it

Mother* *enters, with a copy of the poetry book, unseen by* **Spencer***

23.

Chorus   Four.
"Finally finished my book, sending a copy to my mom . . ."

Mother*   My child wrote a poetry book.
they printed, and binded, and sold it themselves.
and I am proud. They sent me a copy,
holding it in my hands was like holding my grandchild
They spent months, if not years on it
This was their child.
I remember when I first held them,
and my heart was in sync with theirs
their eyes opened and I knew everything they would be
they would be strong
they would be passionate
they would be prepared for the world
And I was right
But nothing will prepare you for their heartbreaks
their battles
their anxiety
My anxiety. I knew there was something in common with me
the way we overthink everything
How I read too far into the little things
I can see how they read deeper

The apple didn't fall far from the tree and I'm afraid that
The roots weren't strong enough to give them the nurture
they needed.
I blame myself for how they turned out. Depressed
I raised them right, they are passionate/strong/prepared
but they're sad
They're lost
They aren't sure what they're doing any more
The words they wrote in that poetry book hurt me.
To see my child in pain
Crying for help, it's a devastating sting I cannot describe.
I ask if they're okay
And they text back "why wouldn't I be?"
but a mother knows. A mother knows.
they claim that they wrote these two years ago
But why weren't they reaching out?
My child wrote this poetry book,
And I can't help think it's not a final letter to the world.

Mother* *is gone*

Spencer* *puts the book away*

somewhere safe

23.

Chorus   Ten.
"I'm scared . . ."
Casey appears, he is very drunk
and aggressive, he is smoking a cigarette
Spencer is not
they are in their house

Casey   No you don't understand!
You'll never know what it's been like
To have a father who loves you
and supports you
You never had that
And it's so sad
My father gave me, so much
and yours didn't even care, and he just
Died

Spencer   Dude, it's okay

Casey   No it's not! You're so strong for this
You have a strength I can't even comprehend

I'm jealous

Spencer   . . .

Casey   Do you know what I've been through

Spencer   . . .
I don't know dude

Casey   I've been through
A lot
You wouldn't understand
I drink to deal

Spencer   . . .

Casey   NO no no
I'm NOT an alcoholic
A drinking problem, maybe
But I'm nowhere near an alcoholic
My dad was an alcoholic
And he drank his twenties away, he doesn't remember
Any of it

Spencer   My dad was also an alcoholic,
You know that

Casey   And he died
Mine is still alive, and he's sober now, but
Him, and my fucking mom, are
poisoning me
And they're all over me and they won't leave me alone
. . .
And and and my mom
my mom is fucking bat shit
She took my car,
did I tell you that
For no goddamn reason, she took my shoes, my good shoes
that my aunt bought me, and then took the car, and I had to fucking chase her down
She isn't my mom anymore,
Since they fucking divorced
My life has gone to shit
. . .
I'm watching them sell, my childhood home, my entire life
gone
Up for sale
To some fucking strangers and all those memories
gone
So that's why I drink okay
Are you happy

Spencer   I don't,
I think I'm gonna // head to bed

Casey   And I drink to forget what I did
All the things I did
I thought everything was normal
I feel like my life is over,
Dude, I need you
I need you
Don't leave me
please
Spencer, I need you more than anything

the most pitiful sob

Casey *sobs uncontrollably on* **Spencer***'s* * knee*

the stars are dim

what feels like an hour passes

Spencer* *starts unpacking boxes*

finds random bric-a-brac like wood figurines, board games, lights, random paper

24.

Chorus   "It's like looking in a mirror . . ."

Therapist *appears*

we are in her office

Casey *is still crying*

Spencer   I can't fucking live with him.

Therapist   Why?

Spencer   He's emotionally manipulative and
reminds me of my father

Casey *is gone*

Therapist   How so?

Spencer   The drinking mainly. He gets really drunk really fast and then becomes
aggressive. I remember the one time we did a power hour, do you know what a power
hour is?

Therapist   No,

Spencer   It's where you take a shot of beer, or wine in some cases, but when you do
a wine power hour you only do half an hour because it's more alcohol content so,

okay anyway. We did a power hour last year, and we would do them all the time because it was like a bonding thing we did after finals to celebrate. And this is the one where I got really drunk, but of course, he was drunker, it was the end of winter quarter, I remember it. We were dancing and I started talking about housing because I was gonna live with some other people but finding housing was difficult for four people and one thing led to another and we decided to live together. I was, so excited. At the time

Therapist   Why?

Spencer   Why was I excited? Oh, because he was my best friend and I really wanted to live with him. Like I would have never thought that I would be living with an upperclassman.

Therapist   Can you move out?

Spencer   I don't know. Getting out of a lease is really hard. I just, I don't know anymore.

Therapist   I think you need to take a step back
evaluate
and get out
If he is causing this much anxiety, I think it's best if you
move

Spencer   I just don't know where
and I'm scared to tell him,
how do I tell him
like, do I find a new roommate for him,
or do i say, good luck doing it yourself bitch

Therapist   I think you should solidify what you're doing first,
then worry about that later
there are plenty of resources on housing
Facebook, Craigslist
Ask around

Spencer   Yeah,
Yeah. It's been a long year for me
. . .

Chorus   Therapist is gone

Spencer* *continues to unpack*

they find an old polaroid of them and **Derek**

Spencer* *unboxes more*

finds an unopened letter,

to **Greg**

25.

Chorus   "My heart fell five hundred feet . . ."

Spencer *stands at a lake,*

the sound of water, there are no stars.

The stars are gone.

they are alone, but surrounded by many

Spencer   Greg, was, is, and will always be the person to make us smile. No matter where he went, he brought the most infectious energy. No one was safe from his happiness. He was my best friend, he put me in a better mood every time I saw him. I felt like I needed to keep him safe, like a mother. I'm not a real mother, but I felt, I uh, I felt like he was a reckless child. You want to protect them. But you can't, not all of them. You have to send them off and let them see the world. If you love something, set them free, you know. I uh, I remember uh, one time, I was in my room and he walked in with this massive smile across his face, and he said "Hey Spencer, I just climbed the giant crane in the courtyard," and I said "what?", and he did what he said, he had climbed the crane. Then with even more happiness he told me that he was going to go do it again, and I told him to be safe. He said he always is. I told him to be safe, and he said he always was, Greg was one of those people who left a room feeling better than when he entered. A ray of sunshine who would give you the shirt off his back, and did, many times. I didn't believe he was gone. I didn't want to believe. You think people like him, uh, people like him are invincible. That nothing can hurt them, that every safety precaution is with them. I know you're all here for him. And um, fuck, wait can I swear here? . . . Y'all don't care do you, it's just I, uh, I had some stuff I rehearsed, but I can't read this. sorry, i thought I was numb to all of this, but I'm not, I can't walk down my hall without sobbing. I would rather be numb, but i'm anything but that, I'm overcome with emotions and I'm overcome with the feeling of wanting one last embrace. I want a lot, but there are things I want that I can't have. Fuck. God, I can't. I feel like I lost a child, a part of me is gone, a part I can't get back. The last time I saw him was so nice, but I wish I knew that was the end. I wish I knew, I would have made that hug last longer, forever. I would have never let go. He was a genuine person, and he will live on forever in our hearts as just that. Uh, I would have never waved goodbye. The kindest person with the biggest sense of adventure. I know he's climbing newer, taller, bigger mountains. He would want us to keep climbing, keep living, find new paths. For him. His heart was bigger than the mountains he climbed.

it's quiet

Spencer* *goes back to unpacking, it's much slower*

They crawl into bed for a depression nap

26.

Spencer *is in a hospital bed, hooked up*

Quinn *is with them*

Spencer   You never think it'll be you
you think, it's always other people,
people in the news, online,
It's scary

. . .

I'm scared
Quinn
I don't want to die

Quinn   . . .

Spencer   . . .

Quinn   . . .

Spencer   . . .

Quinn   Shut the fuck up, you're just dehydrated

Spencer   But I'm dying
    I'm gonna die

Quinn   That's the valium talking

Spencer   The what

Quinn   Oh my god
Did you fucking forget already

Spencer   Listen, I'm just
happy you're here
To hear my final words

Quinn   And what are those going to be

Spencer   Live Fast Die Young, Dumb Bitches Do It Wrong

Quinn   Oh my god

Spencer   Wait, wait, take a photo of me

Quinn   Oh perfect

Spencer *pretends to be dead in the bed*

Quinn   Heheheeheheh

Spencer   I look pretty good
for a dead bitch.
Oh my god send it to Brian,

Quinn   Done and done
He is going to flip

Spencer   Hand me my phone,
I wanna text Derek

Quinn *reaches into their purse, pulls out a small bag of capsules, then shoves it back in*

Quinn   Oh no

Spencer   Did,
is that the fucking molly

Quinn   Yes . . .

Spencer   You brought molly into a hospital
What the fuck

Quinn   I forgot about it okay

Spencer   It has been seven months

Quinn   I'm stupid

They laugh

Quinn *is gone*

27.

Chorus   One.

Doctor *appears*

we are back in her office

Doctor   Well hello again,
let's just look at your charts,
it's been wow, three years since you been in

Spencer   Yeah, I was here to drop a class
like, my freshman year
God that was so long ago

Doctor   It was, indeed. So what brings you back

Spencer   Well, I think I, uh, need meds

Doctor   What for?

Spencer   Anxiety, depression,
I'm not quite sure exactly

Doctor   Let's talk about your symptoms and

we'll see what we can do.
Describe a state of panic for you

Spencer   It's like losing my breath, but my heart is racing.
My entire body sinks to the floor, and
I've had to leave work early
Because I
I just couldn't function
and, I get anxious thinking about my friends,
like, sometimes I'll uh, think they don't like me and my brain starts to go in
every direction of "they hate me, they don't want me" and I get so consumed
by it, and I don't want that. I've seen how my anxiety has affected my friends,
mainly my best friends, some I lost because of my anxiety. It was too much for
them. I thought being on meds would save those friendships, but I think I was
wrong

Doctor   Hmmm

Spencer   The slightest thing has caused me to just, break. Absolutely break. Back in
March I had to go to the hospital because of a mixture of dehydration, and a panic
attack

Doctor   When was the last time you weren't wound up about something,
or in a panic

Spencer   Let's see,
Uh,
. . .
. . .
. . .
I'm going quarter by quarter in my head,
Uh, no that was the Casey thing, . . . summer was hell . . . Hmmm
Hmmm,
. . .
. . .
I wanna say like five, or six years

Doctor   A lot of what you're showing is high levels of panic.
I think it would be beneficial for you to try out some meds
I'm going to prescribe you sertraline,
We'll start off in small doses
I added a sheet with the dosage amount each day
Keep me updated, please

Spencer   Okay, I will
thank you, thank you so much

Doctor *is gone*

Spencer *cleans up more of the room, finally organizing things, making it look nice*

28.

Spencer *is taking notes*

Derek *enters and sits next to them,*

they are in a classroom,

Chorus   Welcome to class,
Introduce yourself to your neighbor and say something cool
or interesting about yourself

Spencer   Hi

Derek   Hi,

Spencer   Nice to meet you, I'm Spencer

Derek   I'm Derek, great to meet you

Chorus   Derek is gone.

Spencer* *tidies up*

29.

Chorus   Five.

Therapist *is here*

We are in her office

Spencer   I think that I became infatuated with the idea
of who they were
and what they could do for me
Not what I could do for them

Therapist   Elaborate

Spencer   like i wanted to be their friends so badly,
that who they were, or how they treated me, was out the window
they could do nothing wrong in my eyes, until,
i finally took those rose tinted glasses off
and i saw the red flags that waved in my face
and it made me feel like shit
Causing me more anxiety
I wanted them to be something completely different
But I never told them what I wanted
it was all in my head and they had to assume what I wanted
and I craved their attention, I craved other people's attention
like, I wanted other people to see me with these totally cool people
and I, by association, would be cool

that wasn't it
it never was. I wanted an Instagram-worthy best friend
which was selfish of me. To use people for my own personal gain
and pretend like I cared about them

Therapist   Hmmm

Spencer   I'm on meds now,
Because I need to start to focus on me
Not keep putting my emotional baggage on other people,
Because that's shitty, and I hate myself for it
but // now

Therapist   // eh hem, yes and

Spencer   I hate myself for it
and, i think I've grown from it
I recognize the toxicity in them
and as well as my own toxic tendencies

Therapist   What do you mean by your own toxic tendencies?

Spencer   I broke someone's relationship up, defended a shitty guy because I wanted
him to like me, tried to control someone and make all his decisions

Therapist   Hmm, okay

Spencer   I feel like I set them up for failure
they were doomed to never live up my expectations from the beginning. I wanted my
friends to use me as an emotional outlet, I wanted to be the one they could come to, I
wanted to be considered. You know, when someone thinks about you when you aren't
in the room, I want that, and I didn't think people would ever consider me. I am still
working on this, it's always a battle but I know that if I work hard, it can only get
better.

Therapist   Sometimes we create false ideas of the people in our life,

Spencer   Oh I definitely did that.

Therapist   That's honesty right there,
how have the meds been treating you

Spencer   Really, really good. I keep track of them every day in my journal

Therapist   Journaling I see?

Spencer   Yes, I have to keep my doctor updated in case anything goes wrong
If any side effects take a toll or anything
I've actually gotten into this really good routine at night, I always journal at 9pm
if I'm home
but I have a reminder for meds and journaling
and each journal entry is just me reflecting on the good and the bad things that day
also for the meds I need to track my emotions.

but I didn't want to make any emotions feel negative?
If that makes sense
so I created a numbering system.
One is lack of emotion, like the days where I feel absolutely nothing,
I wouldn't say it's depressive, but it's def not happy
Ten is just, too much emotion. Like it could be way too happy, or way too much anxiety,
or just a shit ton of sadness

Therapist   So what're you today

Spencer   I'm like a saucy five
I'm not over or underwhelmed
I'm just
whelmed

Therapist   So what's next for you

Spencer   . . .
I don't know

Therapist *is gone*

30.

a door slam is heard

Brian* (*offstage*)   I'm back!
Did you fix the wifi?

Spencer*   No!
I've been cleaning my room

Brian* *enters*

Brian*   Fuck dude!
You really did that

Spencer*   How was hanging out with Derek?

Brian*   It was good, we just played some video games,
got burgers
nothing special

Spencer*   Glad to hear it,
Oh I found your drumsticks, they're on my bed

Brian*   Thank you
You're almost fucking done though

Spencer*   I'm so close. But, Rome wasn't built in a day
    And I can't clean all my room in one day

hehe, Rome, room
Good one Spencer

Brian*   I hated that,
but wow
I forgot you had a floor

Spencer*   Me too,
You forget it's there when your dirty laundry and trash is covering it

Brian*   and you unpacked
I'm actually, very impressed

Spencer*   Thank you,
I thought it was time to finally go through a bunch of stuff
unpack some things I completely forgot about

Brian*   Good
Hopefully, you can take this energy
and show up to my recitals

Spencer*   You get what you get, and this is it

Brian*   Understandable they are boring,
you see the sunset tonight?

Spencer*   Nope, I barely left this room

Brian*   absolutely beautiful,
it was like, this vibrant lilacy purple
and orange, I can't even describe it

Spencer*   I think I can grasp what it is

Brian*   Hell yeah,
Quinn is coming over for drinks
If you wanna join

Spencer*   Nah I'm on a cleaning kick so I'm gonna finish this

Brian* *begins to exit*

Spencer*   Oh uh, bro
I love you

Brian*   I uh, I love you too dude

Brian* *exits*

Spencer* *keeps folding*

then, it hits them

they rush over and grab their old poetry book

they write as quick as they can

Spencer*   at first i felt like the
world was ending. the sky
would fall. and i was
the first to go. but the scent of lilac
-s caught me by surprise. when
my mother picked i
-t from the ground and wanted
me to have it. to
remember the days when i thought kill
-ing myself was the answer. i learned the answer was myself

The room isn't clean, but cleaner than it was before

The colors from the sunset bleed into the room.

End of play.

Part Two
Fraught Spaces

Witnessing the Revolutionary Mundane: Raphaël Amahl Khouri's Queer Documentary Theatre

Melory Mirashrafi

I. Truth

Raphaël Amahl Khouri's plays are full of life. Unabashedly theatrical, brimming with love, pain, and laughter, yet always intimate, Khouri gives voice to queer Muslim and Southwest Asian and North African (SWANA) experiences and communities by listening to, curating, and presenting them on stage as documentary theatre. Carol Martin, author of *Theatre of the Real*, says in her essay "Our Reflection Talks Back" that "In the 21st century, theatre of the real, including documentary theatre, has several defining characteristics, including the particularization of subjectivity, the rejection of a blanket universality, an acknowledgment of the contradictions of staging the real within the frame of the fictional, and questioning the relationship between facts and truth." She continues, "increasingly documentary theatre includes the difficulty of finding out the truth as part of its subject matter" (Martin 2017). Martin unpacks documentary theatre through an interrogation of the real and subjectivity, distinguishing between the objectively "real," and the reality that can be constructed within the confines of a performance—an important delineation when, in the case of Khouri's theatrical process, one might consider the difference between someone's first-hand experience and the presentation of that experience on stage.

Following a Zoom performance of his play *She He Me* in June of 2020, Khouri told the National Queer Theatre, "In terms of the mixture of verbatim and imagination, I very much believe that documentary theatre is close to fiction. [. . .] It's not an objective thing for me, documentary, whether it's film or theatre," on his understanding of documentary theatre as a constructed reality (Khouri 2020). *She He Me* was billed by the National Queer Theatre as the "first trans Arab play," Khouri's depiction of its three Arab characters and their experiences of gender novel not only to documentary theatre as a genre, but to the theatrical landscape at large. While the four defining characteristics of "theatre of the real" as articulated by Carol Martin hold true to Khouri's documentary theatre, Martin's final suggestion, "the difficulty of finding out the truth as part of its subject matter," does not. Khouri's search for truth works not as an end goal, but as a starting point, presenting instead a version of documentary theatre that prioritizes the theatrical as a way of confirming what is true. Through a multilayered process of witnessing, Khouri establishes a methodology for validation—from first-hand experience, to Khouri's witnessing of the stories he would then go on to theatricize, to the artistic process, and finally to the audience, all participating in a layered cycle of testimony and reception that gives not only validity but also value to the lives and stories shared on stage. *She He Me*'s ultimate mission is not to seek a singular truth, but to use collaborative storytelling, multi-casting, and witnessing in order to advocate for a greater collective truth-making experience for its actors and audiences.

II. Witnessing

She He Me begins with a series of questions. As the show starts, Omar, Rok, and Randa, the play's primary storytellers, mingle with the audience, distributing thirty different questions and statements amidst the crowd: "Are you going to have the operation?" "Where are you from, you have kind of an accent? "You pass so well as a woman! I never would have guessed!" (p. 191). Although Khouri's stage directions with regard to the treatment of the questions are spare, Randa, a trans Algerian woman, eventually asks in return: "Why doesn't anyone ask me what I do for a living?" She prompts the audience, "Ask me what made me an activist." She waits, prompting again, "Ask me!" When someone does, she's relieved. "Wow. Thank you. You see, how hard was that?" (p. 191). Randa's interaction with the crowd, addressing her personal life and desires within the first few moments of the play, works two-fold: First, to reveal to the audience the dehumanizing and invasive fixation on trans bodies by cis-gender people, and second, as a moment of connection and mutual experience between audience and actor, inviting the audience into the world of the play. Khouri's inclusion of the audience in the storytelling process by prompting them to ask meaningful questions establishes a space in which listening to and learning about Randa's lived experience is encouraged and validated.

As a documentary play, *She He Me* gives value to the daily lives and stories of queer Arab people by providing a space for them to exist and share, together. The characters of *She He Me* are drawn from interviews and conversations between Khouri and his friends, colleagues, and fellow members of the LGBT+, Muslim, and SWANA communities. *She He Me*'s trio of main characters present a range of queer Arab experiences: Randa, a trans Algerian woman, activist, and refugee in Sweden; Omar, a gay Jordanian man who Khouri has described as "nonbinary . . . but before I had the language for that" (2020); and Rok, a trans Lebanese man living in New Jersey. Throughout the performance, each of the named characters also double and triple as several smaller characters within one another's stories. Khouri establishes an active relationship between audience and actor in *She He Me*, folding the audience into the testimonies and lived experiences depicted within the play by giving them a place in it. Khouri's combination of direct storytelling to the audience and interaction between actors within their own first-person narratives in *She He Me* allows audience members and actors to recognize one another's humanity, laying the foundation for a process of mutual truth building with the goal of developing a deeper understanding of the lives of the people on stage, and for one another.

Raphaël Amahl Khouri, originally from Jordan, has been creating theatre that centers the daily lives of queer people ever since his time at the Lebanese American University in Beirut. In *Queer Dramaturgies: International Perspectives on Where Performance Leads Queer*, Khouri writes that in Beirut in the late nineties "there was not even a semblance of queer activism" (2016: 98) Khouri set out to fill this void, presenting in 2014 what he described as "the first queer Arab performance" (2016: 98). The piece, entitled *No Matter Where I Go*, was performed at the American University of Beirut, and consisted of an adapted transcript of a conversation between friends about navigating their daily experiences as queer people in Lebanon.

Khouri melds modes of public and private performance by focusing on mundane life and every day stories onstage, lifting the experiences of queer Muslim and SWANA people and corroborating them through an exchange of listening to and sharing their personal narratives. "Exhibiting the element of queer mobile everyday experience," Khouri writes, "represents a vital intervention that responds to two noticeable gaps in the academic literature: on the one hand, literature on the public spaces overlooks queer experiences; and on the other hand, queer literature overlooks Arab and Middle Eastern queer experiences in the public space" (2016: 99). Steph, Nisrine, and Lora's conversation in *No Matter Where I Go* is in conversation with the invasive questions distributed in the opening moments of *She He Me*—one of the characters, Steph, says, "Well, we all have these kinds of harassment stories," to Nisrine, who replies, "For sure! We all get harassed." Lora chimes in, "They say you get used to the harassment, but it's not true. It becomes heavier and heavier each day" (Khouri 2016: 106). Steph, Nisrine, and Lora all speak to the truth of the daily harassment they experience as queer women in Lebanon, their confirmation of one another's realities serving as a collective testimony for their audience. The act of testimony, most often seen in courtrooms or religious spaces in the form of oral declaration by a witness under oath, or public declaration of faith, works to build toward and align the testifier with a set of laws or common truths for their listener to confirm. In the case of *She He Me*, the law or common truth built towards and confirmed on stage is that of the play itself; each character's declaration functions as another argument for the value and legitimacy of the lives on stage.

Director Zuleikha Chaudhuri, quoted by Martin in "Our Reflection Talks Back," speaks of art's ability to "disarm frameworks of certainty by insisting on the ethical and epistemic vitality of the intimate, the desired, and the imagined. By doing so, it acts as a caveat to what people think of, or take for granted, as the 'real'" (Martin 2017). Khouri's dedication to the "vitality of the intimate" is present in both *She He Me* and *No Matter Where I Go*—both pieces make room for the stories and paths of their characters to cross and uncross, acknowledging, witnessing, and taking part in the other's existence to create the real anew. Similar to how a testimony in court may lead to a jury believing a case, the "new" reality constructed and backed up by live testimony in Khouri's plays presents a common belief in the worth of the stories and lives of its characters, disarming fiction as a dismissive scapegoat for its audience in favor of fiction as a tool for validity through shared experience.

III. Queering Documentary Theatre

Documentary theatre, or more broadly, theatre of the real, holds a significant place in the history of queer and SWANA theatre—from Moisés Kaufman's *The Laramie Project* (2001), which investigates a small town's response to the murder of Matthew Shepard, to George Packer's *Betrayed* (2008), which weaves together interviews of Iraqi interpretors in 2007 in response to U.S. intervention of Iraq, originally written for a journalistic piece in *New York Magazine*. *She He Me* is perhaps most openly in conversation with Heather Raffo's *9 Parts of Desire* (2003), a set of curated stories centering Iraqi women, set between the 1990 Gulf War and the 2003 United States invasion of Iraq. Both *9 Parts of Desire* and *She He Me* use double casting (or multi-casting; "double" in this case meaning more than one), depicting the self as multiplicitous in its ability to contain many stories and lives. The most significant difference between the two is that while *9 Parts of Desire* was originally written as a one-woman show for Raffo herself, *She He Me* opts to use a cast of three actors. The fragmentation of the self into the nine women, inspired by Raffo's time interviewing women in Iraq as well as her own experiences, contrasts with *She He Me*'s three different, yet interconnected characters. While both depict the multiplicity of the Arab identity, *She He Me* ensures that throughout the performance, no one person is ever alone. The concept of queer chosen family, a cornerstone of queer community-building and safety, shines through in Khouri's script as even the harshest abusers such as Randa's prison guards, or Rok's brother, are performed by someone who has the capacity to empathize, rejecting isolationism for the community-oriented dynamics of both the queer and Arab identities.

Khouri's approach to the documentary form, apparent in both *She He Me* and *No Matter Where I Go*, nods to more traditional pieces documentary theatre such as *The Laramie Project* or *Betrayed* in its use of interviews and personal stories, construction of narrative, and interrogation of identity; however, Khouri's abandonment of the journalistic voice in favor of intimacy, banter, and warmth, a tactic seen in Raffo's work as well, distinguishes his work from its predecessors. "I wanted to have a mixture between people giving testimony and drama. I didn't want it just to be monologues, or straightforward," Khouri said of his process. "I wanted to kind of create this mixed genre, a transgender genre between documentary and fiction" (2020). Khouri's "transgender" docu-fiction sheds the dry and hardened shell of journalistic documentary theatre, and exposes the vibrancy beneath. After a particularly touching moment with Randa followed by one with Rok, Omar breaks in, "Such a waste! You got to be a girl and you threw it all away! As they say in Arabic, God always gives sweets to those without teeth" (p. 203). Khouri's characters have an awareness of performance and theatricality, winking to one another and the audience with their jabs, and expressing a desire for audiences to walk away with an understanding of trans stories as dynamic, and filled with nuanced moments of joy and laughter. Khouri's inclusion of moments in which the characters address the construction of the play, such as Randa setting up a moment to talk about her activism, or Omar teasing Rok, communicates a sense of purpose: a mission to move past queer and SWANA lives and experiences as either news headlines, or tragic stories, by listening to the stories queer Muslim and SWANA people want to tell.

IV. Revolution

In the spirit of Martin's definition of theatre of the real as rejecting "blanket universality," Khouri's reclamation of life and identity in his plays is a concept familiar to the people of Southwest Asia and North Africa. Tunisia, Syria, Egypt, Yemen, Libya, Bahrain, Algeria, Sudan, Iraq, and Lebanon are all countries that have participated in the stream of uprisings in the twenty-first century commonly known as the Arab Spring, and emerged with a shift in power, with other SWANA countries also having smaller yet similar movements. In *She He Me*, Khouri extends the concept of revolution to include not only overhaul and reformation of regional identity, but also the redefinition and reclamation of gender identity in order to accurately and safely self-identify at will.

Revolutionaries of the Arab Spring and beyond challenged governing structures that no longer represented them by working to claim agency over their own narratives, a methodology that can be true of trans narratives as well, working to redefine one's self from the inside out rather than allowing external forces or structures to serve as defining terms.

Khouri defies a myopic understanding of the queer and trans Arab identity in *She He Me* by allowing the trans Arab identity to exist in multiplicity together: all three of the play's characters on stage at the same time, all three stories holding their own truths while helping construct another's. *She He Me* exposes two kinds of revolution: one at the surface of the greater SWANA identity, always churning over power and rebelling for a cause, pushing to break out of the projections thrust upon it by outside forces; and two, the revolution that is unseen, taking place internally as someone reclaims and represents themselves accurately for the first time, be it through community, through language, or through physical changes of the self. The words and stories of LGBT+ Arab people displayed in *She He Me* shows that just as Southwest Asia and North Africa has the capacity for revolution and change, it also has the capacity for queerness and community, and the two phenomena are innately linked.

Throughout *She He Me*, Khouri disrupts and dismantles harmful assumptions about the Arab identity, such as its blind condemnation of queerness and endorsement of archaic gender roles, or its existence solely within the context of constant war or the American news cycle. By grounding the existence of the queer Arab identity in a place of truth, Khouri alternatively pushes myths about Southwest Asia and North Africa or Islam into a place of interrogation. To most of the world, what it means to be Arab, SWANA, or Muslim is a monolith, stemming from the very inception of the region— more recently, the push for Southwest Asian and North African as a replacement for the colonial relic of "Middle Eastern" has been seen in an effort of decolonization and reclamation of the region. In an act of definition and reclamation of the queer SWANA narrative, Khouri fills his scripts with the language and lives of queer SWANA people, focusing on their interactions, details of their daily lives, and specificities of their identities. Randa, who lives in Sweden, reminisces about living in Lebanon: "I miss Beirut all the time. I always say, Randa was born in Algeria and grew up in Beirut. I love Beirut. (Dreamily) I would leave the house at eleven at night, and not come home till eleven in the morning. Having breakfast after staying up all night, going for a walk along the corniche as the sun came up" (p. 213). While the specifics of Lebanese daily life are distinct to Randa, they are likely lost on anyone unfamiliar with the streets of Beirut. Randa's depiction of life in Lebanon, particularly in contrast to Algeria, captures the minute yet monumental differences between the many SWANA, and in this case Arab, cities and cultures often melded together as a result of geography and miseducation.

Along similar lines of delineation and distinction, each Southwest Asian and North African country also has a different governmental and cultural relationship to transness and queerness. Countries such as Kuwait, the United Arab Emirates, and Oman explicitly criminalize gender nonconformity. Jordan, Omar's home, decriminalized "same-sex behavior" in 1951, but freedoms of expression for LGBT+ people are often limited by the government's manipulation of media and censorship, or by the refusal of the Jordanian government to defend or take part in securing the rights of LGBT+ people. In Iran, homosexuality is criminalized, yet gender affirming surgery is legal and partially subsidized by the state. Randa's former home of Algeria criminalizes homosexuality, and Lebanon, Rok's homeland and Randa's found home, allows gender affirmation surgery only with the approval of three psychologists and a doctor (Egypt had a similar process until 2016, when the government stopped issuing permits for gender affirmation surgery after a "debate about the morality of the operations") (Groshal 2018). The wide brush that the treatment of LGBT+ people and issues in SWANA countries is painted with erases the long and complicated history of activism and socio-political evolution present within the region—a history that *She He Me* not only engages with through its characters, but actively participates in as a piece of political theatre. Notably, Lebanon and Egypt both have vocal and vibrant queer and LGBT+ communities and activists that have been present before, throughout, and beyond their respective twenty-first-century revolutions. Pro-LGBT+ rights graffiti and chants, such as, "We want to topple homophobia; it must go," were seen and heard across Lebanon amidst the changes demanded by protestors. Lebanese activist Genwa Samhat says in an article in *Time* magazine about the 2019 uprisings that LGBT+ protesters "are claiming their visibility because they have always been there" (Harb 2019), a nod to the contributions of activists like Khouri and those who came before him in the ongoing fight for LGBT+ rights in Lebanon and beyond.

V. A Note on Futurity

The presence of queer activism during Lebanon's 2019 protests seems in direct conversation with Khouri's body of work. Just as Khouri made space for queer voices in Beirut in 2016, Lebanese revolutionaries continue to advocate for their own validity and visibility, inviting the world to witness their truth through protest. The characters of *She He Me* are those same voices of revolution: three distinct queer Arab experiences, bringing into focus narratives, both regional and personal, that have been overlooked and distorted, granting them humanization and lasting possibility through a layered process of first-person experience, mutual witnessing, and confirmation. Ingrained activism, the many shades of joy and tragedy, and a deep sense of community are all essential elements of Khouri's plays, reflecting the values and experiences of the communities he represents in his work.

She He Me's theatrical process invites everyone involved in its creation to actively participate in the confirmation of what is true throughout the performance, creating a new and collaborative experience in its every iteration. In the final moments of the play, Randa says, "I think us trans people come from the future. We take everything that society holds dear and just shake it up [. . .]," a sentiment that supports Khouri's treatment of documentary theatre as a whole, shaking up gender, what it means to be Arab, or even what it means to truly see someone (p. 214). José Esteban Muñoz speaks In *Cuising Utopia: The Then and There of Queer Futurity* of the "anticipatory illumination of a queer world, a sign of an actually existing queer reality, a kernel of political possibility within a stulifying heterosexual present" (2009: 49). The "anticipatory" nature of the "queer world" denotes it as innately futuristic in its need to see beyond the "heterosexual present," suggesting that futurity exists within the daily lives and experiences of queer people. While Khouri's plays could be "from the future," as Randa ponders, applying Muñoz's framework takes it one step further: the web of testimony and confirmation weaved by Khouri about the queer Arab experience is not only futuristic in and of itself, but brings a bit of the future into the present of every performance. Khouri offers through his queer documentary theatre a version of the present that contains a multitude of futures, identities, realities, and possibilities. A present in which listening is integral to validation, and collaboration to creation. A present in which truth is an ever-evolving organism. A present that is revolutionary.

References

Ghoshal, Neela. 2018. "Audacity in Adversity: LGBT Activism in the Middle East and North Africa." HRW.com, April 16. https://www.hrw.org/report/2018/04/16/audacity-adversity/lgbt-activism-middle-east-and-north-africa#

Harb, Ali. 2019. "'This Revolution Has Raised the Bar.' How Lebanon's Protests Have Created a Surprising Space for LGBT Rights." *Time*, November 13. https://time.com/5726465/lgbt-issues-lebanon-protests/

Kaufman, Moisés. 2001. *The Laramie Project*. New York: Vintage Books.

Khouri, Amahl. 2016. "Queer Dramaturgies: International Perspectives on Where Performance Leads Queer." *Contemporary Performance InterActions*. London: Palgrave Macmillan.

Khouri, Amahl. 2020. Criminal Queerness Festival Zoom Performance and Post-Show Discussion of *She He Me*. National Queer Theatre, June 21.

Martin, Carol. 2017. "Our Reflection Talks Back." *American Theatre*, August 22. https://www.americantheatre.org/2017/08/22/our-reflection-talks-back/

Muñoz, José E. 2009. *Cruising Utopia: The Then and There of Queer Futurity*. New York: New York University Press.

Packer, George. 2008. *Betrayed*. New York: Farrar, Straus and Giroux.

Raffo, Heather. 2003. *9 Parts of Desire*. Evanston, IL: Northwestern University Press.

She He Me

Raphaël Amahl Khouri

Characters

Randa—forty-two, a male-to-female Algerian trans woman living in Sweden.
Omar—twenty-eight, male, Jordanian, a big guy, homosexual, living in Amman.
Rok—twenty-eight, a female-to-male Lebanese man, slight build, facial hair, living in New Jersey.

The actors will play multiple parts.

Casting Policy

Preferably trans people of color; failing that, Randa should be played by a cis woman, not a cis man.

Setting and Time

Anywhere, anytime.

Playwright Notes

Special thanks to: Catherine Coray, Jocelyn Clarke, NYU Abu Dhabi, and Lina Abyad.

Scene One

Questions distributed from ALL ACTORS to the audience:
1. When did you realize you were born in the wrong gender?
2. Are those tits real?
3. Did you have—you know—bottom surgery?
4. Are you planning to?
5. You pass so well as a woman! I never would have guessed!
6. How are you paying for your operations?
7. Do you take it in the pussy or in the ass?
8. Do you have any photos of yourself when you were a man?
9. What was your name?
10. Where are you from, you have kind of an accent?
11. But where are you really from?
12. Wow! Your story is so amazing!
13. You're so brave!
14. Which bathroom do you go to?
15. Are you going to have all the operations?
16. What do you have . . . you know . . . down there?
17. What's the difference between trans and drag?
18. Your life could totally be a song!
19. How do you have sex?
20. Can you have a real orgasm?
21. Do you have a pussy?
22. How did they make it?
23. Do you have sex with men or women?
24. Do you feel it when they penetrate you?
25. Does it hurt?
26. Does your boss at work know?
27. Are you going to tell them?
28. Are those lips real or did you get them from giving blowjobs?
29. Are you a sex worker?
30. Can you have a baby?

Randa   Why doesn't anyone ask me what I do for a living? Or what my favorite book is? Why doesn't anyone ask me where I do my shopping? Or what my favorite city is? Ask me about my activism. Ask me what made me an activist. (*She waits or prompts the audience to ask her.*) *Ask me!*

Audience   What made you an activist?

Randa   Wow. Thank you. You see, how hard was that?

I grew up in the Algerian civil war. I was drafted into the army and worked there as a nurse. That civil war—may it be remembered but not repeated, as they say. Trans women had it very bad in the war. I remember the story about one trans woman back then, she was a sex worker. The men in the street got a hold of her. They beat her and beat her. The police do nothing because it's a war and they can get away with that. People come to watch. They beat her in front of everyone, in the middle of Martyrs

Square, it's the biggest public square in the whole country. No one raised a finger to defend her. No one said a thing. They beat her for two whole hours before an ambulance arrived. By then it was too late.

I know what you're thinking. She endangered herself! She chose to be a sex worker! You want to stop a trans woman from being a sex worker? Start from childhood. Stop kids from bullying her at school. Stop the teachers, the principals, from mistreating her. Keep her from getting beat up on the way home from school. A lot of trans girls just drop out of school early because they can't take it anymore. And if you don't have an education, how are you going to get a job? I mean it's hard for a cis person to get a job, so imagine how hard it is for a trans woman who dropped out of school. You want to stop a trans woman from being a sex worker? Make it easy for her to change her ID to female. Make it easier for her to rent a house. Give her a job. Give her a chance and then see if she still does sex work.

Scene Two

Omar   Location: Amman, Jordan. Time: 4:30. The advertising agency he worked at was trying desperately to look authentic. Its furnishings of skateboards, graffitied walls decorated with vintage posters, just reeked of middle-aged ad executives trying to look "Street," trying to get down with the kids. On one lonely wall hung a framed certificate that licensed OMAR M to pursue the calling of art director, with no one ever suspecting him of being an agent of gender subversion. Just when the sexist macho bigots working at this office begin to find comfort in his big fat bearded man exterior, BAM! He camps it up! He is nothing short of invincible. He was born into a gender dystopia, a fertile ground where the patriarchal villain of bigoted masculinity thrives and reproduces itself from generation to generation. But no matter how they tried, he would not succumb. Nothing short of ending compulsory gender norms would satisfy him. His mission at work today? SHOCK THE BIGOTED MALE COWORKERS INTO RETHINKING GENDER. His outfit? GOPHER MAMBO! (*Campy dance to Yma Sumac's "Gopher Mambo."*)

I remember once when I was around thirteen, my really macho brother was completely in love with an Iraqi girl and my father was very disapproving of it and forbidding and angry, because you know, (*imitating angry dad*) Who is this strange girl? And my brother was just devastated, he was in pieces. I wanted to console him. I literally dragged my brother to the basement. I grabbed him by his hand, and he was a big man. I was caressing him, caressing his hands, I was saying, Shh, don't worry, it's going to be ok, shhh, and I actually suggested he go and do ablutions and pray (*he giggles*), just as a way to find comfort and he did and it helped (*he smiles*). I remember my mom was busy upstairs, she was trying to calm my dad down, and I was with my brother comforting him, and—it just pains me that I actually— that I actually stood up for him. I'm sorry—(*gets emotional*) and then when he was the one attacking me later, there was no one to comfort me. That's what really hurts me.

Scene Three

Rok   The first rule of TV, never watch it with your parents. Because here's what always happens. Every single time. If you're gay and in the closet, by some freakish coincidence, there's going to be a show on about gays and your mom is going to start crying. If you're trans and struggling with it, by some freakish coincidence, there's going to be a show on about trans people and your mother is going to start crying. There I was, breaking the first rule of TV, sitting in the living room, watching with my mom. And who did they bring on *Oprah*? Not a homosexual, not a lesbian, not a recovering alcoholic, not even a serial killer, but a full-blown female-to-male transsexual. (*Points to self.*) Now here's where it got interesting. The transsexual was there, on TV, but my mother was not crying or frowning or wringing her hands. Instead, she said:

Randa as Rok's Mother   In Islam, transitioning is acceptable.

Rok   Now clearly, I was hearing things. What?

Randa as Rok's Mother   Yes, habibti. In Islam, this is halal.

Rok   And I said to myself: ok, man. This is your chance to come out to her. Do it! Do it now! Mama! Mama!

Randa as Rok's Mother   Yiiiiii! Look look! The mother is crying! Ya haram (*poor thing*) tsk tsk.

Rok   Mom . . .

Randa as Rok's Mother   SSSSHHHhhhhh! You know I love *Oprah*!

Rok   A couple days later, it was the third of July. We went to the beach in the south of Lebanon. We took out all the beach stuff from the car, my aunts were getting out the tabbouleh and hooka, my sisters put on their suntan lotion. And I was sitting there, thinking: we're in a beautiful spot, nothing can go wrong, my mom says Islam encourages transition, this is the perfect moment to tell her. Now, my mother and I have always been close, since I was never busy chasing boys. I was home listening to her gossip. So, I put on a sad face, I knew she's going to ask what's wrong.

Randa as Rok's Mother   What's wrong, habibti?

Rok   And I played hard to get, No no, it's nothing, Mama.

Randa as Rok's Mother   Rouwaida, habibti, tell me. What is it?

Rok   I'm fine, it's nothing.

Randa as Rok's Mother   I'm not going to leave you alone until you tell me what's wrong.

Rok   I swear, it's nothing.

Randa as Rok's Mother   Rouwaida, you're my daughter, I know you. You're not telling me something.

Rok   Lak wallah Mama mafi shi, it's nothing.

Randa as Rok's Mother   Rouwaida!

Rok   Mama, do you remember that TV show? With the trans person?

Randa as Rok's Mother   No! Don't tell me! Your friend Mariam, right? She's a man, right? I knew it! I knew it!

Rok (*to the audience*)   Oh great! I just came out to my mom and now I have to come out again. No, Mom! Me! It's me, I'm male!

Randa as Rok's Mother (*total panic*)   Yeeeeeee! Fatimeh, bring the chairs! Yallah yallah! We're going home! Zeinab, put the food in the car! Go get the umbrella. Yallah, yallah! Fatimeh, get the towels and the chair. Yallah! Let's go, everyone back in the car!

Rok   My aunts were hustling and we were all squished back in the car. My sisters were screaming.

Omar as Rok's Sister   Mooo-om! We just got here! It's not fair. What's going on? Are the Israelis bombing or something?

Randa as Rok's Mother   I wish! It's worse! [Alternative line: (*to children*) I hope Israel bombs you!]

Rok   And then nine days after I came out to my mother, the Israelis did bomb Lebanon. My mom and I were back in the living room, watching TV. Not *Oprah* but the news this time. It was the 2006 war. Lebanon was in chaos. My mother and I were back in the living room watching TV. Thirty-four days of war. The airport was bombed. Sixty-four bridges demolished. Sixty-nine roads destroyed. Two billion dollars in damaged buildings. One and a half billion dollars in damaged infrastructure. One thousand two hundred and thirty-three Lebanese people died. Five thousand eighty-nine wounded. A million cluster bombs were dropped on the south of the country. And then our village got bombed. What did she say?

Randa as Rok's Mother   Yiiiii! This month of July has been cursed from the beginning! You know what I'm talking about.

Scene Four

Randa   I've been an activist for a long time. I remember the story of another trans woman during the Algerian war. Amina. She graduated with a degree in psychology. The war ruined her life. She left her job because there was fighting, and kidnapping, and she couldn't get to work. And so many women stopped working in Algeria because the militias threatened to kill them if they went to work. When her brother joined the Islamists, Amina had to leave the house. She worked the streets to survive. And the police raped her more than once. Just because she was trans. In the end, a terrorist group caught Amina. Her brother was among them. He slit her throat himself. They threw her body in the street.

That's what made me an activist. I started an organization for LGBT rights in Algeria with some friends. It was the first one in the country. We called it Abu Nuwas and we fought for women's rights, LGBT rights, and children's rights. We declared October 10 as national day for LGBT people. On that night, LGBT people all over Algeria lit candles in their windows. We also declared an election boycott. Then I realized nobody gives a damn if we boycott the elections, we were too small a number! (*Laughs.*) So, I designed this ballot that said "I vote LGBT" and we posted it on the internet for people to download and print and put in ballot boxes on election day. And we also printed out hundreds of these ballots and went to windows above voting stations and we threw them over the doors.

I was arrested three times. Questioned and then released.

Once, as I was heading to our office, I was stopped by two policemen. I was carrying a briefcase, which was full of documents about Abu Nuwas. It had names and plans. I was terrified. My heart was beating so fast. I thought they would discover the briefcase.

Two policemen accost **Randa** *in the street.*

Rok as Police 1   Where you are going?

Omar as Police 2   What are your political affiliations?

Rok as Police 1   Tell us the names of the people in Abu Nuwas!

Omar as Police 2   Who is this guy Abu Nuwas? Is he your gang leader? One of your friends? Tell us where he lives!

Randa (*laughing*)   He's dead.

Omar as Police 2 (*angry and confounded as fuck that she's laughing and that he is dead*)   What?!

Randa   He was a poet. He died in the ninth century.

Rok as Police 1   I will poetry your ass in jail, faggot.

Omar (*breaking out of police character*)   Haha, did he really ask you who Abu Nuwas was?

Randa   Yes, but what I didn't tell them was that Abu Nuwas wrote homoerotic poetry. They let me go. And by some miracle, they didn't notice the briefcase. We fought harder. More campaigns. More meetings. More members. More danger. We were a clandestine group after all. We secured hormones for trans members and I started taking hormones. My family started to notice. My wife noticed. The government started to notice. Every time I flew out of Algiers for an LGBT conference, they pulled me aside at the airport. They made me wait until everyone else had boarded. An officer escorted me to the plane last. He looked at me and handed me back my passport.

Rok as Police 4   We'll be waiting for you, when you get back.

Randa   When I got back, the threats started. The first threat came by mail.

Omar as Hate Mailer 1   You fucking cunt, we're going to cut your fucking throat–

Randa   One time, someone knocked at the office door. I was alone. When I opened the door, no one was there. But there was a letter on the ground.

Rok as Hate Mailer 2   You fucking fucking faggot whore, fucking tranny—

Randa   Then I got more letters, and more phone calls—

Omar as Creepy Stalker   I'll be waiting for you after work—

Randa   I thought it would go away. Until my brother-in-law and brother came over to my house one night.

Rok as Brother-in-Law   Where is my sister? Where is my nephew?

Randa   They're asleep. It's the middle of the night. What's going on?

Omar as Brother   Are you sure they're asleep?

Randa   What's going on?

Omar as Brother   You need to leave.

Randa   What do you mean I need to leave?

Rok as Brother-in-Law   You need to leave the country. You have ten days.

Randa   What are you talking about, Mohammed?

Omar as Brother   Someone from the secret police came by our house to talk. Word on the street is certain people want you dead. He said they can only guarantee your safety for ten days. After that . . .

Rok as Brother-in-Law   And if you're killed for being a faggot, it will stain the whole family. Everyone will know. I will divorce your sister.

Omar as Brother   And your other two brothers-in-law will divorce your other sisters. You know what divorce means for an Algerian woman.

Rok as Brother-in-Law   I'll have nothing to do with a faggot brother-in-law, killed in the streets like a cheap whore. You think I'll stand people laughing at me in the streets?

Omar as Brother   You bring shame to all of us. Have you thought of our mother and father? Have you ever stopped to think about them? Huh? You only think about yourself.

Randa   I can't leave, this is my home. This is my country. You are my family. What about my son?

Rok as Brother-in-Law   What kind of father are you? Look at you! You will make him a faggot. The scandal will be the talk on everyone's lips. We have to think of the reputation of our families.

Omar as Brother   You will disappear and never ever make yourself heard from again, is that clear? Ten days, no longer, do you understand?!

Randa   Mohammed!

Omar as Brother   Don't ever say my name again. From now on, you have no brother.

Randa *sings an Umm Kulthum song as transition.*

Scene Five

Omar   Mission: Umm Kulthum. Location: The Bathroom. His Age? Fourteen. His Outfit? A scoop cleavage red velvet Valentino dress. Because he's not the fastest of the superheroes, but he knows for a fact: he's the best dressed one.

He came from a family of overachievers and by golly, if his mission was to dismantle oppressive forms of masculinity, he would start with himself and he would do it all the way by letting the greatest diva of all times show him the way. Obsessed with Umm Kulthum, he listened to any tape of hers he could get a hold of on the Walkman his mother had given him. His mother thought that, like everyone who listens to Umm Kulthum, this meant that he was in love. What she didn't know is that he didn't just want to listen to Umm Kulthum. He wanted to be Umm Kulthum.

Omar *stops voguing.*

Omar   My brother's violence started in high school, when he found my diary. No, actually, it started way before, when I was like ten. He saw me get off the school bus. I was waving to my friends and I turned around. There he was, watching me.

Rok as Brother   Why are you swishing your shoulders like that?

Omar   I was ten. I didn't even know what swishy meant. And it hasn't stopped since then. When I was sixteen, he went snooping in my room and found my diary. Hilariously, the cover of my diary was very graphic, it had pictures of celebrities and my name written in glitter. (*Laughing.*) I mean, it was asking for it. There was a Britney Spears picture, a Shakira picture, a Celine Dion picture, yeah, basically, a mélange of contemporary pop artists.

I had a crush on this boy at school and I had written about it truthfully in my diary for the first time. Before that I used to refer to my crush as (*campy, enigmatically*) F.H. or create some safe journal entries pretending I was interested in a girl, but then this one time I decided I was going (*campy voice*) to tell it all, and I described how I used to get shivers when I saw my crush—you know, like from the top of my neck all the way down my back. I remember, I even glued a picture of him from the yearbook onto the page and I revealed everything I felt. (*Mocking his teenage self.*) "I like Shadi, I like Shadi, I don't know why, I like Shadi." Yeah, I actually don't know why, since he didn't even care I was alive—but it was a very important diary entry for me, because I acknowledged it for the first time—I wrote down that I like a boy, which I hadn't done before. And that's when my brother found it.

Scene Six

Randa   I remember I packed my son's teddy bear. A stone from the house. Clothes. Two books. My diplomas.

I went to Lebanon because I couldn't get a visa anywhere else in ten days. I had never made any preparations. I never thought the threats would become an ultimatum. Luckily I had met a Lebanese activist at a conference a year earlier. I don't believe we meet people by accident. I called her and she said she would help me come to Lebanon. I bought a ticket. I told my wife I was going to a conference. As I was leaving, I saw my son standing there in the corridor. He started crying for no reason. I couldn't hug him. I couldn't pick him up. I left the house without saying goodbye. I knew if I did, it would make me weak and I wouldn't be able to leave. You know, even now, eight years later, I can't get out of bed in the morning because I miss him so much. And then I left.

I couldn't even cry. Too much adrenaline. I was worried I would be arrested at the airport. They took my passport and disappeared for a long time. (*Pause.*) Even when they gave it back and let me through, I was convinced they would storm the plane. Only when the plane took off did I feel safe, did I cry. I cried the whole way to Beirut. I kept saying: How could you leave your son behind? How? How could you leave him and go?

Scene Seven

Rok   So, because of the war, the subject gets dropped. Until about six months later, when I beg my mother to take me to a psychiatrist. She decides to take me to her favorite clinic at the American University Hospital. Now, the eighteen religious sects in Lebanon disagree over everything and kill each other over a parking space. But the one thing they can agree on, my mother included, is the American University Hospital. All of them, whether they're Christian—and by this I mean Armenian Catholic, Armenian Orthodox, Assyrian, Syriac Catholic, Chaldean Catholic, Greek Catholic, Latin Catholic, Greek Orthodox, Syriac Orthodox, Maronite, Coptic, Protestant—or they're Jewish, or they're Muslim—and by that I mean Sunni, Shi'a, Alawite, Druze, Isma'ili—they all love the American University Hospital. Because even though it's almost entirely staffed by Lebanese doctors now, it was started by some American dude 109 years ago, so it must be awesome. My mother picks a Lebanese psychiatrist there called Doctor Khoury who tells my mother flat out:

Omar as Dr. Khoury   Your child has what is known as GID, which stands for gender identity disorder. It means your child's gender does not match their sex, which could be the result of hormonal developments in the womb.

Randa as Rok's Mother   Shou ya3ni? What are you trying to say?

Omar as Dr. Khoury   I'm saying it's a perfectly natural—

Randa as Rok's Mother   That it's my fault?

Omar as Dr. Khoury   Of course not, you didn't do anything wrong—

Randa as Rok's Mother   You're saying it's my fault she's this way.

Randa as Rok's Mother   It doesn't mean you did something wrong, it could easily be hormonal developments in the womb.

Randa as Rok's Mother   Hormonal what? What would you know, were you ever bombed by Israel? Do you know what a cluster bomb is?

Omar as Dr. Khoury   No—

Randa as Rok's Mother   Exactly, you people in Beirut, you think you know everything but you know nothing. Rouwaida, get up, let's go!

Rok   Mom, he's a doctor, he knows about GID, he knows what I have!

Randa as Rok's Mother   I know what you have, you have something in your head.

Rok   Mom!

Randa as Rok's Mother   Get in the car, we're going to our village. I know a doctor there. He's much better than these Americans.

Rok   Not only was she taking me to a random doctor in the village, she was taking me to a doctor who happened to also be—

Omar as Doctor (*vampirish*)   Hahahahaha. Dr. Mustafa

Rok   —my mother's first cousin.

Omar as Doctor (*totally sleazy, chauvinist, and generally gross*)   You know this trans nonsense . . . is risky business. You like girls, don't you?

Rok   Oh my god! Yes!

Omar as Doctor   Why don't you just live as a lesbian, instead of all this?

Rok   I was like, you're totally right, oh village doctor uncle's cousin's son's cousin! Here I am thinking I need to change my entire body, disrupt my social and family life, lose my ability to live in my homeland, take injections every two weeks for the rest of my life, go through numerous operations, risk cancer, risk my safety and sanity every time I travel, and jump through countless bureaucratic hoops to change my name and sex, when in fact, all I need to do is find some girl and kiss her. Silly me!

Scene Eight

Randa   When I got to Lebanon, I didn't have anything, just a gold bracelet, which I hoped to sell for a lot of money. I pinned all my hopes on that bracelet. Two weeks after I arrived, the bracelet got lost. I applied for work as a nurse at a hospital and the head nurse stared at my CV and said:

Omar as Head Nurse   Honestly, with a CV like this (*holds it up*) you should have my job, (*pause*) but I can't give you work here, because it's not up to me. Nuns run this hospital, they would never accept you.

Randa   I was taken in by a lesbian community center in Beirut. The women there were nice, but I went hungry a lot. But I was too proud to admit it. Sometimes after the women at the community center would go home, I would eat out of the garbage. When I helped clean up the center, I would wrap the leftover food very carefully when I threw it in the trash because I knew I would eat it later. Eventually some of the women noticed that no one had ever seen me eating.

Omar as Lesbian Friend 1   Hey, Randa, we're all going out for pizza, yallah, go get your stuff!

Randa   You know, I don't really feel like it. I'm kind of tired. I'm going to skip this one.

Omar as Lesbian Friend 1   You're coming with us, no buts about it. Go get your stuff.

Randa   Really. I'm really not in the mood to go out.

Omar as Lesbian Friend 1   It's on me and you're coming.

Rok as Lesbian Friend 2   Yallah! Yallah!

Scene Nine

Omar (*as Naomi Campbell*)   I'm looking for a guy who's a fighter, who knows how to claw his way in. Because I have twenty-eight-plus years in the fashion industry.

I don't want to be a man or woman – I just want to be Naomi Campbell!

Scene Ten

Rok   After the doctor in the village incident, I decided I was going to take things into my own hands. I was still my mother's daughter, so there wasn't much I could do medically. I resolved to transition socially, at least during the daytime. I would just have to live two lives—boy at college and girl at home. Now as you might imagine, going from girl to boy over spring break requires a lot of PR when you get back. The first thing I did was write an article coming out as trans in the college paper to inform everyone. Unfortunately, some people just didn't get the memo. My first problem was a professor, who insisted on addressing me as young lady at every inopportune moment. He would call my name in class.

Omar as Professor   And how are you today, young lady?

Rok   I spoke to you about this yesterday if you remember. I go by male pronouns. And the next day he would pass me in the cafeteria.

Omar as Professor   And how are you today, young lady?

Rok   And I would repeat my little speech again. We've spoken about this before, sir. I go by a male pronouns. I need you to respect that. And the next day, he passed me in the hallways.

Omar as Professor   And how are you today, young lady?

Rok   I couldn't take it anymore. I'm doing very well thank you. And how are you doing, young lady?

He never called me young lady again. My next problem was a student-slash-asshole. I'm standing there with the girl I'm dating and some friends and he shows up. He points to my binded chest:

Randa as Student-Slash-Asshole   What happened here? (*Pointing to* **Rok***'s binded chest.*) Now that you're "a guy," what are you going to do with them? Who's going to believe any of this?

Rok   There are surgeries that people have. Go and educate yourself before you try to humiliate someone!

Randa as Student-Slash-Asshole   What's the surgery going to do for you? This is how God made you! You have to stay that way!

Rok   Great, so go up to people that have a cleft lip and say, "You can't have surgery! God made you this way!" He came up to me a few days later and apologized. He said he didn't understand the process and he asked me questions about how transition works. I explained it.

My biggest problem was and still is my mother. She's done some pop psychology analyzing of my situation and she turns out to have a Ph.D. in blaming my dad. He left when I was very young. They got divorced and he moved to New Jersey. She raised us pretty much on her own.

Randa as Rok's Mother (*bitter, speaking to ex-husband's new wife*)   Hello, Madame. Can I speak to Sameh? Is he asleep? Tell him it's the mother of his children.

Omar as Rok's Dad   Hello.

Randa as Rok's Mother (*very cold*)   Marhaba, Sameh.

Omar as Dad (*awkward silence*)   Oh, Salwa! Marhaba. (*More awkwardness.*) Keefik? How's everything? How are the kids?

Randa as Rok's Mother   Funny you should ask about the kids.

Omar as Dad (*defensive*)   What do you mean! You know I love them. I'll send you money as soon as I can. Things are tight right now.

Randa as Rok's Mother   With a new wife, yeah, I can imagine.

Omar as Dad   Salwa . . . you know what you guys mean to—

Randa as Rok's Mother   —I'm not calling about money

Omar as Dad   Is everything ok?

Randa as Rok's Mother   It's Roqaya. (*On the verge of tears.*)

Omar as Dad   What's wrong? Is she doing okay at school?

Randa as Rok's Mother   Yeah! She is doing fine at school!

Omar as Dad   Well, what is it then?

Randa as Rok's Mother   It's so hard sometimes on my own.

Omar as Dad   Salwa, it wasn't working, you know that.

Randa as Rok's Mother   She wants to be a boy!

Omar as Dad   What?

Randa as Rok's Mother   She says she's a boy.

Omar as Dad   Who says she's a boy?

Randa as Rok's Mother   Roqaya, your daughter, but you're not listening as usual.

Omar as Dad   A boy? Rouwaida?

Randa as Rok's Mother   Yeah. That's right. And where are all you in all this?

Omar as Dad   Give me her, let me talk to her.

Randa as Rok's Mother   Look what you've done.

Omar as Dad   Just give me her—

Randa as Rok's Mother   It's too late. Look at the mess you've made. It's your fault. The children have no father, are you happy?

Omar as Dad   Please, let me talk to her.

Randa as Rok's Mother   She's dressing like a boy and I don't know what to tell people. Are you happy? She's looking through your old clothes for things to wear! She wears them in front of everyone.

Omar as Dad   Salwa, calm down!

Randa as Rok's Mother   You should come home now! We're being humiliated in front of the whole family, thanks to you.

Omar as Dad   I will fix it, just let me talk to her!

Randa as Rok's Mother (*fuming*)   Ya Roqaya, come here, your father wants to speak to you!

Rok   Mom, I'm in the middle of a game, tell him I'll talk to him later I'm finishing the level!

Randa as Rok's Mother (*to* **Rok**)   I'm going to throw that thing away and bury your cousin for bringing that stupid thing to the house. (*Back on the phone.*) Did you hear that? She's even busy playing video games like a boy. This is your fault, Sameh!

Omar as Dad   Please, Salwa—

Randa as Rok's Mother   Ya Roqaya, ta3i, your dad is a very busy man. (*Angry.*) In2ibri ta3i khalsini![1]

Rok   GOOOAAALLL!

Randa as Rok's Mother   Don't make me take off my slipper!

Omar as Dad   . . . Hello? Hello?

Rok   Yo, Dad, sup?

Omar as Dad   How's my baby girl?

Rok   . . .

Omar as Dad (*recovering*)   Keefik habibti?[2]

Rok   I'm okay, Dad.

Omar as Dad   Uh . . . Do you . . . Your mom said you're wearing my clothes . . . I can send you some pocket money, get yourself some nice things, a new dress, some ice cream.

Rok   Ice cream is not going to make me a girl, Dad.

Scene Eleven

Omar (*to* **Rok**)   Such a waste! You got to be a girl and you threw it all away! As they say in Arabic, God always gives sweets to those without teeth.

Omar *vogues down an imaginary catwalk to music*

Omar   LOCATION: Saad's fifteenth birthday party. MISSION: RUNWAY FASHION. TIME: 2:45pm. DATE: June 7, 1997. Once he had worked quite a bit on his own gender, our agent of gender subversion decided it was time to go out there and proselytize to the other victims of the hegemonic and compulsory systems of patriarchal masculinity: his classmates.

Randa as Omar's Mother   Omar! I heard you did a fashion show at Saad's birthday party! Show me your little fashion show!

Omar   It was true, he had done a fashion show for the boys at the party, but he had done it for the cause. To contrast the ungodly colors at the birthday party, he decided to go monochrome, with a little number from Thierry Mugler. It was too hot, but who cares? These boys were already being programmed with a corrupt idea of manhood

1. Get your butt over here! (in the female conjugation).
2. How are you darling? (in the female conjugation).

and the only way he could make it to stop was to march right through that birthday party as a female model. He wanted to show them that gender was something they could experience apart from their biology.

Randa as Omar's Mother   Well, show me the fashion show you did!

Omar   . . . (*Terrified.*)

Rok as Brother (*holding the diary*)   I found your fucking diary. IF I HEAR ABOUT THIS F.H. PERSON ONE MORE TIME I'M GOING TO FUCKING BURY YOU ALIVE.

Omar   I was terrified. My brother beat me badly and I didn't know what was going to happen next. I went to my parents' room. Each of them was sitting on a different corner of the bed, with their back to one another, as if they got the news that someone had died. And then the shitstorm happened. My brother stormed into my room with garbage bags, on a purge. I kept saying I haven't done anything, I haven't done anything, because it was true I hadn't, it was just a crush. And he was beating me up as he was throwing my things away. And he was talking to me like I wasn't even there.

Rok as Brother   HE'S A FUCKING FAGGOT. I'M GOING TO FUCK HIS SHIT UP.

Omar   Then my mom came into the room too.

Randa as Omar's Mother   I just want to know why, Omar – Why? Why? Just tell me why?

Rok as Brother   You're going to bring shame on our house, you're going to bring scandal.

Omar   My brother threw all my school books into the garbage bags, my drawings, everything, my CDs. There was one album that he broke very dramatically. My mom actually bought it for me. He was all like (*Imitates a macho guy mumbling, breaking shit.*), it was my Destiny's Child *Survivor* CD. Sorry, I know it's not edgy enough. (*In a funny campy voice imitating pretentious person.*) It's not David Bowie, sorry. (*Pause.*) I kept trying to talk to my dad. He had collapsed in his bedroom. He had a breakdown.

My dad didn't speak to me for two months after that. My dad is very social and he has a big name in Jordan and he was just obsessed—he didn't want people to find out that he has a faggot for a son. When it was done, my room was totally bare. And then they sent me away to my father's hometown.

Scene Twelve

Randa   And then I went to get residency papers at the central police station in Beirut—

Omar as Policeman 1 (*very troubled—looking at his computer and at the passport as if something is wrong*) (*to Randa*)   Just, uh, wait right here. Don't move.

Randa   You know, when they arrested me I was wearing a sleeveless lace blouse. (*Laughs.*) I loved that blouse.

Rok as Policeman 2   Take your clothes off!

Randa   Excuse me?

Rok as Policeman 2   All of your clothes!

Randa   Can you close the door?

Omar as Policeman 1   Are you a man or a woman?

Randa   What does it say in my passport?

Omar as Policeman 1   It says you're a guy.

Randa   So, let's stick with that.

Omar as Policeman 1   Send him, or her, or whatever *it* is to the secret police!

Randa   That's when I knew this was more than a little bureaucratic problem with my papers.

Rok as Policeman 2   Where are your balls?

Randa   They retract sometimes. (*Pause.*) It's the estrogen, you know. Well, maybe you don't. Of course, you don't. (*Humiliated, trying not to cry, very proud.*) Can you please close the door? If you're scared that I'll escape, then just stay in here with me and close the door.

Rok as Policeman 2   No. We're almost done. (*Sleazy.*) Almost.

Randa   I thought I was here because my residency papers weren't renewed. What does this have to do with my papers?

Rok as Policeman 2   Oooh, you're a spicy little number, aren't you? With a spicy little mouth . . . Mmmm . . . look at those lips . . . What do you do with that mouth? Hmm? I love me some he–she head. How come I haven't seen you on the streets before?

Randa   I'm not a sex worker.

Omar as Policeman 1   You all are.

Rok as Policeman 2   Which street do you work on?

Omar as Policeman 1   Is that how you make a living?

Rok as Policeman 2   Are those tits real or did you get a boob job?

Omar as Policeman 1   Do you sleep with guys or girls?

Rok as Policeman 2   Does your dick ever get erect?

Omar as Policeman 1   Give us the name of your pimp!

Randa   Not one of them ever asked about my papers. The next thing I knew, I was thrown into prison. A men's prison.

Scene Thirteen

Rok   My friend Ali managed to get me an appointment with Sayed Fadlalah.

(*To the audience.*) Sayyed Fadlallah was the highest Shiite religious authority in Lebanon and the only person whose fatwa was stronger than my mom's fatwa. The amazing thing was that he was a progressive man who openly supported transsexuality and I was going to get a fatwa from him giving me permission to transition. After I came out to my mom, she still stood by her claim that Islam accepts trans people, but she seems to have found a clause in the Quran excluding her own children from this amnesty. How was my mom going to say no to my transition when I would get a fatwa from Sayyed Fadlallah himself? There's no way! Overruled!

But the only way to get an audience with Sayyed Fadlallah was to have an insider go with you. Luckily, my friend Ali's dad knew Sayyed Fadlallah personally.

Omar as Ali   Are you ready?

Rok   Just one sec.

Omar as Ali   I brought you a veil.

Rok   What?

Omar as Ali   Yeah, a veil! There's no way Sayyed Fadlallah would receive a woman without a veil.

Rok   Dude! Look at me! What is Sayyed Fadlallah going to say? Is he going to ask why this young man is not wearing a veil to match his tie?

Omar as Ali   There's no way I'm taking you without one.

Rok   There's no way I'm wearing one.

Omar as Ali   What's the big deal?

Rok   I'm a man, that's the big deal.

Omar as Ali   Just put it on and let's go.

Rok   I'm not going.

Omar as Ali (*leaving*)   Whatever!

Rok (*to audience*)   I wish that Ali pushed me to go see the Sayyed anyway, but I just couldn't bring myself to wear a veil. My whole life would have changed. Sayed Fadlallah was supposed to be the hero who saved me, my ticket to surgery, the person who could legitimize me in front of my mother and my faith and my country. I had imagined him giving me his blessing and telling me to go to Iran to have surgery. Instead I had to go to New Jersey.

Scene Fourteen

Omar (*placing a veil stylishly on* **Rok**)   Hijab-a-Man today.

Scene Fifteen

Rok   I immigrated to the States so I could transition. I used to come back
every year to visit my mom. The problem about returning to Lebanon is my ID.
It has my picture from when I was eighteen years old. Back then, I looked like a
young Jennifer Lopez. In the US, it is not a big deal, they just scan my
fingerprint:

Omar as Border Guard 1 (*American accent*)   Welcome to the United States, sir.

Rok   But coming into Lebanon, it's the local version of *Saturday Night Live*. The
officer will look at my ID, then look at me, then look at my ID.

Omar as Border Guard 1   What is this, your mom's ID?

Rok   Then he'll call all his other officer friends to come have a chuckle.

Omar   Maya come and get a load of this freak.

Randa as Border Guard 2 (*laughing hysterically*)   Oh my God. What's next in this
country? Chicks with dicks? How did she even get on the plane?

Rok   And when I leave, it's just as bad. When the plane is boarding they say:

Omar as Border Guard 1   Boarding all our business class passengers, boarding
rows 1 through 22, boarding rows 22 through 34 . . . and . . . boarding that transsexual
over there with his mother's ID.

Scene Sixteen

Randa   "Dear Diary,

Randa decided to stop crying for today."

In the men's prison, I wrote about myself in the third person for the fear the guards
would find my diary.

"The guards threw away all the hormone pills she had in her purse. A year and a half
of hormone therapy—gone. The stubble is reappearing on her face. It's a nightmare.
She is so ashamed."

"She misses her house in Algeria. She misses her son, Rakane, so much. She wonders
if her mother thinks of her, if she prays for her. Her mother never answers her letters."

"In jail, she can't tell if it's Maghreb or Aser. Randa wants her mother to pray for her.
She asks God to forgive her, she can't pray for herself because she hasn't got anything
to cover her head. God, you are her shelter. Protect her. Appease her suffering. Give

her the strength to fight and endure this. You are kindness, be kind to her. Is she doomed to eternal suffering, Lord? If so, give her the strength to bear it. She is merely a frail human being, Lord."

Rok as Prison Guard   Get up, faggot! You have visitors!

Omar as Lesbian Friend 1   How are you holding up, habibti?

Rok as Lesbian Friend 2   We all miss you at the center, hayati.

Omar as Lesbian Friend 1   The officers told us they put you in solitary confinement because they didn't know what to do with you yet. I hope they don't put you with the men.

Rok as Lesbian Friend 2   It must be so hard. Did they tell you what the charges are?

Randa   The lawyer says the Algerian secret police are still after me and they told the Lebanese government I'm wanted in Algeria for subversive activities . . .

Rok as Lesbian Friend 2 (*consolingly*)   Remember what you used to say? That your hormones were like your food?

Randa (*laughs a little*)   Yeah.

Omar as Lesbian Friend 1   Well. We got you some . . . food . . .

Scene Seventeen

Omar *enters with a box on his head with a face hole cut out.*

Omar   Hat prototype from Zolton Tombor's photoshoot for *Twill* magazine.

And after a few months, my brother picked me up to take me back home. On the way back, he kept giving me speeches.

Rok as Brother   You have to be a big strong man and focus on your studies. You can't hang out with bad kids.

Omar   While we were talking he was driving me around my father's hometown in his Mercedes. It was a very theatrical tour—like he was trying to say (*macho voice*) you need to remember your roots, this is where you come from. All I remember was asking for things to go back to the way they were before between us. But they never have.

Now, when we see each other, it's disgustingly civil, you know? Like, very brother to brother:

(*Very cold, fake voice.*) How's it going?

Pause.

Rok as Brother (*very cold voice*)   Fine, fine.

Pause.

Omar (*Still in cold, fake voice*)   How are the kids?

Pause.

Rok as Brother (*very cold voice*)   Fine.

Omar (*to audience*)   You know? Things are never going to go back to the way they were.

He still watches me. Sometimes I'm convinced he's going to finish what he started when I was sixteen, and murder me. He's threatened me several times. He stalks me online. And that's why I wanted to change my last name on Facebook, but I can't, because Facebook needs to have my real name. So be it. He started by stalking me on Flickr, back in the day. He makes these comments online—

Rok as Brother   You should be ashamed of yourself

Omar   He posts comments under a fake name. I didn't know it was him, he actually told me himself later that he was the one commenting. (*Pause.*) He also follows me on Twitter. I know he's watching every single move that I make. And he does it remotely, too—he lives in Saudi Arabia. I watch myself all the time because of him, I self-censor, you know? I even get scared, like, of fixing my hair on my social media pictures, and not just online, everywhere, because I worry it might be too effeminate. I start thinking, "Should I sit in a certain posture? Is how I'm sitting ok?" I watch what I say, like did I crack a joke that might be frowned upon? He just made sure, my brother, that I constantly feel watched. *brother bullying*

I'm a kind of shriveled, shrunken version of Omar in front of him. The fact that he has a mental leash on me is—by far—one of his greatest achievements. But I'm still doing my missions. I don't worry so much about trying to change adult minds. They're on their way out. I'm concentrating more on influencing my nephews, setting an example for them. They're the future.

Scene Eighteen

Rok   By the way, my mom just immigrated to the US and I've been helping her settle in and get her driver's license and all that. She's hooked on Netflix.

Mom have you seen my blue shirt?

Randa as Rok's Mother (*watching intently*)   Hmmmm?

Rok   I thought it was upstairs. Mama? (*Gets closer to see what she's watching.*) Holy shit, Mom! *Orange Is the New Black*?! Lemme guess, *Orange Is the New Black* is halal?

Randa as Rok's Mother   As if you care about halal now? When was the last time you prayed or fasted?   *atheism*

Rok   My mom is absolutely fine with my gender now. She doesn't blame wars on my sex change anymore. Now, it's my atheism that's causing large-scale disasters.

Mom, God doesn't give a damn if I pray or not or do ablutions or not, or fast or not—because God doesn't exist.

Randa as Rok's Mother (*shocked*)   Yiiii! You're worse than your father. I'm sure you learned this kind of nonsense atheism talk from him! Astaghfirullah.

Rok   He's not going to hear you, Mom. He doesn't exist.

(*Changing the channel.*) Tsk tsk tsk, look at this Trump.

Rok   I know, it's a disaster. He won more than 270 electoral votes! Goddammit!

Randa as Rok's Mother   Astaghfirullah! This election has been cursed from the beginning. You know what I'm talking about.

Scene Nineteen

Randa (*in the prison yard writing in her diary*)

"Dear Diary,

Randa has been taken out of solitary confinement and placed in a cell with other men. No one has hurt her though. Because she shares her food with the Sudanese men, they are now protecting her from the other men. It feels good. Also, she's a bit more balanced emotionally now that the women brought her her hormones.

"Randa still has no veil, so she has not been able to pray. God, please understand. She knows you understand—she is a believer but she is also a modest woman.

"What is her future? She has to get out of here. The shadow of death is still following her.

"She thinks about her son and how much she misses him. Prison has made her question everything. Sometimes she wonders if she made a huge mistake by transitioning. She is desperate for a sign from God. Please God, give her a sign, give her a sign, show her that she is doing the right thing." *leaving*

Two nuns enter.   son = masc

Omar as Nun 1   Hello, my child. We're from the convent of Mother Theresa.

Randa   Oh, hello.

Omar as Nun 1   We do the Lord's work in prisons across the world.

Rok as Nun 2   Would you like us to pray for you?

Randa   Yes, Sister, I would.

Omar as Nun 1   We want you to know that the Lord has you in his heart. He's watching you and He never forgets his children.

Randa (*sad*)   Yes.

Rok as Nun 2   What's your name, my child?

Randa   Randa.

Rok as Nun 2   Randa . . . such a beautiful name! We will be praying for you.

Randa   Thank you, Sister.

Omar as Nun 1   Bless you, my child.

They turn to leave. Suddenly **Nun 1** *turns around.*

Omar as Nun 1   I almost forgot. We've got something for you.

She searches in her purse and pulls out a package wrapped in paper.

Randa (*confused*)   What's this?

Omar as Nun 1   It's for you, my child. Open it.

They leave. **Randa** *opens the package: it's a veil. She veils herself as if before prayer.*

Scene Twenty

Randa   My lesbian friends managed to get me a brilliant lawyer. The police had calls from organizations and activists in Lebanon and all over the world demanding my release from prison, which put a lot of pressure on them. I applied for asylum anywhere that would take me. I've been in Sweden for three years now. The minute I learned two words of Swedish, I started causing trouble. Last year, I went to a meeting of the far-right party, the Sweden Democrats. They have these open meetings to pretend they are, you know, (*sarcastically*) just a chill, swell bunch of people. Not the racist fuckers that they are.

Omar as Swedish Right-Wing Party Member (*softly, overly smiley and friendly*)   We'd like to thank all of you for coming to our meeting. We hope that now you've gotten a better idea about the Sweden Democrats and I, uh, also, hope, uh, that we've dispelled a lot of the myths about our party being racist. I'll open the floor to questions now. (*Looks around at the raised questions, trying to decide who to pick.*)

Rok as Swedish Audience Member (*raises hand*)   Can I ask? I'm a journalist? I'm with—

Omar as Swedish Right-Wing Party Member (*doesn't want to pick him, looks around for someone else*)   Um . . . I think we'll take (**Randa** *raises her hand*), uh, yes, you, that nice woman over there with the brown hair. (*To the assistant.*) Could you pass her the mic please?

Randa (*takes the mic*)   Hello.

Omar as Swedish Right-Wing Party Member (*smiles*)   Hello. Why don't you, uh, go ahead and, uh, introduce yourself?

Randa   Yes. (*Laughs.*) I'm a woman, I'm trans, I'm an immigrant, I'm an Arab, and I'm a Muslim. I'm your worst nightmare. My question for you today is this: Since you claim that you are not right-wing, why is that you've aligned yourself with all the right-wing parties in Europe?

(*To audience.*) The next day, my Swedish teacher ran up to me.

Rok as Swedish Teacher (*quickly, excited, in total disbelief*)   Randa! You're all over the papers!

Randa   What? Why?

Rok as Swedish Teacher   At the open meeting! You showed those right-wingers. (*Laughs.*) They didn't know what hit them. The paper says they didn't know how to respond.

Randa (*to audience*)   I've even been elected to the city council here in Umea, the town where I live. I'm the first trans Swedish politician. I started getting involved in LGBT activism here too and giving talks all over the country. Usually after I give a talk, there's a Q&A. And someone in the audience will always stand up.

Rok as Swedish Audience Member 1   What was your name as a guy?

Omar as Swedish Audience Member 2   Is it hard for trans women to have sex? How do they, like, do it?

Rok as Swedish Audience Member 1   Do you have any pictures of yourself as a guy? You must have been really handsome.

Pause.

Omar as Swedish Audience Member 2   What's it like for you here in the Arab community? It must be very hard!

Scene Twenty-One

Rok   I've been on testosterone for ten years now. My voice is significantly deeper, and I can grow a beard faster than most cis guys I know. And truth be told, a lot of people think straight women won't date trans guys because we weren't born as men. And I know the question all of you are asking yourselves: the answer is no. I haven't seen the last episode of *Game of Thrones*. [Change joke according to current events.] But, honestly, the women I've dated didn't really say anything about a missing penis. I've never had an experience where she says, "Pull down your pants or we are not going to date!"

I postponed the hysterectomy for so long because ovaries are not something that affect you every day, like having boobs. I had chest surgery as soon as I could because boobs are something that slap you in the face every day. LITERALLY, BRO. I couldn't even open the door when the doorbell rang, unless, you know, I veiled the ladies!

Scene Twenty-Two

Omar   You know, I thought I left everything behind to go to a new place—the "gay community." And what I found out is that I can't find refuge in this new cluster. I came to the gay community to enjoy sexual liberty—a liberation about my identity. I started to find out this new gay place is not better than the straight one I left behind.

Sadly, I think that the gender identification within the gay community is a result of what the porn industry created as categories—gay men only looking for dynamics that are based on sexual requirements. It's hilarious when someone comes up and they're like, (*campy*) oh, he's a daddy, or oh, he's a bear, or he's masculine, he's straight acting, he's all of that. I see guys who are like,

Rok as Gay Man 1   I only want a manly man

Omar   or

Rok as Gay Man 2   I only want a straight-acting man

Omar   or

Rok as Gay Man 3   NO FEMMES. NO FATTIES.

never felt at home wiin gay community ↓

Omar   Or there's another extreme who do want feminine men—but just because they want to dominate them. I have a kind of sadness and disappointment that we didn't leave all of this sexism behind, we actually brought it in and we made it the basis of our interactions as gays. There is so much micro-discrimination within the gay community. It begins with the definition of a man and what you are expected to be as a man. That's why I came to question my gender. I mean if both mainstream heterosexual society and the gay community are still so hung up on these certain ideals and standards of what a man is, and I can't find myself anywhere there, I—I started to question the whole concept of gender at large. Like, if I can't be a man, do I have to be a woman? And if I can't be a woman, do I have to be a man?

Scene Twenty-Three

Rok   Lot of trans men are ashamed of once living in a female body. Even if I don't talk about it, how can I forget the girl I was? She wasn't me. But she also helped me get through all this. That strong badass female, she's the reason I survived all that time. Her anger, her passion, her urge to live—she's the reason I made it through. I don't want to hide my identity, but I also don't want to air out my laundry, unless the dryer's broken. It is because I lived a lie so long—so much lying that you finally get sick of it. These days I am disgustingly honest. Now, at work, I call my supervisor, I say, "Hey Dawn, just so you know, I came back from lunch three minutes late."

Scene Twenty-Four

Randa   I miss Beirut all the time. I always say, Randa was born in Algeria and grew up in Beirut. I love Beirut. (*Dreamily.*) I would leave the house at eleven at night, and not come home till eleven in the morning. Having breakfast after staying up all night, going for a walk along the corniche as the sun came up. Life was beautiful, despite everything, despite the instability and rough times, life was beautiful. I wish Swedes lived in the moment like people in Beirut do. In Lebanon, people know that at any moment there might be shelling, and the building might collapse, so people need to enjoy life now, right now.

I miss Rakane, my son. When I first got to Sweden there was milk coming out of my breasts. I went to the doctor, he said it happens to mothers who miss their children. But he'd never seen a trans case of that.

I don't know if I'll ever contact him. It will damage him more. I mean, what am I going to say, "Hey, son, it's me, I'm back in your life after all these years?" That wouldn't be fair. Sometimes I fantasize that I'll run into him at an airport. Or that I'll be able to bring him to Sweden one day so he can study. Sometimes I fantasize that I'll contact him and say I'm his dead father's widow. Just to be near him. Oh, who am I kidding? I've destroyed that boy's life.

I'll probably die alone in Sweden, an old maid, a crazy raving activist.

Scene Twenty-Five

Omar   Think about it—there is so much shit that is being put into this category called "man," there is so much shit being put on, stripped down, beaten up, whipped together, frozen for a bit, taken out, you know? Or stick it in the oven, give it two more beats, and it becomes a "woman."

Randa   My dream is to end gender. Why do we need gender on ID cards? To check society's fertility rates?

Omar   How can we achieve liberation from gender? Is it by being organized, systematized, institutionalized? Or is it by your mere fucking existence? Is it by creating yet another category? Can we call it fuckery? But, then, fuckery is still a category.

Randa   I think us trans people come from the future. We take everything that society holds dear and we just shake it up like this!

Omar   You know, I have this fantasy that in the future when mothers give birth, everything will be different.

(*Grabbing the actors together for a scene.*) Okay, you be the nurse and you be a mother who has just given birth. (*Since this is* **Omar**'*s fantasy, all actors are over-the-top campy.*)

Rok as Woman Who Has Just Given Birth   Well, doctor? Is it a girl or a boy?

Omar as Doctor (*coddling baby*)   How should I know?

Randa as Nurse   It's *way* too early to tell.

Omar as Doctor   We're just going to have to wait until it can talk and tell us!

Rok as Woman Who Has Just Given Birth   Yiiii! You are right, doctor. I look forward to that day.

They all smile cheesily at the audience.

labels be hard / limiting

Scene Twenty-Six

Randa   I did my operation finally, two months ago. I remember when I was in the hospital, I kept thinking, I need my mother to be near me, my sisters right now. I need the women in my family. Lilia, Hajar, Oumaima. I want them here. I'm about to be born.

You know what was funny? When I was going in for my operation, I was crying so much. The nurse came over and he kept saying,

Omar as Nurse   Don't worry, honey, don't be scared, everything is going to be fine. Don't be scared.

Randa   I just looked at him and laughed. "I'm not crying because I'm scared. I'm crying because I'm happy."

End of play.

"Challenging Every Memory":
Manifesting Futurity in *The Devils Between Us*

Yasmin Zacaria Mikhaiel and Ali-Reza Mirsajadi

Some futures are so abstract and unwieldy that the most effective, holistic way to reckon with them is to write them down. This is an exercise in liberation, in dreaming realities that one might manifest or avert. In one of the first plays by her hand, Sharifa Yasmin has claimed this space for such an exercise in futurity. Though a director by training, Yasmin has flexed her narrative shaping skills on the page, thus contributing to an emerging canon of revisionist Southern plays uplifting queer and trans women of color. Although she began laboring on this play in 2019 as a way to contend with the intricacies of her identity, heritage, and complicated relationship with her parents (Yasmin 2020a), Yasmin's work also speaks to the ways that micro-scale human interactions are complicated by social forces like masculinity, religion, and shame.

The Devils Between Us follows Latifa, the child of Muslim Egyptian immigrants, as she returns to her hometown in rural South Carolina in order to bury her recently deceased father. Since she last stepped foot in this town ten years ago, Latifa has come out as a trans woman, and she is met with a mixed reception of acceptance and violent transphobia upon reuniting with the members of her childhood community. The play's forward action is driven by Latifa's need to quickly find a Muslim *man* to wash her father's body in preparation for his burial, but Latifa's mere presence serves as a catalyst for each of the characters reconciling with their complicated pasts—their mistakes, regrets, internalized shame, and the cycles of violence and abuse that they must now attempt to disrupt. Yasmin's play functions as a reminder of the space between perception and lived experiences. It is usually vast, bubbling with unconscious bias and knowledge gaps. Grounded in the central metaphor of the Kübler–Ross model for the Five Stages of Grief (which the matriarch Barb cleverly associates with a Southern thunderstorm), *The Devils Between Us* advocates for radical acceptance. The play's characters are only able to prevail once they can find the inner strength, humility, and empathy needed to reconcile interpersonal differences, hold themselves accountable for past actions, and forgive the world's cruelties.

The burden of forgiveness haunts each of the play's characters, as well as its author. In fact, Yasmin describes *The Devils Between Us* as "a love letter of forgiveness to my childhood" (Yasmin 2020b). Born in Saudi Arabia to an Egyptian father and a white, New Yorker mother, Yasmin moved to North Carolina when she was three and spent the next ten years of her life "bouncing around the Carolinas" before settling in Ladson, South Carolina, at the age of thirteen. She and her brother were raised as strictly practicing Muslims, anomalies in the deeply evangelical Christian South. At the time, she still identified as a queer man. She explains, "It's hard to understand something that has never been explained to you, and I had never received exposure to trans people, either through media or the people around me. I just always felt different" (Yasmin 2020b). It wasn't until Yasmin moved to Kentucky for an apprenticeship at the Actors'

Theatre of Louisville that she finally met other openly trans people, "And once I got out of that bubble, that's when I was able to come to terms with who I am and that's when I started to transition" (Yasmin 2020b).

The Devils Between Us serves as Yasmin's meditation on her personal experiences, swirled with fictionalized storytelling of circumstances that she imagines might manifest in her future. Yasmin wrote Latifa for herself, a fierier version of the woman she aspires to be. What audiences might not expect, however, is Yasmin's affection and personal connection to the play's most morally complicated character, George. She attests, "George is as much of me as Latifa is, they are both two sides to my heart" (Yasmin 2020b). In writing George, Yasmin sees the person she almost was, fully consumed by denial and self-loathing. By pairing these characters together, Yasmin has devised a world where her current and past selves can meet, flirt, fight, and find common humanity against the backdrop of a modern South. The remainder of this introduction will explore the tensions between the complex identities that Latifa and George inhabit, diving into the former's position within the context of LGBTQIA+ Muslims, the way Yasmin uses shame as a generative force for communion, and how the intersection of these two characters and the parallel worlds they inhabit positions Yasmin's work within a burgeoning canon of Southern revisionist dramas.

In order to gain a better understanding of the play—and particularly its central character, Latifa—it is important to acknowledge the loaded complexity of trans and queer identities in MENA (Middle East and North Africa) and Islamic cultures.[1] As a diasporic Egyptian Muslim in the U.S., Latifa is already confronted by an endless series of aggressions and exclusions that characterize the followers of Islam as "backwards" and "terrorists," but the intersection of these identities with her transness creates an almost untenable level of marginalization. In recent years, queer and trans Muslims have emerged as the crystallization of a longstanding cultural conflict between the MENA world and "The West." On one side of this conflict, global human rights advocates are (deservedly) pushing against the gross mistreatment of LGBTQIA+ folks in MENA countries and their relative inability to exist openly in society.[2] Unfortunately, this advocacy has also driven the liberal logic of homonationalism, racism, and Islamophobia that sustains the ongoing military violence of U.S. soldiers in the Middle East. Jasbir Puar interrogates the hypocrisy and paradoxical danger of this "pro-queer" mission, writing, "Unraveling discourses of U.S. sexual exceptionalism is vital to critiques of U.S. practices of empire (most of which only intermittently take up questions of gender and rarely sexuality) and to the expansion of queerness beyond narrowly conceptualized frames that foreground sexual identity and sexual acts" (Puar 2017: 9–10).

On the other side of this conflict are conservative MENA groups who view queer and trans folks as emblematic of nihilism, iconoclasm, and a forced Westernization born out of centuries of colonialism and neoliberal imperialism. Even scholars of MENA

---

1. Our use of the identifier "MENA" here was a conscious choice meant to succinctly represent an expansive region with many cultures, although we acknowledge the problematic ways that it positions a people within the language of colonialist geography ("the Middle East") as well as its limitations toward inclusivity.

2. It should be acknowledged, of course, that MENA cultures are not monolithic, and there are many communities, cities, and even countries in the region that afford queer and trans people liveable lives.

queerness have critiqued the ways US sexual cultures have been imposed upon MENA individuals, replicating the systems of categorization popular in the West while erasing the long legacies of gender nonconformity and queer sexual practice in the region. In his influential book *Desiring Arabs*, Joseph Massad terms this colonial mission "the Gay International." He argues, "In a world where no one questions its identifications, gay epistemology and ontology can institute themselves safely. The Gay International's fight is therefore not an epistemological one but rather a simple political struggle that divides the world into those who support and those who oppose 'gay rights'" (Massad 2007: 174). Caught at the center of this ongoing cultural conflict, queer and trans MENA and Muslim people are forced to advocate for their basic humanity with both parties, placing them in a constant state of intense precarity.

Massad's objections to the imposed language and labeling of the Gay International has been critiqued for its occasional erasure of the contemporary lived realities of those who inhabit non-normative genders and sexualities in the MENA region, as well as its implicit glorification of a type of queerness located primarily in centuries-old Arabic literature and poetry. Still, he is certainly correct in acknowledging that queerness has existed in these cultures in various forms long prior to the arrival of the Gay International on MENA soil. For instance, Afsaneh Najmabadi's *Women with Mustaches and Men without Beards* traces a variety of ubiquitous queer sexual practices and nonbinary genders that were prevalent in Persian cultures, coexisting with Islamic practice, as recently as the nineteenth century. Other scholarship has highlighted the presence of the *hijra* in South Asian cultures, people who were assigned male at birth but effectively live and perform femininity as adults, often conceived as "a third gender" (Lal 1999).

Despite the vilification of Islamic teachings as the reason for LGBTQIA+ oppression in the Muslim world, progressive religious scholars and Imams have sought to renegotiate the religion's apparent objection to queer sexuality and gender. Since Islam is a religion that is largely decentralized and explicitly encourages debate and interpretation in its practice, it happens to allow for this style of progressive revision. The renegotiation of queer sexual practice in Islam has focused on reinterpreting the story of Lot and his flight from the city of Sodom, which is mentioned at several points in the Qur'an. Gender nonconformity and trans-adjacent identities are not directly addressed in the Qur'an, however there is mention of *mukhannathun* in the hadiths (the published second-hand accounts of Prophet Muhammad's (pbuh) words and actions).[3] The term *mukhannathun* is traditionally interpreted as lived effeminacy, or those people assigned male at birth who perform femininity through dress, speech, body language, occupation, etc. Although the *mukhannathun* are often described in abject terms in the hadiths, the debate in favor of progressive revisionism has focused on the particularity of this identity's social role in early Islamic cultures, which is far removed from contemporary trans experiences. Furthermore, Islamic practices that are less influenced by the hadiths (like shi'a sects) are more embracing of trans identities. In 1987, then-Supreme Leader of Iran Ayatollah Khomeini released a fatwa stating, "Sex-reassignment surgery is not prohibited in *shari'a* law if reliable medical doctors recommend it" (Alipour 2017: 96). While this problematically frames surgery as a necessity for trans individuals, Iran now provides

---

3. Given the Hadiths' origins in hearsay, its influence on Islamic practice varies widely, although it is mostly considered to be canonical in Sunni circles.

the second highest number of SRS globally, and the government not only subsidizes many of these operations but also reissues birth certificates with the revised gender.

In *The Devils Between Us*, Latifa's trans identity is located at the jarring nexus of the affirming LGBTQIA+ culture and community found in major U.S. cities like New York, and the conservative interpretation of her non-normativity by *both* her father's style of Islamic practice and the rural South Carolina community where she grew up. In doing so, Yasmin pushes back against homonationalist rhetoric that vilifies Muslims, de-exoticizing her Egyptian heritage and finding a space of communion (albeit one rooted in intolerance) that coalesces the two halves of her own Arab-American identity. However, the play consequently joins a complicated canon depicting immense harm and pain amongst society's most socio-economically oppressed peoples, namely black, Indigenous, POC, and LGBTQIA+ folks.[4] On the other hand, since this play is written through the eyes of a trans woman, Yasmin is able to employ a strategic nuance that primarily is found in writings that uplift one's lived experiences and community affinities. She resists digestible "good" vs "bad" binaries in which characters are easily sided with or disposed of, instead underscoring the complexity of layers present wherever BIPOC and LGBTQIA+ stories are rooted. When harm is an undercurrent and strife is plot, we must ask to what end. Since theatre is still a predominately white craft that exists for white consumption (purposefully or not), Yasmin's play serves as a necessary addition to an expanded canon reflecting all bodies and all ranges of experiences. Even so, it remains clear that stories of joy and pleasure are still few and far between when concerning the narratives of the disinvested. Nevertheless, Yasmin offers a window into what it takes to find self and aspire towards joy.

Yasmin's narration of Latifa's journey, one dedicated to accepting her identity and forgiving those who have caused her deep trauma, relies on Latifa's conscious decision to push back against feelings of shame. The postcolonial queer theorist Dina Georgis uses the affective experience of shame as a way to explore "the complex subjectivity of queer Arabs" (2013: 249), positioning shame as a framework through which the intersectionality of LGBTQIA+ MENA individuals can be read outside of the specter of whiteness and the Gay International. Acknowledging the dichotomous tensions between pride and shame and their place in Western queer cultures, Georgis argues for a reading of shame as community and transformation. She locates the significance of shame (or *'ayb*) in Arab societies, claiming that "it is probably not a generalization to say that the fear of social retribution and ostracization in a culture that intensely values family ties and religious/sectarian loyalty is the emotional reality for most Arabs" (2013: 243). In her queer reclaiming of *'ayb*, Georgis labels us "witnesses" who are increasingly attuned to "the fragility of human connection and the power that others have over us. In this way, shame is generative: it activates the imagination for reconstructing the terms of relationality or community, either by reinvesting in them or by finding and creating new ones" (2013: 244–245). Furthermore, Georgis positions shame as a potential locus through which global queer experiences and narratives can be rewritten, empowering the queer subaltern: "If shame is a response to our social environments [. . .], then writing

---

4. Of course there are cases in which such stories of pain and harm featuring BIPOC and LGBTQIA+ communities are of value to the canon, but such must exist in intentional ways that do not center leading whiteness to empathy.

shame offers a queer historiography and insight into queer identities that is both culturally/locally contextual and simultaneously an effect of contaminated histories, globalization, and Western imperialism" (2013: 246).

When looking to *The Devils Between Us*, it is clear such "contaminated histories" erupt out of a spectrum of worldviews and shame, as characters like George and Barb harden or soften when the past comes knocking. This past is now named Latifa, and nearly every facet of her identity is interrogated as she steps foot into a world she had given a decade of space. She invokes memories of past and buried selves. In George's immediate rejection of Latifa, we are attuned to the parts of himself he wishes to hide, and his internalized shame is projected onto her as violence. Though this tension by Yasmin's hand serves to apply pressure upon a detrimental worldview, it also brings to light how an internalized hatred or contradiction within the self is capable of harming others if unchallenged. Barb steps in, demonstrating a more empathetic and socially aware posturing. Her immediate acceptance of Latifa's name and pronouns is the bare minimum of respect that George will not manifest. In his recurring refusals to address and refer to Latifa, we witness the common bigotry that trans folks face both within and outside the home. Here, in George's home, accepting Latifa as who she is would compromise George's standing, one deeply anchored in patriarchy and homophobia. Shame emerges as a space of communion and reconciliation for Latifa and George. Latifa's grueling journey to overcome the feelings of shame thrust upon her and find self-love and acceptance provides a model by which George can reevaluate his own life and find comfort in his queer identity. Barb provides George with the support needed to challenge his self-hatred, functioning as a figure that complicates audience's expectations for a white Southern woman in her sixties. She is quick-witted, pushes back, speaks up, and ultimately makes space for folks to be their whole selves, even if it took a few decades of processing shame and shaking respectability politics for Barb to embrace her power to ally.

Yasmin joins an emerging canon of Southern plays on race and womanhood that complicates the aesthetics of antebellum plantation life evident in the work of Tennessee Williams and similar playwrights. In 2016, Kelundra Smith, an Atlanta-based arts journalist, published the piece "Facing South," in the October issue of *American Theatre* magazine. The article explores five new plays by Southern female playwrights, bringing to light the diversity of experiences in the modern South. The South here is expanded beyond the gentility and respectability of Williams-era drama, and the insidious omnipresence of white supremacy is brought to the fore. The new Southern revisionist drama uses naturalism as a tool for dismantling oppression, challenging these slices of human life by exposing the complex social issues (and intersectional identities) existing beneath them.

For instance, some of these playwrights critique the ways that the South's commitment to evangelical Christianity creates a tension between tradition and sexuality, abandoning the possibility for queerness. In this vein, Christina Quintana's *Scissoring* (2018) follows a lesbian teacher (Abigail) who accepts a job teaching history at a conservative Catholic high school in New Orleans. By taking the position, Abigail must now pretend that her newish girlfriend is a roommate, not a lover. As someone raised in a Catholic household, Abigail was already wrestling with and slowly overcoming her own demons on the path to embracing her sexuality, but the new job forces her to interrogate her shame anew. Her relationships with the church and her lover Josie are too much to manage as she is seemingly thrown back into a past life as a Catholic schoolgirl questioning her desires. Similar to Yasmin's work in *The Devils Between Us*, Quintana integrates her own complex racial and cultural identities as a Cuban and Louisianan within the characters of *Scissoring*. With Yasmin centering her play on queer femmes of color, we are again gifted with a spectrum of lived experiences of the South, pushing against the stifling normativity of whiteness and heteropatriarchy. Like *The Devils Between Us*, Quintana's play narrates the struggle between one's deep-seated relationship with religion and the affirmation of LGBTQIA+ identity. In both Southern-rooted plays, we see characters reckoning with their realized and imagined rejections of acceptance. Although Abigail's upbringing and family are not explicitly explored in *Scissoring*, the weight of these are felt in the guilt and shame that color her everyday interactions with folks who might cast her out should they discover her true identity.

The subtle subversion of *The Devils Between Us* also calls to mind Branden Jacobs-Jenkins' attempt at dismantling Southern cultural and dramatic narratives in his play *Appropriate* (2014). As this sprawling piece unfolds, we watch as the LaFayette clan returns to the Southern Delta region of Arkansas to sell their family's plantation home in the aftermath of the patriarch's death. With this play, Jacobs-Jenkins strategically uses the forms of naturalism and family drama, so precious to Southern performance narratives, as a means to expose the gaps in their storytelling, highlighting *in absentia* those identities and racial sentiments that do not comfortably align with the image of an idyllic South. Amidst conversations about wills, sibling rivalries, and sorrow, the playwright injects constant reminders of the characters' whiteness, the privilege that affords, and their ongoing complicity with histories of racial violence. As Jacobs-Jenkins explains, "I was interested in how invisible I could make blackness but still have it affect the viewing experiences" (Bent 2014). Like *The Devils Between Us*, *Appropriate* marks the whiteness of its Southern characters, refusing to treat this identity as universal (or even "raceless"). Both plays also acknowledge our deeply human desire to feel loved by our parents, as well as the complex interweaving of grief, betrayal, and tarnished legacies that arise from the bigotry of deceased fathers.

Yasmin herself attests that the biggest influence on *The Devils Between Us* (and her own personal journey as an artist) is the work of Naomi Wallace, and especially her play *The War Boys* (2004), which Yasmin directed in August 2019 at the Hangar Theatre in New York. Set on the Texas–Mexico border, this play follows three male vigilantes who spend their nights informally patrolling for Mexicans entering the United States. Onstage, misogyny runs rampant alongside xenophobia. Wallace's trio of white men (one being biracial, Mexican, and white) are generally crude and violent, but on the night in which the play transpires, they spiral into confessionals. One of these men, George, is perhaps the softest of the lot, but he is no less a player in the game of asserting dominance to the degradation of others. In Wallace's reveal of George's backstory, we learn how he was shaped by his father's fist and violent sensibilities. In spite of the power he yields and the violence he enacts on others, Wallace positions George as an underdog. Through the process of working with the actor playing George in her production of *The War Boys*, Yasmin came to feel sympathy for the character, understanding the ways love and violence were intricately connected in his past, and his inability to interrupt that self-perpetuating cycle of abuse. This, in large part, inspired the George we see in *The Devils Between Us*, whose character arc shares space and time with Latifa's own journey. As Yasmin explains, "George is problematic and he is violent, but there's a reason that he is, and that doesn't pardon his behavior, or his actions, but it's something we have to understand if we ever want to change him" (Yasmin 2020b).

There is a world where people of all backgrounds, especially historically disinvested folks, can thrive without the aches of oppressive systems. Yasmin's writing makes space for this imagined reality, but that dream ultimately exists outside of the confines of her playscript, demanding the dismantlement of the ways we flame the fires of power and patriarchy.

References

Alipour, M. 2017. "Islamic Shari'a Law, Neotraditionalist Muslim Scholars and Transgender Sex-reassignment Surgery: A Case Study of Ayatollah Khomeini's and Sheikh al-Tantawi's Fatwas." *International Journal of Transgenderism 18*, 1: 91–103.

Bent, Eliza. 2014. "Branden Jacobs-Jenkins: Feel That Thought." *American Theatre*, May 15. https://www.americantheatre.org/2014/05/15/brandenjacobsjenkins_appropriate_octoroon-2/.

Georgis, Dina. 2013. "Thinking Past Pride: Queer Arab Shame in *Bareed Mista3jil*." *International Journal of Middle Eastern Studies 45*: 233–251.

Jacobs-Jenkins, Branden. 2019. *Appropriate*. New York: Nick Hern Books.

Kugle, Scott Siraj al-Haqq. 2010. *Homosexuality in Islam: Critical Reflection on Gay, Lesbian, and Transgender Muslims*. Oxford, UK: Oneworld Publications.

Lal, Vinay. 1999. "Not This, Not That: The Hijras of India and the Cultural Politics of Sexuality." *Social Text 17*, 4: 119–140.

Massad, Joseph A. *Desiring Arabs*. 2007. Chicago: University of Chicago Press.

Najmabadi, Afsaneh. 2005. *Women with Mustaches and Men without Beards: Gender and Sexual Anxieties of Iranian Modernity*. Los Angeles: University of California Press.

Puar, Jasbir K. 2007. *Terrorist Assemblages: Homonationalism in Queer Times*. Durham, NC: Duke University Press.

Quintana, Christiana. 2019. *Scissoring*. New York: Dramatists Play Service.

Smith, Kelundra. 2016. "Facing South." *American Theatre 33*, 8: 118–121.

Wallace, Naomi. 2005. *The War Boys*. Alexandria, VA: Alexander Street Press.

Yasmin, Sharifa. 2020a. Interview with Yasmin Zacaria Mikhaiel, July 3.

Yasmin, Sharifa. 2020b. Interview with Ali-Reza Mirsajadi, July 9.

The Devils Between Us

Sharifa Yasmin

Characters

George Craver—cis white man. Late twenties. Owner of the auto garage.
Latifa Mubarak—trans Arab woman. Late twenties. Muslim.
Hunter Gabriel—cis man. Any ethnicity. Early thirties. Town coroner.
Barb Craver—cis white woman. Sixties. George's aunt by marriage.

Casting Policy

Latifa must be played by a trans woman of color. No exceptions. Great protections need to be put in place to ensure the actress playing this role is not harmed by the transphobic content that is said to her.

Setting

South Carolina.

Time

2020.

Playwright Notes

Content Warning

The Devils Between Us contains sexual content, transphobic and homophobic language, and mentions of violence against members of the LGBTQ+ community. This show is not meant to re-harm, but to be a release. With that said, its content has the capacity to trigger and it's strongly advised not to read or be a part of this show if any of the above themes might cause harm for you. It is very important that the audience is made aware of these content warnings before embarking on this production.

Transphobia

As a trans writer, it was important that the story reflected the very real moments that TGNC people face all over this country and, more importantly, confronting how problematic those moments are. Dealing with the transphobia in the play is not about the other characters politely learning to respect Latifa; it is about them being confronted for that behavior and being held accountable.

Intimacy

It is strongly advised that an intimacy choreographer be attached to any production of *The Devils Between Us*. Intimacy is an integral component of the play, serving as a catalyst for the characters actions. The actors and their safety, both mentally and physically, should always be the priority; therefore it is vital that those moments are choreographed by a specialist.

Accents

Strong Southern accents tend to immediately bring along a lot of clichés about the South. Many in South Carolina do not have an accent, and it's more reflective of rural areas. *If* one is going to be attempted, it should be a soft hint at the end of the word—a very light twang.

Special thanks to Ari Koontz for their help with editing of this play.
Jasmine B. Gunter for her help with development.
Naomi Wallace for her inspiration.
And to my mother.

Act One

Scene One

11 a.m. Lights up on Gus & Sons Auto Garage. There are three exits: one that leads to the garage, one that leads to the interior of **George***'s house, and the other leads outside. The space should feel cluttered and confining.*

Barb *is sitting at the desk reading a romance novel.* **George** *enters from the house in the process of putting on his work shirt.*

George   I know I'm late.

Barb   For someone whose house is attached to their job, you still seem to have trouble finding your way here.

George   Any drop-offs?

Barb   Nope, town's as silent as a louse.

George   I don't think that one works.

Barb   Do lice speak?

George   No, but—

Barb   Then it works.

George *gives a light chuckle. He goes to his desk and pulls deodorant out of a drawer and starts putting it on.*

Barb   George Craver, I know your daddy taught you manners.

George   I ran out in the house, quit barking.

Barb   How you ever gonna get a wife if you keep acting like an animal?

George   Well, I guess I'm stuck with you then.

Barb   You're about thirty years too late, young buck.

George   One husband in the ground, you ain't looking for another?

Barb   Your uncle was enough man for me in one lifetime, I'm good right here with my books.

George   What's this one about? Renaissance bride falls in love with rival family's prince . . . or cowboy bride falls in love with hunky outlaw?

Barb   You make fun of me all you like, but there's some good life lessons in these books.

George   Like what?

Barb   How to have an orgasm.

George   Barb!

Barb   You wanna know what it's about, you can read it, or you too busy writing that book you're never gonna let me see?

George   It's just a hobby.

Barb   And hell is just a sauna.

George   Maybe one day, when I finish it, but for now we got a shop to run.

Barb   Ah, yes.

George *looks out the window at the road.*

George   Nothing.

Barb   Before I forget, Hunter called.

George (*checks his phone*)   Why didn't he call my phone?

Barb   He did, the line was disconnected.

George   Shit, I didn't pay the bill. Fuck.

Barb   The Lord's always listening.

George   You can say "orgasm" but I can't curse?

Barb   You're an adult and last time I checked that wasn't a curse word. Although the way men in your family act, it might be a foreign one.

George   BARB!

Barb   God rest your uncle's soul.

George   What did Hunt want?

Barb   Something to do with Mr. Mubarak. He wants you to call him back.

George   I will as soon as I get my phone connected.

Barb   That's gonna require money, George.

George   I have money, Barb.

Barb   In that case, there's about three weeks' back pay you owe me.

George   Right . . .

Barb (*beat*)   I'm just playin', I know you'll pay me when you can.

George   I'm gonna have the money, soon.

Barb   Don't worry, honey, I'm doing just fine.

George   I promise as soon as business picks up.

Barb   Well, there's a storm brewin', with any luck we might get the results of some slippery roads.

George   God's gonna strike you down for thinking like that.

Barb   If I'm on the top of his priority list, then something's right with the world.

The sound of a car pulling up is heard. **George** *looks outside.*

George Bless the Lord.

Barb And would you look at that, I'm standing in one piece. Who is it?

George I don't know . . . she looks familiar but I can't place her.

Barb (*goes over to the window*) Isn't she a pretty thing—looks like money.

George I'm not gonna upcharge just because we're desperate. We've talked about this.

Barb Your daddy would've.

George (*under breath*) Yeah, well, God might be giving you a reprieve but he already collected from him.

Latifa *enters from outside. She's carrying a purse and wearing sunglasses.*

George Good morning, ma'am! It's a great day at Gus & Son Auto Garage.

Barb He's Son and I'm not Gus.

George (*shoots* **Barb** *a look*) How can we help you today?

Latifa (*beat*)

George Ma'am?

Latifa Hi . . .

George Are you okay?

Latifa Yeah . . . I'm good . . . I'm . . .

A beat.

George What seems to be the trouble?

Latifa Right, uh . . .

George Ma'am?

Latifa Sorry . . . I've been driving for a while now . . . and the car I'm using is acting a little strange.

George What exactly was it doing?

Latifa I don't really know how to explain it, it just felt harder to control, I guess . . . I'm not really good with cars. This is the first time I've driven in a while, so I thought it was me, like I just forgot how to drive. But turns out I do remember and it's the car that's starting to forget . . . so . . .

George Barb.

Barb On it.

George Barb's gonna go give your car a look over while I get some information from you.

Latifa   Great, um, here—here are the keys.

Barb *takes the keys and exits outside while* **George** *collects paperwork from his desk. He passes by* **Latifa** *and she flinches when he gets close to her.*

George   Sorry . . . didn't mean to scare you.

Latifa   . . . It's fine.

George   What's the make and model of your car, ma'am?

Latifa   It's a Ford Escape, no idea what year.

George   No worries, we'll just look at the registration.

Latifa   The car's not mine. I'm borrowing it from my boyfriend.

George   What's the name of the car's owner?

Latifa   Hussein Abboud.

George   . . . Um, could you spell that for me?

Latifa   Here I have his card.

She pulls a card out of her purse and gives it to him.

George   Great, what's his insurance?

Latifa   I don't know what company, but I'm sure that's all in the glove box. I should have looked before I came in.

George   No worries, ma'am, we'll get it . . . Sorry, but have we met before? You seem—

Latifa   Let me go ahead and call Hussein.

She starts calling. **George** *continues to stare at her. She turns her back to him.*

Latifa   Hey, it's me, I ran into some trouble with the car . . . give me a call back as soon as you get this. (*Hangs up.*) Voicemail. Is there anything else I can answer without him?

George   Yeah, what's your name?

Latifa   My name . . . do you need that if it's not my car?

George   Ma'am?

Latifa   Right . . . okay . . .

She takes a breath and then takes off her sunglasses. **George** *looks at her. And then . . .*

George   Jesus Christ.

Latifa   Yep.

George   Holy shit.

Latifa   Hi, George.

George   Latif?

Latifa   It's Latifa now . . . added an a.

George   Added a lot of things.

Latifa   Yeah, guess I have.

George   What—what are you . . .

Latifa   I've been in New York for a while now.

George   Ten years, it's been ten years.

Latifa   My dad passed away last night.

George (*beat*)

Latifa   I got a call from the coroner, Mr. Gabriel?

George   Hunter?

Latifa   Yeah, I think that was his name. It was a heart attack, apparently.

George   I just saw your daddy the other day . . . he was fine . . .

Latifa   . . . Look, I wasn't planning on . . . the car was acting up and you're the only place in town—

George   We're not anymore, a lot changes in a decade. You should go to Hills Auto over on Chestnut Street. They should be able to help you out.

Latifa   George, please.

George   Do you know what people would think if they saw you? If they saw us? Look at you, Latif.

Latifa   Latifa. My name is Latifa.

George   Fuck!

Barb *enters.*

Barb   You're not too old for me to wash out that mouth of yours. (*To* **Latifa**.) I did a quick look and couldn't find anything wrong, but we can bring it in to do a thorough inspection.

Latifa   That's okay, I'm sorry I wasted your time. Let me pay you for your services.

George   That won't be necessary.

Barb   George?

Latifa   I get it . . . I should head out. I'm sorry for . . . have a nice day.

She exits outside. We hear her car start up and leave.

Barb   What in the hell was that?

George Nothing.

Barb If your daddy had seen that, he would've—

George You didn't know who that was.

Barb I know exactly who that was.

The sound of a car crash is heard.

Well, at least the Lord listens to me.

George (*goes to window*) You have got to be kidding.

Barb What is it?

George She hit a tree.

Barb Son of a biscuit. Well don't just stand there, come on.

George *and* **Barb** *exit outside. A few beats of silence, stillness.* **Barb**, **George**, *and* **Latifa** *enter.*

Latifa I can wait outside.

Barb It's about to rain cats and dogs, you come in here while we figure this out.

Latifa God, Hussein is gonna be so worried. He was already nervous about me driving his car.

Barb What happened?

Latifa I was trying to pull out and I lost control over the steering wheel, it just locked up on me.

George Oh.

Barb She said something was wrong with the car, George.

Latifa It's okay, this is why we pay for insurance.

Barb Insurance, George.

George Hush up.

Latifa I'll, um, I'll call the other auto shop and see if they can tow the car over there.

Barb That won't be necessary.

George It won't?

Barb Latif—

Latifa It's Latifa.

Barb Latifa, you should go grab yourself a cup of coffee in the kitchen, you're probably tired from that drive and I just made a pot . . . a few hours ago but the burner's still on. And you can call your boyfriend.

Latifa That would actually be great. Thank you.

She exits to inside the house.

George   No.

Barb   I didn't even say nothing yet.

George   We're not fixing his car.

Barb   Why the hell not? When you're the reason she hit that tree.

George   Like hell I am.

Barb   She came in looking for help and you turned her out for no good reason.

George   Stop saying she! Listen, Barb, it's not good that Latif is here. If people find out what he is now . . . something bad is gonna happen to him—and us if they think we're involved with him.

Barb   Good thing this shop is a ghost town, no better place to hide her.

George   Something happened before Latif left town and we can't . . . this is a bad idea.

Barb   You want to keep your daddy's shop up and running so badly? Well, her insurance will help with that. You need the money, you know you do. And did I forget to mention, this is your fault.

George   I said no.

Barb   Well, if you're not going to do it for her, do it for her dad.

Latifa *enters with a coffee.*

Barb   How's the coffee?

Latifa   It's good, thanks.

Barb   Were you able to reach Hu- . . . Hasen?

Latifa   Hussein. I left a voicemail, he's out of the country for work so I'm not sure when he'll get back to me. In the meantime, if one of you can give me the number for the other auto shop? I have a lot to do today.

Barb *looks at* **George** *and makes a "come on" sound.* **George** *turns away from her.* **Barb** *makes it again. Finally . . .*

George   You don't need to call 'em, we'll take care of it.

Latifa   Really?

George   I'll need the insurance information.

Latifa   Of course, it's all in the car.

George   I'll go assess the damage.

He exits outside.

Barb   I'm sorry for the hissy fit he's throwing. I haven't seen him like this since . . . well, a long time.

Latifa   I don't know what I was expecting. I was trying to avoid it, if I'm being honest. Things didn't exactly end well between us.

Barb   You got out of town pretty quick.

Latifa   I did . . .

Barb   It must be strange to be back here.

Latifa   Yesterday I was in the city and everything was normal. And today I'm back in my hometown with strangers who used to be family. It's just . . . (*She rubs her head.*)

She loses her balance.

Barb   Whoa there, you okay?

Latifa   Sorry . . . I think I hit my head kind of hard when I crashed into the tree . . .

Barb   Here, let me get you a chair—

George (*entering*)   Well, I'm going to need to get a couple parts, but we should be able to get you out of here by tomorrow morning.

Latifa   Tomorrow? No, that's too late. I need to . . . need to . . . get . . .

Barb   Darling, you okay?

Latifa   I . . . need . . . Baba . . .

She faints. **George** *catches her before she hits the floor.* **George** *looks to* **Barb**, *unsure of what to do.*

Barb   And you thought it was going to be slow today.

Thunder. The sound of a storm enters the space. Lights out.

Scene Two

1 p.m. Lights up on **George** *and* **Barb** *in the shop. The sound of rain outside is heard.*

Barb (*beat*)   It's really blowin' up a storm out there.

George   Yup.

Barb (*beat*)   There wasn't anyone else you could have called?

George   Nope.

Barb   I mean, is he even qualified?

Hunter *enters from the house. A beat between* **Hunter** *and* **George**.

Barb (*clears throat*)   How's Latifa?

Hunter   Uh, she's fine, just tired, and stressed.

Barb   You don't think hitting her head had anything to do with it?

Hunter   The combination of her father and the accident took her for a moment. She's just fine now.

Barb   Are you sure? No offense, Hunter, but your patients aren't normally . . . alive—

George   Thank you for coming in, Hunt.

Hunter   It's no problem. I needed to meet with Ms. Mubarak anyways.

George   Ali?

Hunter   She won't let me proceed with his body until they can perform a religious service. Until then I'm just sitting on my thumbs.

Barb   No other dead bodies to occupy your time?

Hunter   It's always a pleasure, Barb.

Barb   Isn't it.

George   Barb. How about you go start on the car, while I finish up here?

Barb (*under her breath*)   How about you get that stick out ya—

George   What was that?

Barb   Right away, buddy.

She exits to the garage. **George** *and* **Hunter** *are left alone. They take each other in.*

George   Hey . . .

Hunter   How are you . . . Are you okay?

George   Yeah . . . I'm—good. I'm fine.

Hunter   That's good.

George   . . . How's Noah.

Hunter   Still winding down from his birthday.

George   Twelve already, sooner or later he's gonna be doing your job.

Hunter   Well, he'll do a better one than me, that's for sure.

George   I wouldn't sell yourself short.

A breath.

Hunter   Got to say, I agree with Barb. Not many people would reach out to the town coroner for a woman with a pulse.

George   With Latif-a being in town, I haven't even been able to process that he's gone.

Hunter   You've never mentioned Ali's daughter before . . . only his son.

George (*beat*)

Hunter I remember when you told me about him—I'd never seen you drunk before.

George Hunter . . .

Hunter Those are similar names, don't you think? Latif, Latifa.

George *freezes.*

Hunter I'm not gonna say nothing.

George If anyone found out . . . you and I both know it could get real bad for him.

Hunter Secret's safe with me.

George (*breath*) How did you even get Latif's contact information? Ali didn't have it.

Hunter It was all in his will.

George That doesn't make sense? They hadn't spoken since he left. None of us had.

Hunter Well, Latif's here, I don't know what to tell ya.

George *processes, as* **Hunter** *looks at him. Suddenly just like that,* **George** *is lost in thought.* **Hunter** *reels him back in.*

Hunter Latif's different than I imagined . . . not just the obvious stuff.

George You mean the fact he's a damn woman now?

Hunter What does it feel like . . . to see him—her?

George . . . If Latif's good now, I think you're fine to head out. Thanks again for stopping by, Hunt.

He goes to lead **Hunter** *out the door.*

Hunter Did you write her letters too?

George *stops. Air.* **Hunter** *pulls out a piece of paper from his pocket.*

Hunter
> Too bright for my sensibility
> Unshielded, impuissant, I fly too close
> Rising in virulent ecstasy
> Burning to your skin

George (*beat*)

Hunter I had to look up a few words. My vernacular is a bit limiting. (*A breath.*) It's beautiful, Georgie.

George (*beat*)

Hunter You know, I try so hard to get you to talk about what you're feeling, it's like pulling teeth sometimes. But your writing—

George It's time for you to go, Hunter. I'm not gonna ask again.

Hunter (*beat*)   I'm getting a divorce.

George   What?

Hunter   It was her idea, believe it or not . . . I think she met someone but I don't know.

George   I'm sorry.

Hunter   We got married right out of high school, when we found out she was pregnant. She's the only person I've ever been with, the only thing I ever knew. It's like now . . . now I can do all the things I never got to, all those things I wanted to.

Hunter *walks over to* **George***, he gets very close to him. They stay in this as* **Hunter** *speaks softly.*

Hunter   Two years we've been circling this, Georgie.

George (*a breath*)

Hunter   I've been smart my whole life. I've been a faithful husband, a good father. But what use is there in being smart, if you're miserable the whole time?

George   Hunt . . .

Hunter *slowly leans in, to kiss him. Hovering just above his lips, waiting for* **George** *to reciprocate. They live here, a heartbeat from one another, until . . .*

George (*softly*)   No . . . No . . .

George *pushes away; his hand trembles slightly.*

George   NO!

Hunter   Georgie . . .

George   I told you to leave.

Hunter   Can we please talk about it?

George   I'm not playin', Hunter!

Hunter   Don't yell, it's okay—

A dark shift. **George** *balls his fist.*

George   I SAID GET OUT!

Hunter   Hey, calm down!

George *gets in* **Hunter***'s face and stares him down threateningly.*

George   NOW!

A sound from the door. **George** *backs away from* **Hunter***.* **Latifa** *enters from the house. It's unsure if she saw anything.*

Latifa (*beat*)   Hey.

Hunter (*clears his throat*)   How are you feeling?

Latifa (*looks at* **George**)   Better. The nap helped.

Hunter   Good. That's, um . . . good.

Heavy beat.

Latifa   How's the car?

George   Barb's working on it.

Latifa   Alone? She's, like, sixty now?

George   You try telling her that.

Latifa   Well, how soon until it's finished?

George   We're working as fast as we can, okay.

Latifa   I need to bury my father—God, that sounds so strange . . . I need to bury my father, and I can't do that until I do a million other things that are hard to do without a car.

George   You have a couple days.

Latifa   No, I don't. He can't be embalmed, which means I don't have time . . . so he needs to be buried as soon as possible . . . if he's going to move on . . . If God's gonna . . . I have to . . .

George   Latif?

Latifa *is having trouble standing up.* **Hunter** *goes to* **Latifa** *and holds her up.*

Hunter   Take it easy, okay?

Latifa   . . . I just need to sit for a second . . . I'll be fine.

Hunter *guides her to a chair.*

Hunter   Take deep breaths.

Latifa *complies.*

George   Hunter said you can't bury him until a religious service?

Latifa   Yeah. That's correct.

George   How can I help?

Latifa   Now you wanna help?

George   For your dad.

Latifa   You hated him?

George   Just stop fighting me, and tell me what I can do?

Latifa (*breath*)   Do you know of any Muslim men in the area, or any in a nearby town?

George   No, your family's always been the only ones.

Latifa   I was really hoping that changed.

Hunter   I made some calls, beyond the guys that you didn't like—

Latifa   They were Shia.

Hunter   Beyond them, there's a few guys out by Darlingon, but they can't be here until tomorrow.

Latifa   No, that's too late. Is there anyone else?

Hunter   A few Muslim women, but they weren't willing to wash a man.

Latifa   No, that would be haram.

Hunter   Haram?

George   Sinful.

Latifa *looks at* **George**.

George   I remember a few things.

Hunter   Unfortunately those are your only options as of now.

George   Wait, why do you need a Muslim man?

Latifa   So he can wash my father.

George   . . . Wash him?

Latifa   Yes. And shroud him. That has to happen before he goes into the ground, so he can be cleansed of sins—so he can be forgiven by Allah.

Hunter   What are you going to do if you can't find the right person?

Latifa   I will, I just need to call more people . . .

George   After ten years, after he disowned you—said you were dead to him, you came back to bury him?

Latifa   What exactly are you insinuating, George?

George   I just find it hard to belive that's the only reason.

Latifa   And what other reason would there be?

George   Don't play dumb. You were never good at it.

Latifa   I didn't even want to come here. I didn't have a choice because of the car. Trust me, you were the last person I wanted to see.

Hunter   I should step out . . . y'all look like you need a moment.

George   Oh, and miss this grand reunion?

Hunter   I'll talk to you later, Georgie.

He exits.

Latifa *scoffs.*

George   What?

Latifa   Nothing . . . just, you used to hate it when I called you Georgie.

George   Not as much as you hated when I called you LJ.

Latifa   I still don't get it, I don't have a J anywhere in my name.

George   It was a cool nickname.

Latifa   No, it was a white-washed one.

George   Oh here we go. How many times did you call me white trash?

Latifa   You know what, Georgie, if the shoe fits.

George   You called this whole town white trash. Glad to see you didn't lose all that attitude in your little transformation.

Latifa   I mean, we're in the middle of nowhere, South Carolina, was I wrong? You had no idea what it was like for me here. Being the one Muslim kid in the entire town, being one of three people of color in our whole high school.

George   Last I checked, I was there with you for a whole lot of it.

Latifa   Yeah, you were my friend, and you defended me, but it was always different for you than it was for me.

George   Those weren't the only reasons it was different. It might have paid you right to keep your head down sometimes, instead of flaunting certain things.

Latifa   I wasn't ashamed, and I wasn't going to pretend that I was. Could've learned a thing or two.

George   Listen, you need to watch yourself.

Latifa   Or you'll what? What can you do that you haven't already done?

George (*beat*)   If we're gonna get your boyfriend's car fixed ASAP, I should go get back to work.

He exits to the garage. **Latifa** *is left by herself. After a beat, we hear her phone ring.*

Latifa   Hey, habibi. (*Beat.*)—I know you're worried but I'm fine, wallahi.—Yeah, I saw the recommendations you sent. I called them, they weren't right.—I don't need to explain myself, I told you, they just weren't right.—I'm not being picky, Hussein. I don't need you to judge me right now!—. . . I'm sorry. I don't mean to be short. I know I'm being . . . selective, but it's my dad. I have to be.

Barb *enters.*

Latifa   I can't talk about it right now, but everything is okay, habibi.—I can't wait to see you either, you have no idea how much I miss you right now.—Wait, one more thing. That question you asked me before you left . . . let's talk about it when we're both home, inshallah.—Ana bahebak. (*She hangs up.*)

Barb   I saw Hunter and George left.

Latifa   Well, I seem to have a talent for clearing the room.

Barb   George is certainly in one hell of a mood, after talking to you.

Latifa   You know, he was always a little bit of an asshole, but now . . .

Barb   Well, the second they hit puberty their brain moves from their head straight down towards hell.

Latifa   Like father, like son.

Barb   God rest his soul.

Latifa   . . . When did Mr. Craver pass?

Barb   Few years ago. George's been taking care of the shop in his place, it's what Gus wanted.

Latifa   Yeah, who wouldn't want to keep this place going for a man like Gus.

Barb   Well, your dad certainly thought highly of this place. He was our most frequent customer.

Latifa   What?

Barb   Started after you left, he'd come by the shop to fix this on his car, fix that, swear he just started making up things at one point. I mean, the hours George put in on that SUV, the hours your daddy would sit in this shop . . . next thing I knew, George was running errands for him, fixing up his house—

Latifa   Wait, hold up. My dad hated George.

Barb   Used to.

Latifa   What does that even mean?

Barb   George was about your daddy's closest friend in this town.

Latifa (*beat*)

Barb   You're not the only one who's in mourning.

Latifa   He blamed everything he hated about me on George . . .

Barb   Things change, Latifa, you know that better than anyone.

Latifa   Glad to see they formed a little book club over how much they hated me. That's just the cherry on top of the revelation that has been my return.

Barb   No one hates you, honey.

Latifa   . . . When I came out to my dad, he was begging me to—to "not let the devil in." He just took our faith and used it like a dagger. And it wasn't hateful, it just was out of complete desperation for me to stay on God's path. And when I made it clear who I was, and that Allah made me that way—when I made it clear that I wasn't going to pretend anymore . . . he told me I wasn't his son, and you know what, he was right.

Barb   Then why are you back here doing this for him?

Latifa   This is the last thing tying me to this place, so the second I can cut that cord is an opportunity I will jump on.

Barb (*beat*)

Latifa   He didn't want me to be his kid, and that was his choice, but he will always be my dad, as much as I wish he wasn't.

Barb   And what about George?

Latifa   What about him?

Barb   Is he not tying you here too?

A beat. **George** *enters.*

George   Hunter just called. He thinks he found someone who can wash your dad.

Latifa   Alhamdulillah.

Barb   What does that mean?

George   Thank God.

Barb   Well then, Alhamdulillah. (*Mispronounces it.*)

George   We should head out if we're gonna catch him. Hunt's gonna meet us there.

Barb   I'll grab the umbrellas.

She goes to the closet.

Latifa   Thank you, George.

George   It's not for you.

Latifa   . . . Right.

Barb   Why y'all just standing there, let's get going.

She opens her umbrella and exits outside. **George** *opens the door for* **Latifa**. *She looks at him as she passes, he follows. Thunder.*

Lights out.

Scene Three

4 p.m. Lights up on the shop. The storm outside is getting worse. **Latifa** *bursts in, followed by* **George**, **Hunter**, *and* **Barb**. *They are all wet from the storm.*

Latifa   Fuck that guy!

George   Please, calm down.

Latifa   Don't tell me to calm down! Who the hell does he think he is?!

Barb   Don't pay no mind to what he said.

Latifa   He was not Muslim—he was a white trash convert who had no comprehension of Allah's teachings.

Barb   Who was that man, anyway?

Hunter   He was a friend of a friend's nephew, he converted to Islam a little while back.

Barb   Well, the cheese slid off that boy's cracker a long time ago. Latifa, how about I grab you some tea, it'll calm you down.

Latifa   I'm fine. I need to look for someone else.

Hunter   Maybe just take a moment to breathe.

Latifa   What do y'all not get? If he's not washed now, if he's not buried now, he's not going to be forgiven—he'll never be at peace.

George   You said you needed a Muslim man to wash your dad, and this guy was willing to . . . so I don't get why you keep saying no to everyone we find, over some small details that don't matter.

Latifa   Forgive me if I don't think it should be the crazy guy who lives in the woods and hasn't washed himself in God knows how long.

Barb   Is there no one else who can do the washing, Hunter?

Hunter   He was the last option. Everyone else we found who was willing, Latifa didn't think—

Latifa   It's not about finding someone who's willing. That man was not Muslim, no matter how much he wanted to say otherwise. And most of the guys we've found were Shia, not Sunni.

George   I don't get why that matters?

Latifa   It just . . . it . . . it does, okay—Why are y'all grilling me like this?

Hunter   You know, Latifa, you're Muslim, why can't you?

Latifa   It has to be someone of the same gender. It has to be a man.

Hunter   Well . . .

Barb   Hunter!

George   You used to be one.

Latifa   Jesus Christ? No. I never was, and it's really offensive when y'all insinuate that.

Hunter   I didn't mean offense.

Latifa   And yet.

Hunter (*beat*)

Latifa   I've tolerated a lot of really ignorant, offensive things that have been said today. I always was who I am now, just because I don't look it anymore doesn't change that. What has changed are my pronouns and the amount of respect everyone has shown me. So if you or anyone else wants to refer to me, it is by she, her, and hers. Is that understood?

Hunter   Lesson learned.

George   We're just trying to figure out a way to help you resolve this, okay.

Latifa   Listen, you've known me as someone else for so long, and I'm challenging every memory you have of me in a really uncomfortable way, I get that.

Barb   But washing him doesn't change the fact that you're a woman. You get to decide how you celebrate your faith.

Latifa   This isn't about me. This is about what needs to happen in order for God to forgive my father.

George   Well, what if he needs you to forgive him too?

Latifa   I'm not equal to Allah.

George   But you are Ali's kid, and God's not the only one that needs to forgive your daddy for him to be at peace.

Latifa   Why is that important to you? Did you forgive your dad?

George   Watch it. My daddy was a good man trying his best. What you're not gonna do is come in my house and condemn him.

Latifa   He's dead, you don't need to defend that asshole anymore.

Barb   You shouldn't speak ill of him, hun, show some respect.

Latifa   Barb, I really do love you, but we both know you were aware of everything Gus did to George.

Barb *turns away.*

George   Don't put your shit with your old man on mine, it's not the same, / it wasn't the same.

Latifa   It's like he's still breathing down your neck. I mean look at you, you're still in this shitty town, still running his shitty business, and still believing the shitty things / he taught you.

George   You need to shut the hell up!

Hunter   / George, calm down.

Latifa   It's like you enjoy living in this cage, hating yourself, because he taught you to. Maybe I'm fucked up because I can't forgive my father, but at least I'm honest with myself about who he was—

George   Your dad was just trying to protect you! Just like mine. Maybe you've forgotten what it's like here, maybe you've spent too much time in New York fuckin' city where you could be a goddamn alien for all anyone cares. But here? Here! How entitled are you to come back after all these years, preaching and being higher than God, to judge us the way you have.

Latifa   I'm not judging you. I'm just saying that I get it, I'm saying there's a better way.

George   I'm surviving. And I'll continue to survive without your help as I have been doing for the past ten years.

Latifa   Surviving isn't living, George.

George   It's better than being dead!

Latifa   No it's not! I could move through the world as Latif. I could've stayed here, I could've married some girl. I could've lived life as a man, and I would have been fine. I could survive that. But then what would my life be, nothing—nothing but waiting for the next day and the next and the next, because you don't have to be dead to not exist. And that's what happens when you hate yourself, for who you are—who you've always been.

George   ENOUGH!

Latifa   I know what that is and I know the love I have for myself now. One day as "Latifa" beats a lifetime as "Latif." And I want that for you, I just want you to live, really live, because it breaks my heart to think you're never gonna get out of this prison he put you in.

George   You think you're free?! Look at you, Latif!

Latifa   Latifa!

George   LATIF!

Latifa (*beat*)

George   Look at you! How long did you take putting on all that makeup, those clothes, your hair. You're in a whole new prison now, one you built yourself. Your dad would be buried right now if you were thinking straight. But instead, you wanna preach to me about what it means to be free? Well if being free means living like you are—like a freak . . . I'm just fine where I am.

Barb   George!

George   Wash your daddy or not, but stay the hell out of my life!

Latifa Well . . . at least this time you didn't use your fist to push me away, so I guess that's an improvement. Let me know when the car's done, and I'll pick it up.

Barb You don't need to leave.

George Yes, he does.

Latifa Fuck you, George.

She exits.

Barb She's going through something real rough right now and you just sent her out of this house, into that storm.

George Him.

Barb Her. She's her! You're disrespecting your friend, or have you forgotten that's who she is?

George No. Latif is dead. That person I knew, that I grew up with, is not here.

Barb Well, I just saw her with my own two eyes.

George Really? Well that person doesn't give a shit about Ali, and Latif . . . Latif wanted nothing more than his dad to love him. After all the things his family went through, immigrating from Egypt, his mom dying when he was young—his dad was the only person he had.

Barb She had you too, jackass! Ever since y'all were little, she was there for you, and you were there for her.

George Latif, I was there for Latif! God, through everything, even when the other kids made fun of him for not speaking English, or for what he brought for lunch—when they hid his stuff all over the school. I was there to help him, every time—for Latif.

Barb What did they do?

George (*breath*) The other kids—they were jealous he got to leave class to pray, so they used to steal his backpack and put it in the ceiling tiles where he couldn't find it. He would stay after school looking for it, for hours. I would find him crying in the cafeteria, saying his dad was gonna punish him for losing it again, and I just . . . I knew what that meant.

He *looks to* **Barb**. *She looks away from him.*

Barb Things got better.

George For a little while . . . but then September 11th. After that, things got bad for him and his dad. Ali's store kept getting vandalized. People came and spray painted things all over their house. I started to sleep over to make sure he'd be okay.

Hunter That's awful.

George Yeah, it was . . . but Latif never let it get to him though. Just kept showing up to school, stood up to anyone who gave him shit. Just not his dad . . .

Barb   And you're wondering why she's having a hard time processing his death?

George   Ali tried, okay! He just . . . he couldn't get past who Latif was. He was so girly—always causing problems for himself.

Barb   She was just being who she was, George.

George   Well, what did he think was gonna happen, showing up to school with his nails painted pink, piercing his own ears? It's like he just wanted to make it worse. But every time those kids went after him, every time, I stopped them, I was there for him!

Barb   And her dad wasn't! You need to understand that to know what she's going through right now! That person you're talking about, your best friend, your family, she's still that person. All those memories you have, they're all hers too. Latif's not dead, she just got an "a" added to her name. So that excuse you think you have, to act like a little shit to her, is just that, an excuse.

George (*beat*)

Barb   Now while you collect your pride off the ground, I'm going to go fix that nice young woman's car so she can bury her daddy. You join me when you decide to act like the respectful man you were raised to be.

She exits. A beat. **George** *is lost in thought.*

Hunter   George?

George   . . . Ali would tell Latif right to his face that shayatin were inside him.

Hunter   Shayatin?

George   Devils. (*Beat.*) I always thought that's why Latif prayed so much . . . to get them out.

Hunter (*guttural sound*)   Hmm.

George   He just wanted his dad to love him for who he was . . .

He has a realization and goes to his desk to look for something.

Hunter   Can I ask you a question that I really wanna know?

George   Since when do you ask permission?

Hunter   How come you haven't been with anyone since? She's the only person you've ever—

George   Barb is five seconds out the door, could you hush the hell up?

Hunter   It's been ten years, don't you think that's a little extreme?

George (*ignoring him*)   Found it.

Hunter   Found what?

George   Ali left his wallet the other day when I took him to the supermart. He was gonna stop by today to get it.

Hunter   Why do you need it now?

George   'Cause I think I just put two and two together.

He opens the wallet.

(*Under his breath.*) Holy shit.

Hunter   George?

George *doesn't respond; he stares at the wallet.*

Hunter   George.

George   What?

Hunter   You didn't answer my question.

George   I need to help Barb with the car.

Hunter   I know something happened between the two of you. Something that's the reason you can't—the reason you won't . . .

George *goes to leave.*

Hunter   Open up to me, please. Write it down if that's easier, just let me know what you're feeling.

George   . . . Hunt, I can't handle this . . . I can't handle you, and Latifa, and everything inside of me right now . . . So just drop it, okay! Why did you have to ruin everything! We were fine!

Hunter   Georgie, come here.

George   I told you—

Hunter   Just look at me.

George *does. It takes time, but* **George**'s *defenses melt. When they do,* **Hunter** *advances towards him, until there is no space left between them.* **Hunter** *leans in, to kiss* **George**. *Hovering just above his lips, just as he did before, waiting for* **George** *to reciprocate.*

Hunter   Kiss me.

George   Hunt.

Hunter   Kiss.

George   I—

Hunter   Me.

George   Shit.

George *kisses* **Hunter**. *It's long, deep. Just when things are going to evolve further,* **George** *pushes* **Hunter** *off of him. His hand shakes again, his breathing is heavy.*

George   I told you . . . I can't.

Hunter (*softly*)   Let go, Georgie.

George   I can't, Hunt, I just . . . can't.

Hunter   Because of her? Because of what happened?

George (*a shift*)   Stop pushing it!

He pushes **Hunter**.

Hunter   Hey!

George *pushes* **Hunter** *again.*

Hunter   George!

George *pushes* **Hunter** *again. And again. This time* **Hunter** *pushes back. The two men wrestle.*

George   Stay away from me!

Hunter   Relax!

George *has* **Hunter** *pinned on the ground; he is on top of him.* **George** *is shaking.*

George (*primal shout*)   I don't want anything to do with you!

Barb *and* **Latifa** *enter from seperate entrances,* **Latifa** *freezes at the door as she watches* **George** *and* **Hunter**. *She snaps out of it and goes to pull off* **George**.

Latifa   GET OFF OF HIM! I SAID GET OFF OF HIM!

She gets **George** *off of* **Hunter**.

George   It's nothing!

Latifa   Hunter, leave!

Hunter   It's fine—

Barb   What the hell happened!

Latifa   You too, Barb.

Barb   But—

Latifa   Leave.

A look. **Barb** *and* **Hunter** *exit separately.*

George   I thought you left.

Latifa   Hard to do without a car in the middle of nowhere. I heard y'all outside.

George   It wasn't like that.

Latifa   Like what, George? Huh? It's not an excuse, by the way, that you're closeted. That doesn't mean you have a get out of jail free card for not handling your emotions and hurting / others.

George   I need to get back to fixing your / car.

Latifa   I want you to imagine something for me. I want you to imagine the person you care about the most in this world, the person you trust to take care of you—to love you back, imagine how it feels to have that person destroy you.

George   Latif . . .

Latifa   You've been nothing but an absolute dick to me since I came back. An aggressive, violent, mirror image of your father. Is this what you've become?!

George   I'm leaving.

He tries to leave.

Latifa   You are going to stay right here, and you're going to hear every word I have to / say.

George   Fuck off! I don't owe you shit!

Latifa   YES YOU DO!

George (*beat*)

Latifa   Look at me.

George *can't. He's frozen.*

Latifa   Look. At. Me.

George *complies.*

Latifa   I want you to say what you did. From the beginning.

George   Latif . . .

Latifa   From when we got to your house.

George   Please . . .

Latifa   We got to your house and . . .

George   . . . My dad's car wasn't in the driveway. So we . . . so we . . . .

Latifa   Went upstairs. To your room.

George   We did . . .

Latifa   And then?

George   And then we were on my bed, and you . . . I can't do this.

He tries to leave.

Latifa   I just came out to my dad and it was the most painful thing I ever went through, but when he kicked me out, it was okay because you, YOU were my home, YOU were my family. And when we finally—when we were together . . . That was the first time I ever felt safe in this world. I felt invincible. I asked you to leave this town with me.

George   . . . I said yes.

Latifa   But when I came back, after I grabbed my things . . .

George   I wouldn't open the door.

Latifa   A few hours before, do you remember what you were saying to me?

George   That I loved you.

Latifa   And a few hours later, do you remember what you said to me behind that door?

George (*beat*)

Latifa   Say it.

George   Please . . .

Latifa   SAY IT.

George   . . . Faggot.

Latifa   But I kept begging you to open the door. Knocking on it, harder and harder.

George   And then I did.

Latifa   I couldn't even see your face before you grabbed me and pushed me to the floor.

George   Why didn't you leave? Why didn't you—

Latifa   I'm just staring at the ground, trying to process that I was on it. Tell me what you did next.

George   Stop, please.

Latifa   What did you do?!

George   . . . I kicked you.

Latifa   Where?

George   In your side.

Latifa   And what did you say?

George   . . . "Faggot."

Latifa   Over and over again. You wouldn't even let me see you. Every time I tried to turn to you, to beg you.

George   Kick.

Latifa   Faggot.

George   Kick.

Latifa   And when I couldn't move anymore.

George   I grabbed you by the collar.

Latifa   And you threw me out of your house.

George   And I closed the door.

Latifa (*beat*)   Ten years—ten years and I've never moved past it. No matter how good things are now, how much I love my life, me . . . It's still like I never got out of this town. So coming back, burying my dad, seeing you, maybe—Maybe that's what I needed to finally be free of this place, of all the memories I don't want. But now . . . now that I'm here, now that I can look at you—your face . . .

She exhales. She stares at him—into him. **George** *tries to say something, do something, but he can't.* **Latifa** *exits.*

Lights out.

End of Act One.

Intermission.

Act Two

Scene One

7 p.m. Lights up on an empty shop. The storm is still ongoing, but it's softer than it was previously. **Barb** *is at her desk on break.* **Hunter** *enters from outside. Beat.*

Barb   What do you want, Hunter?

Hunter   I need to talk to George and Latifa, are they here?

Barb   Latifa borrowed my car to run an errand, and George is in the garage working on the car.

Hunter   Why didn't he come out, then?

Barb   Ignoring you, if I had to guess.

Hunter   Well, that's just . . . peachy.

Barb   What happened, Hunter? He almost ripped your head off, then Latifa spoke to him and now he's practically catatonic.

Hunter   . . . Why don't you ask him?

Barb   He won't say nothing, won't even look at me, he's just been working on Hussein's car like a madman. Whenever I can get a glimpse of his eyes, he just looks like . . . I don't know.

Hunter   Like what?

Barb   Like he's not there. He gets this way sometimes, especially around when his daddy died. But I've never seen him this bad.

Hunter   Barb, when George and Latifa were arguing about his dad . . . he's never said anything about Mr. Craver to me.

Barb   He doesn't talk about his daddy with anyone.

Hunter   George isn't a bad guy, but whenever his dad is mentioned, whenever . . . I ask him what happened between Latifa and him. He becomes someone else.

Barb   Maybe he got mad 'cause you're sticking your head where it don't belong.

Hunter   You keep changing the subject, but that's not gonna stop me.

Barb   No wonder George was about to strangle ya.

Hunter   He wasn't gonna hurt me, he wouldn't . . . he wouldn't do that.

Barb   You don't know what that boy's been through Hunter.

Hunter   Then tell me! (*He stops himself from yelling.*) Sorry, I didn't mean to—I just . . . I just want to make sure he's okay.

Barb   So do I.

Hunter   Then be honest with me.

Barb (*a breath*)   There are things in the past that I wish I'd . . .

Hunter   Wish you'd what?

Barb (*beat*)   Shouldn't you be getting back home? Don't you have a wife? Kid? Refrigerator door that's open?

Hunter   You really don't trust me, do you.

Barb   You don't make a move unless you gain from it. You want something from George.

Hunter   I want him to be happy.

Barb   No you don't, 'cause you wouldn't be coming round here if you did. He doesn't like who he is when he's with you. In fact, I think he hates that person fiercely. I think that person scares the living crap out of him, and that boy's been through enough hell already.

Hunter (*beat*)

Latifa *enters carrying a box.*

Barb   I should really get back to helping George.

She exits.

Latifa   Can you grab this from me? My hand's slipping.

Hunter (*helping her*)   What's all this?

Latifa   It's what I'm keeping from my dad's house before I sell it.

Hunter   Where's the rest of it?

Latifa   This is it.

Hunter   Over twenty years in that house, and only one box?

Latifa   Everything else is gonna be thrown out, or given to Goodwill.

Hunter   That's a little harsh.

Latifa   This is all I can take back with me to New York. Some of my mom's jewelry, her family photos from Egypt, her Koran.

Hunter   Anything from your dad?

Latifa   Nope.

Hunter   . . . Nice to see you being so practical in a time of mourning.

Latifa   What is that supposed to mean?

Hunter   Your father died, it's okay to be emotional about that.

Latifa   I'm handling this in my own way, and I don't need you or George's judgment for how I'm processing.

Hunter   Yes, ma'am.

Latifa   Right now the most important thing is finding someone to help me bury my dad. That's where my focus needs to be, not sorting through a house I haven't lived in for a decade.

Hunter   Is it important to find someone, though?

Latifa   Excuse me?

Hunter   I just had a real interesting conversation on the ride over here. Hussein called, he got worried 'cause he couldn't reach you, so he looked me up. He spent some time on the phone educating me about Islamic burials. Imagine my surprise finding out that a Christian or a Jew could also perform the practice and that it doesn't have to be a Muslim.

Latifa (*beat*)

Hunter   But you already knew that.

Latifa   Hunter . . .

Hunter   We've been bending over backwards to help you with this, when just about the whole town is eligible to bury your dad . . . why did you lie?

Latifa   I didn't lie, I just didn't . . . I don't know, say the full reality of the situation.

Hunter   Which is?

Latifa   He would have wanted it to be someone who was Muslim.

Hunter   And for someone to not be a convert, or Shia, or the million other reasons you've excluded all the people we've found today, when according to your boyfriend, none of that even matters. So, what's really going on, Latifa?

Latifa   I don't owe you anything.

Hunter   I don't know what the hell you want or need, because you didn't have to come here—Anyone in this town could do the service. Literally anyone.

Latifa   No.

Hunter   Anyone!

Latifa   It's supposed to be me! (*Beat.*) It was . . . it was supposed to be me. The closest family member, of the same gender, that's the one who should wash him. My entire life here, he made that clear to me. That when he died, I was the one who would make sure Allah forgave him. And that's a really big concept to put on a kid.

Hunter   But you're not the same gender . . . and he disowned you.

Latifa   That's the point. . . . I get that call from you, and it's like this invitation, right? To come down here, and finally settle all these things. And I was hoping that I'd feel like—I don't know how to put it into words . . .

Hunter   Try.

Latifa   If I helped him move on, then I could not care that he didn't love me . . . Listen, I'm not a victim, I refuse to be, I'm a survivor and there's a difference. But my dad makes me feel so . . . weak. Because after everything, knowing that he hated me, I still love him. So much. Not a day goes by I don't think about him, and I hate that.

Hunter   How does not letting someone else bury your dad change any of that?

Latifa   It doesn't, but maybe . . . if I'm the one . . . maybe if I see him and I send him off, then . . . I don't know. Everything George said when he suggested it just keeps ringing in my head. I mean not the transphobia, but me needing to forgive my dad to move on. And that's not fair, why do I have to forgive him? Why do I need that, why can't I just hate him?

Hunter   Then wash him. Sounds like you already made up your mind.

Latifa   Did you not hear me before? I can't. If I wash my father, it's like I'm saying he was right. Somewhere deep down in my core, I'm saying to myself, and Allah, I'm not who I am.

Hunter   Jesus, Latifa, then let someone else!

Latifa   I can't do that either!

Hunter   Then what are you gonna do?

Latifa   I don't know, asshole, that's what I've been trying to say!

Hunter (*beat*)

Latifa   I'm not ready to forgive my father.

Hunter   . . . And you're not ready to let God forgive him either.

Latifa   So I'm left in this in-between with a clock ticking in my ear. How do you condense an entire lifetime of anger and resentment into one day of letting that go?

Hunter   You can't, that's impossible.

Latifa   I know, and yet the clock ticks down.

Hunter   So let us help you.

Latifa   God, why do you even care?

Hunter   Alright, now. I've been going out of my way for you—

Latifa   Are you helping me, or are you helping yourself? Because the sooner I bury my father, is the sooner I leave, and that means I'm out of George's life for good.

Hunter   . . . How did you—

Latifa   I know better than anyone how George acts when he's having feelings he wishes he didn't. And I know that you don't like that I'm back in town, and it's not hard to discern why.

Hunter   I'm not . . . he's just never opened up to me the way he's opened up to you.

Latifa   Well, speaking from personal experience, that's not necessarily something you should want.

Hunter   Everyone keeps talking about the past like it's something I should know, but the second I ask about it, y'all want to keep telling me it's not my business. Everything he is now is because of everything that happened to him before. And I might not have been there for that, but I'm the one who's here with him now.

Latifa   You can be with him now, Hunter, but he was screwed the moment he was born. He's not capable of opening up to anyone, and you can't push him to do so.

Hunter   It's a new time, things are different now.

Latifa   We want to think we live in this new era, where there's no ignorance and everyone is equal, but that's a fallacy. He's had an entire lifetime being raised in a place that punishes anyone who goes against the norm. I mean, he protected me from a lot of shit growing up, but he couldn't stop everything. And then you throw his dad on top of that. He can't control his environment, and I pity him for that, but he can control how he acts. Being hurt doesn't justify hurting others. So Hunter, I am just trying to warn you that George is not able to give you what you want, and if you don't respect that . . . you should watch your back.

Hunter   He gets a little . . .

Latifa   Violent?

Hunter   Don't put your shit with him on our relationship. He's never done anything with me.

Latifa   Have you been with him?

Hunter   . . . We've just kissed.

Latifa   And that wouldn't happen to be the time I walked in on him about to punch you into the ground?

Hunter   You know what? You want me to butt out of your business with George, fine. Then you can butt out of our shit as well. I've tried to help you today and all you seem to want to do is fight me and every other person who's giving you a helping hand.

Latifa   I'm not trying to fight you, I'm just . . . (*A breath.*) You know what, you're right, I'm sorry. This is none of my business. I came back to deal with my father, and not George—not any of this.

A moment. A surrender.

. . . I know you've gone out of your way today. Whatever your reasons might be, however awkward it is for you that I'm here, I know you have. So thank you, Hunter, for your help.

Hunter (*beat*)   You know, George doesn't like to drink.

Latifa   Never did . . . hated what it did to his dad.

Hunter   He also never talks about you.

Latifa   Don't see why he should.

Hunter   Well, the one time I saw George drunk, he finally brought you up. Called you a . . . firecracker with a heart so big it'll swallow you whole. (*Beat.*) Call me when you decide what you want to do about your dad.

He goes to leave. He stops when he sees the wallet that **George** *left on the table.*

Latifa   What's that?

Hunter   Your dad's wallet. George said he left it here. You should probably have it.

He hands the wallet to **Latifa** *and she opens it.*

Latifa   Crap, I need to call his card companies—another thing to add to the list.

She pulls out a photo.

Latifa   Oh my God.

Hunter   What is it?

Latifa   Hunter, how did you have my contact info? My dad didn't know where I was, or that I changed my name.

Hunter   You were listed as his next of kin with all your information. Why do you ask?

Latifa   Because he has a photo of me in his wallet.

Hunter   When you were a kid?

Latifa   No. . . as Latifa.

Hunter *and* **Latifa** *look to each other.*

Lights out.

Scene Two

9 p.m. Lights up on the shop. The storm is at its worst. **Barb** *enters from the garage.* **George** *follows her and goes to his desk to finish paperwork.*

Barb   Well, it's done, Latifa's car is all ready to go. I don't know how you finished it so quickly.

George *doesn't respond.*

Barb   She's gonna be real grateful that you got it done this evening.

George *doesn't respond.*

Barb   Now she can just focus on her daddy. You did a good thing, George. Ali would be thankful.

George *doesn't respond.*

Barb   George, say something!

George (*beat*)   I'm filing all the information with her boyfriend's insurance right now. I'm gonna leave the keys on the desk for her, make sure she gets them.

Barb   Why don't you give them to her?

George *doesn't respond.*

Barb   George!

George   What?

Barb   You're scaring me . . . you haven't said nothing for half the day, you can't even look me in the eyes.

George   . . . I've just been focused on getting the car done.

Barb   And you did it, so now you can talk to me.

George   I don't have nothing to say.

Barb   Well, Latifa did. What'd she say to you, hun?

George *doesn't respond.*

Barb   Baby, I care about you, so much, just let me in.

George (*beat*)   . . . Daddy's birthday is coming up.

Barb   Yeah, it is.

George   Been thinking about it a lot.

Barb   He'd be proud of the man you are, George.

George   I don't think he would.

Barb   He would . . . your father loved you . . . he just fell on some hard times, didn't know how to handle himself.

George *doesn't respond. A beat.*

Barb   I know sometimes he was . . . he could be strict with you. I'm sorry that . . . that I . . .

George   That you what?

Barb (*beat*)   . . . Nothing. With Latifa being back, this whole day has been one big trip down memory lane.

George (*beat*)   Yeah.

A silence. **Barb** *wants to say something, but she doesn't.* **George** *just continues to file paperwork.* **Hunter** *enters.*

Hunter (*to* **George**)   Hey.

George *doesn't look at* **Hunter**.

Barb   Is Latifa with you? We finished her car.

Hunter   She left with yours, needed to breathe. She got overwhelmed when she found Ali's wallet.

George   The photo.

Hunter   Yeah.

Barb   What photo?

Hunter   Ali had a picture in his wallet of Latifa. She said it was from an awards ceremony a few years ago. She was being honored for her work with Muslims who are LGBT . . . some other letters in there.

George   . . . I used to see Ali pull out that photo all the time. I never got a good look at it, I just thought it was some . . . long-lost sister or some woman. I had no idea it was Latifa.

Barb   About time.

George   What?

Barb   You finally called her by her name.

George (*beat*)

Barb   Well, I'm pretty beat, I think I'm gonna head home early. Just tell Latifa to leave my keys here, and I'll grab them tomorrow.

George   The storm's still raging.

Barb   I'm not far away.

George   No, you're not going out in this mess. You can stay in Daddy's room for the night.

Barb   You don't need to do that for me.

George   It wasn't a question.

Barb   Thanks, George.

They look at each other. **Barb** *exits to the house.*

Hunter   Hey.

George   . . . Hey.

Hunter   . . . Are you okay?

George   I'm fine.

Hunter   You were really . . . I've never seen you like that.

George (*beat*)

Hunter   And now.

George *looks away.*

Hunter   I'm done being scared, Georgie. I'm finally at this place where I want to live my life and not just watch days go by trying to survive it. Latifa was right when she said that, she really was. She's living her life. She's being who she was always meant to be. Doesn't that spark something in you?

George (*beat*)   I need to finish this paperwork.

He turns to leave. **Hunter** *pulls out a letter.*

Hunter   To release all that fire that's been cooking inside you, that still burns no matter how hard you try to stifle it. To let those flames rage—would you be a better man because of it?

George (*breath*)   I wrote that for you a year ago.

Hunter   I think about it all the time.

He goes to **George**. *When they finally lock eyes, when they breathe each other in,* **Hunter** *slowly kisses* **George**. *A beat and then* **George** *breaks away abruptly. He grabs* **Hunter** *by the shirt threateningly. Just when things seem like they are going to take a dangerous turn,* **George** *pulls* **Hunter** *back in. The kiss is deep, voracious, hungry.*

George   Please . . .

Hunter   Please what?

George   I can't . . .

Hunter   Then stop.

George   . . . I can't.

Hunter *starts kissing* **George**'s *neck.* **George** *is breathing hard between each time he speaks.*

Hunter   We just need a minute. Just let go for one minute.

George   Someone could . . . Could walk in . . . Could . . .

Hunter *is starting to undo* **George**'s *pants, and stops.*

Hunter   Could what?

He meets **George** *at eye level. A beat, a decision.*

George   One minute.

He pulls **Hunter** *back in.* **Hunter** *undoes* **George**'s *pants.*

George   Hunt . . . Hunt . . . Shit. Shit. Fuck.

He climaxes; it's intense. **Hunter** *stops; a heavy beat.* **George** *is catching his breath, he sits in what just happened. His hand begins to shake.*

George (*under his breath*)   Leave.

Hunter   Georgie?

George   Leave . . .

Hunter   What?

George   GET OUT!

Hunter   Hey?!

George *balls his fist.* **Hunter** *is terrified.*

George   GET THE FUCK OUT!

Hunter   . . .

George   NOW!

Hunter *leaves.* **George** *fixes himself, zips up his jeans. He tries to move but slips, and catches himself on the desk. He stops, he breathes, he whispers a prayer. It's a low volume, we don't need to hear it, we probably shouldn't, but* **George** *needs to say it, to move past his breath.*

George   Lord . . . mindful of your mercy . . . and love that took you to the cross . . . I place myself before you . . . and ask your forgiveness . . . for all the times . . . when I have failed to follow you . . .

But it's not working. **George** *is breathing hard. His hand is shaking harder. He tries to still it but he can't. He's getting frustrated.* **George** *takes his aggression out on the wall. Hitting his hand against it. It evolves into punching, kicking, slamming,* *whatever he needs to do to release. It's explosive; we should fear he is going to break something, or hurt himself in the process.*

Barb *enters from the house, as we hear a car pull up outside.*

Barb George, What's wrong?!

George I'm fine!

Barb But your hand—

George I'M FINE!

Barb Does this have to do with Hunter?

George Can you mind your own fucking business, for once in your goddamn life!

Barb If your daddy heard you speaking like that, he would—

George's *shaking gets worse.*

George WHAT? My daddy would what! Whip my hide?! Get me into shape?! Beat some sense into me?!

Barb That's not what I—

George What do you think he would do? What do you think he would do! WHAT DO YOU THINK HE WOULD DO!

Barb *is stunned.* **Latifa** *enters the shop from the outside door.* **George** *and* **Barb** *don't notice her.*

George IF HE WAS HERE! RIGHT NOW! HUH! WHAT WOULD HE DO TO ME! DO YOU THINK HE'D TAKE OFF HIS BELT? NO, THAT WOULD TAKE TOO MUCH TIME. HE'D JUST START WITH HIS FIST. ONE REAL HARD ONE RIGHT TO THE TEMPLE, SO I'M KNOCKED OFF MY BALANCE. SO I CAN'T THINK. SO I DON'T KNOW WHAT THE WORLD IS. AND WHILE I'M TRYING TO FIGURE ALL THAT OUT, HE'S TAKING HIS TIME TOWERING OVER ME. CORNERING ME SO I CAN'T ESCAPE. AND THEN HE JUST LANDS ANOTHER HIT. AND ANOTHER. AND ANOTHER. EACH ONE KNOCKING THE AIR OUT OF ME, EACH ONE BECOMING LESS AND LESS PAINFUL UNTIL I FEEL NOTHING. JUST BLACK NOTHING! NEXT THING I KNOW I'M WAKING UP, AND I CAN'T MOVE. AND ALL THAT HURT I DIDN'T FEEL COMES SURGING BACK. MAKING ME WISH I WAS DEAD, 'CAUSE THEN I WOULDN'T KNOW THAT KIND OF PAIN. AND HE'S JUST STANDING THERE IN A PUDDLE OF MY PISS, MY BLOOD ON HIS KNUCKLES, LOOKING AT ME SO PROUD OF HIMSELF. BECAUSE HE TAUGHT ME A LESSON HE KNOWS I NEEDED TO LEARN. IS THAT WHAT HE WOULD DO?! IS THAT WHAT YOU THINK HE WOULD DO!

A heavy beat passes. And another one. And another one. **Barb** *is unable to speak, but she looks to* **Latifa**, *and exits.* **Latifa** *doesn't say anything, she just stands there.*

George *won't look at her. He looks at his hand that continues to shake; he tries to stop it, tries to breathe.*

George   . . . We were on my bed . . . and you looked at me in this way that . . . seared my soul. And I put my hand on your cheek . . . and I rested my head on yours. My heart was beating so fast, I couldn't stop feeling it thump against my chest. I just wanted to breathe you, be right there with you and breathe you in. I didn't even know that I started to kiss you until I was. Until everything else just stopped moving.

Latifa   George . . .

George   And it felt like a lifetime, and it felt like a second. And I pulled away to look at the door, I was so scared someone would catch us, but I didn't want to stop.

Latifa   You were shaking so bad.

George   Until you held me, and everything just became us. We weren't in this town, we weren't hurting, we were just . . . and you looked right up at me and you asked me . . .

Latifa   If you were sure.

George   I couldn't speak . . . but I unbuttoned my shirt, and then yours. I took off everything. Not just my clothes, not just yours, but everything.

Latifa   We were standing there, a heartbeat away from each other, nothing between us.

George   And I stopped looking at the door.

Latifa   And you stopped stopping yourself.

George   And I let go.

Latifa   And your hands—

George   Your skin—

Latifa   It didn't matter that we didn't know what we were doing. For the first time—

George   We weren't scared. We were really fucking happy.

Latifa   But only for a moment.

George   I've lived in that moment for a lifetime.

Heavy beat.

He caught us . . .

Latifa   What?

George   My dad was there the whole time . . .

Latifa   No, that was—he had that second job at the warehouse, he was at work?

George   His boss sent him home for drinking, and wouldn't let him drive. That's why his car wasn't in the lot, that's why we thought he wasn't here.

Latifa   Oh my God . . .

George   He came in after you left . . . He . . . he . . .

His trembling intensifies.

Latifa   George . . .

George   That's why I didn't want you to see me when you came back, why I didn't open the door . . . I didn't even look like me—I was just bruises and blood.

Latifa   You said all those things . . .

George   I just needed you to leave!

Latifa   Then what made you open the door . . . What made you decide to do that to me? Why?!

George   He heard you, Latifa! He came downstairs and he heard you!

Latifa (*beat*)

George   I had a choice to make, and I made the wrong one. I'm sorry . . . I'm so sorry . . . I'm so—

Latifa   You did it because of him . . .

George   I don't even know how I had the strength, if it was adrenaline, or fear. I was just so scared that if I didn't, he was gonna do something worse to you—that he would . . . but I should have stood up to him. I should've ran out of that house with you. I should've . . . I should've . . .

Latifa   Why are you just telling me this now?

George   When he finally passed out, I went to your house, but it was too late. I tried to find out where you went, a number I could call, an email I could send, but you were gone.

Latifa (*beat*)

George   I destroyed us, not him. I did. He was just watching out for me, it was discipline . . . because he loved me and he wanted me to be a better man . . .

Latifa   NO! He taught you that was love, he taught you that was how to express yourself, what you're feeling; he taught you to hide it. But you're smarter than that. You're stronger than that. He had muscles the size of your truck, but he was the weakest man I ever knew. Your power, your strength, it comes from this.

She holds **George**'s *head gently with her hands. It's a tender action.*

Latifa   And this.

She moves her hands to his chest, above his heart.

That's what makes you a man.

She takes his fist and unclenches it.

Latifa   Not this.

George's *hand stops trembling. A moment. A breath.* **George** *sits.* **Latifa** *sits down next to him.*

A lot of time passes.

Latifa   Did you know about the photo?

George   I didn't know it was you . . . but yeah.

Latifa   All these years he knew about me . . . where I was, who I am.

George (*beat*)   When you left, it was like the whole town moved on, but your dad and I . . . we couldn't. We never talked about you, but we both knew that the closest we could get to you was through each other. And for those moments, when I would help with his car, or drive him to the grocery store, or watch those shitty action movies he loved so much—

Latifa   God, I hated them.

George   When we did those things, you were—it's like you were there . . . That's how we could keep you alive.

Latifa   I didn't think that he . . .

George   Missed you? Every minute of every day.

Latifa   He didn't know how to deal with me when I was here.

George   He didn't know how to deal when you weren't.

Beat. They're weighted in this silence.

Latifa   Our dads really . . .

George   Yeah.

Latifa   Yeah.

George   Sometimes when I get to the shop real early in the morning, when I haven't gotten enough sleep, and I'm just pissed at the world . . . I'll catch a glimpse of my reflection on the cars, and I see him looking right at me.

Latifa   You're not your dad, George. You're not a bad person.

George   Then what am I?

Latifa   A scared one. (*A breath.*) We both are.

George   Do you think one day we won't be?

Latifa   I don't know.

George   Like one day do you think you're going to be okay about who you are, all of you, absolutely all of you. You look in the mirror and you don't see . . .

Latifa   A man looking back at me.

George   A faggot.

Latifa   Worshiping just being okay.

George   Not even happy.

Latifa   Just okay.

George   Yeah.

Latifa   . . . I guess I do. I have to.

He looks at her; she looks at him. They exist, together. A few beats pass, comfortable silence, for the first time.

Latifa   George.

George   Yeah?

Latifa   Will you do something for me?

George   Anything.

Latifa   Will you help me wash my dad?

A beat. The storm stops.

Lights out.

Scene Three

Morning the next day. We hear the quiet sounds of nature. Lights up on the shop. It's empty, quiet. **Hunter**. *He looks around and goes to* **George**'s *desk. There's a packed duffle bag on it.* **Hunter** *leaves a letter. He takes a breath, and then goes to leave, but before he does,* **Barb** *walks in and it stops him.*

Barb (*beat*)   Mornin', Hunter.

Hunter   Mornin', Barb.

Barb   . . . Beautiful day out.

Hunter   Yeah, it's um . . . it's nice. (*Beat.*) I was dropping something off, if you can make sure Georgie—George gets it.

Barb   Yeah, I can.

Hunter   Thanks . . . Have a nice day now.

He goes to exit.

Barb   I never saw you leave one for him . . . I've always seen him sneak them off to you when he thought I wouldn't notice, but never the other way around.

Hunter (*beat*)

Barb   I was jealous of the damn things. To know what he was feeling, how he was doing . . . to be something that made him happy . . . It was easier to think it was the letters. (*Beat.*) What'd you write?

Hunter   Nothin' . . . just silly stuff, I guess.

Barb   Like what?

Hunter   I don't know. (*Beat.*) Like how I'll always catch him smiling when he sees a possum.

Barb   Lord knows why. They're just about the ugliest creatures I've ever seen. What else?

Hunter   How he wiggles his nose when he gets a really good idea for his novel. How he only laughs once in a blue moon, but it warms my whole soul.

Barb   Yeah.

Hunter (*beat*)   How beautiful he is—God he's beautiful . . .

Barb (*breath*)   Yes, he is.

Hunter   And how I can't say goodbye . . . so I wrote it. (*Beat.*) Tell him that, um . . . Tell him I'm sorry for ruining us.

He goes to leave. Right before he can . . .

Barb   He loves you Hunter.

Hunter   . . . And I love him.

He exits. We hear him drive away. **George** *enters.*

George   Was that Hunter's car that just pulled out?

Barb   Yeah.

George *goes to the window and looks out of it.*

George   He's gone . . . .

Barb (*beat*)   You know my mamma used to say that Carolina storms go through the five stages of grief. First they don't know what they want to be, a little drizzle, wind's a little different, airs a little different too. Then they're real mad, come down pouring like God himself. And that part feels like it's never gonna end, just gonna be cats and dogs forever. But when you're not expecting it, it starts to let up . . . and then pours again . . . and then lets up . . . and then pours, and then lets up, and then—

George   Is there a point to this?

Barb   Once those clouds realize they let it all out, everything they've had in 'em, all stored up for years and years—

George   I don't—I don't think that's how meteorology works.

Barb   Once they accept they have to release everything they've been holding . . . that's when the storm passes. And despite the fact it was hell to go through it, everything down here on the ground is a lot clearer because of it. I mean, look at the green bursting from those trees. New life sprouting all around us, all from one big hell of a storm.

George (*beat*)

Barb   I heard you washed Latifa's dad.

George   Yeah. We did it together.

Barb   What was it like?

George   She talked me through it before, but when I saw his face . . . I just froze. Seeing him there, for the first time since . . . and this, I don't know, calm just washed over her. I could see her relax, like physically—I could see her breathing. And then she started saying stuff in Arabic—prayers. I did the stuff she couldn't, it took longer 'cause it was just us, but . . . I don't know, it wasn't scary, it was just . . . a child saying goodbye to her dad.

Barb (*Beat*)   About your daddy, George . . .

George   I shouldn't have yelled at you.

Barb   Yes you should've. Just as I should've done something. I knew . . . I knew . . .

She starts to become emotional.

George   Barb . . .

Barb   I knew, and I . . . I didn't stop him. I didn't try. I didn't think it was my place and I was so scared of . . . I was the adult, and you were a child, I should've done something, I should've stood up for you, I—

George   You couldn't have done anything.

Barb   I could've made sure you knew you could be whatever the hell you wanted to be. I could've made sure he didn't stop that . . . but I didn't.

George *starts to get emotional.*

Barb   I'm sorry, baby. I am so sorry.

George   It's okay. I'm . . . I will be . . . okay.

Barb   You will be, you hear me. I love you. Nothing, and I mean nothing, will ever change that. The only thing I care that you are, is happy. You're my George, you hear me, I love you to the moon and back. (*She wipes away any of* **George**'s *tears. Composes herself.*) Hunter left a letter for you.

Barb *retrieves the letter and hands it to him.*

Barb   When I look back at my life, my only regret is not fighting for the people I love.

She kisses **George** *on the cheek, and exits.* **George** *reads the letter. When he's done, he puts it down, and takes a big breath.* **Latifa** *enters.*

Latifa   Hey . . .

George   . . . How are you feeling?

Latifa   Weird, I guess. Barb was right when she said that washing him wouldn't conflict with who I am. But, um . . . I've carried that man with me for so long, and now I'm . . . lighter.

George (*beat*)   What's next for you?

Latifa   Hussein and I have been talking about marriage. I'm usually the one who changes the subject, but . . . I love him and I think I'm ready for that to be enough.

George   He sounds like a good guy.

Latifa   Well, he puts up with me, so at the very least we know he's brave.

George   He's lucky to have you.

Latifa   Yeah, he is, isn't he. Even with all my baggage. (*Sees the duffel bag.*) Where you headed?

George   I don't know, but I'm getting out of town.

Latifa   Never thought I'd hear that from you.

George   One day I want to be here and not feel . . . I love this place, I know you hate it, but it's mine . . . I'll be walking out in the woods, surrounded by the greenest green, and that Carolina heat goes through me like an awakening.

Latifa   Yeah.

George (*breath*)   I need to figure things out on my own, like you did. I'm just ten years behind.

Latifa   You're not behind. You couldn't ever be behind. (*Beat.*) Is Hunter going with you?

George   . . . No. (*He puts down the letter.*)

Latifa   I'm sorry.

George   Don't be . . . I'm not good for him. I'm not even good for myself . . . After everything I put him through, how could he not hate me, Latifa? How could you not?

Latifa   . . . I did, for a long time. But if I know anything about Hunter—about what it means to love you . . . he just wants you to be happy. The only thing he hates about you is feeling like he's the reason you're not.

George (*beat*)

Latifa   I don't know if I can forgive you, George—or my dad. But if being back here has taught me anything, it's that I don't have to. 'Cause maybe understanding is enough.

A beat. A moment. **George** *and* **Latifa** *take each other in.*

Latifa   I should get on the road. Hussein was able to get a flight in tonight, and I want to pick him up from the airport.

George   Yeah . . . You have a safe drive now, don't go hitting no trees.

Latifa   Well, maybe if you fixed the car like when I asked you to.

George   Maybe if you didn't have that attitude of yours. Hurricane Latifa.

Latifa   Now that's a nickname I can get behind.

George *smiles. A beat.*

Latifa   Take care of yourself.

George   You too.

Latifa *stays for a beat, like she can't leave. And then she hugs* **George***. It takes him by surprise, but the hug quickly becomes familial and he grips her tight. For a brief moment, they're the two best friends they were a decade ago.*

Latifa   I hope you find peace, and love, and life, and everything that's been kept from you.

George   I hope you do too.

Latifa   Go after him, no matter how far away he gets.

They break away. He looks at her. She looks at him.

George   Goodbye, Latifa.

Latifa   Goodbye, George.

She exits. **George** *goes to the window and watches. We hear her car start up and listen as she drives away.* **George** *looks around the room, grabs his bag and the letter. He turns off the lights, leaving the only light source the bright daylight coming from the windows. He takes a breath, and then exits. We hear his car start up. We hear him slowly get further and further away, until he's gone.*

Lights out.

End of play.

Part Three
Familiar/Familial

Cruising Dystopia

Jaclyn I. Pryor

Set in a "near future" America in which queerness and abortion are once again illegal, police surveillance is increasingly pervasive, medical doctors have all but vanished, the nation-state is officially divided into factions of people (and currency) referred to as "Coastal" and "Heartland," and the "planet is cooking itself to death," Leanna Keyes' *Doctor Voynich and Her Children* is as much about this present moment of bio- and necro-politics as it is about some imaginary time yet to come. The play's titular character, a traveling herbalist who calls herself Rue Voynich, grows and sells medicinal herbs from her mobile dispensary "parked on the side of a dusty highway in the Heartland" (p. 282). The opening stage directions indicate that this dispensary "in a previous life [. . .] *may have been* an ambulance" (p. 283, emphasis added), gesturing not only to the breakdown of modern medicine but also to the very uncertainty of history: it is as if this America is in such disrepair that not even the play or the playwright can be certain of its past. Rue is joined by her apprentice, Fade, "an asymmetrical young woman" who gets entangled in the central conflict of the play: a pregnant teen named Hannah comes to the apothecary for a (now illegal) abortion; when Rue's attempts with contraband abortifacient herbs fail, Fade secretly performs the abortion with "an archetypical coat hanger [bent] into a straight rod" (p. 326). The events that follow unleash not only the police state in this near-future dystopia in which the characters live but reveal previously hidden secrets of genealogy and gynecology alike.

Central to the dramaturgy of this play is the transmission (and suppression) of intergenerational folk knowledge about plants and/as medicine, as embodied in the master/apprentice relationship dynamic between Rue and Fade, which persists against a cultural backdrop that seeks to tear it apart. While the exact time of the play is not stated, various context clues place it somewhere in the 2060s—far enough into the future, that is, that Donald Trump's vision for America seems to have prevailed, and we find ourselves in a world in which the full repeal of abortion rights has become the law of the land. Rue explains, "Look, the knowledge [about abortion] didn't just vanish when we lost in the Court. But it's useless without the right tools. They destroyed all actual equipment back in the Trump days" (p. 299). The fact that the government would seek to destroy the medical equipment necessary for the successful execution of abortion reveals not only the regressive political landscape in this not so imaginary near-future but also the disturbing awareness on the part of the state that one particularly effective way to interrupt the transmission of queer and feminist ways of knowing is to take away the literal tools and instruments that make possible our continued access to self-determination.

Between the lines of Keyes' text, we hear the echo of multiple other playwrights in the theatrical canon, including those who have similarly taken up the topic of justice— reproductive and otherwise—and subverted the norms of realist drama. Keyes' title, *Doctor Voynich and Her Children,* clearly evokes twentieth-century German theatre director and playwright Bertolt Brecht's infamous *Mother Courage and Her Children*

(1939).[1] *Mother Courage* is set in the early modern dystopia that was the Thirty Years War in Europe (1618–1648), but its actual inspiration was the rise of Hitler's fascist regime during World War II. Using an "epic theatre" style that Brecht is credited as having invented, *Mother Courage* paints the world in broad strokes: it covers twelve years of history (presented as episodic scenes) and offers a scathing critique of war and capitalism (an itinerant trader, Mother Courage, and her five children travel by wagon, as she profits off of the war by selling her wares). Brecht's critiques are successful, in part, because his theatre aims to rupture the theatrical illusion and awaken its audiences to the political reality *outside* the theatre's doors—deploying various techniques including the use of archetypes (as personified by the character "Mother Courage," as well as "Sergeant," "Cook," and "Chaplain," etc.); the interruption of dramatic action with song and music; and the display of signs and placards that announce the upcoming scenes.

Like Mother Courage, Brecht has many "children"—modern playwrights who have been influenced by his voice, style, and themes. Notable examples include British playwright Caryl Churchill (*Top Girls*; *Vinegar Tom*; *Cloud Nine*; *Love and Information*), and American playwrights Tony Kushner (*A Bright Room Called Day*; *Angels in America*; *Homebody/Kabul*; *Caroline, or Change*), Suzan-Lori Parks (*The America Play*; *Topdog/Underdog*; *The Red Letter Plays*; *White Noise*), and, more recently, Branden Jacobs-Jenkins (*An Octoroon*; *Gloria*; *Appropriate*; *Everybody*)—all of whom have also influenced and been influenced by one another.

It is helpful to place Leanna Keyes' *Doctor Voynich and Her Children* within this genealogy. *Doctor Voynich* bears a particularly strong resonance with Suzan-Lori Parks' body of work, especially her *Red Letter Plays*, which include *In the Blood* (1999) and *Fucking A* (2000). In Parks' first play, for instance—which functions as a black theatrical riff on Nathaniel Hawthorne's *The Scarlet Letter* (1850)—the protagonist is Hester La Negrita, a homeless woman who lives under a bridge with her five beloved children; she's teaching herself how to read and write, always "trying to get a leg up" in a system structured to keep her down (see, for example, Parks 2001: 11 and 21–22). In one telling scene, the character known only as "Doctor" informs Hester that she must be sterilized—before breaking out into the satirical song, "Times Are Tough: What Can We Do?" (2001: 42). Parks' play is citing the long history of forced sterilization that poor, black, and/or disabled women have had to endure at the hands of the state. Her next play, *Fucking A,* turns this history sideways. Like *Doctor Voynich, Fucking A* is set in "a small town in a small country in the middle of nowhere" (Parks 2001: 129), and this Hester—known as Hester Smith—works as an abortionist. Her chest is branded, like Hawthorne's Hester the "adulteress," with the scarlet letter "A" as public indignity. She is what trans theorist C. Riley Snorton might call "captive flesh"—as he traces the central role that black women's bodies have played in the history of gynecology and reproductive medicine (Snorton 2017: 57).[2]

---

1. Thank you to my colleague AB Brown for making this connection.
2. *Fucking A*'s Hester Smith has been portrayed by actors of various races. The premiere, which I saw at The Public Theater in 2003, featured African American actor S. Epatha Merkerson in the lead role as Hester, and this production informs my reception and analysis of the play.

We hear resonances of Parks formally, too. Throughout Keyes' text, we find multiple staged silences. In her brief guide that accompanies the text, "HOW TO READ THIS PLAY," Keyes writes, "Character names without accompanying dialogue indicate a significant action, reaction, or pause" (p. 282). Put differently, they might be read as what Parks has called "spells." A spell, Parks writes, "is a place of great (unspoken) emotion. It's also a place for an emotional transition" (1994: 16–17). Spells—which, too, are Brechtian in nature—might be described as silent, intersubjective beats that transpire between two characters just long enough for time and space to hang in the air, as it were—become felt experience—and for larger social relations to flicker, ever so briefly, into view. With Leanna Keyes' *Doctor Voynich and Her Children,* these larger social relations include the current political moment, in 2020, of division and unrest— marked by increasingly public discourse about police/state violence; the curtailing of (and demand for) civil liberties; and the public upswell of (and resistance to) racism, misogyny, ableism, xenophobia, transphobia, and class warfare in the contemporary United States. In other words, it is an ideological battle over which narratives about our collective past (and collective future) will survive to become the master ones. In *Doctor Voynich,* this is played out, in part, through (an ostensibly private) struggle over the past and future of reproductive medicine in this one small town, and the tools (books, medical equipment, laws) that make its practice possible (or not).

The relationship between Brechtian theatre, in general, and Parks' early plays, in particular, and *Doctor Voynich and Her Children* are thematic as well as formal. As previously noted, epic theatre is always political: like Brazilian theatre director Augusto Boal's Theatre of the Oppressed arsenal, it aims to awaken its spectators to the violent realities in which they currently live. Dispensing with theatrical realism—what Aristotle famously calls *mimesis*—epic theatre uses live performance to make visible the stark inequities of modernity. It is a theatre of gesture—what Brecht calls *gestus*— physical actions that reveal not an individual character's psychology per se but rather point, or gesture, to social relations writ large.[3] In this regard, much like *Mother Courage*'s Mother Courage, or *In the Blood*'s Doctor, we might read *Doctor Voynich*'s Rue as "an herbalist" (as the cast of characters suggests), Fade as "an apprentice," Hannah as 'a young woman seeking an abortion," Jess (her mother) as "a mother," and Harrison (a police officer) as "an officer of the law." Seen in this light, *Doctor Voynich and Her Children* has the capacity to become a play both about and not about these particular women but as representations of a (present and possibly future) social world in which there exists a stark ideological divide between the gatekeepers of power and normativity and those who are said to live on its margins. It is also representative of a late capitalist surveillance culture in which healers, lesbians, mothers, queers, and transgender people are uniquely vulnerable and in which their powers are vilified and feared. As Chicana feminist writer Gloria Anzaldúa argues in her groundbreaking *Borderlands/La Frontera*:

The female, by virtue of creating entities of flesh and blood in her stomach (she bleeds every month but does not die), by virtue of being in tune with nature's

---

3. Elin Diamond's *Unmaking Mimesis* (1997) is particularly useful here, as she explains the feminist politics behind the disruption of mimetic realism in performance and performance criticism, calling this *gestic* feminist criticism.

cycles, is feared. Because, according to Christianity and most other major religions, woman is carnal, animal, and closer to the undivine, she must be protected [. . .] from herself. [. . .] She is man's recognized nightmarish pieces, his Shadow-Beast. The sight of her sends him into a frenzy of anger and fear.

(Anzaldúa 2012: 17)

Bearing this in mind, it is no wonder that abortion is at the center of this (and other) feminist plays: abortion is the perfect (and polarizing) cultural flashpoint precisely because reproductive justice demands that we regard women and transgender people as actually possessing full personhood in the form of bodily autonomy, and such a view defies some of the most fundamental beliefs that society holds to be true.

Doctor Voynich also upends our sense of time and the progression of history. Indeed, time operates queerly in Keyes' new play, placing it into productive conversation with those discourses of "queer temporality" now central to the convergent fields of queer and performance studies.[4] Queer and performance theorist José Muñoz, for instance, argues that while "straight time" conceives of history as progressing in a linear, progress-oriented fashion, what he terms "queer time" acknowledges the ways in which the past and future productively collide, haunting the present. As he succinctly puts it in *Cruising Utopia*, "the future is in the present" (Muñoz 2009: 49).

This dictum is literalized in *Doctor Voynich*. As previously noted, the diegetic present (and past) is set in the non-diegetic future, which means that the non-diegetic present exists, in turn, in the diegetic past. Put differently, our histories and futures—on both sides of the curtain—are bound up with one another. When Leanna Keyes subtitles her play "A Prediction," she is pointing to the ways in which the near-future America that this story calls in view—one in which a "small American flag with no stars dangles from the radio antenna" (p. 283)—has, one could argue, already been set into motion. But this is also a play in which the tensions between fate and free will, choice and chance, are thrown into high relief. When, for instance, Harrison warns Hannah and Fade—somewhat ominously—"I just want to remind you./ Make good choices" (p. 324), we hear not only a moralizing cop speaking to seemingly foolhardy teens but perhaps, too, the playwright speaking to us, her contemporary audience.

A prediction, after all, is a both noun that signifies *the thing predicted*, as well as the *action of predicting* the thing. It exists, that is, in both the future and present tense. Etymologically, it derives from the Latin *praedicere*, which means to "make known beforehand." And the very action of predicting—to make something known beforehand—has the capacity, of course, to alter the course of (seemingly fixed) history.

---

4. The debate within the field about "queer temporalities" can be traced, in part, back to Lee Edelman's polemical *No Future* (2004), in which he argued against reproductive futurism and critiqued the dominant model that situates children, reproduction, and futurity as inherent social goods. Jack Halberstam's subsequent *In a Queer Time and Place* (2005) was foundational in thinking about queer temporalities in relation to cultural production, including film and visual art; Halberstam's theorizing of the relationship between straight time and late capitalism was also crucial to the development of this discourse. In addition to Muñoz, see also Elizabeth Freeman's *Time Binds* (2009); Heather Love's *Feeling Backward* (2009); Juana Rodriguez's *Sexual Futures* (2015); and Kara Keeling's *Queer Times, Black Futures* (2019); as well as my recent book on the subject, *Time Slips* (2017), which takes up the topic as it relates to live performance.

Like Hannah who comes to the dispensary in search of an abortion ("I'm pregnant and I don't want to be" (p. 293)), it is possible to interrupt the course of history. And while the interruption of the linear, progress-oriented flow of time and history may produce a crisis in temporality that dominant culture cannot integrate into their worldview, it is a technique that the theatre has long known well. From Brecht to Parks to Keyes and back again, the theatre has always been a site of utopian imagining—even and especially through the portrayal of those dystopian realities that we, as readers, spectators, and social actors, have the power to disturb.

References

Anzaldúa, Gloria. 2012. *Borderlands/La Frontera: The New Mestiza.* Iowa City, IA: Aunt Lute Books.

Boal, Augusto. 1993. *Theatre of the Oppressed.* New York: TCG.

Brecht, Bertolt. 1991. *Mother Courage and Her Children.* Trans. Eric Bentley. New York: Grove Press.

Churchill, Caryl. 2013. *Love and Information.* New York: TCG.

Churchill, Caryl. 2010. *Cloud 9.* London: Samuel French.

Churchill, Caryl. 1992. *Vinegar Tom.* London: Samuel French.

Churchill, Caryl. 1982. *Top Girls.* London: Samuel French.

Diamond, Elin. 1997. *Unmaking Mimesis: Feminism and the Subversion of Identity.* London: Routledge.

Edelman, Lee. 2004. *No Future: Queer Theory and the Death Drive.* Durham, NC: Duke University Press.

Freeman, Elizabeth. 2010. *Time Binds: Queer Temporalities, Queer Histories.* Durham, NC: Duke University Press.

Halberstam, Jack. 2005. *In a Queer Time and Place: Transgender Bodies, Subcultural Lives.* New York: NYU Press.

Kushner, Tony. 2015. *A Bright Room Called Day.* New York: Broadway Play Publishing.

Kushner, Tony. 2013. *Angels in America: A Gay Fantasia on National Themes.* New York: TCG.

Kushner, Tony. 2005. *Homebody/Kabul.* New York: TCG.

Kushner, Tony. 2004. *Caroline, or Change.* New York: TCG.

Jacobs-Jenkins, Branden. 2021 (forthcoming). *Everybody.* New York: TCG.

Jacobs-Jenkins, Branden. 2020. *Gloria.* New York: TCG.

Jacobs-Jenkins, Branden. 2019. *Appropriate.* New York: Nick Hern Books.

Jacobs-Jenkins, Branden. 2015. *An Octoroon.* New York: Dramatists Play Service.

Keeling, Kara. 2019. *Queer Times, Black Futures.* New York: NYU Press.

Love, Heather. 2009. *Feeling Backward: Loss and the Queer Politics of History.* Cambridge, MA: Harvard University Press.

Muñoz, José Esteban. 2009. *Cruising Utopia: The Then and There of Queer Futurity.* New York: NYU Press.

Parks, Suzan-Lori. 2020. *White Noise.* New York: TCG.

Parks, Suzan-Lori. 2001. *The Red Letter Plays.* New York: TCG.

Parks, Suzan-Lori. 2001. *Topdog/Underdog.* New York: TCG.

Parks, Suzan-Lori. 1994. *The America Play.* New York: TCG.

Parks, Suzan-Lori. 1994. "Elements of Style." *The America Play and Other Works.* New York: TCG.

Pryor, Jaclyn I. 2017. *Time Slips: Queer Temporalities, Contemporary Performance, and the Hole of History.* Evanston, IL: Northwestern University Press.

Rodriguez, Juana. 2015. *Sexual Futures, Queer Gestures, and Other Latina Longings.* New York: NYU Press.

Snorton, C. Riley. 2017. *Black on Both Sides: A Racial History of Trans Identity.* Minneapolis, MN: University of Minnesota Press.

Doctor Voynich and Her Children

A Prediction

Leanna Keyes

Characters

Rue, an herbalist. Forties.
Fade, an apprentice. Late teens.
Hannah, a young woman seeking an abortion. Late teens.
Jess, a mother. Forties.
Harrison, an officer of the law. Fifties.

Casting Policy

No one in this play needs to be white or pretty or skinny. Rue is a trans woman. Please cast responsibly.

Fade is written in this script as using "she/her" pronouns, but may be played as non-binary. In this case, Rue and Hannah will refer to them using "they/them" pronouns, but Jess and Harrison will still call Fade "she/her." Rue or Hannah may tactically decide to call Fade "she/her" when talking to Jess or Harrison, but it extracts a cost.

Setting

The Ambulatory: a mobile dispensary of herbal medicines, parked on the side of a dusty highway in the Heartland.

I am not invested in naturalism of scenery. You don't have to buy an actual ambulance and find a way to put it on stage, though that would be awesome. Scenic descriptions are for your inspiration.

Time

The near future, God help us.

Playwright Notes

Character names without accompanying dialogue indicate a significant action, reaction, or pause.

A line break indicates a choice, or a shift in thought.

Dialogue in [brackets] is plausibly deniable. It's quiet, or implied through a sound.

Everything between sets of //railroad tracks is overlapping.//

This script includes a welcome and content note as part of the action of the play.

Footnotes contain playwright notes, alternate lines, and different ways to stage the play depending on your circumstances.

Scene One

Monday morning, when the sunlight is still more blue than yellow

A large boxy vehicle sits onstage, dusty and warm. In a previous life it may have been an ambulance. It is covered in flourishing flower boxes, planters, and terrariums, strapped and bolted and welded and nailed on. The side is painted with a fading image of a smiling woman carrying a potted pennyroyal, with the words "DOCTOR VOYNICH'S HERBAL AMBULATORY" emblazoned in a curly ribbon. A small American flag with no stars dangles from the radio antenna.

Fade, *an asymmetrical young woman, throws open the back doors of the Ambulatory. Yawning, she goes about unstrapping various planters, setting them up to be perused. This goes on for a while during pre-show—deploying a storefront takes time and care. The birds chirp and caw and heckle. When the performance is ready to begin:*[1]

Fade   Welcome to *Doctor Voynich and Her Children*. This story contains sexual content and discusses abortion in great detail. Should you need to leave at any time, the exits are there and there. Oh, I'm supposed to tell you: turn off your phones. You never know who could be listening.

Fade *goes about her business. Unintelligible folk music pours forth from the Ambulatory radio. It crackles and morphs as the radio operator surfs the frequencies. Eventually it clicks off and the driver's side door opens.* **Rue**, *a middle-aged herbalist, emerges, looking far too awake for this time of the morning.*

Rue   Someday, there will be a Heartland station that doesn't make me want to swallow hemlock, but

Rue/Fade   Today is not that day.

Rue   Oooh, you're comin' out hot this morning.

Fade   You could help me set up, you know.

Rue   Builds character.

Fade   You're the worst.

Rue   I know. Come on, let's get a move on.

Fade   I'm working on it! There's a lot!

Rue (*indicating their ride*)   "Doctor Voynich's Herbal Ambulatory." When you earn your herbalist name, it'll say "Doctor Whatever's Herbal Ambulatory." You can make your apprentice set up the merchandise. But until that day . . . you missed a pot.

Fade *checks. She did miss one. Grumbling, she retrieves it.*

---

1. If you've got a pre-show announcement, Fade can work behind; no one wants to sit in silence watching an actor set up the stage. My dream is that you've managed to gather enough plants that Fade can be setting up for the duration of house-open.

Rue   Should be a good sales day. They'll have used up everything we sold them last time we were here.

Fade   Or the plants will have died in the drought. Think they'll remember us?

Rue   I'm unforgettable.

Fade

Rue   Memorable at the very least. Keep it up, young blood, and I'll leave you out in the sun all day. Dry you up.
But yes, I imagine they remember us. Not many traveling herbalists left around here.

Fade   I was sick the whole time.

Rue (*chuckling*)   Right, right. Nasty.

Fade   Yeah. You used me as a demonstration model.

Rue   Good thing too, we sold more antibiotic starters that stop than in all of Indiana put together.

Fade   I didn't like everyone seeing me that way.

Rue   It was two years ago. Your image is safe. No one will even remember.

Fade   You better hope not! You sold them moldy bread, penicillin barely works.

Rue   "Don't let sentiment cloud your professional judgment." It's not like I could've made you get better any faster.

The sound of a gasoline motor and the crunch of gravel. Car door slams.

Rue   Quick, get the log.

Fade   Here

Fade *pulls out a logbook and opens it.*

Rue   You see the plate?

Fade   Got it.

Fade *confirms these details as* **Rue** *remembers.*

Rue   Okay, the mom, that's . . . that's Jess. She's got a daughter. Named . . .

Fade   Starts with an H.

Rue   Hannah. Jess and Hannah.

Fade   They bought herbs for a sick rabbit. You got it.

Rue   I've always got it. Okay, ready?

Fade   I'll lead.

Rue   I'll lead.

Fade

Rue   You'll get your chance!
"The first customer of a stop colors the whole—"

Fade   "—colors the whole town." I got it.

Rue (*considering her*)   You really want to?

Fade   I—yes!

Jess*, a mother with a practiced smile, and* **Hannah***, her teenaged daughter, approach the Ambulatory. They stop, a little uncertain.* **Rue** *looks at* **Fade***.*

Fade   Hello there! Welcome to Doctor Voynich's.

Jess   And hello to you.

Hannah   Hi.

Fade   What, uh, can I help you with? We've got a variety out today, as you can see.

Jess   Are you Doctor Voynick?

Fade

Rue   That would be me, ma'am. It's "VoyniCH," not "VoyniCK."

Jess   Oh, my apologies.

Rue   Please, call me Rue. "Doctor Voynich" makes a nice logo, but it is a bit of a mouthful.

Jess   Jess. A pleasure.

Rue   Likewise, ma'am.

Fade

Rue   And this is my apprentice.

Fade   Apprentice Fade, at your service, ma'ams.

Hannah

Fade   Just Fade is fine.

Hannah   Hannah.

Rue   Well, then, Jess, and Hannah, what can we help you—wait a moment, here. Ah, yes, of course! Hannah, I remember you from my last stop here! You were a head shorter then, but that smile is unmistakable.

Hannah *smiles.*

Rue   There it is. You came by to pick up some . . . St. John's wort, and fennel, for your . . . bunny, right?

Hannah   Wow! Yeah.

Jess   You have quite a memory, I'd half forgotten that myself.

Fade (*the keeper of the logbook*)   Yeah, her memory's amazing.

Hannah (*to* **Fade**)   And you had the . . .

Hannah *makes a horrible gesture at her face.*

Fade   Yeah, that was me.

Fade *gives* **Rue** *a withering glare.*

Rue   Well, since we're all friends here, Fade, why don't you show the young lady around, while Jess and I talk shop.

Fade   Of course.

Fade *leads* **Hannah** *around the back side of the Ambulatory, pointing out terrariums.*

Rue   Now, what can I help you with?

Jess   You have a lovely daughter.

Rue   Just an apprentice, but thank you.

Jess   I'm sorry?

Rue   Fade's not my blood.

Jess   Oh, I didn't mean to—I just assumed—

Rue   It's an easy mistake. She travels with me and she learns, I'm sure you understand.

Jess (*she doesn't*)   Of course.

Rue   Her parents were Coastal. East Coastals, if you can believe that. Disreputable types. She's much better off with me.

Jess   Even on the road like this?

Rue

Jess   I don't mean to pry.

Rue   With the climate, a lot of these plants don't grow here anymore. They were here for thousands of years. They can cure illness, make you happier. They heal. We're preserving knowledge and plants and rituals that worked for generations of our ancestors. Even if you could afford to see a med-tech, would you want to? Nano-bots crawling in my bloodstream? No thank you, give me a poultice any day.
Fade might not be living a "normal" life, but she's at the tip of a tree with very, very deep roots.

Jess (*awkwardly*)   Well, I'm sure she's learning a lot.

Rue   We're certainly trying. Enough about us. Could you tell me what you were looking for?

Jess   Chamomile, definitely. And maybe some . . . I forget what it was called. We got some last time you were here. Ash? Ashwig . . .

Rue   Ashwagandha.

Jess (*demurring*)   I think that's right.

Rue   I see. You know, the anti-anxiety blend is actually one of our most popular treatments.

Rue *pulls out a satchel with a label.* **Jess**'s *face rises, then falls.*

Jess   I'll take it. But, could you, um.

Rue *pulls off the label, then guides* **Jess** *around the side of the truck.*

Rue   Your privacy is our priority. I don't normally do this, but you seem like good folks. Let's pick up a few plantable versions of these, see if we can't set you up with a long-term solution . . .

Hannah *and* **Fade** *come around the other side of the Ambulatory.*

Fade   . . . so you can see why you wouldn't want to grow the culinary herbs on the same side of the van as the medicinal herbs.

Hannah   Yeah.

Fade   Aaaalright, is there anything you want me to pick up for you while we wait for your mom?

Hannah

Fade   How about . . . wait just a second.

Fade *picks a small yellow flower from a planter. She pulls off a few inches of the stem, breaks it in half, offering half to* **Hannah**. *They eat it.*

Hannah   It's sour!

Fade   Good, isn't it? "Oxalis pes-caprae." Most people just call it sourgrass even though it isn't a grass at all.

Hannah   That's kind of cute.

Fade

Hannah   Like looking at it you wouldn't think it tastes like candy. And you wouldn't know what it is from the fancy name. It's a sneaky plant.

Fade   Ahhh, what else? It tends to grow on mountains or along roads. It's from Africa originally.
"Pes-caprae" means "goat's foot" in Latin.

Hannah   Latin?

Fade   One of the ancient languages. Like, uh, "carpe the diem."
We use it to name plants.

Hannah   Oh. "We" like herbologists?

Fade   Other people too.

Hannah   But you're an herbologist?

Fade   Herbalist. Well, an apprentice. Rue—Doctor Voynich—is teaching me. She's tough, but she knows her stuff.

Hannah   So you know about . . . stuff. Things.

Fade   Plants.

Hannah   You could tell me what plants to take.

Fade   Yeah! Well, maybe. Probably. What seems to be the problem?

Hannah   I'm not . . .
I don't know how to say it.

Fade   I understand that it can be awkward.
Back when there were medical doctors, people used to go years without getting help because they were embarrassed. Their shame was so powerful they just lived in the pain. But for the doctors, their "weird" problem is just a normal day. They didn't care.
Herbalists are different. We care. We know how to handle shame.
Plus I'm gonna be on the road again in like a week. You won't have to see me again for a long time.
What I'm saying is that you can trust me.

Hannah *decides whether that's true or not.*

Hannah   I need an abortion.

Fade   Oh, shit
I'm sorry
I mean, I'm not sorry that you
Need
I just
I didn't think
That's what you needed.
Um.

Hannah   Can you help?

Fade

Hannah   I don't have anywhere else to go.

Fade   Are you a cop?

Hannah   What

Fade   If you're a cop you have to tell me.
But I don't know why you'd think we do anything like that.
What are you trying to say?

Hannah   I'm sorry, I just thought
I don't know what to do.

I need help.
Someone told me to look out for an herbalist, so I
Please help me.
Apprentice Fade.

Fade

Hannah

Another crunch of gravel and a car door slams. **Harrison**, *a middle-aged woman in a sheriff's uniform, saunters up.* **Rue** *and* **Jess** *come from around the back of the Ambulatory carrying potted plants.*

Harrison   Hello, ladies.

Jess   Sheriff, I didn't expect to see you all the way out here!

Harrison   I like to keep an eye out.

Rue   Sheriff? As I recall, last time we were here you were just a deputy. A pleasure to see you again.

Harrison   Don't doubt it.

Something is happening between their eyes. **Fade** *doesn't like it.*

Fade   Ma'am.

Harrison   Didn't know when we'd see you two again 'round here.

Fade   Well, that's the funny thing about routes, they go in circles.

Rue   Down, girl.
Sheriff, do you still take your tea hot?

Harrison   Piping.

Rue   Apprentice, why don't you check out our customers while I brew the officer a cup of our finest.

Fade   Of course.

Harrison   Much obliged.
Jess, you've got to invite me over for dinner again sometime
Your casserole
Just

Jess (*with performative sweetness*)   You'll be the first person I call.

Harrison *shoots her a finger gun—maybe even double finger guns!—and follows* **Rue** *into the Ambulatory. They close the doors.* **Hannah** *makes a face at* **Jess**, *who shushes her.*

Fade   Right this way. Okay, we've got one satchel worth of—ah, one satchel. Two potted plants. Chamomile, ashwagandha. Do you know how to cultivate ashwagandha?

Jess

Fade   That's fine, that's fine, most don't. Let me jot down some notes for you. Doctor Voynich always says, "Plants are like children, give them a little love and attention and they'll do all right."

Hannah   And water.

Fade   Yeah, stay hydrated. You can keep that one in the pot for probably another month, this one will want to be in soil as soon as you can. Dappled sunlight, if you can swing it.

Jess (*uncertain*)   That's a lovely word, "dappled."

Fade   Tell you what, I need to go into town to get supplies. If you don't mind me hitching a ride, I'll help you get that green into the ground.

Jess   You're sure we won't be pulling you away?

Fade   Nah, Rue'll be happy to have me out of here for a while, it was a long trip from Cincy.
Okay, we're all set here. Heartland or Coastal?

Jess (*handing over coins*)   Heartland of course. Do you—do you deal with Coastals?

Fade   You'd be surprised at how much makes it over the border.

Jess   Well, there's nothing like that here. We're not those kind of people.

Fade   Out of fifty.
Okay, let me just—(*making a note in the logbook*)
Let me just finish this up here and I'll be right behind you.

Jess   We'll be in the car.

Jess *departs.* **Hannah** *begins to follow, but* **Fade** *grabs her.*

Fade   Okay listen
I can't help you by myself
Find a reason to come back with me tonight
We'll talk to Rue

Hannah   Promise?

Fade   Promise. Come on, let's go.

Fade *and* **Hannah** *depart. A moment of silence, then the back doors to the Ambulatory fling open and* **Rue** *and* **Harrison** *emerge, wrapped in each other's arms, kissing maybe too hard.*

Harrison   I missed you.

Rue   I know.

Harrison   A year!

Rue   I know.

Harrison   This shop is still illegal.

Rue

Harrison   I'm not arresting you.
I'm just saying.

Rue   If you want to use your handcuffs, you don't have to invent a pretense.

Harrison   I'm not making it up. This is an illegal pharmaceutical establishment.

Rue   We're in a gray zone.

Harrison   Not in my county.

Rue

Harrison   Again, I'm just saying.

Rue   You making out with me is illegal too. You going to arrest yourself?

Harrison   I'm a sheriff now. Being a sheriff comes with certain privileges.

Rue   My lips are a privilege? 'Salittle weird but I'll take it.

Harrison (*somehow thinking this is sexy talk*)   You watch that mouth of yours, vagrant.

Rue   I'm sure I can help you see things my way.
Have dinner with me tonight.

Harrison   I don't have that many privileges.

Rue   Oh come on, who cares? You're in charge now.

Harrison   I didn't get to be sheriff by being open about—well—

Rue   Can't you trust your deputies?

Harrison   With my life? Yes.
With you?

Rue   Secrets are better when they're dirty, anyway.

Harrison   God, I missed you.

Rue   I'm sure you haven't been waiting for me.

Harrison   Well
No.
But that doesn't mean I didn't miss
this
or
these

Rue   What about this?

Harrison   Mmmm
I definitely thought about that a *lot*.

Rue   And you'll have all that and more soon. But not today.

Harrison   Hnng.

Rue   Patience. Good things come to those who wait.

Harrison   How long are you here for?

Rue   Hard to say.

Harrison   Doctor Voynich, are you being cagey with me?

Rue   Not at all, officer.
Probably a week. Depends on how fast word spreads that we're out here.

Harrison (*she's said this a hundred times*)   Settle down. Start a respectable greenhouse. Grow stuff.

Rue (*she's heard that a hundred times*)   Who can afford to see a med-tech in this town?

Harrison   Me. A few.

Rue   Not enough.

Harrison   Don't see how that's my problem.

Rue   Darling. They need these plants, grey zone or not. Either they buy ground sorrel from me or they go out into the woods and try to make medicine themselves. You don't want that any more than I do. They'll end up eating weeds.
Just look the other way, please.

Harrison

Rue   I'll give you plenty of other things to look at.

Harrison   A week?

Rue   A week.

Harrison   And nothing illegal in here?

Rue   Just me.

Harrison (*undeterred*)   Dope. Weed. Emmenagogues. Anything that could kill a person. Or an unborn person.
You don't know anything about that.

Rue   I'm harmless.
Cross my heart, hope to die.

Scene Two

Monday evening, with fringes of orange.

Rue *is closing up shop, covering some of the plants with tarps, putting others back into or onto the Ambulatory. An orchestra of crickets, cicadas, katydids. A pair of folding lawn chairs are set up.*

Footfalls, in sync. **Fade** *and* **Hannah** *emerge from the twilight, carrying bags of supplies.*

Rue (*not looking*)   Took you long enough. The whole day without you! I almost lost out on a sale of that willow root because we got backed up and—
Oh! Hello. Goodness, I didn't expect you back. Is everything okay with your order?
You, put away those supplies.
How can I help you?

Hannah   I need
I, uh

Rue   This isn't about one of your purchases, is it.
Alright, honey, come here, have a seat.

Hannah   Thanks.

Rue   So what seems to be the trouble, my dear?

Hannah   I'm pregnant and I don't want to be.

Rue   And you think that I can do anything about that?
Abortion is illegal, and don't let the "Doctor" in my title fool you, I'm just a glorified gardener.

Hannah   I don't
But
People said

Rue (*intentionally loud*)   I would hate for you to have made the trip all the way out here for nothing, stay for a while.
Fade, make yourself useful. Please take the young lady's purse, it looks quite heavy.
I'm afraid you have the wrong impression.
If you're pregnant, that's God's will, and you'll come to love the little him or her.

Fade *stashes away* **Hannah**'s *purse. She reaches into the cab and turns on the radio.*

Rue   Now that that's taken care of.
Fade, be more careful next time or I'm leaving you on the side of the road.

Hannah   I don't understand.

Fade   You have a phone. Which has a microphone.
They listen sometimes.

Hannah   You should have told me.

Rue   She was supposed to. This is why she's still an apprentice. She gets distracted by a pretty girl.

Hannah & Fade

Rue   So, you're pregnant. How long?

Hannah   I don't know.

Rue   Just your best guest is fine.

Hannah

Rue   Okay, come here. I'm going to feel your belly, is that okay?
Lift up your shirt and brace yourself, there will be some pressure.
When you're ready.

Hannah

Fade   It's okay. Here. Can I?

Fade *cozies up behind* **Hannah** *and braces her.* **Hannah** *lifts her shirt.* **Rue** *feels her.*

Rue   Well, we're still in the first trimester.
That means three months.
When was your last period? You can drop your shirt.

Hannah   Um. I'm not sure.

Rue   You don't track your cycle. Alright. When did you last have unprotected sex?

Hannah   Unprotected?

Rue   Without a condom.

Hannah

Rue   [Christ alive.]

Fade   Rue.

Rue   Okay, let's go back to basics. Hannah, why do you think you're pregnant?

Hannah   Well, I'm sad. Big sad.

Rue   Any symptoms more definitive than feeling sad?

Hannah   Um.
I haven't bled in a while. I've felt a little sick. Here. I threw up last week for like, no reason.
Oh God this is so embarrassing.
But I guess I did
Swallow
A lot recently

Rue & Fade

Hannah   That's bad, right

Fade (*biting the bullet*)   Hannah . . . that's not how you get pregnant.

Hannah   Sure it is. How else does the white stuff, y'know, get to the belly?

Fade   I, It's
The "belly" is just something people say, it's just a saying.
You only get pregnant if someone comes in your vagina.

Hannah

Fade

Hannah   You know I can see that.

Rue   That's good.

Hannah   Yeah that makes a lot more sense.
Well, wait
Like the come in the vagina thing
That does happen sometimes.

Fade   Doctor, may I administer a pregnancy test to our patient?

Rue   You don't think that's contraindicated here?

Hannah   I can pay.

Rue   These tests are rare and getting rarer. At the risk of assuming too much about you, Hannah, I don't know that you have the funding for it.

Hannah

Fade   I'll pay.

Rue & Hannah

Fade

Rue   On your own head.

Rue *retrieves a lockbox from the inside of the Ambulatory. She inputs a complicated combination and pulls out a dusty, faded pregnancy test.*

Rue   There's a little plastic stick inside this box. Take it into the bushes and pee on it.

Hannah

Fade   Yes, really.

Hannah   That's nasty.

Rue   So is giving birth. Go on. It'll give you a little plus sign if you're pregnant.
Good luck.

Hannah *heads off into the bushes to take the test.*

Rue (*calling after her*)   You pee on the stick, not the box!

Hannah (*from off*)   I got it!

Fade

Rue   So. You're being awfully . . . proactive for this one.

Fade   She deserves more than this.

Rue   You're not wrong. But we all deserve more than this.
Planet cooking itself to death. The country broken up. Abortion and birth control lost.
The Supreme Court, Christ. But that's been true for as long as you've been alive,
young blood.

Fade   In another life, I think I could have been her. You know?
If I'd been raised in a Heartland town with no prospects instead of . . . well, with
you.
In her place, I'd want someone to help.

Rue   Has it occurred to you that you might harden your heart deliberately?
Caring is important. Caring too much is dangerous.
You need to channel your feelings to make yourself stronger, not let your feelings
control you.
People you care about can be used against you.

Fade

Rue   Bless your heart.
In the non-sarcastic way.
You're a promising apprentice. But you need to live in this world, not the one you
wish for. You might live for a future time . . . but the people in power don't.

Fade   I . . . I'll think about it.

Hannah *returns from the underbrush, a new look on her face.*

Rue   That's settled, then.
Come here.

Rue *gives her a hug, which* **Hannah** *accepts.* **Fade** *looks at her master, surprised.*

Hannah   Now what?

Rue   Fade, make some tea. Pennyroyal, dittany . . . Queen Anne's lace, and . . . let's
do Artemisia.
(*To* **Hannah**.) You have a decision to make.
I know you came here because you wanted an abortion, but really think about it.
You can't half-ass this, if you'll pardon the expression.
The body knows. There are medications I can give you, but just the herbs aren't
enough. You need to be resolved and diligent.
Can you do that?

Hannah   I think so.

Rue   You need to know so.

Hannah   I . . .

Rue   Tell me about why you want an abortion.

Hannah   Oh, God. Where to start?
My mother. She'll kill me. And I'm only like kind of joking. She'll be so disappointed in me.
"You don't even have a boyfriend."
There's so much I want to do. Get out of this town, go to college, get a real job.
I'm not a mother.
A baby? What do you even do with a baby?
It's too much.
You push a . . . a person? Through *this*? I'll break. I'll come apart.

Rue   Do you ever want a child?

Hannah

Rue   It's okay not to know. You're young.

Hannah   I'm just thinking.
If I had to decide now . . .
No.
If you ask me again tomorrow, maybe I'll say "someday." But right here, right now . . .
No. I don't want this one, and I don't want one ever.
Does that make sense?

Fade   Hmm. "I am whoever I am when I am it, I will live tomorrow as someone I have not yet become."

Hannah

Fade   Angel Haze. Lesbian scripture.

Hannah   I like that.

Rue   Ask me again.

Hannah   Can I have an abortion?

Rue   Yes.

Hannah and **Rue** *share an emotional moment.* **Fade** *hands* **Hannah** *the tea.*

Fade   Here you are.

Hannah   Oh, I don't drink tea, but thank you.

Fade   No, no, it's a tea. That's how this works. That's made with abortifacient herbs.

Hannah   That's it?

Rue   It's not as easy as it sounds. It tastes like the Devil's earwax, for one. Because you're probably pretty late on, we're going to be using a shotgun approach. There are dozens of plants that help induce menstruation, and you'll be on several. Not by accident, most of them are also semi-toxic. There will be side effects, like—

Hannah   As long as one of the side effects is not being pregnant, I'll deal with it.

She downs the tea and hands the cup back.

Rue   You're tougher than people give you credit for, aren't you?

Hannah

Rue   Any questions?

Hannah   So what if it doesn't come out?

Rue   It will. You need to trust the process. Your body and mind will work together with the herbs in the tea. It will work.

Hannah (*trying to believe*)   It'll work.
Okay. So should I go back out into the bushes for this or

Rue   What?

Hannah   When the thing comes out.

Fade   Oh, uh, it doesn't work that fast

Hannah   I drank the tea, we should be done here, right? I drank it.

Rue   This is a course of treatment, not a one-and-done. You'll see results in a week or so.

Hannah   That's too late!

Fade   Why?

Hannah   It's gotta be now. Do it now.

Rue   Hannah, there's nothing I can do to make this happen faster. It takes time.

Hannah   You're not listening. My mom's going to find out.

Rue

Fade   Why do you think that?

Hannah   She's the nosiest bitch alive, she can already tell something's wrong

Rue   [Language . . .]

Hannah   And if I have to keep drinking this stinky tea she's going to figure out it has something to do with you
You've never seen her when she's angry
Take it out.
And don't tell me that you can't because I know that's a thing.
Like you can kick me, or vacuum it out or whatever

Rue   We don't do that.

Hannah   You need to, or—or I'll tell the sheriff about this.

Rue   No, you won't.

Hannah   I will! Take it out. Or I'll report you.

Rue   Do you think you're the first person to threaten me?

Hannah

Rue   I understand that you're upset, so I won't be taking this personally. As long as you stop this foolishness. Now.

Fade   Please, don't say anything. Every herb we've given you has a "legitimate" use. If you combine them in a manner likely to cause an abortion, you can be charged with attempted murder of an unborn person.

Rue   We're doing the best we can for you.
(*To* **Fade**.) Give her the next dosage.
(*To* **Hannah**.) Teenage girls go through all sorts of phases. If your mom asks why you're suddenly drinking tea, just tell her that you're mysterious and full of emotion.

Fade   Don't panic about something that hasn't happened yet. We'll be here for a while.
We are not going to abandon you.

Hannah   This is not okay.

Hannah *departs with the next dosage, upset. The herbalists watch her go.*

Fade   We could have helped her.

Rue   We *are* helping her.

Fade   She's right though. This isn't okay.
There are other ways.

Rue   Not anymore.

Fade *scoffs.*

Rue   Look, the knowledge didn't just vanish when we lost in the Court. But it's useless without the right tools. They destroyed all the actual equipment back in the Trump days.

Fade   Donald?

Rue   Ivanka. Thank you, first woman president.

Fade   I'm worried about her.

Rue   Yeah, well.
Me too.
But there's nothing more we can do to help her than what we're already doing.
Herbs helped people control their fertility for six thousand years. She has more in common with a Greek woman wearing a bedsheet than she does with her great-grandmother, right now.
Christ.

Fade   Do you think she'll . . .

Rue   Turn us in?

Fade   No. Like,
Take matters into her
Own hands.

Rue   I hope not. But that's out of your control.
Listen up. You're giving her the best tools we have, the best option she's going to
come across out here. I don't mean just her. Any patient you treat.
"Do the best you can with what you have."

Fade   I always preferred "Do no harm."

Rue   That's for naïve old men.

Fade   There are other ways that we could try.

Rue   Honey. I'm trying to be patient. With both of you.
We do not do that.
We will never do that.
The back-alley methods are too dangerous for the parents and they're too dangerous
for us.
You know what happens to people who get caught doing this kind of work.
Do you want to be locked up? Carted around as part of the propaganda machine?
I'm sure they'd love to carry around a Coastal abortionist, you can do the whole
talk radio circuit, tell everyone about how you murdered all those unborn people,
ruined their poor mothers' lives, locked them out of the Kingdom of Heaven
forever.
And that's if we're lucky.

Fade   Okay but

Rue   *Ay dios mío.*

Fade   You used to
Right? You did
(*She makes a scooping motion at her vagina.*) Before.

Rue (*indicating the Ambulatory's logo*)   I earned that "Doctor," not that it matters
now.

Fade   So you know how.

Rue   That's enough.
I know that look in your eye.
No.

Fade   Okay look, cards on the table
What do you think her chances are?
There were waaay too many drugs in that tea we gave her
That was a Hail-Mary abortion cocktail.

Rue   Say that a little louder, why don't you
Look, a third of pregnancies end in miscarriage anyway. What we gave her will help,
especially if she believes that it'll help.
But based on the examination . . .

Fade   So we're selling her false hope.

Rue   As I recall, we're not *selling* her anything, Miss "I'll pay."

Fade   This is bullshit.

Rue   No, it's hope, which she desperately needs right now.

Fade   We need to help her!

Rue   God above, what do you think we've been doing? Dicking around?
Lemme just round up some super-illegal plants to give to an emotionally unstable
teenage girl

(*overlapping*)
//—who has already threatened to turn us in, by the way—lemme just gather those up
for her and send her on her way. For no money. Just because my apprentice asked me
to.

Fade (*overlapping*)   But—this is her life! She's gonna get stuck with some baby if
we don't do something
Or or or she's gonna try it herself and
And
God! We can't just throw up our hands and tell her good luck.//

Rue   This. This is why I tell you to harden your heart.
Because you get wrapped up in these people.

Fade   Maybe it's easy for you to just give it your best shot and walk away
You never have to stick around and deal with the consequences
You just give them their plants and it's on to the next town, the next job, the next
route.

Rue   Dammit!

Fade   Maybe if you were able to get pregnant—

Rue

Fade

Rue   Get out of here.

Fade   I didn't

Rue   Go

Fade   You know I

Rue   Come back
But not soon

Fade   I

Rue   Now.

Fade *grabs her shit and leaves.* **Rue** *looks at the sky.*

Rue   Wade, if you're up there, it's your turn to be the bad cop. Fuuuuuuck.

Rue *retrieves a hidden canister. She opens it and retrieves one of very few precious blunts. She is about to put the container away, then looks after* **Fade**—

Rue   Treat yo' self.

—and pulls out a second blunt. She tucks it behind her ear. Then she puts the canister back, and lights up. Inhale, exhale. Inhale, exhale.

The crunch of gravel, but **Rue** *doesn't notice.* **Jess** *walks up.* **Rue** *still doesn't notice.* **Jess** *clears her throat.*

Rue   Oh! Hello, ma'am, we're not open right now, but
Well.
Shit.

Jess *walks over to* **Rue***, then snags the second joint from behind her ear.*

Jess   Hi again.

She takes the lighter and blazes like a pro. **Rue** *regards her in astonishment.*

Jess   We'll call it a bribe not to tell Sheriff Harrison that you're smuggling contraband across state lines.

Rue   Huh.

Jess   I wasn't always an insurance agent, you know.
I did things. Went to college. I acted. I managed a hardware store. I served people food.
I've felt things.

Rue   Mmm.

Jess   The anti-anxiety herbs you gave me were good, mind you. But this, well.
The lungs remember.

Rue   They do.

Jess   Bodies remember.

Rue (*serious*)   Yeah.
So, what brings you to my Ambulatory?

Jess   Doctor Voynich.

Rue   Rue.

Jess   Doctor Rue. Okay. Why, do.
Why do we bleed.

Rue   I . . . can you be more specific.

Jess   Like . . .
(*She gestures at her vagina.*) Bleaaggghhh.
I'm asking for your perspective. You know . . . Lore. "Science."

Rue   Okay. So basically we bleed to get rid of eggs.

Jess   Eggs? I have—?

Rue   No no, like human eggs, they're tiny, like they become babies if you—
You do know how . . .?

Jess   Oh right right yeah right.
Totes. Totes ma goats.

Rue

Jess   My mom used to say that.

Rue   [Anyway . . .]
Your body releases the eggs—puts them in your—situation—starting with puberty,
then if they don't get
Fertilized
Then you need to get rid of it so you can have a fresh one ready.
Now, cats and dogs and stuff, they can get rid of just the egg, blood pretty much stays
where it is.
But humans have to bleed out the whole thing. Every time.

Jess   That's
That is messed up.

Rue   I guess at some point, evolution—or God—decided that it was more important
for
For humans to suffer their way through reproduction.
From blood to egg to
Teenager
Suffering, all the way down

Jess   Sad.

Rue   [Yeah.]

Jess   I think I screwed up my kid.

Rue (*spluttering and coughing as her inhale goes down the wrong tube*)   No, no,
nah—I mean—why—why would you say that.

Jess   I just
She didn't come out right. There's just something not quite
It's
Did you trust your mother?

Rue   I am not high enough to have that conversation. Look, let's just, hold on a second.

Rue *reaches into the Ambulatory and flicks on the radio for some slow music from the 2000s.*

Jess   I didn't take you for a golden oldies kind of woman.

Rue   Do you know the last time I got to talk to an adult? Someone who actually remembers this music? My mom loved it. God, she probably danced to this song at her prom.

Jess   It's nice.
Hey.
Come here.

Jess *pulls* **Rue** *to her and starts to slow dance.*

Rue   What are
What?

Jess   Just relax. Relax into me, and tell me about her.
I'll lead.

Rue   I'll lead.

Jess

Rue   Sorry, that's just how I am
I don't really have any chill.

Jess   Well, let me lead. Pretend you know how to have chill. What went wrong between you?

Rue   When I was nineteen, I took an STI test. Very routine. Came back clean. Good job, Rue. Went home to my partner at the time. We had sex. Like a lot.
The next morning the med-tech office called me back. "Hey we used expired reagents on your first test, so we re-did it, and I'm sorry to tell you this over the phone, but the test came back positive for HIV."

Jess   Lord almighty.

Rue   They were sending it off to another lab to confirm-confirm, but they'd done the test three times. Those tests are wrong once in 30,000 times.
Keep in mind, this is happening while my partner was in bed next to me, wondering what was wrong.

Jess   Did he

Rue   It was the longest week of my life. I didn't call my mom. I didn't know what to say to her, what to ask. How to get help. AIDS was a death sentence again by then—it wasn't long after the drug cocktails stopped working, but it was long enough.
A week later, the med-tech office called back. False positive. Or, three false positives in a row, I guess.

Jess   Praise Jesus, for He is good.

Rue   For He is good. Good with a sense of humor. The odds of three false positives in a row is less than one in a quadrillion. So, the next time I was home was Thanksgiving. My mother asked me how I was. I told her, "Mom, everything is fine now, everything's totally fine, but can I talk with you about this thing that happened that was scary?"

Jess   What did she say?

Rue   She said if she knew that something had gone wrong with me, she would be too worried, so she only wanted to hear good news.

Jess

Rue   That's when I lost my faith in my mother.

Jess   Shit.

Rue   Yeah.
If you could talk to your daughter about something that was scary but now was fine
That might be enough for her.
You could be enough.

Rue *and* **Jess** *may have stopped dancing by now, or maybe they haven't. Maybe they're cuddling.*

Jess   She's
She used to tell me things.
Small things. Childish things. But they were real to her. They mattered.
There wasn't just one moment where it stopped. But I went into her room one day to clean
It was springtime
I lifted up the mattress
There was a sea of red
Just dozens of underwears, covered in blood
She hadn't told me, I hadn't noticed
Why didn't I notice?
I took them all away and I started giving her pads but
We never talked about it. That was years ago. I'm sure it wasn't her first secret, but it's when I realized.
Now, I wonder what else I haven't noticed.
(*Gesturing to her now-smoked joint.*) Christ up in Heaven knows I was up to no good at her age.
I mean, hell, I smoked when I was pregnant.
I didn't even want to get pregnant. I didn't want to pass this all on. But then here she is. All the worst parts of me, she's got them. And it's not like there's anyone else around she picked up her habits from. Loser number one, right here. The wellspring.
She's acting strange.
I hope she's not in trouble.

Rue   Have you tried asking her?

Jess   Have you tried asking your daughter what's going on with her?

Rue   Fade's not my daughter.

Jess

Rue   No. No, I suppose I haven't.
I could.

Jess   Last week, I tried to ask her how she was doing.
Not like, "how was your day at school," or "how was the sleepover,"
But really ask her.
Her eyes were just
Just
Fear.

Rue

Jess   It's not right. I—
My mother wasn't around. I'm around. I'm not perfect, but I'm trying.
I take her to stuff. I put her in classes. Buy her instruments and clothes and
Dogs and things. Take her to church. We pray.
Everything I do just bounces off.
She's scared of me.

Rue   You've got to open up to her if you want her to do it for you.

Jess   Maybe.
(*Toasting.*) To our hellraisers
May they be better at getting out of trouble than their mothers

Rue   Or their master and their mother

Jess   You can just call her your daughter.
No one would ever know.

Rue   She's not. I like her fine, but we're not
I'm no mother.
I don't have the courage.

They both know something could happen.

Rue   I'm not scared of you.

Jess   Yeah?

Rue   I mean this isn't where I expected my evening to go but
Yeah, this is nice.

Jess   I'm not this kind of person. I want you to know that.

Rue   What kind of person?

Jess   I don't have the courage either.

They both know something won't.

Jess (*at weed*)   This is some powerful shit.

Rue   It helps.

Jess (*starting to leave*)   You've been very
Accommodating.
Thank you.

Rue   Why did you come out?
Here, tonight, I mean.

Jess   Because there's something wrong with Hannah.

That implication sits heavily in the air. **Jess** *exits. The crunch of gravel.* **Rue** *tidies up.*
Another crunch of gravel. **Rue** *looks up, hopeful. It's* **Harrison**. **Rue** *tries to conceal*
her dismay—and the evidence of pot.

Rue   Sheriff! So good
So good to see you
I just
I was just

Harrison   Babe, don't worry, this isn't a professional visit
I wanted to see you.
I brought you

She holds out flowers.

Rue   Oh wow

Harrison   I know, I know. You grow plants for a living
But they're all so practical. I thought you might like
Something beautiful
Like you
Maybe it's stupid

Rue   No they're very nice, thank you

Harrison *goes in for a kiss, which* **Rue** *diverts into a quick hug.* **Harrison** *looks at*
her suspiciously.

Harrison   Uh, okay

Rue   Just wanna put these in water real fast
They'll die here, with the heat
Thank you, again

Rue *ducks into the Ambulatory.* **Harrison** *pokes around and sniffs.*

Rue (*from inside*)   How kind of you to bring these to me
(*With the bouquet, leaving the Ambulatory.*) There we are, just the thing
Just the very thing

Harrison   Voynich.

Rue   Are we on a last-name basis today?

Harrison   Do you think I'm an idiot
I know what weed smells like, dumbass.
What else do you have here
(*Going through the plants.*) How many of these would land you in jail? What about
this one? Huh?

Rue

Harrison   I trusted you
God, I bend so many rules just by letting you park here and sell your stupid
herbs.
You lied to my face.

Rue   Harrison . . .

Harrison (*at that tone of voice*)   NO.

Rue   I wish it were different. But it isn't.
Because people need this. They do!
Not the weed, but the rest of it. These plants keep people from dying, Sheriff. I keep
them from dying. The weed is just
I need an escape sometimes

Harrison

Rue   I don't sell it. Fade doesn't use it. It's me. It's just me. I don't even grow it. I
bought this down in Cincy.
I'm sorry, I'm sorry
So so sorry
Look, I can make it up to you

Harrison   My hands are tied. I can't just keep looking the other way.
I have to bring you in.

Rue   Wellwellwell
Okay
But first
Let's go have dinner

Harrison

Rue   Please, Harri, let's
Just let's go have dinner. Somewhere that serves things covered in cheese, just like
you like it.
We can talk about this. I'll tell you all about it. We can—we can pray about it.
Then afterwards, we'll go for a walk
We'll go to that meadow

Harrison   Mmm

Rue   Our meadow.
We'll walk beneath the stars and the eyes of God
Beneath angels' wings and above the souls in the dirt
And you can decide whether you'll be taking me to jail
Or to bed.

Harrison (*not sure if she means it*)   You're going to jail.

Rue   That may be true, my dear,
But after we eat.

They exit together. **Rue** *looks back nervously at the Ambulatory—she never leaves it alone for obvious reasons. But she must, so she does. Perhaps she performs a small ritual or prayer.*[2]

Scene Three

Tuesday night, when the sky is at its deepest and everything feels a little more possible

Hannah *bikes onstage with* **Fade** *riding on her pegs.*[3] *They fall off their bike. They've clearly been drinking.*

Fade   Holy shit! You do that all the time?

Hannah   I mean not like *all* the time
It's kind of a kid thing
Did you never pegdrift when you were a kid?

Fade   "Pegdrift"?
I love the Heartland.

Hannah   It's what it's called!
There's like three things to do in this town:
You watch TV
You do drugs
Or you ride your bike.

Fade   I love it.
Doctor! Doctor Voynich! Rue?

Hannah   Doctor Voynich!

Fade   Rue!
Weird.
Super-weird.

Hannah   What is?

2. If you want an intermission, this is where it goes.
3. For safety or financial reasons, you can have this commotion happen offstage. I just think it's beautiful if
    you can pull it off.

Fade   She's just always here. She never leaves unless I'm here to watch it. 'Cause
Well you know

Hannah   Totes.

Fade

Hannah   It's something my mom says.

Fade   Totes.
Doctor Voynich?

Hannah   What kind of name is Voynich anyway? It's not her real name is it?

Fade   Wilfrid Voynich was a collector of manuscripts in twentieth-century Poland
He found this book, it used to be quite famous actually. It was written in an
uncrackable code. No one has ever been able to figure out what it says.

Hannah

Fade   Rue is kind of a nerd about stuff like that

Hannah   Yeah. Rue's the nerd.

Fade   Whatever, dude.
Well, she's not here right now apparently. Weird as balls.

Hannah   That phrase is worse than "pegdrift."
Well okay
There is not a doctor in the house. What do we do?

Fade   What do you wanna do?

Hannah   Get an abortion.

Fade

Hannah   Sorry that was maybe abrupt

Fade   Ya think?

Hannah   Please? You're my doctor.

Fade   I'm the doctor's apprentice

Hannah   How hard can it be?

Fade   Probably pretty hard

Hannah   Well sure but
You could figure it out.
(*Indicating the Ambulatory.*) And like, what about this thing? This thing is huge.[4]
There's gotta be something in there that would help.

---

4. If you've designed it so the Ambulatory is offstage, Hannah can say "that" thing rather than "this" thing.

Fade   Doctor Voynich doesn't like me to poke around too much.
I think it's booby trapped.

Hannah   Very funny.
What are you, chicken?

Fade   She's my boss! And my teacher and my guardian and the person who could
destroy my entire life. Do I think I could do it, if somehow we found out how? Sure,
why not? But I also don't wanna die.

Hannah   I will die.
If the tea doesn't work and I have this baby
I will expire. My hips will break apart and my insides will fall onto the dirt. I will
pass from this earth.
Help me.

Fade

Hannah   Please.

Fade   Well, there is one thing we could try.

Hannah   Yes! Thank you thank you thank you

Hannah *kisses* **Fade** *on the cheek, with feeling.* **Fade** *climbs into the Ambulatory and
pulls out a locked box. She begins to try combinations.*

Fade   God, Rue's gonna kill me. I'm not supposed to get in here.
But I'm pretty good at guessing things like this. She can be kind of
Predictable
It's usually either her birthday or my birthday or 05-13-16 . . . Yes!

It opens. **Hannah** *pulls out a speculum and uses it like a duck bill, quacking.*

Hannah   What is this?

Fade   I'm not sure
But look at it. Like the shape. I'm pretty sure it
I think it goes (*indicating*)

Hannah   Ugh! Gross!

Fade   You let a penis inside you but this is gross?

Hannah   I liked the penis. It was good to me. This looks like a torture device.

Fade *works through a collection of scissors, hooks, scalpels, and delivery forceps.*

Hannah   Pretty sure you don't need those for herbology.

Fade   No, you don't.
Careful, sharp.
(*Reaching the bottom of the box.*) Here it is.
Okay, listen. Before I show you this: you cannot tell Doctor Voynich. You CAN'T.
I'm not allowed to read this without her.

Fade *pulls forth a huge leather-bound tome. It looks ancient. It's magnificent; there are several sections of different types of paper: parchment, printer paper, what might be papyrus.*

Hannah   Wooaaaah.
"The Voynich Manuscript, Rescued from the Ruins of the Beinecke Rare Book and Manuscript Library at Yale University by Wade Johnson, M.D., with Annotations and Expansions."
This is the thing! The thing that the Polish guy found!
Rue named herself after a book?
Open it up

Fade (*paging through*)   Crazy, right?

Hannah   You can read that?

Fade   This is herbalist shorthand. It's really, really hard to read, because the name of the person who writes it changes how you translate and parse each letter.

Hannah   This is old.
Like look at this, it's like a treasure map

Fade   Parchment. Or maybe vellum?

Hannah   This is like, serious shit.
Wow. These illustrations.

Fade   Yeah. They're kind of hard to make out. They've started to . . .

Hannah   Fade.

Fade   What?

Hannah   "They've started to . . ."
Never mind.
So this is like, an herbalist . . . instruction manual?

Fade   Well, sort of. Like look, look here, this part is written by someone called Madame de Monteferra, she's talking about how to dose birthwort, but this part, with the picture of . . .

Hannah   Gross.

Fade   This part is by someone else—this part here, that's her signature—and she disagrees with Monteferra. It hasn't faded as much, this must have come later. This is about as far as I've gotten in my lessons.

Hannah   Rue taught you to read this kind of writing?

Fade   Yeah, once I grew up a bit and decided I really did want to be an herbalist
Like on my own, not just because she was

Hannah   Wait. So she somehow translated this manuscript that no one in the world can understand?

Fade   She didn't just figure it out by herself. When Doctor Voynich was still an apprentice, she learned it from her teacher, who learned it from her teacher . . . and so on. Wilfred Voynich found the book in 1912, but according to herbalist lore it's from the 1400s. And it's been added to ever since. It takes like two years to learn how to read herbalist code even with a really good teacher.

Hannah   And you can read it.
That's hot.
Keep flipping.
What in the world is that?

Fade   Yeah, that's a sort of, well it's a kind of occult-theurgical-astrology-alchemy . . . thing, I honestly, I have no idea. Renaissance witches had their own stuff going on.

Hannah *admires that. They keep flipping.*

Fade   We're getting to the part of the book that Rue won't let me read. God, she's gonna kill me.

Hannah   What's that stuff there?

Fade   Where's the signature?
Wade Johnson. Her again.

Hannah   How do you know it's a her?

Fade   I just know.
Look at this bit, it's just paper, this was added recently. Well, recently compared to the rest.
Woah, look at this illustration.

Hannah   Is that
Is that what my vagina looks like?

Fade   I mean not your vagina specifically, but yeah, that's a vagina. Well, that part's a . . . in English I think that would be . . . ucher? Uter. Uterus?
Oh damn. Yeah, I was right.

Hannah   What?

Fade   I'm pretty sure this is about abortion. Like, back-alley abortion.

Hannah   Oh my God

Fade   I can see why this section is forbidden.
Yeah yeah yeah, look here, that's a . . . Chure-viche? Service? Cervice?

Hannah   That little knubby thing?

Fade   Mmm.

Hannah   I've felt that before
I always thought
Huh

Fade   What?

Hannah   I thought that's where the pee comes out.
It feels like a spout

Fade   No.
Well, maybe?
No, this is definitely where the babies come out.

Hannah   But it's so small.
Fade, could you . . . you could give me an abortion with this.

Fade   It'll take me a while to decipher this, but
I think this means that there's a way to do it, even without the real medical equipment.

Hannah   Oh my God.

Fade   We're not going to do anything until I talk to Rue. Okay?

Hannah   What? No, she'll just say no, or hide the book, or
Or take you away from here.
From me.
No, we have to do this on our own.

Fade   I'm already going to be in a ton of trouble just for showing you this, do you
know how mad she's going to be if I try to give you a secret abortion?
We need her help. You'd be a lot safer with her.

Hannah   She won't do it. You heard her before. She won't. And this tea isn't gonna
work, is it?

Fade

Hannah   I'm not gonna stop taking it
But I feel like garbage and it hasn't worked
This is a sure thing.

Fade   I I I I don't know about that
I mean we just found it
It's
I'm not

Hannah   You can learn. You are smart.
I trust you. Read the gross book.
Just, just learn it, and we'll decide what to do then, okay?

Fade   It's just knowledge . . .

Hannah   Exactly. It's just knowledge.

Fade   Okay. Yeah, yeah, I'll study it.
We'll figure this out.

Hannah   Are we a we, now?

Fade

Hannah   Because I like the way "we" sounds.

Fade   It feels good to say.

Hannah   "We."

Fade   We. "Oui oui, mademoiselle."

Hannah

Fade   French.

Hannah

Fade   They still speak French.

Hannah

Fade   In
Places

Hannah *kisses* **Fade**.

Like, a lot.

Fade   Woah.

Hannah

Fade   That was
Okay wow

Hannah   You're such a dork.
Where do you sleep?

Fade   ?!

Hannah (*indicating the Ambulatory*)   Is there a bed somewhere in this thing?
Because I wanna put you on it.

Fade   You don't
This isn't a trade, Hannah. I'm not
You don't need to

Hannah   I know, that's what makes me so nice.

Fade   No, really

Hannah   You don't want me to?
Look I may be pregnant and maybe that implies something about my tastes
But this wouldn't be my first time being
Pretty in pink

Fade   I well uh you I didn't haven't exactly well you know how
I haven't

Hannah

Fade   Not yet

Hannah   Ever?
What the
Aren't you Coastal? You're supposed to be a bunch of sexy freaky sex freaks

Fade   And Heartland people are all supposed to be like
Repressed and pure

Hannah   You believed that?

Fade   And it's illegal!

Hannah   Have you seen our sheriff? Like that bitch is going to flip a shit about a little carpet munching between friends.

Fade   So, no, I haven't

Hannah   God, why?

Fade   I wanted to wait for
Someone special

Hannah   Have you never been bored?
Like okay I've never been "on the road" or whatever you call it, but I feel like I would get bored
And I would have sex. Like a lot of sex.

Fade   And Rue is always around . . .

Hannah   She's not now.
Okay, um,
I'm not going to pressure you into doing anything you don't want to do
But a girl gets hungry, and you are delicious.
Maybe I'm not the special girl you were saving yourself for,
But maybe I could be.

Fade

Hannah

Fade   You could be.

Fade *kisses* **Hannah**.

Like, a lot.

Eventually she pulls away and pulls the bed out of the Ambulatory. At one point it was a medical stretcher. It has gynecological stirrups at the end.

Hannah   Woah. This is some hardware.

Fade   "We do what we can with what we have." I think it's called a stretcher.[5]

5. If you don't have the resources for a stretcher and just wanna use like a table or something, I'm not picky. You can cut "I think it's called a stretcher" through to the end of "Those are for."

Hannah   Does it stretch you? Is that what these are for?

Fade   Nah. Like you stretch out on it. Those are for (*indicating the stirrups*)

Hannah   Oooooh. Oh, that could be fun.

Fade (*low-key freaking out about that idea*)   Totally

Hannah   Would you like to
Stretch out?

Fade   Yeeeeesssss?
I mean, yes!
But
Oh, shit
Shit!

Hannah   What?

Fade   I'm on my period.

Hannah

Fade

Hannah   Alright, let's get to it then

Fade   Hannah!

Hannah   What? It's blood.
If it can feed a baby it can feed me.

Fade   The babies don't eat the blood.

Hannah   What? Sure they do, that's why you don't bleed when you're pregnant, and
you do when it's gone.

Fade   I—
Huh. That does kind of make sense and I don't know enough about babies to
dispute it
But it's still
You don't have to

Hannah   I know I don't have to, but here we are.
To be honest I've always wanted to earn my red wings.

Fade   Your red wings?

Hannah *gestures at her cheeks with both hands.*

Fade   [Oh]

Hannah   Mmmhmmmmmmmmm.
I'm not going to feed you a line here, I'm not going to tell you I love you, because I
don't. Yet.
But I will tell you this:

When I touch you, it feels like our bodies are having a conversation.
You make me vibrate deep down to my core
I am trusting my body to tell me what it wants, and listening when I hear,
"You want her."

Fade   That works for me.

They have sex.[6]

Hannah *earns her red wings, and* **Fade** *ends up in the bed with her thighs bloody.*
Hannah *kisses* **Fade** *goodnight and whispers something just for her. She gets on her*
bike and departs. **Fade** *falls asleep in the bed, smiling up at the stars, her pants still off.*

Scene Four

Wednesday morning, the morning after

Rue *walks up to the Ambulatory, looking rather the worse for wear. Her "stride of*
pride" doesn't look very proud. **Fade** *continues dozing on the bed.* **Rue** *sees her.*

Rue (*crying out*)   Wade!
Christ alive!
WADE!

Rue *runs up to her.* **Fade** *jumps awake and falls off the bed. She tries to cover herself.*
Rue *snaps back to reality and looks away.*

Fade (*overlapping*)   //Oh my God
Rue, Doctor Voynich
Oh my God you were never
I'm so sorry
Please, let me just get
Where are my pants
Oh god

Rue (*overlapping*)   What the hell
How could you
What happened here? Are you okay?
Holy shit, Fade,
I didn't know if you were hurt
What is wrong with you?
How could you do this//

Fade *has gotten her pants on.*

Fade   Rue, I am so, so sorry, I don't

6. I'm not going to tell you how to stage this. Hire an intimacy director if you can. This is a collaborative
    consent-based process between director and actors. Fade to black, show some skin, make it a dance that
    rhymes with Rue and Jess's slow dance from earlier, make it contact improv. It's as poetic or as dusty as
    the rest of your world.

I don't know what to say

Rue You can start with what the hell this was!

Fade There's no
I have no excuse, ma'am.

Rue I didn't ask for an excuse
I asked WHAT THE HELL.

Fade I just
I don't know what to say
I got carried away

Rue Laying there exposed to the world
Do you realize what could have happened?
And God, the blood.
I've raised you better than to make such a mess.
Get some water from the tank and clean yourself up. God in Heaven.

Fade I'm sorry.
(*Noticing.*) What is [that], is that a bruise?
Are you okay?

Rue What? You mind your own business.

Fade Your neck, that doesn't
I mean that doesn't look like it was fun

Rue I was making sure your ungrateful ass wasn't left on its lonesome, okay?
Knock it off.

Fade

Rue

Fade Rounds.

Rue Rounds? Now? Really?

Fade Now.

Rue Okay. Apprentice Fade, present.

They sit together.

Fade Patient presents with intense anxiety about their primary caregiver's health
and state of mind. She's experiencing tightness of the throat when she sees what looks
like a bruise. She's worried that her caregiver is in over her head. End of chart.

Rue You're smart enough to know how this works.
To survive, sometimes we have to do things we aren't
Well, it's not my favorite part of my job.
(*Gesturing at her neck.*) Sheriff Harrison is a good woman, in her own way.
Our arrangement works. I don't tell the other officers of the law she . . . cares

about a woman. She looks the other way, most of the time. I push, she pulls. Balance.

Fade   That's really dangerous for both of you.

Rue   She thinks she's doing the right thing, I suppose.

Fade   Everyone thinks they're doing the right thing, or they would do something else.

Rue   Maybe.
Some people like doing wrong.

This has never even occurred to **Fade**.

Rue   Since we're doing rounds . . . how about that blood?
Hey, no squirming out of this, you're the one who called it. What's the scoop?

Fade   I, that is,
Um. Me and Hannah

Rue   You and Hannah?
Like

Fade   Yeah.

Rue   Oh. And it was

Fade   Oh my God, I'm not giving you details

Rue   Fine, fine. Just checking that you're
Well, you're okay?

Fade   Yeah.

Rue   Good. I mean, professionally, I'm supposed to scold you right now about not getting involved with your patients, but
(*She gestures at her bruised neck, then refocuses.*) I'm glad it was good.

Fade   Yeah. Yeah, it was.

Rue   Okay. I need to go get washed up. Which you should do too, by the way.
Can you mind the shop today?
I'm going to be . . . occupied, all day, and probably tonight.

Fade   I understand.

Rue (*rising from her seat*)   Good. You'll do alright. And for God's sake . . . no more sleeping outside with your pants off.

Fade   I'll do my best.

Rue   That's my girl.[7] Rounds over?

---

7. If Fade is being played as nonbinary: "That's my apprentice."

Fade   Why did you call me Wade?

Rue (*stopping dead in her tracks*)   What?

Fade   You called me Wade, earlier.

Rue   What? No I didn't.

Fade   You did.

Rue   You misheard. Wade, Fade.

Fade   Don't lie to me

Rue   Fade, I never

Fade   MOM.

Rue

Fade

Rue   I'm not your mom.
Not when we're in front of other people, not when we're alone, not to St. Peter at the
Pearly Gates.
You are not my daughter.[8]
Don't
Ever.

Fade   I'm sorry.

Rue   Good.

Fade   You called me Wade because that's my real mom's name, right?

Rue

Fade (*misinterpreting* **Rue***'s pain*)   She isn't news to me. Wade Johnson, M.D. It's
her book.

Rue (*covering*)   It's
You just looked like her, in the light. Took me back for a second.

Fade   How did you meet her?

Rue   She's someone I knew.

Fade (*unsure*)   Because she was a doctor? And she knew you, and
Gave me to you? Before she died?

Rue   Do you trust me?

Fade   Of course I do.

Rue   I mean really trust me.

8   Alt for enby Fade: "You are not my blood."

I'll tell you about her when the time is right.
And I'll let you take lead on cases when the time is right,
And I'll turn this whole operation over to you when the time is right.
Today is not that day.
I'm not going to harvest you before you're ripe.
I will tell you how you came to me, but not yet.

Fade   "Today is not that day."

Rue   Do you understand?

Fade   Sure.

Rue

Fade   I said sure!

Rue   I'll take it.
I'm going to drop off Hannah's next dosage of tea before I
Well. Before the rest of my day. Rounds over?
(**Fade** *nods her assent.*) Be safe, young blood.

Rue *departs.* **Fade** *waits until she's far enough away, then pulls out the Voynich Manuscript.*

Fade   "Rescued . . . by Wade Johnson, M.D."
Mom.

She hugs the book, then begins to read. She reads and reads.

Scene Five

Wednesday evening, when Mars starts to shine

Fade *continues to read. You'd think she'd be bored by now, but she's not. Her notes cover several planters. She's intent.*

The crunch of gravel. Car door slams. **Harrison** *walks up, escorting* **Hannah**.

Harrison   Hi there.

Fade   Oh, shit!

She slams the book shut and begins to gather up her papers.

Harrison   You wanna try that again?

Fade   Hello, Sheriff. Welcome to Doctor Voynich's.

Harrison (*teasing*)   Why, hello to you too.

Fade   Hannah.

Hannah   Fade.

Fade   What's going on? Is everything okay?

Harrison   Everything's fine. Just fine.

Hannah   Sheriff Harrison saw me heading this way, so she gave me a ride. Because I'm supposed to pick up those seed packets from you.

Fade   Yes, right, the seed packets, let me just

Harrison   What are you working on, here?

Fade (*cleaning her papers up, trying not to look frantic*)   Just notes.

Harrison   Notes on what? That looks like

Fade   They're just plants. Ma'am.
Botanical illustrations.

Harrison   Now, I'm no expert, but that looks like a
Well, you know what it looks like.
It's like one of those paintings by that Georgia lady that's a flower but it's
actually a

Fade & Hannah

Harrison   I've seen paintings.

Fade   Really, they're just plants.
I'm thinking of putting them in a book.

Harrison (*eyeing the Voynich Manuscript*)   Like that one there?
Rue says hello, by the way.

Fade   Where is she?

Harrison   Oh, she's fine. She asked me to come out here and check on you. Make sure everything's okay.

Fade

Harrison   She's at my house. Getting ready.
You know how women are.

Fade

Harrison (*so sly*)   Now you two ladies behave yourselves. I'd offer you a ride back into town, but I know how long it can take to find good seed packets.

Fade & Hannah

Harrison   I don't expect that Rue will be home tonight.
But you're . . .
Old enough to look after yourself, aren't you?

Hannah   We'll behave, Sheriff. Actually, Fade was going to

We wanted to look at the stars, and it's so much darker out here on the road

Harrison   Sure is.

Fade   Yeah.

Harrison   Hannah, could I have a word with you?

Hannah   Anything you want to say to me, you can say in front of Fade.

Harrison   Alright, then.
I just wanted to remind you.
Make good choices.

Hannah   I am, Sheriff.

Hannah *takes* **Fade**'s *hand.* **Harrison** *and* **Hannah** *stare each other down.*

Harrison   Listen you little wiseass. I didn't get to be in the position in life, in this job, by flaunting it. Be more careful.
"Seed packets?" Come on. I get it. You're teenagers. But you're lucky I'm me instead of, well, just about any of the other officers in this county.
Be smarter. You think you're brave, but you're just stupid.
(*To* **Fade**.) Best be off.
I'll be sure to tell Rue you said hello.

She exits.

Fade   God what a cunt.

Hannah   I hope I didn't just make it worse

Fade   What? By holding my hand?

Hannah   I thought it would be better if she just thought we were a bunch of
Well, like her
I wanted her to think it was cute
You know, nothing to see here, just gals being pals,[9] nothing else to be suspicious about

Fade   I mean, if I were her, I'd buy it.
We were pretty cute.

Hannah *kisses her.*

Hannah   So what have you learned?

Fade   You're kind of a babe.

Hannah *flounces.*

Fade   Anyway, yes, I've started interpreting the section we saw, and it's slow going, but . . .

---

9. If you're playing Fade as nonbinary, "just gals being pals" can be cut, or not, at your discretion.

It's Wade Johnson's guide to performing abortions without a hospital.

Hannah   So you know how to help me now.

Fade   Take a look at this.
This is a diagram of your

Hannah   I got it.

Fade   And that duck bill thing you were using yesterday, that goes there. Then you take something long and pointy and it passes through the

Hannah   I don't want the details.

Fade

Hannah   It's gross.

Fade   Hannah . . . do you want me to do this or not?
Because it's important to me that you know what you're signing up for.
I'm not going to just . . . zap you and it's all better.

Hannah   I know, I just
I wouldn't ask a dentist for all the details either.

Fade   I'm not a dentist. And we're not extracting a tooth.
We're extracting a fetus.
Or, well, we sort of damage the fetus and irritate your uterus and your body takes it from there.

Hannah   It comes out on its own?

Fade   If it's not too far along, yes.

Hannah   What if it is too far along?

Fade   Then you say you had a miscarriage and the med-techs take it out.

Hannah   Absolutely not. No way. Mom would find out that I've
She would lose her shit if she knew I'd actually had sex, it's not—it's just not acceptable, okay, so, just, do better, okay, and

Fade   This is happening.
You are pregnant.
You can become not pregnant one of two ways: you can give birth, or you can
Not give birth.
Either way, there's something in there that's coming out.
There's nothing I can give you to just make it dissolve.

Hannah   No, you're right, you're right. Okay.
So you take the long pointy thing, stick it through the little spout thing, stab the baby, wha-bam.

Fade   Wha-bam?

Hannah   Yeah. Let's do it.

Fade   What? Just like that?

Hannah   Yeah. I understand everything.

Fade   Hannah, I barely understand the basic anatomy. I started learning this shit last night.

Hannah   I caught my mom snooping around my room this morning. She's suspicious. Sheriff Harrison is suspicious. Rue isn't here and isn't coming back tonight. There is never going to be a better opportunity.

Fade   I haven't had time to read all the instructions. The translation—

Hannah   You could study for the next week. But that's just words. You just study the pictures,
Trust your instincts and do it.

Fade   I haven't earned your faith.

Hannah

Fade   I will hurt you.

Hannah *kisses her.*

Hannah   You might hurt me.
But no matter what I'm going to stop being pregnant.
With or without your help.
I want it to be with, but I'm out of time.
If you can't have faith in yourself, have faith in Wade Johnson, M.D.

Fade   That I can do.

Hannah *gets up on the bed and prepares.* **Fade**, *consulting her notes, uses the speculum on her. Then, she takes an archetypical coat hanger and bends it into a straight rod.*[10]

Hannah   I need to go home after.

Fade   What? No, you should stay
Rest.

Hannah   No. If my mom sees that I'm not home, she'll know something's up.
She's like a shark.
She smells blood in the water.
I need to be home tonight.

Fade   You could bleed out. I need to monitor you . . .

Hannah   If it gets dangerous, I'll
I won't, but if it does
I'll be good. I'll deal with it.
If my mom finds me here with blood in the sand, it's all over.

---

10. You can overlap this with the following dialogue, or play it in silence.

Fade   I don't

Hannah   We.

Fade   Okay.

The two women share a moment. **Hannah** *grips* **Fade***'s hand very, very tightly.* **Fade** *extracts her hand. She removes* **Hannah***'s underwear. She begins the procedure.*

Hannah *arcs her back with a violent inhalation—pain and pleasure sound the same. Eventually,* **Fade** *helps her put her underwear back on.* **Hannah** *says a nonverbal goodbye, and leaves.* **Fade** *wants so badly to go, but she can't, so she doesn't. She goes into the Ambulatory.*

Scene Six

Thursday afternoon, with the dark on the horizon

Jess *runs in. She carries* **Hannah***'s bloody underwear and smears bright blood across the illustration of* **Rue** *on the side of the Ambulatory as she kicks and smacks it.*

Jess   PIECE OF SHIT
I KNOW YOU'RE IN THERE
COME OUT
YOU GODDAMN COWARD
MURDERING BITCH
OPEN UP

Fade *emerges from the Ambulatory.*

Fade   What the hell?

Jess   YOU!

Jess *comes at her.* **Fade** *fends her off.*

Fade (*overlapping*)   //Step the hell back
Calm down
What's wrong?
What did you do to our
I don't understand

Jess (*overlapping*)   YOU PIECE OF SHIT
SHE TRUSTED YOU
HOW COULD YOU DO THIS
SHE TRUSTED YOU
MY BABY GIRL//
My Hannah . . .

Fade   What happened?

(*Noticing the bloody underwear.*) Those are hers—

Jess   This morning, I just wanted to check on her,
There was so much blood, her underwear

Fade   Shit.

Jess   I took her to the hospital. She tried to tell me no
But, oh God, the sheets on her bed
Just . . . red.

Fade   Is she going to
Is she

Jess   I know it was you.

Fade

Jess   You, or Rue, or . . .
Something you did. Something you gave her.
It's not natural.

Fade   Ma'am, I

Jess   Don't.
Lie.
To me.

Fade   Rue's not here right now, but when she's back
I'm sure she'll tell you
There's nothing we could have given her that would cause that.

Jess   She told me.
What you did.

Fade

Jess   You can be honest with me.
Just say it.
Please.
Say it. Say it!
I need you to say it.

Fade   I didn't do anything.

Jess   Rue, then.
Please, Fade. I need to know the specifics. So we can, [oh God]
So we can save her life. The med-techs, they need to know.

Fade

Jess

Fade   It's that bad?

Jess   She's dying.

You can save her.
Just tell me what you did.

Fade

Jess   Please.

Fade   She . . . she came to me . . .
I want you to understand, she was desperate.
If it hadn't been me, she would have thrown herself down the stairs.

Jess   [Oh]

Fade   I did everything I could to
To make it safe
But
I'm not
I don't know
Didn't know

Jess   You gave her
An abortion, didn't you?

Fade   Yeah.
Yeah, I did.

Jess   Is this what you do?
You go from town to town murdering children?
Rue taught you how to do this, didn't she?

Fade *begins to realize that something's wrong about this.*

Jess   Didn't she? You're in this together.
Tell me. Rue is the master, you're just learning from her. This is her. Tell me.
Tell me!

Fade

The sound of slow clapping. **Harrison** *enters from offstage, pushing* **Rue** *ahead of her.* **Hannah** *comes too, looking defeated.*

Fade   What the fuck?

Rue   Fade!

Fade   What the fuck is happening?

Hannah   I'm so sorry.

Fade   Hannah! Are you okay? Oh my God, I thought you were

Harrison (*to* **Jess**)   Thank you for your assistance, ma'am, but you went a little far at the end.
You can turn off your wire now.

Fade   You son of a bitch!

Fade *comes at* **Jess**, *but* **Harrison** *steps between them.*

Harrison   Ah ah ah! You're under arrest for the murder of an unborn person. You want to add assault?
You have the right to . . .
Actually, you don't have those rights here. Hands behind your head.

Jess (*fumbling with her wire*)   I don't actually know how to turn this off

Harrison (*to* **Fade**)   So young . . . we're going to have you for eighty years.

Rue   Harrison, please
She didn't do it.

Harrison   We know that Hannah had it done. She confessed to it this morning.
She gave you up, Fade.

Hannah   That's not how it happened

Harrison   Jess found that tea and saw the blood. She figured it all out and gave me a call.
And now I have you on tape confessing to the murder of Hannah's child.

Hannah   I asked them to do it! It's my fault, I

Jess   Shut up.

Harrison (*to* **Hannah**)   A deal's a deal. Your mom helped me get this confession. I won't be bringing you in . . .
Unless you keep talking.
(*To* **Fade**.) Hands behind your head, now.

Rue   It was me!
It was always me.

Harrison   Come now, I saw Fade and Hannah conspiring just yesterday.
All those notes and drawings. The situation is clear.
. . . I knew, Rue. I knew you weren't just some gardener. But to use a child to do your dirty work.

Fade   She never

Rue   FADE! Be quiet.
Sheriff, you've got it all wrong.
My apprentice is just trying to protect me.

Fade   But

Rue   Not another word!
Please, listen to me.
Let her go, and I'll tell you all about it.
And not just this one. All the others.

Harrison   The others?

Rue   I've been a traveling herbalist for twenty years.
Do you really think this is the first time?
I'll tell you everything.
Every one.
All of the children I've killed.
Just let this one go.

Fade   Rue, don't!

Rue   "Don't let sentiment cloud your professional judgment."
I appreciate what you tried to do, but it's time we told the truth.
This is all me. Let her go.

Harrison   I would've loved to have both of you, but you heard her. She's confessed.

Rue   No! Take me!
If you bring her in, it's off the table, and you've got nothing.

Harrison   I have her on tape!

Rue   And so what? That's one person. Think about what I'm offering you. Hundreds of abortions. I can tell you about every single one.
But not if you bring her in. She was just trying to protect me. I'm the one you want.

Jess   Sheriff, let's bring them both in. I messed up, I didn't get the full confession. But there's enough here. We can get them both. Please, we made a deal.

Hannah *has a lightbulb moment. She works it out.*

Harrison (*not noticing*)   No, no, I've got the apprentice. It's not like the master can do anything now, can she? Can you, Voynich? Because you know what will happen if you start working again.
If you take any more lives, I'll find out about it, and who could say what would happen to little Fade? The prison system is a dangerous place for an abortionist.
Your deal's tempting, but this is the safest way.

Hannah   Why is it just you?

Everyone looks at her.

Why is it just you here? Why not the whole sheriff's department? Where are all your deputies?
This is a big deal.

Rue   She's right. We could be the biggest catch of your career.
Why aren't you arresting me?

Harrison   Look I
I already told you, I have the evidence on her, I didn't get a recording about you

Rue (*to **Jess***'s *wire*)   MY NAME IS RUE VOYNICH. I AM AN ABORTIONIST.
I PROVIDE ABORTIONS TO PEOPLE ACROSS THE HEARTLAND.

Everyone

Harrison   Enough of this. Jess, we're done. Turn off that wire right now, or I'm placing you under arrest too for disobeying an officer of the law. NOW.

Jess *does, confused at* **Harrison**'s *anger.*

Harrison (*to* **Fade**)   You. Hands behind your head. Let's go.

No one moves.

Hannah   It's you, Rue. She doesn't actually want to bring you in.

Jess   What? Why?

Hannah   Because if she does, her career is over.

Harrison

Jess   Oh my God. Oh my Lord in Heaven.

Rue   If she brings me in, it's going to come out that she's a lesbian. A lesbian in love with a Coastal abortionist.

Fade   Your entire life would fall apart. We were working right under your nose and you did nothing.

Harrison   Stop it. You stop it. This is over. Okay? I can't let you go.

Rue   No. It doesn't have to be this way. What's the point? Look, we'll leave. We'll go far away. You'll never hear from us again. Your secret will be safe. Our secret will be safe. We all just walk away.

Harrison (*mostly to* **Rue**)   You really don't understand me at all.
You think this is just a job, or or
Or it's about the badge. No.
What I do, I do for them. For the unborn.
You kill people.
Both of you. People who never get a chance at life because their mothers make bad decisions.
This is war. We're soldiers, you and me. You kill hundreds. You tell yourselves that they're not people, but they are.
People die in war all the time. If I bring you both in, then you can't kill any more.
You'll tell them all about me, but . . .
If I have to be a casualty of the war, then
Well, maybe I do.

Fade   WAIT!
Wait. I'll trade you.
I'll trade you the book.

Rue   No!

Harrison   That book I saw.

Fade   Yes. That one. It's everything. All our knowledge. Thousands of years of it. Everything we know. I'll destroy it.

Rue   No, no, absolutely not. You can't.

Fade   I can and I will.
But you have to let us go.

Harrison   I can't do that. You'll just go out. Rewrite the book. Kill more people.

Fade   No we won't.
I swear.

Harrison   How dumb do you think I am? I could never trust a person like you.

Fade   No.
You don't need to trust me. Because you have the recording.

Harrison

Fade   You have both of us on tape confessing to giving abortions. If we leave here and we try to rewrite the book or we keep practicing, you'll find out eventually. You'll have everything you need to destroy us.

Rue   This can't work. There's nothing to stop her from taking us in as soon as we destroy the Manuscript. It'll be her word against the word of two confessed abortionists.
Sometimes there's no way to win.

Jess (*unable to help herself*)   You need some insurance.

Harrison   Will you shut your goddam mouth?

Fade   No, she's right. You have your blackmail material, with the recording of us. So let's make a recording of our own. Our insurance.

Harrison (*getting the implication*)   Go to hell.

Fade   It's the only way this works. You get everything you want, Sheriff. We'll be gone. The book will be gone. No more abortions. You'll be safe. We all walk away.

Harrison *stares her down.* **Fade** *stares right back and doesn't shy away.*

Harrison   Do it.

Rue   No!
Fade, I won't let you do this.
Wade Johnson, M.D. Your mother. Thousands of years of herbalist knowledge, decades of abortion experience, written in the blood of the people who died in back alleys. It meant more to her than her own life.

Fade   What does that mean?

Rue   It wasn't long after the abortion ban, and Wade and I were still practicing. We knew people in the Heartland were going to need our help, so we stole an ambulance and made it across the border before it closed.

She was pregnant again, this was maybe a year after you were born. We did the best we could. But she was ectopic—that's a really serious complication.

Fade   There were hospitals . . .

Rue   Wade refused. She knew. If we went to a hospital, we'd be picked up. We couldn't continue the work.
I'm sorry.

Fade   You let her die
So you could keep doing "the work"
For strangers

Rue   You were a baby, you never knew her. I did.
I was her fucking wife! We made you! It's what she wanted.
I tried so, so hard. To save her. For hours.
But she
Died
On the table.[11]
I'm sorry I never told you. They use the people you care about against you.
You can't destroy this book, Fade. This is bigger than us.
She knew she was sacrificing herself. And her future with you.
She didn't do that lightly, on a whim. It was her choice to make.
I'm sorry you never knew her, but I do. I know her still.
You don't have the right to throw her legacy away.

Fade   She deserved better than
To die
On some roadside
Just to protect
What? What is that book, really?
Some scraps of vellum.

Rue   Six thousand years of inheritance.

Fade   I got lucky.
When Jess came to me and said that Hannah was hurt, in the hospital,
That I'd hurt her . . .
We don't have the tools. This Manuscript, it gives us just enough knowledge to be dangerous.
It's not worth it. I got lucky. THIS—ALL OF THIS—is the version where we got lucky.
No. No more.
What happens the next time a girl comes to me? Thinks I'm going to solve all her problems with . . .
What, a coat hanger. It's not right.
Sheriff, the book, and you let us go. Both of us.

---

11. If you want to be especially cruel, this is the same table/stretcher that Fade sleeps on.

I'll burn it right here, right now.

Fade *pulls out a bin of plant scraps and a lighter.*[12] *She starts a fire.*

Rue   You can't do this.

Fade (*to* **Harrison**)   Final offer. Or Rue goes her own way. You can bring me in, but you can't bring her in or you'll lose it all. She'll leave. You'll never find her again. But she'll find lots and lots of Hannahs. There are always Hannahs.

Harrison   Do it, then.

Rue   You can't! This isn't

Fade *gets out the Voynich Manuscript.* **Harrison** *inspects it, then nods her agreement. She grabs* **Rue** *to her just behind the burning bin in preparation of making their "insurance recording."*

Fade   Hannah, use your phone, film this.

Rue   Fade, please. Wade died for this book.
I'm not her. I'm not worth it.

Fade   Wade Johnson was my mother.
She was an abortionist. She died.
But you're my mom.

Fade *drops the Voynich Manuscript into the flames. It screams as it falls into the burning plants, cracking and lost forever.* **Harrison** *kisses* **Rue**. *It's real.*

Hannah   We got it. We have the insurance video.

Harrison *pushes* **Rue** *away. Rue falls to the ground, shell-shocked by the enormity of her loss.*

Harrison (*to* **Fade** *and* **Rue**)   You're free to go. The whole Heartland will be on watch for you. You've killed your last baby. I don't want to see you here ever again. God have mercy on all our souls.

Harrison *exits to her squad car.*

Jess   Come on, Hannah. Let's go home.
Hannah. It's over.
It's time to go home.
Now!

Hannah   I'm not going.

Jess & Fade   What?

Jess   Of course you're going.
Let's go.

---

12. Or maybe you have a campfire in your set design.

Hannah   This was wrong.
Rue didn't deserve this. Fade didn't.

Jess   Do you
I did this for you. For you.
The sheriff knew what you'd done. You were going to jail until I

Hannah   Was this your idea?

Jess   It
Well, not
It's not like that

Hannah   Then what's it like?

Jess   I have responsibilities. I'm your mother.
I wasn't going to let you

Hannah   THIS WAS MY CHOICE TO MAKE.

Jess   It's my fault.
You're my fault. I'm—I'm sorry you're this way.
It's in my blood, I gave you all the fuck-up genes. I'm so sorry, baby.
I wanted to make you better

Hannah   I'm not bad.

Jess   Don't be ridiculous, you're
You were pregnant, that doesn't just happen
You were making wrong choices and I needed to

Hannah (*hurt and hurting*)   I loved every minute of it.
Flirting. Kissing. The way he smelled.
Sucking his dick. Getting eaten out. Sex.
I'm glad. Glad I did it. I'd do it again.

Jess   How did it work out for you, Hannah?
Pregnant. Alone.
Men leave, Hannah. Because they can.
They don't know what it's like for us and they don't care.
Men leave. Yours did. Mine did. They always do.
Look what all this got you.
No man. No baby.

Hannah   I am enough for me.
I don't need you. Or him. Or a baby or anyone.
I need me.
Get out of here.

Jess   Hannah, you're the best thing that I've ever done and you're still screwed up.
I am begging you. Give me another chance to get one thing in my life right.

Hannah   Am I that broken to you?

The answer is no.
NO.

Jess   . . . My door is always open, baby.

Hannah *will never get what she needs from her mother, so there's nothing more to say.* **Jess** *exits. The sound of a slamming car door, then the squad car pulls away.* **Fade** *watches it go—***Hannah** *doesn't.*

Hannah   I'm
I'll go.

Rue   No.

She rises.

Fade (*uncertain*)   Rue . . .

Rue *and* **Fade** *look at each other.*

Fade   I'm not sorry.

Rue *looks into* **Fade**'s *eyes.*

Fade   We can . . .

Rue

Fade

Rue   Oxalis.

Fade   What?

Rue   Your herbalist name is Oxalis.

Fade   I'm

Words fail her.

Rue   You're a woman.[13]
I see you.
I would never have done what you just did. I would have gone down with the ship. Found a way to get the book out. You didn't. You're your own person, not just my apprentice.
It's time.

Fade   I don't know what to say.

Rue   You could say that you're sorry for sacrificing the life's work of two hundred generations of herbalists, but,
You're not sorry.

Fade   No. Our ancestors worked it all out before. We'll figure it out again.

---

13. If Fade is being played as nonbinary: "You're an adult."

Rue   It was the last thing of Wade's, I . . .
But I guess that's not true, is it?

Rue *holds* **Fade** *by the shoulders.*

Rue   You're my daughter.[14] What do you say?

Fade   I say . . .

She breathes. The weight of her heritage settles on her shoulders. She likes the way it feels.

Oxalis   Let's get to work.

Rue   Yes, Doctor.

Hannah *sobs a little.* **Rue** *and* **Oxalis** *give her a look.*

Hannah   It's just so
Goddammit.

Oxalis   Hannah, if you're
I mean, if you want.
There's a place for you here.

Hannah   What do we
Where would we go from here?

Rue   It's been a while since I've been on the run.
(*To* **Oxalis**.) You were right, Doctor.
There are a lot of Hannahs out there,
And they need us. We can't work safely in the Heartland anymore, but.
There's Hannahs everywhere.

Oxalis   You're welcome to join us as an apprentice.

Rue   Or
(*Making a significant glance at* **Oxalis**.) Whatever.

Oxalis   How does it sound?

Hannah   No.
Apprentice isn't right.
Maybe . . . advocate.
I'm going to start a new Manuscript.
The story of how we won the fight for abortion. Again.
Day . . . one.

Oxalis *and* **Rue** *get to work cleaning off the Ambulatory.* **Hannah** *starts the new Manuscript, doing what she can with what she has. The sun goes down.*

End of play.

---

14. Alt for enby Fade: "You're my blood."

Transcending Gender to "Soar Above the Earth" in Ty Defoe's *Firebird Tattoo*

Courtney Mohler

I sit in my home in Indianapolis, Indiana, early in the summer of 2020 as I write this introduction to Ty Defoe's deeply personal play *Firebird Tattoo*. Exemplary of Native American storytelling, Defoe's tale simultaneously takes me to the settings it evokes (an Ojibwe reservation, a tattoo shop in Chicago, "on top of a drum, in created sacred circles, other places that symbolically represent a mysterious woodland environment"; p. 348) and also crystallizes my awareness of the place I am in as I write.

The world has been connected over the past many moons by COVID-19; we are connected too through mounting evidence of the wealth and health disparities the powerful actively (or passively) work to render invisible year after year. My family's brick and wood paneled house, which is about a half mile from the White River, is blessed with mature trees: Red Maple, Sycamore, Walnut, Red Bud, Norway Spruce . . . Their grandeur creates a maze of sun and shade patchwork in which the cotton tails, ground squirrels, robins, and cardinals dodge and play. These are the traditional lands of the Miami, Delaware, Potawatomi, and Shawnee peoples, who traded, farmed, hunted, loved, prayed, mourned, created, invented, and passed on wisdom for generations in advance of and throughout white settler colonial violence, biological and militarized warfare, land theft, and removal policies.

"Indianapolis, Indiana." A place name that perfectly illustrates the seductive trick of "surrogation," performing the active forgetting of the material lives, past and present, of the regions' Indigenous peoples through a gesture of remembering (Roach 1996: 3). In this case, the very names of city and state make meaningless the violent historical experience of the Miami, Delaware, Potawatomi, and Shawnee peoples who presumably "once lived," but now are treated as though "vanished," leaving the space open for settler colonialism.

These kinds of sleight-of-hand illusions are ubiquitous in the relatively short story of the European and white-American conquest and occupation of North America. One such example is how settler colonialism has constructed, regulated, and constrained gender and sexuality norms for Indigenous people. The success of this effort can be measured in part by how Christian-Judeo constructions of "woman" and "man" are internalized and hold power within the Indigenous communities themselves.

In his foreword to *Two-Spirit Acts: Queer Indigenous Performances*, edited by Jean Elizabeth O'Hara, Cree playwright Tomson Highway explains how Western monotheism, which anthropomorphizes God into a (presumably straight, cis-gendered) male, subsumes Indigenous spirituality, which traditionally made room for spirit in all animate forms:

> In pantheism [. . .] the idea of divinity has NO human form. It is simply an energy, a "great spirit" that functions like an electrical bolt that shoots its way through the universe animating everyone and all that it touches and/or passes through, which is one reason why pantheistic languages don't even have a "he"

or a "she." In that system, therefore, we are all he/shes. As is god, one would think. Meaning to say that, within the pantheistic system, there is at least room for the idea of divinity in the female form.

(2013: xvi)

He goes on to explain that in the process of colonization, Christian ideas about divinity and humanity as closed patriarchal systems waged war against Native spiritual and social practices; colonialism operates most effectively in the realm of gender conditioning. "On the vertical straight line of monotheism [. . .] there is room for two genders only, male and female, with the former having complete power over the other. On the circle of pantheism, on the other hand, there is room for many genders" (2013: xv–xvi). Indigenous communities, from time immemorial, had traditional methods for recognizing and empowering all of the peoples in their communities, including those who did not match the usual life-paths of most males or most females. Highway states, "the people who were physically, emotionally, psychologically, and spiritually equipped for neither role – that is, the people who were both male and female, who were spiritual hermaphrodites – they took care of the emotional and spiritual life of the family, the community" (2013: xvi).

In his one-man play *Agokwe,* Grassy Narrows First Nation playwright Waawaate Fobister plays the trickster spirit Nanabush, who tells the audience, "If they (two-spirits, *agokwe*) did extraordinary things in their lives that broke with tradition it was assumed they had the spiritual authority to do so [. . .] They were shamans, healers, mediators, and interpreters of dreams whose lives were devoted to the welfare of the group" (O'Hara 2013: 101). Unfortunately, colonial notions of binary gender expression and compulsory heterosexuality infiltrated Indigenous communities for decades, replacing traditional spiritual reverence for those on the gender or sexuality spectrum with homophobia, transphobia, and sexism.

The pantribal term "two-spirit," sometimes abbreviated as 2S, can be seen as both recuperative and generative as it looks to pre-conquest wisdom to address contemporary issues of identity, belonging, and decolonization.[1] The editors of *Sovereign Erotics: A Collection of Two-Spirit Literature* posit this helpful definition of "two-spirit":

Two-spirit or two-spirited is an umbrella term in English that (1) refers to the gender constructions and roles that occur historically in many Native gender systems that are outside of the colonial binaries (2) refers to contemporary Native people who are continuing and/or reclaiming these roles within their communities. It is also [. . .] meant to be inclusive of those who identify as two-spirit or with tribally specific terms, but also GLBTQ Native people more broadly.

(Driskill, et al. 2001: 4)

Whereas colonial, linear thinking and (even liberal, progressive) identity politics might challenge the inherent specificity and inclusivity of "two-spirit" as contradictory,

1. For a detailed analysis on the pantribal adoption of the term "two-spirit" and away from the term "berdache," as well as the limitations Native American suprabinary folx experienced in both their tribal communities which had largely adopted colonized notions of gender and sexuality, as well as the gay and lesbian communities of the 1990s which for all their progressive values, were ingrained within settler systems that were often "more focused on sexuality than on gender," see Robinson (2019: 3–8).

2S activists, educators, artists, and writers value this flexibility as rooted in Indigenous ways of knowing and being in community. Cherokee 2S dancer and scholar Qui-li Driskill writes, "Indigenous Two-Spirit/GLBTQ people are asserting uniquely Native-centered and tribally specific understandings of gender and sexuality as a way to critique colonialism, queerphobia, racism and misogyny as part of decolonial struggles" (2010: 69). This kind of celebration of boundary-surfing and norm-shaking is the personal lived experience of 2S individuals, and at the same time has critically important consequences for Native communities moving beyond colonially enforced notions of gender and sexuality.

The need to strictly define and categorize identities, which has been strategically essential for many marginalized groups (including trans and queer activists), is in some ways itself a product of settler colonialism. The lines are purposely blurred between two-spirit and other GLBTQ terms and identities in part because two-spirit identity is rooted in Indigenous wisdom systems, which do not adhere to binaries no neat categorizations easily. They are fluid and always in a dance with tradition and community's present and future realities and needs. In an interview for the "Teaching Artistry Podcast," Defoe explains:

> Two-spirit is a term that's coined by many Indigenous communities as someone that identifies on a type of gender spectrum [. . .] I say *niizh maindoowag* and the real translation of something like that is "two-spirit" but even further than that the verb means "to transcend gender" [. . .] Not meaning you're above gender, and that's like beyond something, or below it, but you're transcending gender meaning it's just something else.

> (Boddie 2016)

This specifically Indigenous way of framing gender and/or sexuality identification and expression is widely inclusive; two-spirit identity can include people who would be identified or self-identify as trans, but also applies to those who would self-identify as queer, gay, or lesbian. Some 2S folx identify as 2S and trans, or 2S and queer, for example; others only identify as 2S. As there is no singular path toward cultural sovereignty, each tribal community navigates and challenges settler colonialism, racism, sexism, patriarchy, climate destruction, and imperialist capitalism with vastly different approaches. There are ongoing debates throughout Indigenous America over how, when, and whether to eradicate these colonial systems. Such debates offer fertile ground for Indigenous art-makers, creators empowered by the Great Spirit to transform the discourse around Native life.

Ty Defoe (Giizhig) is one such Indigenous artist, "rooted in words, a shape-shifter of artistic expression, bringing stories to life," as his website indicates. Defoe is a two-spirit interdisciplinary artist, storyteller, writer, actor, dancer, musician, performance artist, and educator now based in New York City. In addition to his own creative work, he is known for his Grammy Award-winning music and his 2018 Broadway performance in Young Jean Lee's experimental play *Straight White Men*. Embodying a multiplicity of identities, all important manifestations of his spirit and artistic practice, he writes, "These ways of identifying are only parts of me, but as I move through the world, I find that I can't take off my identities like a jacket and simply hang them in a closet. They are interwoven, and in creating any theatre that has verisimilitude or humanity, I must lean into the intersection of identities" (2015). Defoe shape-shifts through his spiritual and creative practices, describing his transformation into two-spirit as an embodiment of shape-shifting power that he does not separate from his identity as an interdisciplinary story-teller.

Defoe grew up in Wisconsin, rooted in his parents' Ojibwe and Oneida traditions. As a child, he learned to hoop dance as soon as he could walk; at the age of seven he began to study and practice the traditional arts and storytelling with esteemed Hoop Dancer and Lakota flute player Kevin Locke (Mistry 2016). For years Defoe and Locke toured the globe, enacting creative reciprocity by sharing their traditional artistry in exchange with other communities and cultures. He describes this practice of cultural, artistic, and linguistic exchange as "a type of gift-giving." He shares, "that (gift-giving) is essential for what I like to think of as art: the reciprocity of exchange or the reciprocity of teachings" (Boddie 2019). This belief propels Defoe to not only dedicate his life to making art, but also inspires how he willingly writes his own story into his work, as an act of gift-giving he hopes illustrates the interconnections between us all. He writes:

> I want to honor the past of my ancestors and pave roads for future generations who are coming to the theatre and will have a multitude of racial and gender identities. I want them to see and hear themselves on the American stage [. . .] There is a teaching I received when I was given a sacred hoop dance. It was that we are all connected in this great circle of life [. . .] In a circle there are no corners in which to hide, and in this circle unifying all living things, we must stand next to and across from each other equals.
>
> (2015)

But, before we can regard each other as equals, we must see each other. *Firebird Tattoo* is one of his gifts to us all, trans and cis, queer and straight, Indigenous and non-Indigenous, "all living things," to see two-spirit in story, in community, in theatre.

To make visible a two-spirit story within one's tribe itself may be a tremendous challenge; to bring that story to an audience who may have little if any experience with Indigenous cultures or two-spirit identities may also prove complicated. Preceding a 2016 interview with Defoe in *Fader* magazine, Anupa Mistry writes, "You might say that Defoe's identity – political, social, spiritual – is defined by a kind of *Un*freedom. To be native and two spirit in America [. . .] is to inhabit fraught territory, geographically and physically" (2016). *Firebird Tattoo*, a theatrical gift intended to create and hold space across multiple communities, explores the exhilarating, painful, complex, spiritual journeys of three 2S Ojibwe characters.

Firebird Tattoo evokes themes of interconnection, shape-shifting, transcending above linear, colonial notions of gender, sexuality, and tradition within a tribal community. This tightly crafted work connects the stories of Sky, an Ojibwe girl on the cusp of her eighteenth birthday, who is resistant to participate in her own womanhood ceremony, and her late father Eagle, whose constant presence in the play takes the form of Landa Lakes. Landa Lakes is a beautiful two-spirit/queer dancer and "an actual/ spirit," who sings and dances during key moments within the play (p. 348). Landa Lakes lovingly haunts Sky's mother, Shinood/Ma, to whom Eagle was once married, and guides Sky to learn about Eagle's past so that Sky might find her own truth.

We also meet Sky's Uncle Philip, a two-spirit comic with secrets to tell. At the play's opening, Sky's overbearing Ma feverishly prepares for Sky's moon cycle ceremony, biting birch bark and picking strawberries for the traditional give-away portion of the celebration, despite Sky's disinterest. Ma ignores Sky's questions about Eagle's disappearance from their lives, emotionally closed to her late husband's truth and to why Sky seeks answers. Against Ma's knowledge or consent, Uncle Philip takes Sky to Chicago, where she finds the Sacred Skin tattoo parlor and meets D. Chance, the "rough and tumble" white lesbian owner of the shop (p. 348). Over a ten-hour inking session, which Landa Lakes closely haunts, D. gives Sky her first tattoo: an elaborate depiction of a firebird, copied from Sky's journal. They share intimate stories, and begin to weave threads of their pasts together with romantic tension bubbling between them.

D   What does this design mean to you?

SKY   The bird means one day

   I'll fly from it all

   And leave it all behind

   I'll soar above the earth.

(pp. 369–370)

The theme of discovering oneself, and seeing who one is and where one belongs in relationship with community, is central in *Firebird Tattoo*. Even as Sky discovers that she needs to separate from her controlling Ma and the stifling smallness of her reservation, she goes to the city to connect with her father, and helps Eagle/Landa to move on to the next world.

Sky finds herself in the position to help her father's spirit because Eagle died without resolving his "unfinished business," leaving his daughter in the dark about who he was and why he left (p. 369). Eagle and Uncle Philip each left the reservation, with their two-spirit identities shrouded in secrecy and shame. In sharing the darkness of these 2S stories, *Firebird Tattoo* dramatizes the ways in which some tribal communities have internalized colonial notions of gender and sexuality. Through Sky's journey into her father's "unfinished business," Defoe holds up a mirror to Indigenous and settler audiences, inviting reflection on how narrow concepts of identity can hurt families, individuals, and communities.

In a 2013 interview with Miccosukee Magazine TV, a younger Defoe educates a riveted audience on the power of the Eagle dance, beginning with the beauty of the Eagle:

It speaks to us about the peace and the nobility that the eagle brings to us [. . .] We see this bird all the time depicted in pictures and movies and we look at the beautiful, beautiful wings that the eagle has, we see it soaring in the sky. This dance you are about to see is an emulation, a depicting of having a human being like that eagle, okay. What that means is to imagine ourselves having the ability to soar above all things.

Defoe then goes on to indeed shape-shift into the soaring eagle, transforming from human to eagle and back again, but also merging the two spirits at once. Before Sky's journey, Eagle was not permitted to merge his two spirits, because he died believing the reservation would find his dressing in his wife's feminine regalia, his two-spirit expression, "ugly" (p. 353). At one point Uncle Philip explains to Sky that he too left the rez because "If anyone found out I'm Two-Spirit/That's it./I'd be erased" (p. 354). In the city, Landa shows Sky visions of past encounters between Ma and Eagle, Eagle and Uncle Philip, and Uncle Philip and Ma.

The play's structure follows what Christy Stanlake calls "Native American dramaturgy," as the story folds scenes from the past into the present, weaves dreams with waking reality, and merges the spirit world with the physical world. "Such earthly/ spiritual interconnections open dramaturgical possibilities as [. . .] the synthesis of distant eras, and in doing, Native dramaturgy capitalizes on the extreme possibilities of human potential" (Stanlake 2009: 23–24). *Firebird Tattoo*'s Native dramaturgy leads its audience in a sacred circle; questions from the first scene regarding tradition, identity, and the role of change within survival are resolved by the play's last scene. In Scene 1, Ma states her investment in Sky's womanhood ceremony: "It's what our people have done for over 10,000 years!" (p. 351). Ma clings to certain traditions, in this case the ceremony designed to cement Sky's gender as woman, but ignores the diverse two-spirit needs and identities of her brother, her late husband, and her daughter. This tension reveals the complexity of Ojibwe society in the context of settler colonialism.

When Sky pleads with her that she needs a change, her Ma responds, "Change is bad medicine" (p. 352). But Sky does not accept that. She replies, "We need change to survive" (p. 352). Here Sky speaks with the wisdom of the ancestors who honored two-spirit people, *niizh maindoowag*, within their communities. The ancestors who lived before colonial gendered thinking took root in Native America understood that difference, transformation, and shape-shifting hold powerful medicine for the people. By the play's final scene, Sky receives a new name, "Ode'imm, the heart berry" (p. 385). Her journey and realization of her sexual desire and gender non-conformity does not come at the price of her identity as Ojibwe. Rather, she is two-spirit, and full of forgiveness for anyone that would have her choose between these aspects of herself. In the play's final moments, "Sky's family and all the spirits including D. face the four directions as Sky tosses her notebook into the fire" (p. 385), releasing her "deepest thoughts" (p. 382), from the secrecy of heart into the world through the regenerative spirit of fire.

Firebird Tattoo articulates the spiritual and creative responsibilities of the two-spirit artist in the twenty-first century. The audience does not ultimately learn whether the character, Sky, will choose to transition, but it witnesses her reject completing the ceremony to become a "woman" simply because her biology gave her a moon cycle. By rejecting this gender-specific ritual, she leaves room for her 2S expression to develop, and she connects with a pre-colonial Indigenous understanding of gender. The characters, plot, and structure of *Firebird Tattoo* transform audience expectations of Indigenous tradition, spirituality, and intergenerational responsibility to accept non-normative gender identity and sexuality. The different kinds of 2S identity expressed through the characters Sky, Uncle Philip, and Eagle/Landa, indicate how fluid, flexible, and expansive two-spirit identity can be.

As a two-spirit play, *Firebird Tattoo* reflects Indigenous ways of knowing, loving, and being that transcend colonial notions of gender and sexuality. This radical transcendence multiplies, includes, and embraces Indigenous traditions and values that served the people for generations before colonial gender construction took hold. Like two-spirit identity itself, *Firebird Tattoo* actively decolonizes by rejecting closed definitions of "woman," "man," and "traditional," instead offering an open window into the limitless blue sky of "just something else" (Bodie 2016).

References

Boddie, Courtney. 2019. "Episode 20: Ty Defoe – Story Nurturer." Boddie interviews Ty Defoe, Teaching Artistry Podcast, July 11. New York City, https://soundcloud.com/user-4096609/tawcjb-ep-20-final

Darby, Jaye T., et al. 2020. *Critical Companion to Native American and First Nations Theatre and Performance: Indigenous Spaces.* London: Bloomsbury.

Defoe, Ty. 2015. "A Red Face in the Crowd: Identities of a Native Americans Two-Spirit Writer." Howlround.com, February 25. https://howlround.com/red-face-crowd§hash.4ggSRhGW.dpuf

Defoe, Ty. 2020. "TyDefoe.com." www.TyDefoe.com

Driskill, Quo-Li. 2010. "Two-Spirit Critiques: Building Alliances between Native and Queer Studies." *GLQ: A Journal of Lesbian and Gay Studies* 16, 1–2: 69–92.

Driskill, Quo-Li, et al., editors. 2001. *Sovereign Erotics: A Collection of Two-Spirit Literature.* Tucson, AZ: University Arizona Press.

Highway, Tomson. 2013. "Where Is God's Wife? Or Is he Gay?" In *Two-Spirit Acts: Queer Indigenous Performances*, edited by Jean O'Hara, xii–xvii. Toronto: Playwrights Canada Press.

Miccosukee Magazine TV. 2013. "Thirza Defoe, OV-307-3," YouTube, March 20. https://www.youtube.com/watch?v=2ODXIL12frs

Mistry, Anupa. 2016. "How Two-Spirit Fits into LGBTQ America: Ty Defoe Talks about Finding an Identity other than Trans that was Part of His Native American Heritage All Along." *Fader Magazine*, September 8. http://thefader.com/2016/09/09/two-spirit-america-ty-defoe

O'Hara, Jean, editor. 2013. *Two-Spirit Acts: Queer Indigenous Performances.* Toronto: Playwrights Canada Press.

Roach, Joseph. 1996. *Cities of the Dead: Circum-Atlantic Performance.* New York: Columbia University Press.

Robinson, Margaret. 2019. "Two-Spirit Identity in a Time of Gender Fluidity," *Journal of Homosexuality*, May 24. https://doi.org/10.1080/00918369.2019.1613853

Stanlake, Christy. 2009. *Native American Drama: A Critical Perspective.* Cambridge, UK: Cambridge University Press.

Firebird Tattoo

Ty Defoe

Characters

Sky | Ojibwe, eighteen, two-spirit/queer, innocent. Bookish and boyish and nerdy. She is young with an old spirit. Seeks adventure and self-discovery.

Shinood | "Ma," Ojibwe female, Sky's mother. Takes up a lot of space in a room. Snide, yet paranoid, easily distrusts and dismisses others.

Eagle | Ojibwe, two-spirit/queer, Sky's father. Can be self-loathing at times. Has an urgent need to run away. Is sincere and hides who he is. Same actor plays Landa Lakes, who is an actual dead/spirit and is two-spirit/queer. She is very fabulous and feminine. Speaks with a sense of candor and honesty. A peacemaker.

Uncle Phillip | Ojibwe two-spirit/queer male, Sky's uncle, brother of Shinood. Aspires to be the best stand-up comedian in the world. Avoids conflicts. There is a likable zest about his presence.

D. Chance | twentysomething, white queer female. Tattoo artist. She is rough-and-tumble and, at times, awkward.

Announcer | (can be played by someone in the ensemble or voiceover recording)

Setting

Various locations in poetic and fluid worlds: Inside a tattoo shop, on top of a drum, in created sacred circles, other places that symbolically represent a mysterious woodland environment.

Time

In Strawberry Moon, *Ode-imini-giizis*, present, past, and future.

Playwright Notes

Expressionist with a dash of hyper-realism and tons of rez humor! This production could be viewed as novella-like.

/ Indicates actor interrupting dialog.

Scenes are there as a guide and places flow from one scene to the next like a river or circles or fragments.

Scene One: That Queer Stirring Feeling . . . You Know the Kind

The sun rises over water on a small reservation in the north.

Sky, *Ojibwe, black hair in Timberland boots, black hipster glasses, and a flannel. She always carries her pocket knife and her notebook.*

Sky *performs a song to herself with a guitar as if she were at an open mic.*

Then a rainbow.

As **Sky** *sings,* **Eagle** *as* **Landa Lakes** *appears from the sage that burns in a shell. She places a buckskin medicine pouch like a prayer song around her neck, then joins her in song.*

Sky *does not see* **Landa Lakes**.

Sky and Landa Lakes
    EAGLE GIRL, EAGLE GIRL
    THERE YOU ARE SITTING
    IN A TREE LOOKING
    DOWN AT ME WHERE
    ARE YOU GOING?
    WHERE ARE YOU OFF TO NEXT?
    YOU ARE LEAVIN' THE NEST.

    EAGLE GIRL, EAGLE GIRL
    YOU LIKE THE WATER
    LET ME TOUCH YOUR FEATHERS

    GO A LITTLE FURTHER FOR ME
    YOU MADE ME CRY
    LET ME TELL YOU WHY
    YOU TAKE THE CITY LIGHTS
    AND PUT THEM ON A STRING
    YOU'RE MEANT TO DO SOMETHING.

    THERE YOU GO UP YOU GO . . .
    THERE YOU GO UP YOU GO . . .
    THERE YOU GO UP YOU GO . . .
    THERE YOU GO UP YOU GO . . .

    EAGLE GIRL, EAGLE GIRL
    WITH ALL YOUR MIGHT WHEN DO YOU TAKE FLIGHT?
    EAGLE GIRL OFF YOU GO IN THE NIGHT . . .

    OOOOOO
    OOOOOO

Landa Lakes *fades.*

Sky *riffs until interrupted.*

Yellow sun.

Ma *is heard in a panic.*

Ma   Sky! Get out of the clouds and get to helping me bite this birch bark for the giveaway!

Sky *bites a piece of birch bark.*

Sky   How many of these do we have to make for the ceremony thing-a-ma-jig? My teeth already hurt. Lah!

Ma   Enough gifts for everyone and anyone who ever cared about you and their children.
The grandmas
The grandpas
Aunties
Uncles
And their children.

Ma *takes a bite of birch bark.*

Sky   That's too many people.

Ma   You're becoming a woman.

Sky *spits out the birch bark.*

Sky   I am a woman.

Ma   Not yet, girl.

Ma *spits out the bark.*

Sky   I turn eighteen tomorrow.

Ma   That doesn't matter here.

Sky   This ceremony thing is long overdue. I started bleeding like four years ago.

Ma   I don't care what age you were when you had your moon cycle/

Sky   Can we just call it bleeding?

Sky *takes a bite of bark.*

Ma   Ah-ah-ah! Don't speak of it like that. It's your moon cycle. Sky/

Sky   Cycle.
Moon.
Blood.
Rag. Whatever.
Been there done that.
Why does this have to happen?
It's awful.
And I don't get why there's some "special event" for it.

Sky *spits out the bark.*

Ma   It's a ritual.
Celebration.
Gathering.
It connects women to the moon and lets us know we are celebrating life.

Sky   Gross.

Ma   It's special.

Sky   Why?! I don't get it, the rest of the world doesn't operate like this/

Ma   It's our tradition.

Sky   Why don't we just say "my hormones-are-raging" and call that tradish!

Ma   This tradition is the survival of our people—it keeps people alive and rituals continuing. These gifts here contain lots of medicine—we have strawberries to pick yet, so keep on biting that bark, girl!

Ma *takes a bite.*

Sky   Well, whatever this ritual is, feels like pow-wow drums are pounding on the inside of my stomach.

Ma   Now you're being dramatic.

Sky   If you were in this much pain you'd be dramatic too.

Ma   I was when I had you.

Ma *takes a bite of bark and spits it out.*

Sky   We're going to be here all night, for days.

Sky *bites and spits.*

Ma   If that's what it takes.
All of us will gather next week for you and I just want you to be prepared.

Sky   I wish dad was still here, he wouldn't make me do this.

Ma *takes a bite of the bark and spits.*

Ma   You know, Sky, we couldn't do this when you were younger.
I couldn't do it alone.
We could n't afford it either.
If your father was around more, maybe it would have been different.

Sky   Then let's not do it.
This ritual lady thing is the last thing I want to do.
It's so archaic!

Ma   It's what our people have done for over 10,000 years!

Sky   I want to go to the city.

Ma *chokes on the birch bark and swallows.*

Ma   Ain't nobody got time for that!

Sky   Uncle Phil said I should see what it's like.

Ma   What did I tell you about the city?

Overlapping:

Sky   It's filled with people who are crooks. They'll rob you, take your money. Use you for everything you're worth.

Ma: It's filled with people who are crooks! They'll rob you blind, take your money. Use you for everything you are worth.

End of overlap.

Sky   But, I don't have any money.

Ma   Worth isn't always money—think about that, Sky.
Value.
Who invented money?
Listen to me, Sky—
I've been to the city before.
It smells like rotten socks and you can't even see the stars at night.
The city lights will blind you.

Sky   But, Ma, that's exactly what I want to experience/

Ma   Nah! Gives me a migraine!

Sky   No, those lights are just like the sun and moon.

Ma   That's all in your head.

Sky   I'm so sick of it here!

Sky *spits.*

Ma   Sky . . . when you were a baby, did you know, I would look down at my skirt and there you were hanging on to me for dear life, like a little wood tick. A little ezi-gaa. Sticking to me.

Ma *takes a bite and spits.*

Sky   I'm going to visit the city. I've saved up money for it.

Ma   All these years I never left your side.

Sky   I need a change, Ma.

Ma   Change is bad medicine.

Sky   We need change to survive.

Ma   Survive on my big toe! (*She spits.*)
You know what? Go then. Go, Sky.

Go and leave me just like Eagle did. Good for nothin' father/

Sky   Ma, don't/

Ma   But I don't know why he keeps showing me his ugly second spirit.

Sky   Because you're still holding on to him!

Ma   I'm not the only one.

Sky   I still don't understand what happened to him.

Ma   He left you for the city.
He left me for the war.
He left us
—and never came back the same. But,
his gosh darn spirit will show up.

Sky   That doesn't make sense to me, something is missing.

Ma   Gaa-ween.
You'll learn.
If it's the hard way, you'll learn.
I have work to finish.

Ma *spits out bark and fades into a shadow.*

Sky *spits out bark.*

The moon shifts.

Landa Lakes *does a whirl as her braid sweeps the floor.*

Scene Two: Sky and Uncle Make a Promise

Uncle Phillip *lights a cigarette with a lighter.*

The sun rises like bread.

He sings as he carves a piece of wood.

Uncle Phillip   Way hey, hey, hey yo
Ode'imi
yah, hey yo,
hey yah, yah.

Sky *sees* **Uncle Phillip** *and the carving.*

Sky   She's beautiful, Uncle.

Uncle Phillip *holds it up.*

Uncle Phillip   Not sure what she wants to be yet.

Sky   She has two heads.

Uncle Phillip   A double-headed bird, good one.

Sky *picks up the carving.*

Sky   Hey, this looks like the tattoo on your arm. It's so smooth.

Uncle Phillip   It is!
Gotta have lotta patience.

Uncle Phillip *whistles and animates the bird.* **Sky** *and* **Uncle Phillip** *share a moment.*

Uncle Phillip   You know, I started this carving the day your father passed. I
found this piece of wood.
I could only stare at it for weeks.
Just the other day I picked it back up again . . .

Time passes.

Sky   Why did you leave here and move to Chicago.

Uncle Phillip   I dunno, I dunno.

Sky   I'm not going to tell anyone. Is it because—

Uncle Phillip   This reservation is way too small.
If anyone found out I'm two-spirit
That's it.
I'd be erased.

Sky   Why? I don't understand. I think
No.
That's just it. You shouldn't have to.
—And I dunno.

You're just really, really smart, and funny, and you only listen to pow-wow music and
Barbara Streisand, and I didn't even know who that was until I saw some Facebook GIF.

Uncle Phillip   Okay, okay, okay now.
—And you missed the part that I'm really, really, really good looking, whollay
wah!

Uncle Phillip *animates the bird again as they share a laugh.*

Sky   Uncle, will you take me to the city?

Uncle Phillip   Sky, baby girl, you know I want to, but you got a big thing coming up
next week.

Sky   Don't remind me.

Uncle Phillip   The timing is really bad and you know your ma will chew me out.

Sky   If you won't take me, then I'll hitchhike.

Uncle Phillip   Absolutely not.
Dangerous.

Sky   I'll take a bus then.

Uncle Phillip   There ain't no bus around here for miles, you know that.

Sky   Then I'll find a way.

Uncle Phillip   Girl, you are the daughter of your father.

Sky   Ya. And he went, didn't he?

Uncle Phillip   What you going to tell that ma of yours?

Sky   I'll just tell her.

Uncle Phillip   She's not going to let you.

Sky   Uncle, my ceremony is next week, there are things I need to know about my dad before I can go through with this lady ceremony or whatever. I need answers. I need you to help me. Please.

Beat.

Uncle Phillip   Okay.

Beat.

Sky   Okay?

Uncle Phillip   Be ready tomorrow morning.
Bags packed and all.
We'll go.
I'll talk to your ma.

Sky   I can't wait!

Sky *gives* **Uncle Phillip** *a big hug.*

Uncle   Hey.
I was waiting for the right time to give you these. (*He hands her two photos.*)
Here.

Sky *examines the photos.*

Sky   These are hip.

Uncle   They're called Polaroids. You know, I am very hip.

One photo is of **Eagle** *dressed in a ribbon dress and the other is* **Eagle** *and* **Uncle Phillip** *in front of a tattoo shop in Chicago.*

Sky   I miss him.

Uncle Phillip   I know.
Me too.

The sun is copper.

Landa Lakes *is present, spins her braid like a short lasso.*

Scene Three: The Funny Bone Cafe: Ha-Ha-Ha

A fun Funny Bone Café song like Johnny Cash's "A Boy Named Sue" plays.

A spotlight whirls around the room looking for **Uncle Phillip**.

A stage, a microphone, a glass of water.

Announcer   Welcome, you funny people, to the Funny Bone Café!
We are pleased to welcome you to amateur night!
Tonight, directly off the reservation,
The Funny Bone Café would like welcome Chief King Phillip!
He speaks English,
stands six feet tall
and can play the Indian love flute while tribal chanting.
He's here to give us some ancient Indian wisdom!

An applause sign is held up.

Announcer   Put your funny bones together for Chief King Phillip!

An applause sign is held up.

Uncle Phillip *takes a sip from the glass and taps on the microphone; it reverbs.*

He is in his best Western wear.

Uncle Phillip   Um, howdy, hello everyone,
The name's Phillip, that's Phil as in Phillip or Philly.
Named after Metacomet.
And I don't mean comet from outer space.

Beat.
I have my niece visiting me here tonight.
And no, her name isn't Denise!
It's Sky.

Beat.
Okay, well . . .
A Cherokee man
goes into a grocery store
and asks for a package of toilet paper.
The clerk offers him three kinds,
Charmin, best brand, and generic.
The Cherokee man takes the generic.
He comes back a week later,
throws what's left of the toilet paper at the store clerk, and says, "I
don't want no cheap John Wayne toilet paper!"
The clerk laughs and says, "It's not John Wayne toilet paper, it's *generic* toilet paper."
The Cherokee guy tells him,

'You can call it whatever you want, but it's rough, tough, and won't take the crap off nobody!"

Laughter from the audience.

The sound of a drum beating like a heartbeat.

So, what do you call a white guy surrounded by ten Indians?

Beat.
A bartender!

A few laughs.
Well, then, what do you call a white guy surrounded by 100 Indians?

Beat.
A bingo caller!

A few more laughs.
What do you get when you go to an Indian garage sale?

Beat.
All your stuff back.

Laughter as he takes another sip from the glass.
Anyone in the audience want to volunteer?
I need ten white people.
You, sir?
How about you, ma'am?
You?

He looks through audience to find people and hands them fake plastic headbands and feathers.

Now, you will be dropped on the reservation where you will have to endure one week of: hardship, gossiping, backstabbing, jealousy, tipi creeping, and 49-ing, and be able to survive on high-fat cholesterol foods that are USDA approved. (My favorite is the Velveeta cheese blocks.)

He uses his cheesiest announcer voice.
The contestants will be given:
Four to five sacred rocks. A car with no doors.
Unwinterized HUD housing.
Three days' worth of food stamps.
Cigarettes without filters.
Five days of continuous *Pow-Wow Highway* and *Dances with Wolves* clips.
Moccasins and feathers to wear around the reservation—which demonstrates cultural sensitivity to inhabitants.

He is deep into his routine.
Survivors will then receive:
Authentic handmade Indian Dream Catchers, from China!
Homemade tattoos!

Pendleton blankets *and*
a medicine bag!

He does a "war-hoop" and throws his fist in the air.

There is "lu-lu" heard from somewhere in the room.

Hey, I'm not a racist, I have colored TV!

He takes another drink from the glass sitting on the stool.

He downs the glass completely and flips over the glass on the stool.

Beat.

Silence.

Beat.

Announcer   Um, thank you, thank you, King Phillip.

Uncle Phillip   Know these two things from an average Indian and you'll get your very own Indian name.
One.
Never take life seriously, nobody gets out alive anyway.
Two.
Behind every successful man is a surprised woman.

Announcer   Alright, please get off the stage, Chief, make your way to the next camp, thank you!

Uncle Phillip *is staggering and pacing the stage like a wolf.*

A spotlight follows.

Uncle Phillip   In God we trust everybody, all others must pay cash!

He tangles his legs in the microphone wire.

Music is a blur.

The moon is blue outside. Drunk **Uncle Phillip** *is over* **Sky**'s *shoulder as she holds him up.*

Sky   You're so heavy, Uncle.

Uncle Phillip   You think I'm fat?

Sky   No!

Uncle Phillip   So, I gained a little weight in the past two months.
I'll get back on the wagon.

Sky   You were really funny tonight.

Uncle Phillip   I don't feel so good.

Sky   Let's chill a moment.

They find a place for a minute to rest.

Uncle Phillip   CHI MIIGWEEEETTTCCCCCHHHH, my girl.
You are going to do great things in life. I know it. I know it, I know it. I
knew it when you were a little bitty Sky.

Sky   Ya and now look who is carrying who.

Uncle Phillip   Oh dear crazy-horse-and-all-those-followers-from-Wanderlust . . .
When will it end?!

Sky   Here, have some water.

Uncle Phillip   Miigwetch, my girl. (*He takes a few sips.*)
Did you know I watch Disney movies for material? (*He guzzles the water.*)
I'm sorry you have to see me like this.

Sky   It's okay.

Uncle Phillip   Your dad was my bestie.

Sky   I know.

Uncle Phillip   It's just been so hard you know.

Sky   Ya.
Uncle?

Uncle Phillip   Anything for you.
Anything, anything.

Sky   Can you tell me about my dad?

Uncle Phillip   The only thing I will tell you is . . .
he was a beautiful man.
That's all I can tell you.
That's all I can say . . .
That's all I know.
a beautiful, beautiful,
beautiful man.

He falls sleep.

Sky *holds* **Uncle Phillip**.

Landa Lakes *is present. Neither* **Sky** *nor* **Uncle Phillip** *see or hear as they dance
with a feather fan and detachable braid.*

Sky *takes out her photos.*

She falls asleep.

The moon is brilliant and reveals a firebird inside of it.

Scene Four

Landa Lakes *pours silver water onto the moon.*

Whispers and voices are heard.

D *and* **Sky** *are both in tattoo chairs.*

The buzzing of a tattoo motor is laced throughout the lines.

Sky   Dreams are my scars
while pictures of ashes are rising
Following flames.

D   Tattoos are my journal,
my skin is my canvas.
The buzzing is in the air.

D *shows her forearm and reads.*

Sky   I dream of change,
I write on birch bark
or paper.

Sky *reads from her notebook.*

D   Nightmares and night sweats.
I lost her in war
Sketch on my skin . . .

Sky   I'll find the pulse of a new place
The pulse of love.

D   I'll tattoo my past, here.
A new sketch.
The heart is for love.

Sky   A Polaroid of dad . . . In a dress with ribbons
I need more truth.

Sky and D   Painful, beautiful
Disasters

Sky   Raindrops like sequins
Sewn on a black shawl
my dad wore.

D   It only looks painful but it's not . . .
If I could just get through it . . .
It will rain today . . .

Sky   Falling asleep at night
humming his song
Way hey ya hey ya hey ya . . .

Sky and D   This I know . . .

Sky *sings a song.*

She has her notebook.

> EAGLE'S GIRL, EAGLE'S GIRL
> YOU LIKE THE WATER
> LET ME TOUCH YOUR FEATHERS
> GO A LITTLE FURTHER FOR ME.
>
> YOU MADE ME CRY LET ME TELL YOU WHY
>
> YOU TAKE THE CITY LIGHTS
> AND PUT THEM ON A STRING,
> YOU/I WAS MEANT TO DO SOMETHING.
>
> EAGLE'S GIRL, EAGLE'S GIRL
> WITH ALL YOUR MIGHT
> WHEN DO YOU TAKE FLIGHT?
>
> EAGLE'S GIRL OFF YOU GO IN THE NIGHT.
> OOOOOO

D *fades in shadows.*

Landa Lakes *combs her hair as if she is getting ready in the morning.*

Scene Five: Sky Meets D

The sun becomes orange.

The tattoo shop.

Pictures of tattooed body parts and sexy people hang on the wall.

D *is dirty and sexy. Boots and jeans.*

D   Christ. Not again.

D *sweeps broken glass from the small window.*

Sky *looks hungry—was she just busking outside? Probably.*

Sky   Um. Hi, there.
I need your help.

D   It's 6a.m.?

Sky   This isn't going to take long/

D   Wait, who are you?

Sky   Sky.

D   Sky?—like above?

Sky   Yes.
The sky
Above.

D *stops sweeping.*

D   Wait, were you in my dream?
I think I'm having déjà vu/

Sky   Me too.

D   Did you come in before?

There is this weird attraction between them.

D *test buzzes an ink motor.*

Sky   No.
Is your tongue pierced?

D   So forward.
Yep.
Sure is.

Look darlin'.
If you want to get painted on, come back tonight.

Sky   I'm just needin' info about the people in this photo.

Sky *pulls out a photo.*

D *looks at it.*

D   WOW. A Polaroid.
This was so long ago
When I first got this shop.
I gave that guy a tattoo.

Sky   So, this is the tattoo shop in the photo.

D   Yep. Sacred Skin!
At the time, tribal tattoos were in.

Sky   That's weird.

D   What is?

Sky   Giving out tribal tattoos when they aren't earned.

D   Well, aren't you woke, someone call the PC police.

Sky   Which guy did you give the tat to?

D   The funny one.

Sky   EAGLE?!

D   Listen, I have so much work to do.

Can you believe this happened last—(**D** *begins to sweep.*)
Broken glass, spilled ink, needles everywhere. Also, watch your step.

Sky   Sounds dangerous.

D   Yah. Very nasty.

Sky   Awful.

D   Disgusting.

Sky   And dirty.

Beat.

D   Yep. Very dirty.

Sky   Heeeeeyyyy, I don't know you. You don't know me.
I appreciate any help.
I'm just finding my way around this city. It's
different from back home.
Can I give you my info in case someone does know them?

D   Yah. We have a message board.

Sky bends down to her bag.

She begins to write.

Sky *hands* **D** *the paper.*

D *checks her out and gets caught.*

Sky   What?

D   Nothing.

Sky   No, what?

D   Nothing.

Sky   You were just staring at me like an animal.

D   Just noticing your long hair.

Sky   Feels like a blanket on my back in this heat.

D   It's very pretty.

Sky   It makes me very hot.

D   It sure does.

Sky *pulls out her hair from her shirt.*

Sky   Too long.

D   It's so long.

Sky   —I'm not allowed to cut it.

D   Allowed?

Sky   Indians don't cut their hair/

D   Whose permission do you have to earn?

Sky   My tribe.

D   You own a tribe?

Sky   Well, my mom.
I have to ask her.

D   So, you can't cut your hair?
Is it against your religion?

Sky   Today Natives cut their hair all the time.
Except in my family.

D   I see, strict family thing.

Sky   No, it represents like some spiritual stuff.
Only when someone passes away can we cut it.

D   Spiritual stuff? Like some sort of shamen thang?

Sky   My mom said hair is like a connection to the spirit world.

D   I'm lost between the hair and the connection.

Sky   Only when someone passes on can we cut our hair.
Mine might be on its way out.

D   —you're going to chop your hair off?

Sky   I thought about it.
My uncle told me hair cutting is all "Indian talk."

D   Why would you go and get rid of something so pretty?

Sky   It's just a symbol.

D   A symbol of what?

Sky   Of attachment.

D   You should think about getting a tattoo instead.

Sky   Wouldn't that defeat the whole purpose?

D   Of what?

Sky   Of detaching from something.
Someone.

D   Could also be to remember them. To celebrate.

Sky *writes a note.*

Sky   Can you please make sure it gets where it needs to go?

D   Sure. Depends.

Sky   On what?

Beat.

D   On what you'll do for me?

Sky   Do for you?

D   Can you make a promise?

Sky   A promise?

D   A promise, yea.

Sky   What is it first?

D   I want to get to know you.

Sky   I'm not here very long.

D   Come back and see me.

Sky   I will sometime.

D   Tonight.

Sky   Tonight?

D   Yes.

Sky   I can't.

D   —Why?

Sky   It's a long story.

D   I like long stories.

Sky   This one is too long.

D   To be specific: stories told by women in glasses,
with long hair,
and who look like they are made from the sky.

Sky   I thought you said you were closed.

D   We are.
I own the shop.
So, we're not.

Sky   Wow, the force is with you.

D   Got to live,
Got to survive,
Got to clean this mess up.

Sky   Looks clean to me.

D   Oh no, the glass spreads like glitter.
You can never clean it all up at once.

Sky   Magical.

D   Someone kicked the window to get in. Always looking for needles, meds, rubbing alcohol . . . anything they can get their hands on.

Sky   Rubbing alcohol?

D   Yeah, that's when they're real desperate.

Sky   Sounds like something that happens on the rez.

D   It's the addicts here.

Sky   Home too! Mouthwash even.

D   Anything to sell for money. Had to call it in.
Took the cops over an hour and a half to get here.

Sky   Just like the tribal police.

D   The reservation has their own cops?

Sky   Yeah but no one wants that job. Breaking up the 49's going all night long. Everyone hates you. Someone might toss some bad medicine in your hair because they are jealous and call you a sellout. You might have to throw your own brother in jail. Then people start to disappear. Women disappear.
You live in fear because you might be knocked off by some vicious family member seeking revenge.

D   Sounds like a war zone.

Sky   I'm sorry I'm babbling on. I just haven't talked to anyone in a long time . . . like a friend.

D *begins to sweep.*

D   You can stay if you want. Don't want to force you to stay.

Sky   I better go.

D   Or you can hang around and get a tattoo by yours truly?

Sky   Um, oh no . . . I didn't come here to get tattooed. I mean . . . I wasn't planning on it.

D   I dare you.

Sky   What?! You dare me?!

D   Why not?

Sky   Always thought it had to be the right time . . . place . . . person . . . I can't randomly just get—

D   —are you afraid it's going to hurt?

Sky   Isn't that the point?

D   Of a tattoo?

Sky   Yea, to cause physical pain.

D   Some people are addicted to pain, not all. Some people come and want to cover something up.

Sky   I always thought it would be my back.

D   Others want to celebrate a memory.

Sky   I dunno. This is crazy . . . My ma would kill me if she ever found out—

D *gracefully yanks a chair and puts it center.*

D   Yea, come on . . . what's your story?

Sky   My story?

D   Yea, everyone has one.

Sky   I have too many . . . stories . . . words . . . memories . . .

D   I'm into the ones you told so far.
Just one then.

Sky   I come from a long line of stories, memories—

D   See, you already have me hooked, brown eyes.

Sky   Do you have a seat belt?
Because this is going to be a long bumpy ride.

D *pushes up her sleeves and reveals her partial tattooed arms.*

Her breasts stand at attention.

D   I think I can handle it. Try me.

Sky *heads for the chair to sit like she is getting to take off for a flight.*

A loud knock is heard. Shadows.

Landa Lakes *uses her braid as a whip.*

Scene Six: Taking a Polaroid of Eagle as Landa Lakes

Sun turns red, then white.

D *and* **Sky** *are in shadow.*

Uncle Phillip *and* **Eagle** *are full of spunk.*

Uncle Phillip   Come on, let me take your picture, Eagle.

Eagle   Where did you get the Polaroid from?

Uncle Phillip   The antique shop in the town
across the way.

Eagle   How'd you get the money for that?

Uncle Phillip   I had my eye on it and then I won a few bucks over at the casino.
Now, stand over there . . .

Eagle   You're trying to capture my spirit, aren't you?

Uncle Phillip   Wah! You caught me.
Wait, hold on a minute.
What about this?

Uncle Phillip *sees a shawl and dress. He places it over* **Eagle***'s shoulders and
arranges it.*

Uncle Phillip   Put this on.

Eagle   No, I can't. Are you crazy? That's Shinood's. She would kill me. She would
kill you.

Uncle Phillip   How will she ever find out? I'm not going tell her unless you are!

Eagle   Philly, she knows every bead, thread, and fringe on her regalia.

Uncle Phillip   No, she doesn't!

Eagle   You should know that, she's your sister.

Uncle Phillip   We'll put it back when we're done. Come on, it's just for fun.

Eagle   I might like it too much and then what?

Uncle Phillip   Or I might like it too much.

Eagle   You're not funny.

Uncle Phillip   I'm a comedian.

Eagle   If we get caught then this is all your fault.

Uncle Phillip   I'll take the fall.
It's worth it.

Eagle *slips the ribbon dress on.*

Eagle   What are you going to do with the picture anyway?

Uncle Phillip   Don't worry, it's just for me.

Eagle *models the shawl and dress and has a moment. . . .*

Eagle   I like this.

Uncle Phillip   Beautiful.

Eagle   When I make it back from over there and I come home to you, will you call me Landa Lakes?

Uncle Phillip   Yes.

Eagle   You feel right.

Uncle Phillip   We are right.

Uncle Phillip *kisses* **Landa Lakes**.

Landa Lakes *kisses him back.*

Uncle Phillip *takes a Polaroid.*

Uncle Phillip   I'm taking a polaroid because it literally lasts longer.

Scene Seven: The Design

D *is looking at papers with* **Sky**.

Landa *is also looking at designs and is not seen or heard but is part of the action.*

D   What does your tribe or community think about your uncle?

Sky   People on the rez look at my family and think we are complete freaks.
They call me white girl.
I'm not even white, just because I like to read.

D   So, if I don't like to read, does that make me not white?

Sky   Not how it works.

D   Oh.

Sky   When my father passed away over winter solstice my ma was never the same.
She said his spirit is trapped here.
My dad has unfinished business.

Landa Lakes   I was stuck in winter and couldn't make it till spring.

A rainbow appears.

Sky   Maybe my family are just freaks.

D   Everyone has a freaky family.

Sky   No, they are like really freaky
like freak fest freaky.

D *and* **Sky** *look at a design in* **Sky**'s *notebook.*

D   What does this design mean to you?

Sky   The bird means one day
I'll fly from it all

and leave it all behind
I'll soar above the earth.

D   Is this something you can live with forever?

Sky   Yes.

D   Let's do it.

Scene Eight: Climate Change

Sky *stares into the sky.*

She has her notebook.

Landa Lakes *buzzes an ink motor.* **D** *is focused and inking.*

Sky   I'm not going to show you every page, what's in here.
Cause if I tell you, I might have to kill you.

D   What if I told you I used to be in the military?

Sky   You were? Army?

D   Marines.

Sky   How long?

D   Two years.

Sky   That's a long time.

Landa Lakes *starts skipping with her braid.*

D   This is looking soo good.

Sky   I use my notebooks to draw out maps,
Sometimes I need to find out where I'm going.
Aren't you wondering what my spirit totem is?

D   Spirit totem, I'm not that much of a hippie.
I am, but I also know you are Ojibwe Tribe and you follow the flowers, right?

Sky   Correct . . . the vines and leaves . . .
If we view nature as our relative, we will take good care of her.

D   I wish more people thought like you.

Sky   I didn't ask for this crazy ass rez life . . . I just learned all this stuff from my
ma. I was just born into it . . . Sometimes I wish I was adopted like you.

D   I think your ma has a point about climate justice and all that.

Sky   I'm also tired of everyone telling me what to do.

Landa Lakes *whips her braid around and the ink buzz increases in volume.*

Ma *has glasses on.*

Uncle Phillip *has glasses on.*

Eagle *has glasses on.*

They are in their own worlds in a circle and overlap talking to **Sky**.

Ma (*overlapping*)   Sky, I think that one day the earth will turn against everyone and all the people. There will be storms and natural disasters.
You will be lucky, Sky, because you will know about the natural instruction from the creator to seek refuge.
Does that make sense, Sky?
Sky?
Sky?

Uncle Phillip (*overlapping*)   Sky, I think sometimes you just have to listen for the signs, you know.
Watch nature and see what it reveals to you. Everything is related in some way.
Does that make sense, Sky?
Sky?
Sky?

Eagle (*overlapping*)   Sky, it's like one day I will be here and maybe one day I won't be. You can always find me in the water. I will give you signs of my return and you will just know that it is me. Does that make sense, Sky?
Sky
?
Sky
?
Sky
?

Ma, **Eagle**, **Uncle Phillip** *fade as* **Sky** *closes her notebook.*

Scene Nine: Tattoo and Strings

Inside the moon an Ojibwe pictograph of woodland animals.

Landa Lakes *enters with a hand-held mirror and watches herself part-time and watches* **Sky**.

Sky *does not see* **Landa Lakes**, *nor does* **D**. *The ink buzzing happens.*

Sky   My dad once had a tattoo of seven animals tied together by their hearts.

D   Where was his tattoo?

Sky   On his chest. I once had this postcard that he sent me with this picture on it.

Landa Lakes   Ew. I looked so manly then.

Sky   He also had "mom" tattooed on his arm.

Landa Lakes   Well, at least I didn't have a ton of hair on my chest.

Sky   He was an artist and a drum-maker. There's a chicken bone stuck in my throat every time I think about him

She pulls out her knife.

D   Um. Do you usually carry a knife?

Sky   Always.
It was the last thing my dad gifted me the very last time I saw him. Well, my uncle. He always tucked in his pocket and said . . .

Sky and Landa Lakes   Desire to sharpen will make it dull.

Sky   My uncle also gave me the photographs when my dad passed away. I keep the knife tucked under my pillow. At night, when I'm alone. I take it out and write.

D   You are so strange. But I like it.

The sun is yellow.

Sky *writes in her notebook*

Scene Ten: Brother–Sister Confrontation

Ma *holds a basket.*

She begins to hang up animal hides on a clothesline with pictographs painted on them.

Uncle Phillip *is five starring the Earth, weeping.*

Ma   Phillip, what the hell are you doing out here? Gizhaate, so bright and hotter than hell.

Uncle Phillip   Gaween, nothing.

Ma   For crime's sakes your face is all wet—

Uncle Phillip   —real hot out here.

Ma   and you're sweating like a fat little koo-koosh!

Uncle Phillip   Sister, you've called me that since we were kids.

Ma   It was that little pig nose of yours.

Uncle Phillip   You have the same one.

Ma   Nii-ba-win, get up. These hides will dry quickly out here.

Uncle Phillip *stands he wipes his face on his clothes.*

Ma   This weather is real crazy. It's that global warming they keep talking about. Turning everything white and dirty brown.

Uncle Phillip   Like us Indians?

Ma   First it was el Nino, Hurricane Rick, Hurricane Diana over in the west. Made an impact all the way over here. Those bodies in the graveyard were floating down the streets. Then that darn Katrina/

Uncle Phillip   She was misunderstood.

Ma   Ayeee gah! Stop it with the jokes already, eh? Oh brother, what next.

Uncle Phillip   Another winter.

Ma   They keep talking about that over at the roundhouse fire you know. It's that eighth prophecy. They say there will be a day when the world will have to come together for that internal fire. I know where I am going to be when the world comes an end. At home right here.

Uncle Phillip   Shinood, the world is not going to end.

Ma   It sure is, little brother. You're not supposed to take what isn't yours.

Uncle Phillip   What is this about, Shinood?

Ma   It's about you stealing my husband.

Uncle Phillip   You already forgave me. She is gone now.

Ma   I still hurt.

Uncle Phillip   He loved you.

Ma   Help me get the rest of those hides ready for Sky's ceremony. I'll never forget.

Uncle Phillip (*offstage*)   You have to talk about this sometime, sister.

Ma *hisses and hauls the empty basket off.*

Landa Lakes *enters and blows* **Uncle Phillip** *a kiss.*

Scene Eleven: The Tat

The sun is saturated.

Unrecognizable chants. **Landa Lakes** *places ink motor down.*

D *picks it up.*

D   —wait a minute, sure you're old enough to be getting one of these? You and your uncle lied to your mother about you coming to the city?

Sky   I told her, uncle and I are having a rites of passage weekend. I showed you my I.D. card, didn't I?

She pulls out her identification from her back pocket and holds it up.

D *continues to sketch out a pattern on* **Sky** *'s back, while trying to read the card.*

D   Sky Red Rope, tribal member, roll number 15190, what is this? Doesn't even have your picture on it.

Sky   A tribal I.D.?

D   What?

Sky   A tribal I.D.

D   Oh, you really are American Indian.

Sky   Don't I look it?

D   Umm, I dunno. What does an Ojibwe look like?

Sky   Me.

D *gives her a long stare.* **Sky** *stares back.*

Sky   Do I have long or short hair?

D   Long.

Sky   Brown eyes?

D   Two brown eyes, of course.

Sky   Yea.

D   Yea.

Sky   Feathers?

D   What?

Sky   Drums?

D   Wait, are you flirting with me?

Sky   What do you see?

D   Just a beautiful topless woman hugging a chair.

Sky *suddenly feels her nudity.*

Sky   I'm cold.

D   I see that.
Wanna take a break?

Sky   Yeah.

D   Here, put this on.

D *tosses* **Sky** *a loose hospital gown.*

Sky   Thank you.

D   So, what's up with Sky?

Sky   What'd ya mean?

D   Why that name?

Sky   I was named after the sky.

D   Profound.

Sky   My ma told me this story about Sky Woman who fell from a hole in the sky and landed on the Earth. She connected to the strawberry with her tears and planted tobacco plants into the earth.

D   Ouch. How did that happen?

Sky *laughs.*

Sky   No, it's just a legend.
Sometime the lady or the figure changes forms—
Did you know that? But, I think it's shape shifting!

D   Oh.

Sky   So, what's your mysterious name mean anyway?

D   D?

Sky   Yea, D. Like D as in the letter D? D as in destiny?

D   Desperado.

Sky   That's your name?

D   The famous western outlaws of the American frontier, the Dalton Family.

Sky   You're dangerous for Indians aren't ya, cowgirl!

D   Hold on, I want to get some aloe for your skin.

D *disappears* . . .

Scene Thirteen: Landa Lakes and Sky

A heartbeat from a drum is heard. **Landa Lakes** *enters with an opened black umbrella.*

Landa Lakes   The moon is rising in the sun.

Sky   Who are you?

Landa Lakes   Are you sure you need to be getting one of those?

Sky   One of what?

Landa Lakes   One of those.

Sky   A tattoo?

Landa Lakes   Smart.

Sky   It's my birthday next week. I'm having a ceremony.

Landa Lakes   Oh you are.

Sky   Yeah, coming of age.

Landa Lakes   Am I invited, Sky?

Sky   It's back home on the rez . . . Hey wait, how did you know my name?

Landa Lakes   Been waiting for you.

Sky   Why are you carrying umbrella?

Landa Lakes   Might rain.

Sky   And why are you being so mysterious?

Landa Lakes   Did you think I would come in a vision?

Sky   You're really creeping me out.

Landa Lakes   Sky who is always getting ready to fly . . .

Landa Lakes *take umbrella and delicately dances.*

Landa Lakes (*offstage*)   Your old ma told me!

Sky *takes out her knife.*

Rubs her hand on the edge and puts it away.

Sky's *face is grey and glistening with tears.*

D *appears and buzzing ink motor.*

D   The ink stinging?

Sky   No. It feels good.

D   Tell me about this design, what does this mean?

Sky   It's for my father.

D   Your father?

Sky   Eagle.
Awkward beat.

She pulls her top off.

D   Come here.
Lay down here.
Tell me . . .

Sky *is on her side.*

The buzzing on inking needle louder and faster.

Eventually white lights.

Sky   I told my ma.

"This place has nothing for me."
Trees for miles, dead leaves in the
fall,
white blaring sun in the summer beating
down on my back like a bull whip.
Mosquitos robbing me of my blood.
The sound of silence like a knife, cutting my ear.
That sound of absolutely nothing.
The sound of silence. Empty.

The buzzing of an ink needle.

Scene Fourteen: That's My Dress

On one side of the drum a figurine.

Eagle *as* **Landa Lakes** *is wearing some of* **Ma**'s *clothes. A ribbon skirt, with a beautiful beaded necklace.*

Landa Lakes *puts on lipstick and braids his hair and doesn't notice* **Ma** *watching and glaring.*

Eagle   The moon is beaded with flowers.
Three parts to braid the hair.
Crossing one section over the other.
The part is the most important thing. No fish scales.
Perfect.
Well, Miss Landa, look at you.

Ma   Well . . . Well . . . Well . . . I see . . .

Eagle *begins to dance in a small circle.*

Eagle   Shinood.

Ma   Don't you dare Shinood me!

Eagle   How long were you standing there?

Ma   Long enough to see this with the white of my eyes!

Eagle   I was trying these on.

Ma   Those are mine!
You gifted that dress to me.

Eagle   I know.

Ma   Why in the hell are you wearing it?

Eagle   I wanted to feel beautiful.

Ma   Now, that's just weird now, ennit? I used to get you, Eagle.

Eagle   No, no, I don't think you ever got me, Shinood.

Ma   You weren't always like this.

Eagle   Like what?

Ma   Like this.

Eagle   I've always been two-spirit, Shinood. I've been trying to telling you.

Ma   My husband is wearing my goddam dress is what!

Eagle *holds out his hand to* **Ma**. *She refuses.*

Ma   The day you went into that man's lodge, you never came out the same.

Eagle   The war changed my life. It
made me realize who I really am.

Ma   Or what you really are!
I thought I changed your life?
Or our daughter changed your life?

Uncle Phillip *appears in the moon with a small drum pounding softly like a heartbeat.*

Ma   Who is it?

Eagle   There.

Eagle *points to the moon.*

Ma   —Look at your red tail pointed up like you did nothing wrong.

Eagle   I had to leave.

Ma   Oh, you did? Why didn't you tell that to Sky?

Eagle   I can't.

Ma   You can't?

Eagle   I can't/

Ma   You can't warrior up and tell your own daughter why you left?!

Eagle   Don't do this, Shinood.

Ma   Do what? Take my clothes back?

She rips a piece of cloth from **Eagle**.

Eagle *screeches!*

Ma   We both know why.

She rips another piece of cloth from **Eagle**.

Eagle *screeches!*

Ma   What does that feel like, Eagle?

To have clothes ripped off your own back?

Eagle *weeps on his knees.*

Ma   There is only room for one momma here and that one ain't you. The way you pretended to love me. I shoulda never believed a damn thing you said.
Why can't you treat me how you treat your eagle feathers?!

Eagle   Stop, Shinood.

Ma   You're a damn fool if you think that I ever will trust again.

Eagle   I'm weak.
I know, I am weak.

Ma   You think I care after you left us with what?
Lies about you and who you are?

Eagle   Please don't punish, Phil. It's not his fault.

Ma   I love my baby brother, he will always be my baby brother.

The moon bleeds.

Scene Fifteen: Long Time Sitting

Overcast clouds hang in the window.

A long buzz from an ink motor increases.

Sky   Ouhahahah! I can't take it anymore, Desperado.

D   Let's take a break. I like how you say my full name.

Sky   It stings.

She tries to sneak a peak in the mirror at her naked back.

D   You're pretty brave for this being your first time, Sky Red Rope.

Sky   Thanks, ahhh, ouuwee . . . it stings.

D   Ten-hour sitting, impressive.

Sky   I'm determined.

D   I take it your ma is not going to approve of you getting this.

Sky   Bingo. Do you have any tattoos?

D   Lots.

Sky   Well, where are they?

D   Under my clothes.

Sky   Why do you cover them up?

D   Dunno, I got them for me to look at. I have been through a lot.

Sky   Do they remind you of someone or something?

D   Getting inked really turned into a ritual for me.

Sky   I see. What is your favorite one?

D   You really are trying to get me to take off my clothes, aren't ya, darlin?

D *takes off her tank top. She is in a sports bra, arms are covered with designs.*

Sky   Wow. I didn't realize you had so many.

D   This one. It's my favorite.

Sky   It's beautiful. Who is she?

D   She was my lover.

Sky   Oh you're/a lesbian?

D   Queer? Yeah, can't you tell?

Sky   Not really. (*She is obviously lying.*)
My uncle is Niizh-manito-wag, two-spirit?

D   Two-spirit?

Sky   In Ojibwe it means he has both parts.

D   Like a hermaphrodite?

Sky   No, like two spirits.
Means he has masculine and feminine sides of him.

D   Right. I didn't know what you meant when you said he has two parts. (**D**
references to her crotch.)
Doesn't everyone.

Sky   I think so. Does your tat wrap all the way around your body?

D   Yep.

Sky *notices a symbol from the military on* **D**'*s tattoo.*

Sky   You really were in the Marines. Semper Fi.

D   Yes, I was. So was she. (**D** *shows more of her tattoo.*)
And the AmeriCorps, here in the US. The Southwest.
Then after that we went to the Middle East together.

Sky   Where is she?

D   Was.
We were there together.

Sky   Is she still there?

D   We almost made it back.

D *has a stone. She holds it up.*

Sky   What happened? I'm sorry—

D   —No it's alright. She would be smiling at me right now anyway.

Sky   Why?

D   Because she said if she ever kicks the bucket I should continue on with my queer self.

Sky   . . .

D   and I talked you into getting stamped by me.

Sky   It just had to be the right time, place/

D   And person. Don't take this the wrong way but, in some ways, you kinda remind me of her.

Sky   I do?
In what way?

D   She was really sweet and tough.
She was living on the streets.
She didn't have anything.

Sky   Did she have her family?

D   Kicked out of the house by her mother and father for bringing a girl home,
Religious fanatic types . . . we tattooed each other for practice when we were in high school.

Sky   Where is your family?

D   We were each other's family for years.
My parents died when I was a teen.
Abused and kicked out from every foster home in middle America for being queer.
Everyone told me I was going to hell.

Sky   So, you enlisted.

D   Not until years later.

Landa Lakes *enters with a shawl folded on her arm.*

D   I met a Native lady dude over there and he sang a song as I was bringing her ashes back to the States. The war was his freedom from the life he had to return to. He has a daughter a couple years younger than your age and said I should try to meet her one day.

Landa Lakes *and* **Uncle Phillip** *sing a stomp song in the moon.*

D   I wanted to find this guy last winter and

Sky *compares the photo and* **D**'s *tattoo.*

Sky (*to herself*)   A chief wearing a copper medallion, canoes, and seven animals with leashes. The animals are strung by their hearts and tied together. It looked like it was just finished.
Chance. I got the chance at life.

D   I add on every year.

Sky *touches* **D**'s *arm for comfort. She hugs her and then kisses her tattoo.*

Moon shifts red, then white, then brilliant silver.

The sun is a phoenix.

Scene Sixteen: Day of the Ceremony

The sound of thunder.

Ma *is in the middle of the drum, pacing in her ribbon dress.*

There is a pile of strawberries.

The fire is burning.

Landa Lakes *is dressed impeccably with moccasin pumps and holds a closed umbrella.*

Landa Lakes   Shinood, Sky is an explorer.

Ma   Today is her big day. She will be a woman.
My fingers are red from berry picking and my mouth sore from biting.

Landa Lakes   Poor Shinood, picked all the strawberries for the ceremony/

Ma   —and prayer ties for the elders.

Landa Lakes   Maybe she decided to leave her ma here alone?

Ma   I am her mother. I know all. Once and for all, Landa Lakes, get the hell out of my hair.

She has **Landa Lakes** *by the braids.* **Landa Lakes** *reveals* **Sky**'s *notebook.*

Landa Lakes   Sky's deepest thoughts. The pages that follow may scare you. If anyone finds this notebook, the spirits will rain down on you.

Ma *releases* **Landa Lakes**'s *detachable braid.*

Ma   You have been working against me from the start, haven't you?

Landa Lakes   I am the one who is there acting as the moonlight.
When you cry I am the hand placed on your back to make you feel better.
I loved you when I was on Earth.

Ma   Get out of here before I throw you in the fire. I'll make you go away once and for all. (*She grabs the notebook.*)

"I must warn you. They are my deepest thoughts." (**Ma** *turns pages and gasps.*)
"This is my map. I dare you to read on . . . without permission." (**Ma** *turns pages and gasps.*)
"I am going to the city. I don't care what anyone says." Oh, after all I have done for her. Disrespectful! Bii-Zaa-Nii-Yaan! (**Ma** *continues to read.*)
"Uncle said to tell Ma that we are going on a rites of passage weekend. I don't care about lying to her. Anything to get away." (**Ma** *turns pages and gasps.*)
"I must find out who he was. I feel as though I cannot live on if I cannot find out who he was to me."
(*To herself.*) He was a good-for-nothing father, that's what he was. (**Ma** *continues to read.*)
"I can understand why Eagle left Ma. I don't want to stay with her anymore. I know it would kill her but if that doesn't, I might."

Uncle Phillip *enters from the sun.*

Ma   I don't need your charity!

Uncle Phillip   Good afternoon to you too, sunshine.

Ma   Where is she?

Uncle Phillip   Thought she was already here.

Ma   No, you are supposed to bring her here. What will everyone think?

Uncle Phillip   Maybe she is on Indian time. Aye!

Ma   Don't give me that crap, Phillip. You know. Endaso-diba'iganek?

Uncle Phillip   Sundown. You said be here then. Here I am. She said she found a ride with a friend.

Ma   Oh, don't give me that bunch of boloney.

Uncle Phillip   I don't know, Shinood. Calm down. How many of those strawberries did you eat?

Ma   What friend? Who is it? Who are they and what do they want with her?

Singers sound a big drum in the distance.

She starts to pace even faster.

The singers are here. Where is she? I told her not to do this to me.

Uncle Phillip   Don't worry, sister, she will be here.

Ma   The singers have started. The berries are sitting out.

Landa Lakes *swirls in circles around* **Ma** *in his black shawl.*

A crack of thunder is heard, the sun starting to sleep.

Uncle Phillip   Sky! Where are your glasses?

Enter **Sky** *and* **D**; *they are holding hands.*

Sky is in a tank top covered in tattoos. **Ma** *snatches* **Sky**'*s knife.*

Ma   Where were you, young lady?

Sky   Ma, I'm here.

Ma   Where were you?

Sky   Ma, please. Put that down, that's mine! Dad gave that to me!

Ma   Don't you "Ma, please" me.
Who is this white lady?

Sky   This is D.

Ma   D? What kind of name is D?

D   I'm Desperado Chance, named after my grandmother, ma'am.

Ma   Stop talking that white talk with me, missy!

Sky   Ma! Put my knife down.

Ma *holds up* **Sky**'*s notebook.*

Ma   This is yours too, isn't it?
Your deepest darkest thoughts, ha?
Your map of life, right?
All the truth in this little notebook.

Sky   HOW DARE YOU READ MY STUFF!

Ma *throws the notebook at* **Sky** *and she catches it.*

Sky *throws the birch bark bitings into the fire with her notebook.*

The moon is blazing and the brands make tattoos in the stars.

Sky   You know what, Ma. Forget it. All of this.
This isn't for me. This is not traditional. All
of this is just to make me stay with you. I
know about Eagle. I found out.
Why wouldn't you just tell me.
You say he lied to you, that Uncle lied to you.
You know what, you lied to me. I lied to you.
Yes, I left to go to city because I had to.
I had to find me. Find out who I am.
I needed to fly and I am soaring.
I can't attach myself here anymore.
This isn't me.
This reservation.

She circles over to **Ma**, *rips her shirt off. Revealing* **Ma**'*s tattoos and scars.*

Ma *faints.*

The moon turns black.

A crack of thunder is heard, a lightning bolt hits the ground and starts a fire.

The singers are still singing in the distance.

Whispers, war cries, and shouts are heard.

Ma *is laid out on the ground covered in red juice.*

Uncle Phillip, **D**, **Sky**, *and* **Landa Lakes** *are watching the orange fire blaze in the distance.*

Sky   There is a time when an Ojibwe girl receives a new name. She has a dream for the future.

Uncle   A vision.

D   A symbol.

Ma *joins them.*

Ma   Ode'imin.

Sky   Ode'imin, the heart berry. It is red and white in color. It is the only fruit with the seeds that grow on the outside. On the inside the white bitter color represents the physical growth of adolescence, the struggles, and the forgiveness. It is searching for a place in this life. The red symbolizes blood. The maturing into womanhood, those unfamiliar feelings of fearlessness. Leaving it all behind like ashes.

Sky's *family and all the spirits including* **D** *face the four directions as* **Sky** *tosses the notebook into the fire.*

Sky   I forgive. I forgive. I forgive.

The heartbeat of the drum.

Ashes rain in the air.

The moon is tattooed with Ojibwe designs.

End of play, for now.

All In and Out of the Family: A Critical Introduction to Azure Osborne-Lee's *Crooked Parts*

Marquis Bey

It is rare, even in a contemporary moment that has been heralded as the "Transgender Tipping Point," that one encounters the complexity of trans life (Steinmetz 2014). That is, trans *lives* in all their nuance and complexity, all their vicissitudes, are still often eclipsed by popular mythologies of extravagant balls and surgeries, skewed life chances, and death. Trans life in the popular imaginary continues to be subject to a certain transnormative depiction—being distilled through only the most acceptable, palatable kinds of trans representation—which thus disallows certain trans stories from being known, shared, and constitutive of the panoply of experiences of living while trans.

In light of this, it is even rarer to find meditations on *black* trans life. What passes for trans representation, in the context of the above mentioned transnormativity, is often white trans life. And, too, when racialized trans life is given airplay, such identity is often restricted to the same figures we are all used to seeing: Janet Mock and Laverne Cox—affluent, post-operative, black trans *femininity*. While surely this is nothing to scoff at, as black and trans representation of any kind is to be celebrated (though critiques of representational logics have been usefully put forth, as in the anthology *Trap Door: Trans Cultural Production and the Politics of Visibility* (Gossett, Stanley, and Burton 2017)), it remains that the kind of images seen nevertheless construct only a certain kind of trans life as viable, which then excludes the possibility—and thus livability—of other forms of trans subjectivity. In other words, when we see only certain images of a certain demographic, especially a marginalized demographic such as people of transgender experience, those images stand in for the totality of that demographic and consequently impact how it is thought about, understood, and encountered. And furthermore, when a subject of that demographic is encountered yet does not measure up, so to speak, to the hegemonic image of that demographic—which is to say, when that subject is written out of the demographic and excised from being a valid member of that demographic—there is a further kind of violence that occurs. Often, the nexus of black and trans *is* that part of trans life violently written out.

Azure D. Osborne-Lee's *Crooked Parts* provides a much-needed alternative to the typical offerings of trans life of whiteness and spectacularized femininity. Osborne-Lee's play asserts boldly the convergence of blackness, queerness, and trans masculinity into the theatrical landscape, shifting its terrain. The net result is a force to be reckoned with, to be sure, not simply because it has as its protagonist a black trans man, not simply because it is a "positive" representation of trans life (or, one that is not subject to the narrative tropes of trans deception or joke-worthy gendered failure), but because it depicts the minutiae of what it means to be black *and* trans and what effect that has for oneself and others who are encountering that gender transition and transgression. *Crooked Parts* gives viewers something more than the mere "trans character"; it gives viewers a deep meditation on what burgeoning transness does to one's family, how transness manifests in subtle and nuanced ways, how racialized identity might complicate gendered identity, and the ways we are called to task when love is met with unexpected difficulties.

The play takes place now and then, today and yesterday, shifting back and forth between the years 1995 and 2013. Its 2013 protagonist Freddy Clark, a black queer trans man, returns to his family's home after a break-up and must deal with the effects his gender transition has on the family. Its 1995 protagonist, Winifred Clark, is a thirteen-year-old who is struggling to navigate her relationship with her mother while also navigating a desire to fit in with her peers, causing a rift between the mother and child. Even more than this, what strikes readers is the way the Clark family—brother, Stephen; father, Michael; and mother, Angela—orbit around Winifred and Freddy in their own unique trajectories. This is not a play simply about Freddy's transitioning but one about how others are required to transition, in different but significant ways, alongside Freddy's gender transition; it is not a play simply about Winifred growing distant from her mother because of the implication of feelings of being "different" but one about the slow, subtle, complex ways that decisions are made and effects result because of feelings that one does not understand or, sometimes, even know are there.

There seem to be two major thematic strands in the play that deserve close consideration. The first is temporality. Temporality describes not simply time but the interpretation and the effects of time. It is, in other words, how time is fractured, bent, reconfigured, misread and reread. Numerous scholars across queer theory, cultural studies, black studies, and transgender studies have noted the significance of temporality for marginalized subjects; they have detailed how time is "queered" (Halberstam 2005), how blackness exists in "black time" (Warren 2016) or in "epiphenomenal time" (Wright 2015), and how trans masculinity is "complex" and "out of sync" (Eckstein 2018; see also Amin 2014). *Crooked Parts* expresses both a playfulness with time as well as a sustained meditation on it as it relates to its effects on gender.

First, of note is the play's title: *Crooked Parts*. In the context of temporality, one might first approach the theme with the understanding that it is not teleological—that is, linear and untroubled, passive, from A to B—but rather comprised of different assemblages that organize around a conception, then, of a sort of time-scape. This is similar to the works of black playwright Suzan-Lori Parks, wherein Parks demonstrates what scholar Mehdi Ghasemi calls "omnitemporality," where time "no longer presents a progressive, coherent linear movement, and it intermingles past, present and future" (Ghasemi 2016: 6). So the "parts" that comprise the temporality of the play are alluded to as "crooked," nonlinear. First, we are off-balanced, crooked, when it comes to chronology: we are in multiple years and cannot firmly situate ourselves, or the characters, in one time. This affects onlookers' experience of the characters, the characters exceeding themselves as individuals and being encountered on multiple temporal grounds. If it can be assumed that who a person is is a result of a history of experiences and subjective changes that often go unseen by another's initial encounter with them, the multiple temporalities present in the play have the effect of allowing the characters to exceed the theatrical "now"; like Ghasemi's description of Parks's omnitemporality, *Crooked Parts* too "leaps backward and forward at once" (Ghasemi 2018: 6). Chronological temporality, thus, is "crooked," which does not diminish our understanding of the characters but enhances it.

Additionally, temporality bears acutely on the overarching topic of the play: gender. It is well known in trans studies and trans communities that pronouns are often an issue, for many involved. And often it is remarked upon as an identificatory issue, one for which the choice of pronoun must ring true for the gender identification and is expected to be used by others. While this is undoubtedly true, pronouns are also a *temporal* issue: What pronouns, in other words, does one use for the self I was before this "new" self? Does one use "she" pronouns for Winifred when discussing *Crooked Parts* or does one project Freddy's "he" pronouns back into the past, giving the child Freddy a kind of gendered constancy? It becomes a question of where, and how, one temporally locates a given person's gender, and how and when one *becomes* a gender. A remixing, as it were, of the oft-quoted line by Simone de Beauvoir that one is not born but rather becomes a woman (Beauvoir 2012: 330). Through Freddy, Osborne-Lee makes us ask the question: If this is true, which surely it is on many levels, *when* does one finally "become" that woman—and, in Freddy's case, when did he stop being the "she" that Winifred purportedly was and "become" the he that he is eighteen years later?

Crooked Parts gives a more robust treatment of pronouns than does popular discourse, not to gainsay the popular wisdom—which the play in fact affirms—but to complicate it. Osborne-Lee depicts on multiple occasions a familiar pronounial scene:

Stephen   Okay. Sounds good, sis!

Freddy   Bro.

Stephen   What?

Freddy   I'm your brother, Stephen. Bro.

Stephen   Oh. Right. Sorry.

(p. 398)

And another, between the not-so-accepting mother, Angela, and her husband, Freddy's father Michael:

Angela   No, Mike. I don't think it's dramatic. Stephen's running around here drinking and taking drugs and doing God-knows-what. In prison half his adult life and waiting tables when he's out. And Winifred? Well, I don't even know what to say about her running around here looking like some fucking he-she!

Stephen   We can hear you, you know!

(p. 435)

In both of these instances, Freddy is thrown outside of himself, (mis)gendered in a way that nonconsensually thrusts him back to a moment simultaneously familiar and unfamiliar to him. Stephen's misgendering stems from seeing his "sister" in front of him, the misgendering a product of holding Winifred in the body or as the image of Freddy. Angela's misgendering, however, is purposefully malicious and an attempt to derogate Freddy by both propelling his subjectivity back to a moment in time where he effectively had less control over his gendered self-determination *and* invalidating his potential occupancy in either pole of the gender binary, as implied in her concluding phrase "some fucking he-she!"

Here we see, then, the complex workings of gendered temporality. In the case of Stephen's misgendering, it is a matter of 1995 holding sway over 2013; it is a matter of an assumed temporal teleology wherein what was the case of someone's gender in 1995 must be and is assumed to be the case eighteen years later. Even though Stephen ultimately, and happily, understands Freddy as his brother, there is still a normative, hegemonic temporal pull that impacts him, subjecting him to an engagement with it. In the case of Angela, there is more of an insistence on the authority of what might be understood as temporal originarity: that is, whatever gender existed, or was made to exist, first is the only gender that will ever be considered valid. That gender was made to hold sway for not only Winifred but Angela as well.

Note how each Sunday Angela and Winifred wash their hair and talk and laugh with one another, just the two of them, calling this time "Girls' Time," at one point demanding that Stephen "hush!" and "Get on out of here and go play" (p. 403). Angela's use of "Winifred" and "her" for Freddy in the above scene is given strength by way of Winifred's "girlness" constituting Angela's "womanness" too, making Freddy, then, an affront to Angela (xx). So, Freddy is temporally curtailed in order to maintain the integrity of Angela and the family as a whole. But furthermore, even more than insisting on gendered temporal originarity, when this is ultimately seen as untenable Freddy is effectively *thrown out of time*. To exist in time is to be made to occupy a distinct pole in the gender binary, as indexed by a "he" or "she" pronoun. Too, the gender binary dictates gendered immutability and mutual exclusivity. Thus, for Angela to refer to Freddy as a "he-she" disallows Freddy's occupation of a valid gendered subjectivity; "he-she" is an improper gender, which, by the logics of the gender binary, is no gender at all. Freddy, then, in this vein is disallowed temporal existence—existence as such. Freddy is the "part" of the family that is "crooked."

The second major thematic strand is embodiment. A very common theme throughout trans narratives—as showcased by people like C. Riley Snorton (2009), Gayle Salamon (2010), Eric Stanley and Nat Smith (2011), and Jay Prosser (1998), embodiment is deeply important precisely because the body is the site of gendered expectations, assumptions, violence, joy, and recognition. Embodiment, in other words, is often where trans identity is felt and where transantagonism happens. There are many aspects through which to tackle the topic of embodiment, but the two I will focus on here are hair and corporeal difference.

An early scene describes Winifred pretending that she is a famous musician and model, giving an interview to doting fans and a reporter. She is asked about the secret of her success, to which a fan jumps in to respond, "It's the hair!" (p. 399). This sets up hair as a thematic thread throughout the play. Stephen comes in to interrupt her pretend time and witnesses that Winifred has a t-shirt draped over her head to mimic long, flowing hair, which Stephen jokingly ridicules, making Winifred self-conscious. As the play progresses, a mass of t-shirt hair begins to hauntingly follow Winifred around, collecting more and more literal hair, magazines, and the like, growing in size. As well, each Sunday night—Girls' Time, as mentioned above—consists of, among other things, Angela and Winifred giving attention to their hair, Angela braiding Winifred's hair for school. It becomes apparent, however, that the way her mother styles Winifred's hair is less than ideal, the (white) children at school and in church spewing racialized and racist comments toward her about her hair (one child at church, whose racial identity is unclear, says, "Oh, Winnie, just look at your hair! That must be how the Africans wear their hair" (p. 406)).

The complexity of this scene, and the topic in general, cannot be overstated. First, there is the fact that hair, especially long hair as signified by a flowing and growing t-shirt mass, implies a certain kind of femininity. We might wonder if the growing mass is indicative of the specter of femininity that Winifred ultimately rejects and that is met with a dismal fate later in the play. Secondly, though, hair is deeply racialized for black women. Often not possessing the long, flowing hair that signifies "proper" femininity, and also often subject to the ways black women's hair is pathologized, black women and girls are forced to combat responses to their hair on multiple fronts. With the addition of Angela styling Winifred's hair as hers was styled when she was a girl, what Winifred experiences in terms of ridicule becomes a transgenerational insult, and Winifred's ultimate response to desire a permed hairstyle going forward becomes one of the first moments when her transition away from womanhood manifests.

There is another scene that expresses the deeply (trans)gendered significance of hair. After Freddy storms out of the house in response to his mother's disrespect of his gender, he drives his car away and finds a place where he ultimately falls asleep. He begins to envision or hallucinate or imagine (the genre of the scene is unclear, one might argue purposely so) a conversation between himself and Winifred.

Winifred   Is that the best mustache you can grow?

Freddy *covers his upper lip in embarrassment, then, recovering, lets his hand fall away from his face.*

Freddy   For now. It's getting better, though.

Winifred   *(generously)* It's not bad!

Freddy   Yeah?

Winifred   Yeah!

Freddy   *(laughing)* I think it's pretty bad, but that's okay. It's what I've got for now and it gets the job done.

Winifred   That's cool.

They share a moment. **Winifred** *drops to the floor and starts to fiddle with the wallpaper strips.*

Freddy   What happened to your hair?

Winifred *touches her hair, embarrassed.*

Winifred   Fire.

Freddy   Right.

Winifred   Yeah. *(Pause.)* Does it look bad?

Freddy   Honestly?

Winifred *nods.*

Freddy   Yeah. It's pretty bad.

(p. 439)

They bond and connect over variously gendered modes of hair possession. Winifred points out Freddy's mustache hair, a signifier of masculinity, which embarrasses Freddy. It is not up to "normal" masculine standards, it is implied, but Winifred assures him that it is not bad, and Freddy acknowledges that it is a stage in his unfolding masculinity, not the end of it. When asked about *her* hair, Winifred too is embarrassed, and Freddy cannot propitiate her self-consciousness. And perhaps he does not want to. There is a deep significance to the gendered aspects of hair. Freddy and Winifred, on one reading, are the same person, which means that in order for Freddy to progress in his existence as validly subjectivated through (trans) masculinity his mustache hair must grow. Winifred's hair, however, must be forsaken, as the solidification and growth of her hair—a feminine signifier—would imply the diminishment of Freddy's hair, a masculine signifier.

When it comes to corporeal difference, or the ways the body shifts in appearance and is registered as different from another or the same body, the most salient factor in this is Freddy's gender transition. Freddy has not seen his family, it is implied, since he began transitioning, and there is an initial shock at his appearance. Stephen mostly adjusts, but still manages to slight Freddy in this regard, remarking, "I had no idea what you were gonna look like now ... but you're not so different," to which Freddy responds, "Oh. Um ... thanks?" (p. 397). It is a nimble space to navigate, both as assessor and as subject to corporeal assessments: *Should* you look different? How different? Should you be recognized; in what ways should others recognize you and in what ways should they not? Do you *feel* different? Does that matter more or less than how you look? An antagonism emerges in the space of Freddy wanting to look different to himself and others as a way to mark the progression of his transition to himself and, importantly too, to his family. But to look different, in his family's eyes, would mean that he becomes, effectively, less and less part of the family.

This antagonism is given precedent in Winifred's birthday wish for a cloak of chameleon skin. She wishes for this not to "turn purple and pink and blue all over," as Stephen assumed, but perhaps to be able to solve the antagonism: to have the cloak of chameleon skin might mean that she can look different when she wants to and look familiar when she wants to; the best of both worlds (p. 409). Dexterously, Osborne-Lee leaves this question open, writing Winifred's response to Stephen's desire to know exactly why she wants chameleon as "Duh, Stephen! If I tell you, my wish won't come true" (p. 410).

Such generative open questions give the play a depth that deserves serious engagement in not only black and trans studies, but in the larger field of theater and literary studies. *Crooked Parts* promises to add to the growing but still paltry conversation surrounding black trans representation. Via its nuanced meditations on trans masculinity, temporality, and embodiment, *Crooked Parts* gives us more than black trans "representation"; it gives us, in addition to this, the substantive minutiae of what black trans life is and does, how it feels and what effects it has—on oneself and one's loved ones. The play depicts a tiny moment in the grand landscape, but a tiny moment—across time—that manages to sustainedly meditate on pressing questions of race, gender, and family.

References

Amin, Kadji. 2014. "Temporality." *Transgender Studies Quarterly* 1, 1–2: 219–222.

Beauvoir, Simone de. 2012. *The Second Sex*. Translated by Constance Borde and Sheila Malovany-Chevallier. New York: Knopf Doubleday Publishing Group.

Eckstein, Ace J. 2018. "Out of Sync: Complex Temporality in Transgender Men's YouTube Transition Channels." *QED: A Journal in GLBTQ Worldmaking* 5, 1: 24–47.

Ghasemi, Mehdi. 2016. "Quest/ion of Identities in Suzan-Lori Parks's Post-revolutionary Drama." *European Journal of American Studies* 11, 11–2.

Gossett, Reina, Eric A. Stanley, and Johanna Burton, eds. 2017. *Trap Door: Trans Cultural Production and the Politics of Visibility*. Cambridge, MA: Massachusetts Institute of Technology Press.

Halberstam, Jack. 2005. *In a Queer Time and Place: Transgender Bodies, Subcultural Lives*. New York: New York University Press.

Prosser, Jay. 1998. *Second Skins*. New York: Columbia University Press.

Salamon, Gayle. 2010. *Assuming a Body: Transgender and Rhetorics of Materiality*. New York: Columbia University Press.

Snorton, C. Riley. 2009. "'A New Hope': The Psychic Life of Passing." *Hypatia* 24, 3: 77–92.

Stanley, Eric A., and Nat Smith, eds. 2011. *Captive Genders: Trans Embodiment and the Prison Industrial Complex*. Oakland, CA: AK Press.

Steinmetz, Katy. 2014. "The Transgender Tipping Point." *Time*, May 29.

Warren, Calvin L. 2016. "Black Time: Slavery, Metaphysics, and the Logic of Wellness." In *The Psychic Hold of Slavery: Legacies in American Expressive Culture*, edited by Soyica Diggs Colbert, Robert J. Patterson, and Aida Levy-Hussen, 55–68. New Brunswick, NJ: Rutgers University Press.

Wright, Michelle M. 2015. *Physics of Blackness: Beyond the Middle Passage Epistemology*. Minneapolis, MN: University of Minnesota Press.

Crooked Parts

Azure D. Osborne-Lee

Characters

1995:

Winifred "Winnie" Clark A twelve-year-old black girl experiencing upheaval for the first time in her life. She does her best to be prepared for any given situation.
Angela Clark/Reporter Winifred's mother, in her thirties or early forties. Expresses love for her family through acts of service and the creation of routine and ritual.
Stephen Clark/Fan 2 Winifred's brother, eight years old. He loves to annoy his older sibling and fancies himself a cowboy.
Michael Clark/Fan 1 Winifred's father, in his late thirties or early forties. An engineer, and an air sign surrounded by earth signs.

2013:

Freddy Clark A black pre-op transman in his late twenties. A writer going through a big breakup and his Saturn Return.
Angela Clark Freddy's mother, now in her late forties or early fifties. She now wears her hair in a natural rather than in a curl.
Stephen Clark Freddy's brother, in his mid-twenties. Life takes away his horse but not his white hat.
Michael Clark Freddy's father, now in his early fifties.

Casting Policy

Freddy must be played by an actual trans actor.

Winifred may or may not be played by an actual child actor.

Setting & Time

A midsize house in a small city in the American South, the fall of 1995 at the beginning of the school year.

A large house in a large city in the American South, the summer of 2013 at the beginning of the summer.

Act One

Scene One

2013. Lights up on the large Clark house. It is nighttime, somewhere between midnight and 2 a.m. The house is quiet and dark. Headlights flash in the frosted windows of the front door and, softly, the chorus of "We Are Young" by Fun. plays on the car's radio. The music stops as the car is shut off.

A car door opens and shuts, and someone tries the front door of the house. It's locked. There's a quiet knock. Nobody answers. Another knock, this time a little louder. Nothing. A loud sigh and muttered profanity.

A text message sounds upstairs, and **Stephen** *enters, jogging down the staircase into the living room. He opens the front door. On the other side stands* **Freddy** *smoking a cigarette. When he sees* **Stephen,** **Freddy** *hastily throws away the cigarette, picks up a bag, and comes inside.*

Stephen   Freddy!

Freddy *shushes* **Stephen** *and goes into the darkness of the house. When he's satisfied that nothing will happen, he embraces* **Stephen.**

Freddy   Happy birthday, little bro! Sorry I couldn't make it earlier. The drive took a lot longer than I thought.

Stephen (*laughing*)   Yeah, yeah. You suck!

Freddy   I know, I know. But you still went out with some friends, right?

Stephen   Nah. I couldn't find anybody to go out with me tonight.

Freddy   Oh. (*Pause.*) Well, let me get a look at you. It's been so long I was afraid I wouldn't recognize you!

They look each other over.

Stephen   What about you? I had no idea what you were gonna look like now . . . but you're not so different.

Freddy   Oh. Um . . . thanks? (*Beat.*) (*indicating* **Stephen**'s *t-shirt*) So you're into fishing now?

Stephen   Nah. This is my work uniform.

Freddy   Okay. Fair enough. (**Freddy** *sniffs* **Stephen**.) You been drinking? All by yourself?

Stephen   Maybe. It is my birthday, after all.

Freddy   Hey, I'm not judging. Just a second. I'll be right back. I really gotta pee!

He dashes into the nearby first-floor bathroom and shuts the door. **Stephen** *stands awkwardly, then picks up* **Freddy**'s *bag.*

Stephen   Is this all you brought?

Freddy *emerges from the bathroom.*

Freddy   Shh! No. My car's stuffed to the very top. That's just my overnight bag.

Stephen   Oh. So, you're only staying for one night? I thought maybe you were moving back in.

Freddy   I'm kind of playing it by ear, ya know? Waiting to see what happens.

Stephen   Got it.

Freddy (*beat*)   Is she here?

Stephen   Yeah. I think she's sleeping.

Freddy   And where's Daddy? Is he in his bedroom?

Stephen (*shrugging*)   I think he's out of town.

Freddy   Do you know when he'll be back?

Stephen *shrugs.*

Freddy   Huh. Okay, well, I'm going up to bed now, but let's have birthday breakfast in the morning, okay? My treat!

Stephen   Okay. Sounds good, sis!

Freddy   Bro.

Stephen   What?

Freddy   I'm your brother, Stephen. Bro.

Stephen   Oh. Right. Sorry.

Freddy   Don't forget. Goodnight.

Stephen   Goodnight.

Freddy *creeps upstairs with his overnight bag.* **Stephen** *goes to the kitchen to make a midnight snack.* **Freddy** *enters his room and closes the door. He sets the bag on the bed and takes out a few articles of clothing. He pauses and looks around the room taking in his surroundings. He sighs and, back to the door, begins to undress. He takes off his pants and shirt. Next, he peels off a compression garment. He sighs with relief as he tosses his binder onto a nearby chair. Just then, there's a knock on the door.*

Freddy   Just a second!

He looks around, then hastily pulls on his discarded t-shirt. He jumps into bed, yanking the covers up past his chest.

Freddy   Come in!

Stephen *enters carrying a full plate.*

Stephen Hey, bro . . . uh . . . I made us some nachos. I thought you might be hungry.

Freddy *relaxes a bit, scooting over to make room for* **Stephen** *on the bed. Still, with his left hand, he keeps a tight grip on the comforter.*

Freddy Oh. Thanks.

Stephen *sits down, and they begin to eat. Lights dim as a deep subterranean rumbling begins and continues into the darkness.*

Scene Two

1995. Lights up in the living room of the house. **Winifred** *is standing next to the* **Reporter**. *She is wearing a school uniform and has a black t-shirt pulled up over her scalp. As the* **Reporter** *interviews her,* **Winifred** *flips her t-shirt "hair" and unsuccessfully attempts to look humble.*

Reporter I'm here with Winifred Clark—musician, model, and all-around adolescent superstar! Winifred, this has been a banner year for you! Not only were you awarded the Student of the Year Award at Whitley Academy, I understand that a number of conservatories are fighting to see which one you will attend after you graduate from high school. As if that weren't enough, you've released two albums and you're giving sold-out concerts all across the nation. Your fans just cannot get enough of you. You're America's newest teen sensation! What do you think of it all, Winifred?

Winifred (*graciously*) Well, I . . .

Fan 1 *and* **Fan 2** *enter and begin fawning over* **Winifred**.

Fan 1 Ooooooh, Winnie! I'm your biggest fan! I've loved you ever since you were discovered walking home from school and recorded your first album. I play your music every night—I can't sleep without it! I have posters of you all around my room. I even named my turtle Winifred! Seriously, Winnie! I love you!

Fan 2 What she said times twenty! I'm a fan from way back. I know where you grew up. I know you started playing the violin when you were nine. I never spend my allowance on anything except your music, concert tickets, posters, and magazines with you on the cover! I'm the one who really loves you, Winnie!

Reporter Well, Winifred, it seems you have cast a spell over the nation. These two represent just a small fraction of your fan base. What *is* your secret?

Winifred I'd like to think that it's a lot of hard work and . . .

Fan 1 It's the hair! I hope you don't mind me answering, Winnie, but I just had to tell her. It's just that you're really talented and all, but the first thing that I ever noticed about you was how pretty you are and how gorgeous your hair is! In fact, I'll admit it. I was a little jealous. I mean, my hair is fine and all, but yours is fantastic! Me and my friends, we all want to know . . . how do you get it to look that way?

Winifred *smiles and takes the microphone from the* **Reporter**. *As she begins to speak, the* **Reporter**, **Fan 1**, *and* **Fan 2** *quietly leave the stage.* **Winifred** *does not notice. As the others fade away, we see that* **Winifred** *is alone in her living room, looking into a mirror and speaking into a round brush, a backpack and a violin case near her feet.*

Winifred (*swinging and stroking the t-shirt hair*)   Aw, you guys are so sweet! Seriously, you're the best! Well, to answer your question about my hair, I don't do much of anything to it. I guess you could say I'm just blessed that way. I just roll out of bed in the morning and . . .

Stephen *enters riding an imaginary horse. He is wearing his school clothes and a cowboy hat.*

Stephen (*pointing and laughing*)   Nice hair, Winnie! What are you doing? Who are you talking to?

Mortified, **Winifred** *whirls around to face* **Stephen***, dropping the brush, snatching the t-shirt off of her head, revealing a head full of beaded braids.* **Winifred** *throws the t-shirt on the floor.*

Winifred   None of your business, Stephen! I was just getting ready for school. I've got to go. You're going to make me late.

She puts on her backpack and snatches up her violin case.

And, Stephen, you had better not tell anybody about this, or you're dead meat! I mean it!

She stomps out of the living room. **Stephen** *waits to make sure that she is gone, then takes off his cowboy hat and pulls the t-shirt onto his head. He goes to look at himself in the mirror, flipping the t-shirt a little as he goes. Satisfied, he snatches the shirt off of his head and drops it back on the floor. He crams his cowboy hat back on, mounts his steed, and rides offstage.*

Scene Three

Later that morning, on the street. **Winifred** *enters. She is on her way to school, and she is trailed by the t-shirt, which has become grotesquely animated.* **Stephen** *enters, running to catch up with* **Winifred**.

Stephen   Bye, Winnie! Have fun at your new school today with all the white people!

He performs a gesture of flipping invisible hair over his shoulder and grins widely.

Winifred (*embarrassed and angry*)   Shut up, Stephen! You just mind your own business and remember what I told you, or you're gonna get it!

Stephen *sticks his tongue out at* **Winifred** *and runs offstage. Flustered,* **Winifred** *addresses the t-shirt.*

Winifred   Sorry about that. My little brother's such a pain. As you can see, he doesn't know when to keep his mouth shut. Anyway, what was I saying? Oh, right! So, my Daddy's an engineer and travels a lot for his job. My mom . . . well, she's an engineer too, but she lost her job . . . so she's at home a lot now. Every Sunday me and her spend a lot of time together. See, after church and Sunday school, everybody—my mom, my daddy, my brother, and me—we go out to eat, usually to the Chinese place down the street from my church because it's all you can eat and my daddy says, (*imitating her father*) "It's a good value."

After we get home from dinner, that's when it's Girls' Time. My mama and I change clothes and we spend the rest of the afternoon just the two of us. We sing along to all the best singers—Anita Baker, Patti LaBelle, and Gladys Knight—and I help her make all the dinners for the week.

And then it's hair time! I stand on a step stool with my head in the sink, and Mama washes my hair with that little spray gun thingy. I sit down in a chair in the middle of the kitchen with a towel on my shoulders, and Mama braids my hair. It takes a while, but it's not boring because we spend the whole time talking and singing. Sometimes when she finishes, Mama takes pictures of my hairstyles so she can show them to relatives later. (*She laughs nervously.*)

Anyway, my name's Winifred. What's yours?

Scene Four

Sunday. Lights up on **Angela** *in the kitchen, dressed in a comfortable feminine dress. She ties on an apron as* **Winifred** *runs into the kitchen dressed in old play clothes.* **Winifred** *drapes a couple of ratty towels over the back of a chair and pulls a step stool up to the refrigerator so that she can insert a tape into the boombox. "Superwoman" by Gladys Knight, or something similar, begins, and* **Angela** *and* **Winifred** *immediately sing along.* **Angela** *gives* **Winifred** *things to open or chop and they move in sync with one another.* **Winifred** *picks up a vegetable and sings into it as if it were a microphone.* **Angela** *follows suit. They continue to perform until they finish the song grandly.* **Winifred** *sits in the chair.* **Angela** *begins to comb* **Winifred**'*s hair.*

Angela   So how was your first week at school?

She hands **Winifred** *a ball of shed hair pulled from the comb. The t-shirt appears in the corner of the kitchen.* **Winifred** *pauses before answering.*

Winifred   It was alright.

Angela   Just alright? That's all you have to say about the fancy magnet school that you begged us to let you go to?

Winifred *begins to worry the hairball in her hands.*

Winifred   Well, no . . . my teachers seem okay. They didn't give me too much homework, and my new locker is big enough to fit all of my books and my violin.

Angela   That's it?

Winifred   And they serve pizza every day, not just on Fridays like at my old school.

Angela   I'm not asking about the cafeteria food, Winifred. What about the other children? Are you making any friends? I saw you talking to that little girl from down the street at the bus stop. She goes to your school, doesn't she? What's her name? Jennifer?

Winifred   Um . . . Julie.

Angela   That's right. Julie. Well? What's Julie like?

Winifred   Julie's cool. She's got a little sister and a dog, and she's on the swim team.

Angela   Well, that's nice. Do you have any classes with Julie? Are you two sitting next to each other on the bus? Do you eat lunch together?

Winifred (*shrugging*)   Yeah. I guess we hang out.

The t-shirt moves closer to **Winifred**.

Angela   Well, that's good! Are you gonna to invite her to your birthday dinner?

Winifred   No. I thought . . . just family is nice, right?

The t-shirt moves even closer.

Angela (*brightly*)   Well, sure! (*Beat.*) Are you making friends with any of the black girls at your school?

Winifred *drops the shed hair on the floor. The t-shirt immediately snatches it up.*

Winifred   There aren't really any. (*Pause.*) Mama, can we please talk about something else? I'm tired of thinking about school.

Angela *looks into* **Winifred**'s *face, but can't catch her eye.*

Angela   Alright, Winnie. What do you want to talk about?

Winifred *shrugs.*

Angela   Okay. We don't have to talk if you don't want to.

She turns up the volume on the boombox. "Somebody Loves You Baby" by Patti LaBelle fills the room. **Angela** *works in silence and, after a few moments, the t-shirt/ hairball leaves the room. "That's What Friends Are For" by Dionne Warwick begins to play.*

Winifred (*giggling*)   Mama, can you believe Mrs. Jones today in church, sitting right in the front row wearing that big 'ole blue hat that looked like Saturn and all of its rings?

Angela   I know! That hat was so bright that I thought I was gonna have to shut my eyes so I could focus on the sermon!

Stephen *enters the kitchen and goes to the refrigerator.*

Winifred (*giggling*)   And did you see the way the rings bounced when she got up and started clapping and singing along with the choir? They looked like a giant Slinky!

Angela   More like a U.F.O.!

Stephen (*loudly, laughing*)   I heard Sister Jackson say after church that it looked like a hula hoop convention! She said that's why Sister Jones's husband—

Angela   Stephen, hush! Get on out of here and go play. You know this is Girls' Time.

Stephen   Yes, ma'am.

Winifred *leans over in the chair and sticks her tongue out at* **Stephen**.

Angela   Winifred, sit like a lady.

Winifred (*sitting back and closing her legs*)   Yes, ma'am.

At the door, **Stephen** *sticks his tongue out at* **Winifred** *and runs away.*

Winifred   Why doesn't anybody say anything to her about those hats?

Angela   Now, Winnie, you know people do. (*Imitating a nosy church woman.*) Why, Sister Jones, you always wear the most impressive and creative hats! Wherever do you manage to find them?

Angela *and* **Winifred** *laugh again. Lights dim. Music fades out as the subterranean rumbling begins again.*

Scene Five

2013. Morning. **Freddy** *and* **Stephen** *enter through the front door carrying boxes.*

Stephen   So that old thing got you all the way here from New York?

Freddy   Hey! Athena's a classic. She's a solid twenty-five years old.

Stephen (*laughing*)   My point exactly!

Freddy   I'll have you know we made it down here just fine! Well, except for the stopover in Philadelphia. Stupid cops.

Stephen (*laughs*)   Tell me about it! What happened?

Freddy   Ugh. I don't want to get into all the details right now, but let's just say that they're quite eager to take possession of vehicles in the City of Brotherly Love.

Stephen   Ahhh. Gotcha.

He heads up the stairs with the boxes he's carrying while **Freddy** *comes in and out of the front door staging some boxes and bags inside the living room.*

Suddenly **Angela** *bursts through the kitchen door. She is wearing a sharp pantsuit and walks quickly, not looking at* **Freddy**. *After entering her bedroom, she crosses the house, retracing her steps.* **Freddy** *raises his hand in greeting.*

Freddy   Hi, Mama!

Angela *barely slows her pace and doesn't look directly at* **Freddy** *as she passes him.*

Angela   I gotta get downtown. I've got a bunch of appointments today.

She exits. **Freddy** *watches her go.*

Freddy   Oh. Okay.

Stephen *comes back downstairs.*

Stephen   Was that Mama?

Freddy   Yeah. I guess she was in a hurry. (*Beat.*) Say, how 'bout we go get that birthday breakfast now?

Stephen   But what about the rest of your stuff?

Freddy   It can wait. Let's go!

Lights down as **Freddy** *and* **Stephen** *exit through the front door. Deep rumblings begin again.*

Scene Six

1995. Sunday. Lights up on **Angela** *cooking in the kitchen. "Sweet Love" by Anita Baker plays on the radio.* **Michael** *enters.*

Michael   Aww, yeah! That's our song!

He turns the radio up and embraces **Angela***, trying to get her to dance.*

Angela (*laughing*)   Mike! I'm trying to cook!

Michael   That food'll be alright. Dance with me. Ms. Baker waits for no one!

Angela *gives in and lets herself be led.*

Michael   Do you remember the first time we heard this song?

Angela (*chuckling*)   How could I forget? It was the best part of that horrible first date you took me on!

Michael   Horrible? It must not've been too bad! After all, you did agree to go out with me again.

Angela   That's because I wanted my money back! I wasn't just gonna let you stick me with the bill!

Michael   Aww, come on, Angie! You know the only reason I forgot my wallet was because I was so nervous about taking out the woman of my dreams! Besides . . . I heard the real reason you went out with me a second time is because you thought I had a nice butt.

Angela   Oh, is that so?

Michael   Mm hmm.

Angela   That's what you heard?

Michael   Absolutely.

Angela *grabs* **Michael***'s butt.* **Michael** *kisses her just as* **Winifred** *and* **Stephen** *enter.*

Winifred   Ewwww!   **Stephen**   Kissing! BLECH!

Stephen *melodramatically throws himself onto the floor.*

Angela (*laughing*)   If it weren't for your father and me kissing, neither one of you would be here today, so you better be grateful! Stephen, get up off the floor before you ruin your church clothes. Both of you get changed.

Winifred   Okay, Mama!

Stephen (*saluting* **Angela**)   Aye aye, cap'n!

He jumps up and rides his imaginary horse out of the kitchen, snatching a bow from **Winifred***'s hair as he goes.*

Winifred   Stephen!

She runs after him.

Angela   Now where were we?

Leaning back into **Michael***.*

Michael   Oh, I like a woman who can run things!

The t-shirt/hairball appears in the corner.

Angela   And what's that supposed to mean?

Michael (*surprised*)   Just . . . nothing, Angie. It was a compliment. I'm saying I like that way you have about you. What did I do now?

Angela   Nothing, nothing . . . Winnie will be back soon. Raincheck?

Michael   Yeah. Okay. Raincheck.

He gives **Angela** *a quick peck. He and the t-shirt/hairball exit together.*

Winifred *runs back into the kitchen.*

Winifred   Mama, the best thing happened today! You know Brittany Williams, who's in my Sunday school class?

Angela   Yes, I do.

Winifred   Well, Brittany's a grade ahead of me, and she's not very nice to me. She's always making little comments about the way I'm dressed, and she'll say them like she's trying to be nice when we both know that she's trying to make me feel bad. Like last week in church when I wore my black shiny shoes, she said, "Hi, Winnie! Those are really nice shoes. I haven't seen anyone wear shoes like that since I was in elementary school."

Angela   Well, that's not very nice of her.

Winifred   I know, Mama! That's what I said! Anyway, today when she saw me she started laughing and said, "Oh, Winnie, just look at your hair! That must be how the Africans wear their hair."

Angela   And what's that supposed to mean? You look just like I did when I was your age.

Winifred   I know, Mama! Let me finish. Well, Sister Murphy came into the classroom as Brittany said it, but Brittany didn't see her because her back's to the door. Sister Murphy heard just what Brittany said, and so she goes, (*imitating Sister Murphy*) "Brittany Williams, I think that you should be less concerned with Winifred's hair and more concerned about your relationship with God. Making observations about other people's appearances certainly isn't going to get you into heaven. Now please take your seat." Ooooh, you should have seen Brittany's face! She couldn't say nothing but, "Yes, ma'am!"

Angela (*frowning*)   Well, I'm glad Sister Murphy said something to Brittany. Do you want me to talk to her parents? I know they taught her better than that.

Winifred   Mama, no! I don't want her to think I'm some tattletale. I just told you because I thought you'd think it was funny.

Angela (*wipes her hands on her apron*)   Alright, Winnie. I just don't find other children picking on you very funny.

Winifred (*quietly*)   Well, neither do I. That wasn't the funny part. (*Beat.*) Never mind. I'm sorry I brought it up.

Angela   Let's forget about Brittany Williams. She's not worth talking about. How do you want me to do your hair this week?

A tangled mass of t-shirts and hair appears in the corner of the kitchen. **Winifred** *looks at it, then quickly looks back at* **Angela**.

Winifred (*seriously*)   I want something grown-up looking. Nothing with beads and no pigtails!

Silence.

Angela   Okay, Winnie. I think I can handle that. Let's get started.

Scene Seven

Lights up on the sidewalk outside the 1995 Clark house. **Winifred** *enters wearing her backpack. She is trailed by the mass of t-shirts, which now includes some photos from glossy magazines as well as balls of hair.*

Winifred   I think I need a new look. What do you think?

She stops walking and turns to regard the mass. After a moment, she starts walking again.

It's just that, well, I think I need a change. I want a more mature hairstyle. None of the other girls at school wear their hair this way, not even the other black girls. I don't want to stick out so much anymore. (*Beat.*) Maybe I can ask for a makeover for my birthday? What do you think?

She approaches the mass, gazing into its glossy faces.

Am I more of a Tatiana Ali? Or a Whitney Houston?

The mass does not respond.

Maybe a Queen Latifah?

No answer. She sighs.

You're lucky. You don't have to worry about these kinds of things. Nobody laughs at you. You just . . . blend in.

Scene Eight

Evening. Lights come up on the kitchen. **Michael** *enters holding a shopping bag.*

Angela   Where's the cake?

Michael   What cake?

Angela   The cake that I sent you out to pick up for your daughter's birthday. I took her out to dinner! Mike, are you serious? You forgot the cake?

Michael   Nope! Just kidding, baby. It's right here!

He exits and quickly returns with a cake box, which he places on the counter beside **Angela**.

Angela   I can't take your practical jokes right now, Mike. Tonight is important! Thirteen is a milestone, and something isn't right with her.

Michael   I know, I know. Thirteen's big deal. You know I was just playing.

He leans in for a kiss.

Angela   Mmm . . . Mike, have you been smoking?

Michael   Of course not, Angie! I told you I quit.

Angela   Then why do you taste like an ashtray?

Michael (*shrugging*)   Must've been something I ate.

Angela   I thought we agreed we were going to set an example for the children, Mike.

Michael   And I *ám*. I said I wasn't smoking, Angie. Damn! Can we drop it, please?

Angela   Fine. Will you help me set the table, please?

Michael   Sure.

He takes off his jacket, drapes it over the back of a chair, and begins to set the table.
Angela *removes the cake from the box, then looks through the shopping bag.*

Angela   Where are the birthday candles?

Michael   Oh, damn! I knew I forgot something. I can go back and get some right now.

Angela   No, I need you here. I'll just . . . I'll figure something out. Can you get the presents from the bedroom?

Michael   Sure.

Angela *exits.* **Michael** *follows. After a moment,* **Winifred** *creeps into the kitchen and begins to snoop. She sees the cake on the counter and goes to get a taste of the icing.*

Winifred   Chocolate. Yes!

She sees her father's jacket on the back of his chair and decides to try it on. She struts around the kitchen with her hands in the jacket pockets, then does a pirouette. She hears her parents approaching and hastily throws the jacket back onto the chair. A Zippo lighter falls out of a jacket pocket. She picks it up and decides to keep it. She quickly exits. **Michael** *and* **Angela** *enter carrying birthday presents.*

Michael   Where do you want these?

Angela   Put them on the floor next to Winifred's chair.

Angela *takes a step back and considers her handiwork.*

Angela   Okay. I think we're ready. Will you go get Stephen? And tell Winifred to wait in the living room until we say she can come in.

Michael   You got it!

He exits. **Angela** *rushes to the junk drawer. She finds a previously lit #1 candle, three stubby rainbow-striped birthday candles, and one thick emergency candle. She plants them in the cake.*

Michael (*from the living room*)   Here we are!

Stephen *runs in and sits at the table.* **Michael** *enters with* **Winifred**, *his hands over her eyes.*

Angela   Mike!

Winifred   Can I look yet?

Michael   Not yet, baby.

He jerks his head meaningfully in the direction of the light switch. **Stephen** *jumps up and turns off the lights.*

Winifred   Now?

Michael   Not yet.

Angela *looks for matches, but can't find any.*

Angela (*whispering loudly*)   I need a match, Michael! I said for her to wait!

Michael (*chuckling*)   Ah, but birthdays don't wait! (*Whispering back.*) Just look in my jacket pocket!

Angela *looks in* **Michael***'s pockets and finds nothing.*

Winifred (*playfully*)   Who's out there?

Angela   Just give us a second, baby girl. (*To* **Michael**.) Where?!

Michael   Inside. Check the inside pocket.

Angela *reaches into the inside pocket of* **Michael***'s jacket and pulls out a loose cigarette. She gives* **Michael** *an icy look and puts the cigarette back.* **Angela** *looks around and decides to light the candles on the stove.*

Angela   Now!

Michael *removes his hands from* **Winifred***'s eyes.* **Michael** *and* **Angela** *begin an overly enthusiastic rendition of Stevie Wonder's "Happy Birthday," as* **Angela** *dances the cake over to the table. They end with a flourish, presenting the cake to* **Winifred**.

Angela   Well . . . blow out the candles, birthday girl!

Winifred *closes her eyes and blows out her birthday candles.* **Angela** *takes the cake back.*

Angela   Mike? Help me cut the cake?

Michael   . . . okay, Angie.

Michael *and* **Angela** *go to a corner of the kitchen, whispering to each other fiercely.*

Stephen   Did you make a wish, Winnie?

Winifred   Yup. I sure did!

Stephen   Tell me! Tell me! What was it?

Winifred   I don't know, Stephen . . .

Stephen   Please! I won't tell anybody else. I promise.

Winifred *looks back at* **Michael** *and* **Angela**.

Winifred   Okay. I'll tell you. (*Lowering her voice.*) I wished for a cloak of chameleon skin.

Stephen (*bugging*)   Ooh! So you can turn purple and pink and blue all over?

Winifred (*seriously*)   No. Not for that.

Stephen   Oh. That's no fun. What for then?

Winifred   Duh, Stephen! If I tell you, my wish won't come true.

Stephen   Oh.

Michael *and* **Angela** *stop whispering and approach the table with saccharine smiles and slices of cake. Deep rumblings. Lights out.*

Scene Nine

2013. Late morning. Kitchen. The banter of talk radio. **Freddy** *enters and crosses to the fridge. He opens it and begins a close inspection of its contents.* **Angela** *enters behind* **Freddy** *and stands there watching him. Then she walks over to the counter and starts to make coffee.*

Angela (*concentrating on the coffee maker*)   So what are your plans?

Freddy *jumps at the sound of her voice.*

Freddy   Oh. Hi. Well, uh, New Orleans is still the plan right now. I just need to stay here long enough to register my car and get the title transferred over. Then I can get back on the road.

Angela   Okay. And what are you going to do in New Orleans? Where are you going to live?

Freddy   Well, you know, I've got a couple of friends from grad school out there. I thought I might stay with them for a while and maybe go around to some of the shops and see if they're interested in selling my work.

Silence.

Angela (*still not looking up*)   Okay.

Freddy   I wanted to ask you—do you think you could lend me some money for just a little while? The drive down cost more than I thought it would, and I've got some bills I need to catch up on.

Little silence.

Angela   No, I don't think that's a good idea.

Freddy (*little pause*)   Oh.

He hastily re-opens the refrigerator and grabs a snack out of it. He exits the kitchen, calling over his shoulder.

Okay, well, I've got some writing to do, so I'm just gonna get to it.

Angela (*turning quickly*)   Maybe we can work out a . . .

She sees **Freddy** *walking away and exhales loudly. As* **Freddy** *enters the living room,* **Michael** *enters the house carrying an overnight bag. When he sees* **Freddy**, *he immediately puts the bag down and embraces him.* **Angela** *pokes her head out from the kitchen. When she sees* **Michael**, *she goes back into the kitchen and busies herself.*

Michael   Is it my Winifred?

Angela (*yelling from the kitchen*)   Is that you, Michael?

Michael (*yelling back*)   Yeah, Angie!

Freddy   It's Freddy now, remember?

Michael   Right. Right. Freddy.

He releases **Freddy** *and steps back to get a good look at him.*

Angela (*still yelling from the kitchen*)   Don't forget about dinner on Sunday! I put it on the calendar!

Michael (*yelling back*)   Looking forward to it!

He turns back to **Freddy**. **Angela**, *still in front of the coffee maker, sighs with impatience, then opens a cabinet and begins to noisily rearrange the pots and pans.*

Freddy   Oh, damn!

Michael   What is it?

Freddy   I forgot about Sunday dinner and made other plans. I got asked to read some of my poetry downtown.

Michael   Oh.

Freddy (*looking torn*)   But I guess I can just tell them I can't . . .

Michael   Why don't you let me take care of this? What day works for you?

Freddy   Any other day.

Michael   Are you sure?

Freddy   I'm sure.

Michael   Okay. Wait right here. I'll be right back.

He enters the kitchen.

Michael   Hey, sweetheart.

Angela (*in a low voice*)   Is it bad?

Michael   Is what bad?

Angela   What she looks like . . . is it bad?

Michael   What do you mean? You haven't talked to her yet? I thought y'all were just . . .

Angela   I have. I just couldn't bring myself to look at her.

Michael   Well, I don't know what to tell you. I guess it depends on your definition of bad. Unrecognizable? No. Different? Yeah.

Angela   I don't know if I can take this.

Michael   It'll be alright, Angie.

Angela   You don't know that.

Michael   I do. I've got a feeling.

Angela   A feeling? Michael . . .

Michael   Say, do you think we can push that dinner to Monday night? I just remembered I've got a meeting on Sunday.

Angela (*flatly*)   On a Sunday?

Michael   Yup.

Angela   You've got a meeting on a Sunday night?

Michael   Yes, Angie.

Angela   Fine.

Michael   Great! Thanks, honey.

Angela *walks to the calendar and draws a line through Sunday. While her back is turned,* **Michael** *exits the kitchen and returns to* **Freddy**.

Angela   I think we should send her to some kind of therapy . . .

She turns around and finds herself alone again.

Michael   Okay! It's taken care of. On Monday night, we dine!

Freddy   Phew! Thanks, Daddy!

Michael   Right. Well, I didn't see any plates on your car out there.

Angela *storms out of the kitchen, past them, and into her room, slamming the door.*

Freddy   I'm taking care of it. As soon as the office opens tomorrow morning, I'm going to get the paperwork. It's legal for now, though. I've got a transit permit for it.

Michael   Okay, then. Just don't give the cops any excuses. You know with your brother's history they're already too well acquainted with this family.

Freddy (*scratching his neck and chin*)   I know. I won't. Daddy, do you think you can show me how to shave without getting a rash? These bumps are killing me!

Michael (*beat*)   That was a long trip home. I think I'm gonna hit the hay.

He reaches in his pocket and pulls out a small wad of bills.

But here's a little welcome home gift for you.

Freddy   Oh. Thanks, Daddy.

Michael   You're welcome, Winifred.

Freddy *cringes and touches his neck.* **Michael** *picks up his bag.*

Freddy   Daddy, wait . . .

Michael   Yeah?

Freddy   What about the . . . do you think I could borrow a bit more? Just until I get settled?

Michael   How much more?

Freddy   I thought . . . 3,000?

Michael (*beat*)   Is Monday morning okay?

Freddy   Sure.

Michael   Okay.

He heads for the stairs.

It's nice to have you back.

Freddy   Thanks.

Michael *exits.* **Freddy** *pockets the money. Deep rumbling. Lights down.*

Scene Ten

1995. The following Sunday. Lights up on **Angela** *cooking in the kitchen. Occasionally she looks towards the kitchen door. She wipes her hands and pushes play on the boombox on top of the refrigerator. Anita Baker's "You Belong to Me" plays.* **Angela** *softly sings along.* **Michael** *enters holding some papers.*

Angela   Have you seen Winifred?

Michael   No. I thought she was in here with you.

Angela   Not yet. I don't know where that girl is! I thought she might've been in the study with you.

Michael   Nope.

Angela   She's around here somewhere. I'll find her in just a minute. What's that?

Michael   The estimate for our foundation repairs. It's not good, Angie.

Angela   How much is it?

Michael   A lot more than we can afford on just my salary.

Angela   I'm looking for work, Michael!

Michael   I know you are. I'm just saying that your severance is almost gone, and with Winifred starting high school next year . . . This house needs a lot of work . . . if it can be fixed at all.

Angela (*a little too loudly*)   What do you mean, "If it can be fixed at all?"

Michael   Shh!

Stephen *enters.*

Angela   Stephen, baby, go see what's keeping Winnie. Tell her I'm waiting on her.

Stephen   Okay, Mama.

He exits.

Angela (*softer this time*)   What does it mean, Mike?

Michael   He said other families on the street have been having the same problems, that it's not just us. The houses are crumbling. We might have to move, Angie.

Angela   What about our homeowners' insurance? They have to cover this, don't they?

Michael   Without any visible depressions in the ground, they don't have to do shit. Like I said, Angie, it's not good.

Stephen *enters.*

Stephen   Winnie isn't coming, Mama. She says she doesn't feel good.

Angela (*to* **Michael**)   Let's finish talking about this later?

Michael   Yeah.

He pats **Stephen**'*s head as he exits.*

Angela (*sighing*)   Your sister said she feels sick? She was just fine at church.

Stephen   That's what she said, Mama . . . but I think she's lying.

Angela   And why is that?

Stephen   Well, I heard her tell Julie Meyers while they were waiting for the bus that she doesn't want you to do her hair anymore. She said some of the kids in her class have been making fun of her, telling her she looks like Coolio. She told Julie that some of the other kids have started calling her Medusa and sometimes they scream or pretend to be frozen when she looks at them.

Silence.

Angela   Is that so? Well, thank you, Stephen. You can go play now.

Stephen   Okay, Mama.

He exits.

Angela (*angrily*)   Winifred! Winifred Josephine Clark, come in here!

Winifred *enters the kitchen walking slowly with her head down. She is wearing her school clothes and a hat. A tangled mass of t-shirt, magazines, and hair enters just behind her.*

Angela   Well?

Winifred (*innocently*)   Well, what, Mama?

Angela   Well, it's Sunday, Winifred. You know that.

Winifred   Yes, ma'am.

Angela (*gesturing at* **Winifred**'s *clothing*)   Then what are you doing in that getup? Why aren't you ready to get your hair done, young lady?

Winifred   I don't feel good.

Angela   You look just fine to me.

Winifred   I've got a stomach ache, and I feel light-headed, like I might just faint at any moment. Also my head hurts.

Silence.

Angela   Winifred, you know you don't come from the kind of people who just "faint at any moment." What's really going on here?

Winifred *shrugs.*

Angela   Is there anything you want to tell me?

Winifred   I don't think so.

Angela   Your brother told me that you don't want me to do your hair anymore. Is this true?

Winifred (*after a moment, weakly*)   Yes, ma'am.

Angela   I see.

She struggles.

And would you care to tell me why?

Winifred *shrugs her shoulders again, still avoiding* **Angela**'s *gaze.*

Angela (*sighs*)   Well, you are thirteen years old. I guess you're old enough now to decide. Would you prefer for me to take you to a salon to get your hair done from now on?

Winifred   A perm? Oh, Mama, yes!

Angela   Well now, Winnie, I wasn't necessarily suggesting that you get a relaxer.

Winifred   But I thought you just said that I was old enough to choose?

Angela   I did say that. It's just . . . are you sure about straight hair, Winnie? (*Patting her own hair unconsciously.*) I have always thought that a curl would look very becoming on you.

Winifred *looks stricken.*

Winifred   Oh, Mama, no. Ewwww!

Angela (*with some difficulty*)   Okay, then. I'll call Sears and see if they can fit you in for a relaxer today. Go get ready.

Relieved, **Winifred** *turns to leave the kitchen.*

Angela   Winnie?

Winifred *stops and turns to look back expectantly at* **Angela**.

Angela   Are you sure that this is what you want?

Winifred   Yes!

Angela   Fine then. I'll set it up. Hurry up now.

Winifred   Thank you, Mama!

She exits. The mass stays in the kitchen and begins to follow **Angela** *as she paces. After a moment she turns off the music and retrieves the Yellow Pages. She sighs as she picks up the phone. Deep rumbling. Lights out.*

Scene Eleven

2013. Later that week. Evening. **Freddy** *and* **Stephen** *stand in the kitchen of the large Clark house.* **Freddy** *cooks at the stove while* **Stephen** *tidies the counter. They're both having a great time.*

Freddy   So then they asked me to sign the tickets and told me to get out of the car! (*Imitating police officer.*) Uh, sir, I'm gonna need you to step out of the vehicle. The tow truck is on its way. Do you have the keys?

Stephen (*laughing*)   That sucks!

Freddy   Yeah! And they asked me if I had the keys as if I had hotwired it. I *told* them it was mine! The police totally jacked my ride and *then* they broke it!

Angela *walks into the kitchen.* **Freddy** *and* **Stephen** *fall silent and become very busy.* **Angela**'s *gaze skips over* **Freddy** *and falls on* **Stephen**.

Angela   Stephen, did you get your prescription filled?

Stephen   Uh, yeah. I took it to the pharmacy.

Angela   That's not what I asked you. I said, "Did you get it filled?" Do you see the difference?

Stephen   Yes.

Angela   Yes what?

Stephen   Yes, I see the difference.

Angela   So, where is it then?

Stephen   My prescription?

Angela (*losing her patience*)   Yes, your prescription! Are you high right now? Let me see your pupils!

Stephen   Mama, I'm not high.

Angela   I've heard that before! Let me see your eyes.

Angela *gets very close to* **Stephen**'*s face, inspecting his pupils.* **Freddy** *shifts uncomfortably, but doesn't interrupt.* **Angela** *begrudgingly concludes that* **Stephen** *is not high.*

Angela   Hmph. Okay. So why don't you have your prescription?

Stephen   Well, I haven't picked it up yet.

Angela   And why not?

Stephen   There was a little bit of a wait, so I thought I'd come home and pick it up later.

Angela   Did you ask them when it was going to be ready?

Stephen   I don't know. I mean, no.

Angela *sighs and rubs her temples.*

Stephen (*rushing to explain*)   Well, there was a sign that said prescriptions are guaranteed to be ready in two hours or less, so I just assumed that mine would . . .

Angela   After I paid for you to see that doctor, you *assumed* that it would be okay to put off taking the medication that you need in order to breathe.

Stephen   But I was going to . . .

Angela   What time is it?

Stephen   What?

Angela   What time is it?

Stephen   Um . . .

Stephen *squints at the clock.*

Freddy   8:05

Stephen   It's 8:05.

Angela   Right. It's now after 8 o'clock at night, and the pharmacy has closed. Just when do you think it's going to be time for you to act like a responsible adult, Stephen?

She exits without waiting for an answer. Silence.

Freddy   Hey, Stephen, I . . .

Stephen (*quietly*)   It's getting late. I think I'm gonna go read. See ya tomorrow, bro.

Freddy   Oh okay, Stephen. Goodnight.

Stephen *exits.*

Freddy (*calling after him*)   Hey, let's do something in the morning! Breakfast! Me and you! My treat!

Lights down.

Scene Twelve

Late morning. **Freddy**'s *parked car.* **Freddy** *and* **Stephen** *sit with the windows down and the doors wide open. Wrappers and empty coffee cups from breakfast are scattered around them. Wale's "Bad" plays quietly on the radio.* **Freddy** *and* **Stephen** *watch cars go by on the busy cross-street, sometimes craning their necks and twisting in their seats to see what's coming next.*

Freddy   Texas. Texas. Texas. Stephen, this is boring. They're all the same.

Stephen   I come here all the time. Keep looking. It'll get better.

Freddy *and* **Stephen** *continue to watch cars go by.*

Freddy   Texas. Texas. Texas.

Stephen (*pointing*)   Arkansas!

Freddy   What?! Where?

Stephen   There!

Freddy   I don't see it.

Stephen   Cuz you're too slow, old man! Keep looking.

Freddy (*frowning*)   Texas. Texas. Texas. Illinois!

Stephen   Georgia!

Freddy   Kentucky!

Stephen   South Carolina!

Freddy   New York. Punch buggy!

He punches **Stephen** *in the arm.*

Stephen   Hey! We didn't say we were doing punch buggies!

Freddy   My car, my rules! Louisiana!

Stephen   Chicago. I mean . . .

Freddy *makes a sound like the buzzer and punches* **Stephen** *in the arm again.*

Stephen   Oww! Hey!

Freddy   Wrong! That's a city.

Stephen   What was that for?

Freddy   I already told you—house rules. You mess up the flow, a-punchin' I will go!

Stephen *grumbles and rubs his arm.*

Freddy   Pumpernickel!

Stephen   What?

Freddy   Word association. Don't think. Just go! Pumpernickel!

Stephen   Uh . . . crust!

Freddy   Sandwich!

Stephen   Pickle!

Freddy   Sauerkraut!

Stephen   Um . . . um . . .

Freddy *makes the sound of a buzzer again and punches* **Stephen** *in the arm.*

Stephen   Ow! Freddy, I'm tired of this. Can we stop?

Freddy   Oh come on! What's the matter? You used to love this game when we were kids!

Stephen   No, I didn't. I used to hate it. You and Daddy used to love this game when we were kids. *I* liked the license plates.

Freddy   Oh. Huh. I never knew. (*Beat.*) So what now? Do you want to go catch a movie or something? We don't have to go home yet if we don't want to.

Stephen   Nah. No time. I gotta go to work in a couple of hours and I wanna shower before I go in.

Freddy   Oh. You're waiting tables again, right?

Stephen   Yeah. And sometimes they let me bartend.

Freddy   How is it?

Stephen (*shrugging*)   It's okay. I'm pretty sure the manager hates me, though. She keeps scheduling me on Mondays. That's the slowest day. I basically don't make any money.

Freddy   That sucks. Have you tried talking to her about it?

Stephen   Yeah, but she says everybody has to work slow days. (*Shrugs.*) Hey, you should come visit me at work some time. I'll buy you an appetizer!

Freddy   Cool. Maybe I will.

Stephen   Cool. (*Beat.*) Can I ask you something?

Freddy   Sure.

Stephen   Why's your backseat full of coffeemakers?

Freddy   Oh, those. They're nice, right?

Stephen   Yeah, I guess . . . but why do you have eight of them? Did you boost them from somewhere?

Freddy   Not exactly. The first one I found on the curb a few blocks from our house. Had a sign that said "works sometimes" and I thought, "Hell! So do I!" So I figured I'd take it home. Maybe I could fix it.

Stephen   Did you?

Freddy   Nope. Not even close! But I did find this comment on a message board that said I could take it to Showers & Such and exchange it for a brand new one.

Stephen   Okay . . .

Freddy   So I did! It went so well that I thought maybe I could make some extra money working the system. You know, see how far it could go.

Stephen   So it's a hustle. Gotcha.

Freddy   I wouldn't call it a hustle.

Stephen   What would you call it, then?

Freddy   Entrepreneurship!

Stephen   Okay, bro, whatever you say!

Freddy   Would you do me a favor and just make sure those boxes are covered by that blanket back there?

Stephen   I'm on it!

Stephen *leans into the backseat and covers the boxes.* **Freddy** *reaches for the keys.*

Freddy   Ready?

Stephen   Almost. Punch buggy!

He punches **Freddy** *on the arm.*

Freddy   Hey! That was one of the new ones. You know those don't count!

Stephen   My birthday, my rules. Deal with it!

Freddy   It's not your birthday anymore.

Stephen   It's my birthmonth!

Freddy (*laughing*)   Okay. Fair enough.

He starts the car. Lights down.

Scene Thirteen

That night. The darkened living room. **Freddy** *looks around to make sure that he is alone.*

Freddy   Do you remember . . .

His voice breaks. He coughs and clears his throat. He starts again.

Do you remember the first time we went to California?

A light comes on upstairs. From deep within the house, the sound of footsteps. **Freddy** *holds his breath and waits.* **Stephen** *enters.*

Stephen   Hey.

Freddy (*exhaling*)   Oh, hey. It's you. I didn't realize anybody else was up.

Stephen *coughs, as he will continue to at odd intervals.* **Freddy** *looks at his watch.*

Stephen   Yeah. I'm always up at this hour.

Freddy   Don't you have to work in the morning?

Stephen   Yeah, but I still wake up twice a night like I did in prison. Bed checks. I tried taking sleeping pills, but it doesn't help much. Habits are hard to break, ya know?

Freddy   Oh, I know.

Stephen *pulls a crumpled pack of cigarettes out of his pocket.*

Stephen   Want one?

Freddy   I don't smoke.

Stephen   You don't have to lie. I saw you the other night.

Freddy (*chuckling*)   Right, right. You totally did. Well, don't tell Mama.

Stephen   Don't worry. I won't.

The two step outside and begin to smoke.

She's already busting my balls about quitting and nagging me about my cough. Do you know she made me buy some nicotine gum from her? She found it on clearance.

Freddy   That sucks. Did you ask her to get it for you?

Stephen   Well, she called me to ask if I wanted it, but I didn't think she was going to make me pay for it myself!

Freddy   Yeah.

Stephen   Yeah. She tried to get me to go AA, too . . . keeps giving me these pamphlets. I went to a meeting or two, but they're just not my thing.

Freddy *grunts his reply. Silence. They gaze at the sky.*

Freddy   So how long have you been home?

Stephen (*shrugging*)   I don't know. A couple of months? I didn't have anywhere to go after I got out, so I ended up back here. Again.

Freddy   I know the feeling.

Stephen   Yeah. So when are you leaving?

Freddy   To be honest with you, I'm not really sure. I've gotta get my car registered and everything, but then . . . well, I was going to go to New Orleans, but I get so exhausted every time I think about it. I'm tired of making blind moves, ya know?

Stephen   So do you think you might stay?

Freddy   I don't know about that.

Stephen   Oh.

Freddy   What about you?

Stephen (*shrugging*)   Like I said, I don't really have anywhere else to go right now.

Freddy   What about Tina? Can you stay with her?

Stephen   We're not dating anymore. And anyway, I'm not really supposed to be in her apartment complex. They don't like people with criminal records hanging around.

Freddy   Oh, right.

Silence.

Stephen   What about that guy you were with? I thought you two were going to get married.

Freddy   Yeah. I thought so, too. I guess he had other plans.

Silence.

Stephen   I was thinking about getting out of this city.

Freddy (*turning to look at* **Stephen**)   Yeah? I'm glad to hear that. You know I've been saying for years that you should get out of here.

Stephen   I want a fresh start. I can't seem to save up enough money, though.

Freddy   Well, it might help if you quit these. It'd probably help that cough of yours, too.

Stephen *shrugs.*

Stephen   Habit's a bitch to break.

Freddy   Yeah.

He stubs out his cigarette and puts the butt in his pocket.

Anyway, it's pretty late. I'm gonna try to go back to sleep.

Stephen   Alright.

Freddy   Thanks for the smoke.

Stephen (*chuckling*)   Anytime.

Freddy   And thanks for the talk.

He starts to go back inside.

Stephen   Freddy!

Freddy (*turning around*)   Yeah?

Stephen   Stay a little longer?

Freddy   Yeah . . . okay.

They stand quietly next to each other.

Stephen   Can I ask you something?

Freddy   Okay.

Stephen   When did you first know you were different?

Freddy   Different how?

Stephen   . . . you know.

Freddy   Um . . .

Stephen   Sorry. Is that rude?

Freddy   Kind of.

Stephen   It's just . . . you remember the fire? When we had to move?

Freddy   How could I forget?

Stephen   Well, that's when everything changed for me. Before that I felt just like a regular kid. You know, playing cops and robbers and making up games and stuff. And it was cool. But when we moved into this house . . . well, Mama and Daddy never really looked at me the same way after. Especially Mama. When we got here, it was like I was always fucking up in some way or another—I was too loud or making too much of a mess. I could never quite get it right. I think they stopped liking me, but they never just came out and said it.

Freddy   Damn.

Stephen   Yeah. I think that was it for me.

Freddy   What do you mean? You've still got plenty of chances.

Stephen   Not like when we were kids. You never get back to that.

Silence.

Freddy   Do you remember that time I went to California?

Stephen (*squinting, trying to remember*)   No. I don't think so.

Freddy   Oh, right. I guess you probably weren't out then. Well it was last year, back when Terrence and I were still together. We took this trip to California to go to a conference. It was my first time out there. Anyway, it was then, on that trip that I knew.

Stephen   Only then?

Freddy *shrugs.*

Freddy   I had an idea before then, I guess. But on this trip . . . something shifted for me. We were on the B A R T, Terrence and me, after this long-ass flight from New York to San Francisco. I get on the train, and it's like I'm in shock. Like I can't trust my senses. There's trees and mountains and this super-fresh air, and my body just can't take it all in. Spending too long in New York City will do that to you, I guess.

So we were there on that train and I finally start to relax. I have a vision. I see two paths open up before me, two possibilities of the future. One is Winifred and the other is Freddy.

I see her, Winifred, twenty years in the future, working hard as ever and making a real difference healing her community. But she looks so serious, so full of responsibility. There's no joy in her face or in her body, at least not that I can see. She is in her home all alone. After all her clients left at the end of the day, there is nobody there with her. No lovers. No children. Nobody. Just her sitting in silence.

Then I see him. Freddy. I see him twenty years in the future, wearing vibrant colors and smiling brightly. He's laughing! And I know that he, too, has community. And he's doing the work. Of course he is! But he's joyful. He's at ease. And he's having great sex. I can just tell from the way he holds his shoulders. He has opened up and he has somebody waiting for him.

So I decided that's what I wanted for myself. I decided it was worth the risk. I guess . . . that's when I knew for sure.

Silence.

Stephen   Wow.

Freddy   Weird, right?

Stephen (*chuckling*)   Yeah. A little.

Freddy   I've been wanting to tell somebody that. That's the first time I've said it all out loud.

Stephen (*beat*)   I've always wanted my own island, you know?

Freddy *laughs.*

Freddy   What?

Stephen   An island. I always wanted one of my own. I had lots of time to think about it when I was locked up. It started when we were kids. Sometimes there would be a Gilligan's Island rerun on, and I would think about how lucky they were—on a permanent vacation. But later I realized that it would be so much better if it were just me, away from everybody else. No bars. No demands. Just me and my two hands. Well, and maybe a pet parrot.

I'd build myself a house out of branches and coconut timber, and then I'd spend my days eating all-coconut everything. Unless, you know, I decided that I wanted to go out and do some hunting.

In the mornings I'd go swimming and take naps on the beach, and in the afternoons and late into the evenings I'd lay in a hammock watching the stars and talking to the moon.

Freddy   Wow.

Stephen   Yeah. Weird, right?

Freddy   No. I think it's nice. A permanent vacation. Yeah.

Stephen   At least your vision was real. You've got a chance of making your dreams come true.

Deep rumblings. Lights down.

Scene Fourteen

1995. **Winifred** *sits on the floor of the living room. Near her is a giant web of t-shirts, magazines, hair and hair extensions. She addresses the mass.*

Winifred (*shaking her hair*)   Well? Do you notice anything different about me?

No response.

It's my hair, silly! Since my hair is straight, it blows in the wind on the bus now. Well, except that it doesn't just fall back into place once the bus stops. That's okay, though. All I have to do is make sure I have a mirror and a comb so that I can fix it before the other kids see it sticking up.

Silence.

And, I'm doing my own hair these days. Well, I'm learning to. Mama doesn't wash my hair for me on Sundays anymore. She says that I'm old enough to wash it myself in the shower on the weeks that I don't go to the ladies at Sears. Mama showed me how to comb my hair and set it in rollers with the little papers and how to grease my scalp, but it's hard. I can't seem to figure out which way is up and which is down when I'm trying to make a part, and my arms get tired. Mama says she'll show me again how to do it, but that she won't do it for me. Now I sit in the living room with the TV on while Mama cooks in the kitchen. She comes out once in a while to show me what I'm doing wrong. (*Pause.*) Still, now I've got hair that moves in the wind. It doesn't look like snakes anymore.

Stephen *enters skipping and stops right next to* **Winifred**. *He's wearing a cowboy hat again.*

Stephen   Heeeeeey, Winnie! Emily from my Sunday school class told me to ask you why your hair got so greasy and stringy all of a sudden. She told me her big sister Pamela who goes to your school says it's because you've been rolling your hair up in fried chicken at night, but I told Emily that wasn't true. I said, "Nuh-uh! Just because my sister Winnie's hair is greasy and stringy doesn't mean she's rolling it with fried chicken. My mama takes her to Sears to get it to look like that, stupid!" and then I stuck my tongue out at her.

He smiles at **Winifred**, *grabs a toy, and runs out of the living room.* **Winifred** *stares after him.*

Winifred (*to herself*)   My hair doesn't look greasy and stringy does it? It's shiny and manageable, just like in the commercials.

She picks up the hand mirror and looks in it.

Isn't it?

Scene Fifteen

Lights up. The kitchen. **Angela** *is cooking alone. "If Only You Knew" by Patti LaBelle is playing on the stereo.* **Angela** *sings along softly.* **Winifred** *enters. The mass of shirts, magazines, and hair follows her and lingers in the doorway.* **Angela** *glances up at* **Winifred**.

Angela   What is it, Winifred? Shouldn't you be getting started on your hair by now? Don't think I'm going to let you stay up late every night just because you're not finished doing your hair. Your father and I gave you a bedtime for a reason.

Winifred   Yes, Mama, I know. I was just wondering—can you help me? I found this picture of Whitney Houston in a magazine, and I want to make my hair look like hers for picture day tomorrow.

Angela *stops what she's doing and looks up at* **Winifred**.

Angela   Well, I don't know about looking like Whitney Houston, but if you'd like, I can still braid your hair into a nice modern . . .

Winifred (*passionately*)   No, Mama! I don't want to look like you! I don't want that! I don't want you to braid my hair ever again!

Angela *turns her back to* **Winifred** *and continues cooking.*

Winifred   I just . . . what I meant was that I want my hair to look like Whitney Houston's for picture day tomorrow. That's all. All the kids at my school, they pay a lot of attention to the yearbook, and I thought that maybe if I looked good they'd see me the way they do the other girls.

Angela   Winifred, I'm sure your picture will turn out just fine. I just don't have time to deal with your hair right now. You're the one who decided that you wanted to have straight hair. Now you're just going to have to deal with everything that comes along with it. Go work it out.

Winifred *doesn't move.*

Angela   In the living room, Winifred.

She goes to the stereo and turns "If Only You Knew" up to a higher volume. She hums along as **Winifred** *slowly turns and exits the kitchen followed by the mass. Lights down.*

Scene Sixteen

Sunday. Lights up on the kitchen. "How Can You Mend a Broken Heart" by Al Green plays on the stereo. **Angela** *stands at the kitchen counter circling job postings in the classifieds. She notices a pot boiling and turns suddenly, knocking over a box of pasta.*

Angela   Hellfire and damnation!

Stephen *enters wearing his cowboy hat.*

Stephen (*amazed*)   Mama, you cursed!

Angela (*distractedly*)   Yes, I did.

She hands **Stephen** *a bowl to hold, then starts picking up pasta and dropping it in the bowl.*

Stephen   Really? Me?

Angela   Sure, baby. Why not?

She continues to pick up pasta.

Stephen   Well, it's just . . . things have been so different around here lately. Winnie's sitting in the living room talking to herself, and you're in here frowning and cursing at the chicken. You and Winnie are always arguing and yelling about combs and stuff. How come you and Winnie don't spend time together anymore? You usually do girly stuff all day on Sundays, but now Winnie spends the whole day at Sears or in the living room and you just stay in the kitchen by yourself. Are you mad at each other?

Angela   Well, Stephen, I think your sister is just getting to the point where she doesn't want to spend as much time with me. She's a teenager now, after all. You all are just growing up so fast.

Stephen   But, Mama, I don't think that's true. I listen to Winnie's conversations a lot and she never said that she doesn't want to spend time with you. She just said that she doesn't like the way that you do her hair. You two should make up.

He plops the bowl down on the counters and gallops off on his invisible horse.
Angela *watches him go, then realizes her sauce is burning. She rushes to turn the burner off.*

Angela   Goddamn it!

Lights down.

Scene Seventeen

Friday evening. The living room. Lights up on **Michael** *sharing a pizza with* **Stephen** *and* **Winifred**. **Stephen***'s backpack, jacket, and cowboy hat lay on the floor in a heap with* **Winifred***'s backpack, jacket, and violin case.*

Winifred (*reading from a piece of paper*) "Sinkholes may form gradually or suddenly, and are found worldwide. Cover collapse occurs when a large void develops underground and, no longer able to support the weight of what's above, the ground caves in. Entire homes can suddenly give way."

Stephen   Is our house gonna fall down?

Michael   No, Stephen. We're doing something about it now before that can happen.

Stephen   But are you *sure* it's not gonna fall down?

Michael   Well, I guess . . . no. I can't guarantee that. But I'm pretty sure it's not going to.

Stephen (*shouting*)   We're gonna fall all the way to China!

Michael   Stephen, lower your voice. Your mother's trying to rest.

Winifred   Where are we going?

Michael   Not too far away. We've been looking at apartments that are in the same school district.

Winifred   Apartments?!

Michael   Stephen, you'll keep going to the school you're in now.

Stephen   Yes!

Winifred   But we live in a house now! How are we going to fit into an apartment?

Michael   Stephen, why don't you go see if we have any more ice cream in the freezer?

Stephen   Alright!

He runs out of the living room.

Michael   Winifred . . .

Winifred   But what about my friends?

Michael   We're not exactly moving away. Yes, we have to move out of this house because it's not safe for us, but we'll still be here, just on the other side of town. So you'll still be able to see your friends. It just might have to be on the weekends.

Winifred   What about school?

Michael (*laughing*)   You're both going to stay in school, of course! Don't think I'm going to let you drop out just because of a little construction. Education first!

Winifred   That's not what I meant, Daddy. I mean, are we going to the same schools?

Michael   Your mother and I were going to talk to you about that, Winifred. There's no bus to Whitley Academy from that side of town, but we found you a school with a great orchestra program and lots of advanced classes.

Winifred   So I have to change schools? Again?

Michael   Think of it like one of our camping trips. It's an opportunity to meet new people and try new things, to see what you're made of.

Winifred (*mumbling*)   I hate camping.

Michael   What's that, Winnie?

Winifred   Can I see that paper again?

Michael   Sure.

He hands **Winifred** *the sheet of paper. She reads it again.*

Winifred (*looking up at* **Michael**)   When do we have to go?

Michael   We'll try to wait until the end of the term, but we need to be out of the house soon.

Winifred *gives the paper back to* **Michael**.

Winifred   I guess I should start packing then.

Michael   Wait a minute, Winnie! You don't have to do that tonight. Don't you want to finish watching TGIF with your brother and me?

Winifred *shrugs and pulls at her hair.*

Winifred   Why are we moving into an apartment? Are we broke?

Michael   You know that your mother isn't working right now.

Winifred   So? Don't we have insurance or something?

Michael (*exasperated*)   You're the oldest, Winifred. We expect you to be mature about this.

Winifred   But I just started at Whitley! Daddy, please! I think I have a chance here! I just started making some friends. Please don't make me change schools again!

Michael   Enough! There's no bus to Whitley from the neighborhood we're moving to, and your mother's not going to have time to drive you once she starts law school in the fall. We all have to make sacrifices for the good of the family. This is what's happening, and that's all there is to it!

Winifred   What does Stephen have to sacrifice?! He gets to have everything!

Michael   Winifred, Stephen is eight! (*Beat.*) Go on then. Try not to disturb your mother while you're packing. She's got a headache.

Winifred (*sullenly*)   Fine.

She snatches up her backpack, violin, and **Stephen**'s *cowboy hat as she exits.* **Stephen** *enters with a carton of ice cream and three spoons.*

Stephen   Winnie doesn't want ice cream?

Michael   I think your sister's had enough for tonight.

Stephen   Oh. More for us!

He climbs onto the couch next to **Michael**.

Michael (*chuckling*)   Well, that's a way to find the bright side! More for us indeed, son.

Deep rumbling. Lights down.

Scene Eighteen

2013. Monday night. Lights up on the kitchen of the large Clark house. **Angela** *carries the last dish of food to the table and places it carefully.*

Angela (*shouting*)   Dinner's ready!

Freddy *and* **Stephen** *run down the stairs shoving each other a bit, but slow down significantly before they enter the kitchen.* **Stephen** *enters the kitchen first and finds* **Angela** *sitting at her spot at the table. He sits.* **Freddy** *enters after* **Stephen**. *He is studiously looking down at his feet. When he reaches the table, he meets* **Angela**'s *gaze and they stare at each other for a moment.* **Angela** *looks away first and starts rearranging dishes on the table.* **Michael** *enters last and sits down at the table.*

Michael (*looking around*)   Well, isn't this nice? Thank you for preparing this lovely meal, Angie.

Angela   Thank you, Michael.

Stephen   Yeah. Nice spread, Mama!

Angela   Mm hmm.

Michael (*rubbing his belly*)   Well, no time like the present I always say!

He grabs a serving utensil and starts to scoop food onto his plate.

Angela   Here, let me do it.

She takes charge of the serving spoons and deposits fat wads of food on everyone's plates. Once everyone has been served, there's silence. **Freddy** *looks around and picks up his fork.*

Freddy (*timidly*)   This looks great, Mama.

Angela *silently acknowledges* **Freddy**. **Freddy** *starts to take a bite.*

Michael   Hold on now. Don't you think we ought to give thanks first?

Freddy (*putting down his fork*)   Oh, right. Sorry. I forgot. And thanks for making dinner, Mama. Sorry I wasn't available to help.

Angela   That's alright. I'm used to cooking alone these days.

Freddy *picks up his fork again and turns back to his plate.*

Michael (*chuckling*)   Yes! Absolutely you should thank your mother for all of her hard work. But I meant we should have a little grace and thank the Lord for all that he's done for us. Don't you think? Let's join hands.

Embarrassed, **Freddy** *puts his fork down again and takes his parents' outstretched hands. All bow their heads and close their eyes. There is a long silence. Finally,* **Freddy** *opens one eye.*

Freddy   Daddy?

Michael   Yes, Freddy?

Angela *opens one eye, then closes it.*

Freddy   I thought we were gonna say grace?

Michael   We're waiting on you.

Freddy   Me? But you always . . .

Michael   Almost always. Tonight I thought you might bless the food for us.

Freddy   Oh.

He pauses and shuts his eyes, then opens them again.

Is it okay if you just do it this time? I'm not really . . .

Michael   To God. Tell it to God, not to me.

Freddy   Okay. (*Long silence.*) The Lord is my light and my salvation; whom shall I fear? The Lord is the strength of my life; of whom shall I be afraid? When the wicked, even mine enemies and my foes, came upon me to eat my flesh, they stumbled and fell. Though a host should encamp against me, my heart shall not fear: though war should rise against me, in this I will be confident. One thing have I desired of the Lord, that will I seek after; that I may dwell in the house of the Lord all the days of my life, to behold the beauty of the Lord, and to enquire in his temple. For in the time of trouble he shall hide me in his pavilion: in the secret of his tabernacle shall he hide me; he shall set me up upon a rock. And now shall mine head be lifted up above mine enemies round about me: therefore will I offer in his tabernacle sacrifices of joy; I will sing, yea, I will sing praises unto the Lord. Hear, O Lord, when I cry with my voice: have mercy also upon me, and answer me. When thou saidst, Seek ye my face, my heart said unto thee, Thy face, Lord, will I seek. Hide not thy face far from me; put not thy servant away in anger: thou hast been my help; leave me not, neither forsake me, O God of my salvation. When my father and my mother forsake me, then the Lord will take me up. Teach me thy way, O Lord, and lead me in a plain path, because of mine enemies. Deliver me not over unto the will of mine enemies: for false witnesses are risen up against me, and such as breathe out cruelty. I had fainted, unless I had believed to see the goodness of the Lord in the land of the living. Wait on the Lord: be of good courage, and he shall strengthen thine heart: wait, I say, on the Lord.

Silence.

All   Amen.

They drop each other's hands and pick up their utensils.

Michael   Thank you for that, Winifred. (*Clears his throat.*) Freddy.

Angela *stands up suddenly.*

Michael   Do you need help with something, Angie? Stephen, help your mother.

Angela   I don't need help. I just need my wine.

She walks to the counter and retrieves a mostly empty wine glass. She drains it, then gets a bottle of wine. She returns to the table, fills her glass up to the top, and takes a long drink.

Michael   So how was everyone's day?

Silence.

Angie? How was your day?

Angela (*taking another drink*)   Thank you for asking, Mike. It was trying. I was supposed to appear in court this morning for this pro-bono case I took on, but when I got there my client was nowhere to be found! I waited for her for over an hour and tried every number I have for her, but she never showed up. This after I explained to her repeatedly the consequences of failing to appear in court.

She shakes her head.

Michael   Wow, Angie, that sounds frustrating.

Angela (*interrupting* **Michael**)   The thing that gets me is this—you do your best to do right by someone, you give them your best advice and, well . . . I burned my whole morning driving around town just trying to help her out! I called her repeatedly and she didn't have the decency to answer. It's just amazing to me how some people don't think about how their actions might affect those who are just trying to do what's best for them.

She looks pointedly at **Freddy** *and* **Stephen***, then drains her glass of wine.*

Michael   Well, what about you Stephen? How was work?

Stephen   Oh, I haven't gone in yet. I'm closing tonight.

Angela (*gesturing with her fork*)   Ask him what he did with his day.

Michael   Okay. What'd you do with your day, Stephen?

Stephen (*shrugging*)   Um, well, nothing much. I slept a lot and read a book.

Angela *pours herself another glass of wine.*

Michael   That sounds nice. What book was it?

Stephen   It's this sci-fi book that I got from . . .

Angela (*interrupting*)   He was supposed to be researching new meetings to attend, weren't you, Stephen? Did you manage to get any of that done?

Stephen   Well . . . not yet. I was going to, but then I was really tired from being up so late last night, so I just . . .

Angela (*interrupting again*)   And why were you up so late?

Stephen (*shrugging*)   I don't know.

Angela   It wasn't because you were out getting drunk in some bar?

Stephen   No, Mama.

Angela   Or smoking reefer in the backyard as soon as it got dark? I know you've done it.

Stephen   No, Mama.

Angela   SO YOU'RE TRYING TO TELL ME THAT YOU WEREN'T OUT GETTING TRASHED LAST NIGHT?

Stephen   No, Mama, I wasn't.

Angela   I don't believe you. You weren't home when I got in, and . . .

Freddy (*interrupting*)   He was with me, Mama.

All turn to look at **Freddy***.*

Angela   Oh?

Freddy   Yeah. I was feeling kind of restless last night, so I picked Stephen up from work and we went to the House of Pies to hang out. I didn't realize we were supposed to check in with you when we went out.

Angela   Well, it's just basic courtesy to check in when you're going to . . .

Freddy   I'll leave you a note or call next time.

Angela   Well, okay then.

Silence.

Michael   Well, I had a wonderful day if you really want to know!

Nobody responds.

Well, come on now! Isn't anybody going to ask me what was so wonderful about it?

Angela *sighs and rolls her eyes.* **Freddy** *and* **Stephen** *exchange a look.*

Stephen   Okay, Daddy. What was so wonderful about your day?

Michael   I knew that I was coming home to finally have dinner with all of you!

Freddy   Daddy, that's corny.

Michael (*looking around feigning confusion*)   I don't see any corn. Angie, did you make corn on the cob tonight? Or maybe some creamed corn? Wait! Is that some cornbread I smell baking in the oven?

Angela *rolls her eyes even harder and takes another drink of wine.* **Freddy** *and* **Stephen** *both groan loudly.*

Angela   Michael, can you help me with the dessert?

Stephen *and* **Freddy** *exchange a look.*

Michael   Dessert?

Angela (*tightly*)   Yes, Michael. Dessert.

Michael   Well . . . alright, Angie.

Angela *pushes her chair back and stalks upstage to the far part of the kitchen.* **Michael** *follows. When they reach the counter* **Angela** *rounds on* **Michael**.

Angela (*whispering loudly*)   How can you just sit there at the table cracking jokes and not say anything?!

Michael   I was making conversation, Angie, enjoying the company of my family.

Angela (*hissing*)   Small talk and jokes aren't what they need, Michael! Why don't you say something? Tell the truth for once! Back me up here! Why does it always look like I'm the one who has a problem here?

Michael (*diplomatically*)   You're not always the easiest person to get along with, Angie, especially when you're drinking.

Angela   Oh, Mike, don't give me that! Just look at them. They need a parent, not some brokedown wannabe comedian!

Michael   Our children are grown now. They're going to live their lives. Stop trying to control everything and enjoy them while they're around!

Angela   Oh, so I'm just supposed to sit there with an idiotic smile on my face? Like you? Just sit there and act like everything is hunky dory? Well, I can't. I won't!

Michael (*sighing*)   Not everything has to be a fight, Angie.

Angela   Not everything, Mike, but some things! Some things you should fight for! Like family! This family! Don't think I don't know what you all say about me. I know you all think of me as the Wicked Witch of the West, always sweeping in trying to choke somebody's puppy!

Michael   Nobody says that about you.

Angela   Oh no? I'm not blind, Mike! I see the way the three of you band together against me. Everybody loves a bad guy, somebody to fight against, and you're no exception. You get to be the hero, the person everybody admires, while I'm the one keeping our children alive!

Michael   Keeping them alive? Don't you think that's a bit dramatic? Nobody's dying, Angie.

Angela   No, Mike. I don't think it's dramatic. Stephen's running around here drinking and taking drugs and doing God-knows-what. In prison half his adult life and waiting tables when he's out. And Winifred? Well, I don't even know what to say about her running around here looking like some fucking he-she!

Stephen   We can hear you, you know!

Angela   Mind your own fucking business, you damn firebug! (*To herself.*) Don't know why we keep letting you back in the house in the first damn place. (*To* **Stephen**.) Are you planning on destroying this house, too?

Michael   Angela . . .

Stephen   I don't know what you mean.

Michael (*to* **Angela**)   I thought we agreed we weren't going to tell him that.

Angela (*loudly, ignoring* **Michael**)   Oh, Stephen doesn't understand. What a surprise! We know it was you who did it, you fuckup!

Michael   Angela!

Freddy   Come on, Mama. Don't talk to him like that!

Angela   I'll talk to him any way I goddamn please, Winifred!

Freddy   My name isn't Winifred anymore! Get it right!

Angela   That's the name I gave you, and that's the name I'm going to call you!

Michael   Angela . . .

Angela   You think everybody else likes the hands they were dealt? You think nobody else wishes things were different for them? But do we force that on other people? No. We deal with it, because that's life, Winifred!

Freddy   I won't be disrespected like this!

Angela   Oh, *you* won't be disrespected? This is *my* fucking house! If you don't like the way it is here, you can get the hell out!

Michael   Freddy. Angela.

Freddy   Fine! I will! I'm fucking gone!

He storms out of the kitchen. **Michael** *follows him.*

Michael   Freddy, you don't have to go. You know how your mother is.

Freddy   Exactly. I know how she is, and I've had enough.

He goes upstairs, grabs his bags, and heads for the door. When he returns, **Angela** *is standing in the doorway of the kitchen.*

Michael   Wait! At least take this with you.

Michael *hands* **Freddy** *an envelope of money.*

Freddy (*looking at* **Angela**)   Thanks, Daddy. I love you!

Freddy *picks up his bags and exits.* **Angela**, **Stephen**, *and* **Michael** *watch him go.* **Angela** *crosses to her room with her bottle of wine and slams the door.*

Deep rumbling. Lights down.

Scene Nineteen

1995. The living room. Lights up on **Winifred** *sitting on the couch, wearing her brother's cowboy hat and holding her violin like a guitar. She plucks a few melancholy notes as she looks down at her school pictures. The mass of t-shirts, magazines, hair extensions, and combs looms over her, blocking out much of the light.*

Winifred   My picture turned out terrible this year. Stupid smile. Horrible hair. I look like Urkel's ugly sister! I know that's what they're saying. I hear them whispering about me every time I walk by. Geek. Freak. Dyke.

She stops plucking the violin and sets it down next to her. She takes the hat off and tosses it to the floor, then picks up the sheet of pictures and examines it closely.

I spend all my time trying to change the way they see me, but it seems like I can never get it right. And Mama doesn't help me anymore. She just says that she's got too much to do, and that she's shown me a thousand times and that I need to figure it out. It isn't fair!

She takes off the cowboy hat and hurls it at the mass. It doesn't go far. Unsatisfied, she picks up her violin and throws that, too. She likes it. She picks up the sheet of pictures and rips it once, twice. Suddenly inspired, she pulls out her father's Zippo and sets the pictures on fire. She watches them burn until the fire nips her fingers. She yelps and throws the burning photos down. They fall onto the cowboy hat, which immediately ignites. The mass quickly catches and begins to blaze. **Winifred** *lunges for her violin, but the fire is too hot and her hair is singed. She backs away from the burning mass and runs.*

Crackling. Rumbling. Fissures.

Scene Twenty

2013. A dirty beach. Lights up on **Freddy** *leaning on his car, which is once again fully packed. The sky is a greyish yellow, and a strong wind blows, bringing with it all manner of litter and seaweed.*

Freddy (*spinning around taking it all in*)   Ah! I love this place! Don't you? The sun and the wind! The sky! The trees! I've never felt so free!

He gestures grandly. Nothing.

(*Shouting.*) I said I've never felt so free!

The wind blows and birds call. More garbage washes up on the beach. **Freddy** *sighs and plops down on the beach. The wind blows harder.* **Freddy** *begins to shiver. He inches closer and closer to the car until he's leaning against it.*

(*Sighing.*) Solitude.

The sky darkens and he shivers more violently. Finally, he gives in and gets in the car.

Peace and quiet. Nature.

He stares out of the car window at the filthy water, then gets bored and pulls out his phone. He checks his email. The phone pings.

Angela   I thought you'd want to know that your brother is back in jail again. No word yet on what the charges are. Your father and I are fine. I hope you're well. Me

Freddy   Well, fuck.

He tosses the phone onto the dash of the car and settles in, grabbing a jacket from the backseat to cover himself with. His stomach growls. He opens the glove compartment of the car and finds a granola bar. He unwraps it and eats.

It's great not having to make conversation at meals, ya know? No awkward revelations. No forced prayers. Right? (*Louder.*) Right?!

He sighs and gropes around for his phone. He finds it and pushes a button.

Stephen   Hi, Freddy. I'm not at home anymore, but I guess you probably already knew that. Mama and I got into an argument. She woke me up in the middle of the night screaming at me to contribute more and to get my life together. I called her a hypocrite and told her she was rude and mean, and then I guess I said some other things that I probably shouldn't've said. I probably should've just kept my mouth shut and nodded, but I just couldn't stand the thought of staying there anymore without you. Anyway, I miss you, big brother. I hope we get to talk soon. Love, Stephen.

Freddy   I miss you, too.

He drops the phone, gets out of the car, and stretches. He grabs the jacket and puts it on, zipping it all the way up. He jogs around the car a few times. Winded, he stops and leans against the car again. He pulls out a cigarette and pats his pockets for a

lighter. Nothing. Inspired, he pops the cigarette lighter out of the dash of his car, but it doesn't work. His phone pings again. Sighing, he grabs it and reads.

Michael   I hope you're safe out there. Things aren't the same here without you and your brother. Your mother won't say it, but she's sorry. You can come back whenever you're ready.

Freddy   Fuck that.

He throws the phone back into the car, then drops into the driver's seat. A strong, dirty wind blows, bringing with it a cloud of ash. **Freddy** *coughs and tries to shut the car door, but the wind is too strong. A voice rises over the wind.*

Winifred   I know lots of time has passed by now and you might not remember me. But I've been thinking about you a lot lately and I wish that you were here or that I were there with you. I'm old enough to know that what I'm asking for is an impossible thing, but I'm wishing for it anyway. I included a key with this message. You know how to use it. Please come if you can. Right now . . . I could really use a friend.

A slip of paper drifts out of the ash and sticks to the inside of the windshield. **Freddy** *snatches it up and clenches it in his fist, closing his eyes against the ash. The lighting changes, becoming more and more brilliant until all of a sudden there's a blackout. The sound of wind blowing grows and grows until it is almost unbearable.*

Silence.

Scene Twenty-One

Lights up on a liminal place. **Freddy** *and* **Winifred** *stumble in from opposite directions, both as if pushed.* **Winifred** *stands clutching a fistful of wallpaper in her right hand. She looks at the floor and kicks some of the wreckage.* **Freddy** *takes in the room but sneaks frequent glances at* **Winifred**. **Winifred**, *aware of his scrutiny, remains withdrawn until . . .*

Winifred   Is that the best mustache you can grow?

Freddy *covers his upper lip in embarrassment, then, recovering, lets his hand fall away from his face.*

Freddy   For now. It's getting better, though.

Winifred (*generously*)   It's not bad!

Freddy   Yeah?

Winifred   Yeah!

Freddy (*laughing*)   I think it's pretty bad, but that's okay. It's what I've got for now and it gets the job done.

Winifred   That's cool.

They share a moment. Winifred drops to the floor and starts to fiddle with the wallpaper strips.

Freddy   What happened to your hair?

Winifred *touches her hair, embarrassed.*

Winifred   Fire.

Freddy   Right.

Winifred   Yeah. (*Pause.*) Does it look bad?

Freddy   Honestly?

Winifred *nods.*

Freddy   Yeah. It's pretty bad.

Winifred   The kids at my new school are never gonna like me like this.

Freddy   Is that what's bothering you? Cuz it'll definitely grow back . . . and if you cut it all off, you might find you like it short.

Winifred *looks skeptical.*

Freddy   Come on, give me some credit. I do know a thing or two about you.

Silence.

Freddy   You asked for me. So why don't you tell me what's bothering you?

Winifred   It doesn't matter.

Freddy   Who says?

Winifred   I just feel so bad. My chest hurts. (*Pause.*) I don't know how else to say it.

She shrugs. Silence.

Freddy   I'm going to tell you something really important, something I wish I'd realized a long time ago.

Winifred   Okay.

Freddy   Most people are full of shit.

Winifred *snorts.*

Freddy   No, but seriously. Those people giving you a hard time, those kids making fun of you, those boys who run and those girls who shy away from you, they're mostly if not entirely full of shit. You're an easy target for them because you can't hide who you are. Not for long, at least. So just be yourself. Cuz those people are too afraid to even try to tell the truth about themselves. They're cowards and they're full of shit. Does that make sense?

Silence.

Winifred   What if I can't do it?

Freddy   Oh, believe me, you'll fail plenty.

Winifred   What?

Freddy   I mean you'll fail and you'll survive. You'll get up and you'll try again. You're tenacious.

Winifred   Tenacious?

Freddy   Trust me. It's one of the best things about you.

Silence.

Winifred   I don't know if that helped.

Freddy   Yeah, sorry. I'm not always great at making people feel better about things.

Silence.

Winifred   Can I ask you a question?

Freddy *pulls out his pack of cigarettes.*

Freddy   Sure.

He looks for a lighter, then remembers he doesn't have one.

Winifred   Does it hurt, getting the way you are now?

Freddy   Honestly?

Winifred *nods.*

Freddy   Yeah. It did. But I think it might be getting easier.

Winifred *nods again.* **Freddy** *sighs and puts the cigarettes in his pocket.* **Winifred** *reaches in her pocket and presents him with her father's Zippo.*

Freddy   Wow, thanks! I just . . . I don't know if I should accept a light from a kid?

Winifred   Be prepared! It's the Girl Scout motto you know.

She gathers her wallpaper scraps.

And it's the Boy Scout motto too!

She nods matter-of-factly.

Freddy (*under his breath*)   Be prepared.

Winifred *starts to walk away.*

Freddy   Hey, Winifred!

Winifred *turns.*

Freddy   Be nicer to your brother. He could use it.

Winifred *nods. Deep rumbling.*

Scene Twenty-Two

2013. Lights up on the living room of the large Clark house. **Freddy** *enters holding his overnight bag. He stands alone in the entryway for a moment.* **Angela** *enters from the kitchen.*

Angela   You're back.

Freddy (*wryly*)   Yeah. Looks like it. (*Pause.*) I got your message.

Michael *enters from the kitchen and goes to hug* **Freddy**.

Michael   Freddy! It's nice to have you back.

Angela   How long are you here for?

Freddy   I don't really know. Until I can find a job, I guess. (*Pause.*) Is that okay?

Angela   I guess that's okay.

Freddy *puts the bags down, relaxing a bit. Silence.*

Angela   I've got a luncheon to attend tomorrow afternoon, an Association of Black Female Lawyers' thing. (*Pause.*) I have an outfit picked out, but my hair . . . what do you think? Can you do something with it?

Freddy   I can try! (*Pause.*) Is the morning okay? I'm pretty tired.

Angela   That'll work.

Silence.

Freddy   I got you something.

He unzips his overnight bag and pulls out a large box.

Angela   A new coffee maker!

Freddy   I figured you could use it for your office.

Angela   Thank you! But what's the occasion?

Freddy   Let's just say I got a really good deal on it. There's more. Look inside.

Angela *opens the box and pulls out a CD.*

Angela   What's this?

Freddy   I made you a mixtape. Here. I'll put it on.

He takes the CD from **Angela** *and puts it in the stereo. "Sing to the Moon" by Laura Mvula plays.*

Angela   This is nice.

Freddy   I'm glad you like it. (*Pause.*) Well, I'm gonna hop in the shower. I'm pretty grimy. But I'll see you in the morning?

Angela   Yeah. Okay.

Freddy *takes a few steps then stops.*

Freddy   Can I ask you something?

Angela   Sure.

Freddy   Why'd you stop calling me? I mean, before I came back. Why didn't you call?

Angela *stiffens.*

Angela   I didn't realize I was supposed to.

Freddy   But you used to. You used to call me every Saturday morning without fail. If I wasn't at home, you called.

Angela   I guess I felt like you didn't want to hear from me.

Freddy   What made you think that?

Silence.

Angela   I don't have an answer for that right now.

Freddy   Well, I do. I do want to hear from you. So now you know.

Lights down.

End of play.